SAINTS

Studies in Hagiography

MEDIEVAL & RENAISSANCE TEXTS & STUDIES

VOLUME 141

SAINTS

Studies in Hagiography

Edited by

Sandro Sticca

medieval & Renaissance texts & studies
Binghamton, New York
1996

© Copyright 1996
Center for Medieval and Early Renaissance Studies
State University of New York at Binghamton

Library of Congress Cataloging-in-Publication Data

Saints : studies in hagiography / edited by Sandro Sticca.
    p.   cm. — (Medieval & Renaissance Texts & Studies; v. 141)
Includes bibliographical references and index.
ISBN 0–86698–179–9 (alk. paper)
    1. Christian hagiography—Congresses. 2. Europe—Church history—
600–1500—Congresses. I. Sticca, Sandro, 1931– . II. Series.
BX4662.S24   1995
235'.2—dc20
          95–4768
          CIP

This book is made to last.
It is set in Bembo, smyth-sewn,
and printed on acid-free paper
to library specifications.

Printed in the United States of America

Contents

Acknowledgment

I wish to thank all those who waited patiently for the publication of this volume, mindful of Horace's comment that *levius fit patientia, quidquid corrigere est nefas*. Now that the work is done I wish also to thank Mario A. Di Cesare, Director and General Editor of MRTS for the guidance provided along the way and Lori Vandermark, Anne E. Healy, Chava Burman, Tracy Youells, and Jennifer Pashley for their editorial skills and compositional expertise. To all of them, a sincere appreciation for their courtesy and help always so graciously extended to me.

Preface

SANDRO STICCA

his volume consists of fifteen papers selected from those given at the twenty-third conference sponsored by the Center for Medieval and Early Renaissance Studies at Binghamton University, "The Cult of the Saints." The arrangement of the essays in the volume reflects a framework suggested by certain recognizable features, critical methodologies, historical and religious concerns that lend themselves, in their diverse critical and intellectual discourse, to categorizing in four distinct groups: saints in hagiographic texts (historical and literary studies), saints in liturgy and drama, St. Francis of Assisi (iconography and hagiography) and a section on the public, private, and popular cult of the saints.

In reviewing, two years after its publication in 1927, Hippolyte Delehaye's seminal and monumental work of hagiographical research, *Sanctus. Essai sur le culte des saints dans l'antiquité*, Marc Bloch, commenting on the book's contribution to the history of sainthood in the Church, remarked that if ever a scholar could be found foolhardy enough to undertake such a history and learned enough to realize it, his book would be without equal in the vistas it would open on the human spirit.[1] Although the wealth of research on hagiographical liter-

---

[1] André Vauchez, *La sainteté en Occident aux derniers siècles du moyen âge* (Rome: Ecole Française de Rome, 1988), revised edition, 1. Marc Bloch's review of Delehaye's book appeared in *Revue de Synthèse* 47 (1929): 88–90.

ature, art and music, diverse and specialized in nature, that has since ac-
cumulated allows us to look upon the history of the saints as no longer
a *terra incognita*, the vast corpus of hagiographical literature bequeathed
to posterity by the Christian tradition still awaits fuller scholarly attention, especially since the saint's life is a genre little studied in most universities' curricula.[2]

Indeed, although enjoying wide popularity in the eastern and western Christian world, the hagiographical genre has often been taken to
task by modern historians who reproach hagiographers for their peculiar concept and vision of history. On the positive side, the resurgence
of interest in hagiography in the past thirty years has resulted not only
in a substantial increase in scholarly studies devoted to the subject but
in the creation in England, France, Germany, and Italy, of special
groups and associations of scholars—under the leadership, in France, of
André Vauchez and Jacques Le Goff and in Italy of Sofia Boesch
Gajano and Lucetta Scaraffia on the one hand, and Edith Pasztor on
the other—whose commitment to hagiographical research has culmi-
nated, in the past decade, in a period of critical activity characterized
by distinguished publications and international sumposia and congresses.

These research groups on hagiography have brought together scholars from diverse disciplines who, for years, had been engaged in different aspects of hagiographical studies. Their intent was not only to
promote hagiographical studies *de novo* but to establish forms of coordi-
nation and intersection of individual research around thematic and
problematic nuclei, while respecting the importance and value of personal interests and scholarly expertise. The first international meeting of
these groups took the form of a seminar on the rapport between the
cult of saints, ecclesiastical and lay institutions, and society in general,
and subsequently a published volume, *Culto dei Santi, istituzioni e classi
sociali in età preindustriale*, which appeared in 1984.[3] This particular
project fit well with a research direction the most significant stages of
which had been identified in the congress organized by Evelyne Patlagean and Pierre Riché, (proceedings published in 1981), in the provoc-

---

[2] William W. Heist, "Irish Saints' Lives, Romance, and Cultural History," *Medi-
evalia et Humanistica* 6 (1975): 25.

[3] Edited by Sofia Boesch Gajano and Lucia Sebastiani, (Rome/L'Aquila: Japadre,
1984).

ative and fundamental volume by André Vauchez which appeared in 1980, and in Jean-Claude Schmitt's original research which came out in 1979.[4]

Under the impulse provided by these publications the research groups embarked on a line of hagiographical studies characterized by a diachronic and multi-disciplinary critical method. One of the first results of this approach was a volume on the lives of saints from the thirteenth to the eighteenth centuries published by the university of Rome "La Sapienza" in 1988.[5] Renewed interest in the *legendae novae* was exemplified within a short period of time by such activities as a congress on the *Legenda Aurea: sept siècles de diffusion*, Alain Boureau's volume on *La Légende dorée. Le système narratif de Jacques de Voragine*, Sherry Reames' *The Legenda Aurea: A Re-examination of its Paradoxical History*, Williams and Williams-Krapp's *Die Elsässische "Legenda Aurea,"* and the appearance of *Jacopo da Voragine. Atti del I Convegno di Studi.*[6]

---

[4] Evelyne Patlagean and Pierre Riché, eds., *Hagiographie, cultures et sociétés. IVe–XIIe siècles*, Actes du Colloque organisé à Nanterre et à Paris, 2–5 mai, 1979 (Paris: Etudes Augustiniennes, 1981); André Vauchez, *La sainteté en Occident* aux derniers siècles du Moyen Âge (Rome: Ecole Française de Rome, 1980); Jean-Claude Schmitt, *Le saint lévrier. Guinéfort guérisseur d'enfants depuis le XIIIe siècle* (Paris: Flammarion, 1979).

[5] Sofia Boesch Gajano, ed., *Le raccolte di vite di santi dal XIII al XVIII secolo. Strutture, messaggi, fruizione*, Collana del Dipartimento di Studi Storici dal medioevo all'Età contemporanea dell'Università degli Studi di Roma "La Sapienza" (Fasano: Schena, 1988). Under the stimulus provided by Gajano the Italian group engaged in a rich critical activity evidenced by their publications: Sofia Boesch Gajano and Lucetta Scaraffia, eds., *Luoghi sacri e spazi di santità* (Turin: Rosenberg and Sellier, 1990); Anna Benvenuti Papi and Elena Gennarelli, eds., *Bambini santi* (Turin: Rosenberg and Sellier, 1991); Marilena Modica, ed., *Esperienze religiose e scritture femminili tra Medioevo ed età moderna* (Acireale: Bonanno, 1991); Gabriella Zarri, *Le sante vive. Cultura e religiosità femminile nella prima età moderna* (Turin: Rosenberg and Sellier, 1990); Lucetta Scaraffia, *La santa degli impossibili. Vicende e significati della devozione a Santa Rita* (Turin: Rosenberg and Sellier, 1990); Sofia Boesch Gajano, *Chelidonia. Storia di un culto* (Turin: Rosenberg and Sellier, 1992); Paolo Golinelli, *"Indiscreta sanctitas." Studi sui rapporti tra culti, poteri e società nel pieno Medioevo* (Roma: Istituto Storico Italiano per il Medioevo, 1988); Paolo Golinelli, *Città e culto dei santi nel Medioevo italiano* (Bologna: Clueb, 1991); Anna Benvenuti Papi, *"In castro poenitentiae." Santità e società femminile nell'Italia medievale* (Roma: Herder, 1990); Gabriella Zarri, ed., *Falsi santi. Santità e simulazione in età moderna* (Turin: Rosenberg and Sellier, 1991).

[6] Brenda Dunn-Lardeau, ed., Actes du Colloque International sur la "Legenda Aurea: texte latin et branches vernaculaires," Université de Québec à Montréal, 11–12 mai, 1983 (Montréal-Paris: Bellarmin et Vrin, 1986); Boureau (Paris: Editions du Cerf, 1984); Reames (Madison: Univ. of Wisconsin Press, 1985); Ulla Williams and Werner Williams-Krapp

Of significant importance for the history of hagiography are the seven volumes—the results of seven congresses—that, beginning with 1987, have been dedicated, under the leadership of Pasztor, to a systematic study of Celestine V and his hagiographical context.[7] To these must be added the trail blazing studies which burst upon the scholarly scene within two years of each other: Müller's *Gemeinschaft und Verehrung der Heiligen* which adovocated a fundamental revision of the traditional understanding of sainthood by proposing a new "theology of the saints" within a perspective based on three models: the secular world, the ongoing ecumenical dialogue, and the traditional Catholic concept of Christianity; and the volume offering reflections by some thirty scholars—at the colloquium organized in Rome in 1988 by l'Ecole Française—on the topic of the place occupied and the role played by sainthood between the third and the thirteenth centuries, in the Church's doctrine, in the collective and individual religious experience, and in the organization of social life of the periods and places considered.[8]

The decade of the 1980s proved to be equally well-represented throughout the Western world by the quantity, quality, and diversity of publications on hagiography.[9] The widespread scholarly interest in

---

(Tübingen: Niemeyer, 1980–83); (Varazze: presso la Sede del Centro, 1987).

[7] Alessandro Clementi, ed., *Indulgenza nel medioevo e perdonanza di papa Celestino*, Atti del Convegno storico internazionale, L'Aquila, 5–6 ottobre 1984 (L'Aquila: Centro Celestiniano, 1987). This seminal congress featured papers by Raoul Manselli, Franco Cardini, Pierre Péano, Edith Pasztor, Alessandro Clementi, and Sandro Sticca; Walter Capezzali, ed., *Celestino V Papa Angelico*, Atti del 2 Convegno storico internazionale, L'Aquila, 26–27 agosto 1987 (L'Aquila: Centro Celestiniano, 1988); Walter Capezzali, ed., *S. Pietro del Morrone. Celestino V nel medioevo monastico*, Atti del 3 Convegno storico internazionale, L'Aquila, 26–27 agosto 1988 (L'Aquila: Centro Celestiniano, 1989); Walter Capezzali, ed., *Celestino V e i suoi tempi: realtà spirituale e realtà politica*, Atti del 4 Convegno storico internazionale, L'Aquila, 26–27 agosto 1989 (L'Aquila: Centro Celestiniano, 1990); Walter Capezzali, ed., *"Magisterium et Exemplum": Celestino V e le sue fonti più antiche*, Atti del 5 Convegno storico internazionale, L'Aquila, 31 agosto–1 settembre 1990 (L'Aquila: Centro Celestiniano, 1991); Walter Capezzali, ed., *Celestino V e le sue immagini del Medio Evo*, Atti del 6 Convegno storico internazionale, L'Aquila, 24–25 maggio 1991 (L'Aquila: Centro Celestiniano, 1993); and the seventh volume, *Celestino a Vieste*, Atti del Convegno storico, Vieste, 24 maggio 1992 (Vieste: Centro di Cultura "N. Cimaglia," 1993).

[8] Gerhard Ludwig Müller (Freiburg: Herder, 1991); *Les fonctions des saints dans le monde occidental (IIIe–XIIIe siècles)*, Actes du Colloque organisé par l'Ecole Française de Rome avec le concours de l'Université de "La Sapienza," Rome, 27–29 octobre 1988 (Rome: Ecole Française de Rome, 1991).

[9] For the United States and Canada see the rich bibliography of publications and

hagiography and the abundance of significant and original publications that accompanied it during that period, are evident when one mentions the works, among others, of Brown, Van Kessel, Becker-Nielsen, Morghen, Gélis, Kieckhefer, Hackel, Grégoire, Sigal, Ward, Wilson, Corbet, Passarelli, Schmitt, Goodich, Di Febo, Giannarelli, Goffen, Davidson, Frugoni, Pernoud, Heffernan, Bynum, Airaldi, Sharpe, Whatley;[10] also two studies on hagiography in the High Middle Ages:

---

of research in progress by Gordon Whatley, "North American Research in Hagiography," *Analecta Bollandiana* 105 (1987): 425–44.

[10] Peter Brown, *The Cult of the Saints: Its Rise and Function in Latin Christianity* (Chicago: Univ. of Chicago Press, 1981); Elisja Schulte Van Kessel, ed., *Women and Men in Spiritual Culture, XIV–XVII Centuries. A Meeting of South and North* (The Hague: Netherlands Govt. Pub. Office, 1986); Hand Becker-Nielsen, Peter Foote, Jørgen Højgaard Jørgensen, Tore Nyberg, eds., *Hagiography and Medieval Literature* (Odense: Odense Univ. Press, 1981); Enrico Cerulli and Raffaello Morghen, eds., *Agiografia nell'Occidente cristiano, secoli XIII–XIV* (Rome: Accademia Nazionale dei Lincei, 1980); J. Gélis and O. Redon, eds., *Les miracles des corps* (Paris: Presses et Publications de l'Université de Paris VIII, 1983); R. Kieckhefer, *Unquiet Souls: Fourteenth-Century Saints and their Religious Milieu* (Chicago: Univ. of Chicago Press, 1984); R. Kieckhefer and George D. Bond, eds., *Sainthood: its Manifestation in World Religions* (Berkeley: Univ. of California Press, 1988); Sergei Hackel, ed., *The Byzantine Saint* (London: Fellowship of St. Alban and St. Sergius, 1981); Reginald Grégoire, *Manuale di agiologia. Introduzione alla letteratura agiografica* (Fabriano: Monastero San Silvestro, 1987); Pierre André Sigal, *L'homme et le miracle dans la France médiévale (XIe–XIIe siècles)* (Paris: Editions du Cerf, 1985); Benedicta Ward, *Miracles and the Medieval Mind: Theory, Record and Event. 1100–1225* (Philadelphia: Univ. of Pennsylvania Press, 1982); Benedicta Ward, *Harlots of the Desert: A Study of Repentance in Early Monastic Sources* (Kalamazoo: Mich. Cistercians Publications, 1987); S. Wilson, ed., *Saints and their Cults. Studies in Religious Sociology, Folklore and History* (Cambridge: Cambridge Univ. Press, 1983); P. Corbet, *Les saints ottoniens* (Sigmarinsen: J. Thorbecke, 1986); G. Passarelli, ed., *Il santo patrono nella città medievale: il culto di S. Valentino nella città di Terni*, Atti del Convegno di Studi, 9–12 febbraio, 1974 (Rome: La Goliardica, 1984); Jean-Claude Schmitt, ed., *Les saints et les stars: le texte hagiographique dans la culture populaire* (Paris: Beauchesne, 1983); Michael Goodich, *Vita Perfecta: The Ideal of Sainthood in the Thirteenth Century* (Stuttgart: A. Hiersemann, 1982); Giuliana Di Febo, *Teresa d'Avila: un culto barocco nella Spagna franchista* (Naples: Liguori, 1988); Elena Giannarelli, *La tipologia femminile nella biografia e nell'autobiografia cristiana del IV secolo*, Studi Storici, fasc. 127 (Rome: Istituto Storico Italiano per il Medio Evo, 1980); Rona Goffen, *Spirituality in Conflict: Saint Francis and Giotto's Bardi Chapel* (University Park: Pennsylvania State Univ. Press, 1987); Clifford Davidson, ed., *The Saint Play in Medieval Europe* (Kalamazoo, Mich.: Medieval Institute Publications, 1986); Chiara Frugoni, *Francesco: un'altra storia* (Genoa: Marietti, 1988); Régine Pernoud, *Les saints au Moyen Age* (Paris: Presses-Pocket, 1988); Thomas J. Heffernan, *Sacred Biography: Saints and their Biographers in the Middle Ages* (Berkeley: Univ. of California Press, 1982); Caroline Walker Bynum, *Jesus as Mother: Studies in the Spirituality of the High Middle Ages* (Berkeley: Univ. of California Press, 1982); Caroline Walker Bynum, *Holy*

a collection of essays published in *Schede Medievali*, and a two-volume mine of hagiographic research on *Santi e demoni nell'Alto Medioevo occidentale*.[11]

Notwithstanding the existence of a large body of significant scholarship and criticism on different areas and aspects of medieval and Renaissance hagiography, scholars at times still engage, at the beginning of their studies, in discussions meant to define, clarify, and interpret the meaning of the term *hagiography* and the original purpose and function of it. The problem is not of little import especially if one considers the lack of regard traditionally shown by modern historians for hagiographical accounts,[12] and the differences of opinion still held, in the study of the history of saints, by what have been defined as *l'école critique*, *l'école conservatrice*, and *l'école hypercritique*.[13] It was left up to Peter Brown, in his provocative study, *The Cult of the Saints. Its Rise and Function in Latin Christianity* (1981)[14] to have created a fourth category, *l'école politique*, by showing the uses and exploitations of saints fostered and practised by the political powers of the late-Imperial period.

As a timely and fitting overview and assessment of this intellectual

---

Feast and Holy Fast: The Religious Significance of Food to Medieval Women (Berkeley: Univ. of California Press, 1987); Gabriella Airaldi, *Jacopo da Voragine: tra santi e mercanti* (Milan: Camunia, 1988); Richard Sharpe, *Medieval Irish Saints' Lives* (New York: Oxford Univ. Press, 1991); E. Gordon Whatley, ed. and trans., *The Saint of London: The Life and Miracles of St. Erkenwald* Medieval & Renaissance Texts & Studies, vol. 58 (Binghamton: 1989).

[11] *Aspetti dell'agiografia nell'Alto Medioevo*, Testi del II Colloquio medievale, Palermo, 20–21 marzo, 1983 , published in *Schede Medievali* 5 (luglio–dicembre, 1983): 303–82; *Santi e demoni nell'Alto Medioevo occidentale*, Settimane di Studio del Centro Italiano di Studi sull'Alto Medioevo, Spoleto, 7–13 aprile, 1988, vols. 1–2 (Spoleto: Presso la Sede del Centro, 1989).

[12] Baudoin de Gaiffier, *Recueil d'hagiographie*, Subsidia Hagiogragraphica 61 (Brussels: Société des Bollandistes, 1977), chap. 4: "Hagiographie et Historiographie," p. 139: "En général, les textes hagiographiques n'ont pas bonne presse chez les historiens, et dire d'une biographie qu'elle rentre dans le genre hagiographique n'est pas un éloge." René Aigrain, *L'hagiographie* (Paris: Bloud et Gay, 1953), 128, observes: "C'est sans doute à la mauvaise réputation d'un trop grand nombre de ces 'légendes' auprès des historiens qu'est due la signification péjorative attachée le plus souvent à ce terme par le langage courant."

[13] Hippolite Delehaye, *Cinq leçons sur la méthode hagiographique*, Subsidia Hagiographica 21 (Brussels: Société des Bollandistes, 1934): 19.

[14] See note 10.

ferment, historically and critically, the Center for Medieval and Early Renaissance Studies at Binghamton University, in the fall of 1989, sponsored the twenty-third conference on the theme of "The Cult of the Saints in the Middle Ages and Early Renaissance: Formation and Transformation."

The fifteen essays that make up this volume encompass a variety of critical methodologies and thematic ranges, and offer insights and perspectives into such areas as art, history, literature, liturgy, theology, spirituality, monasticism, mysticism, theater, and into such topics as sexuality, patronage, childhood and sanctity, desert saints, urban saints, royal saints, shrines and relics.

In an introductory paper that is both an assessment of recent hagiographical studies and a commentary on their unfulfilled promises, Patrick J. Geary suggests some of the reasons for the disappointing results by reviewing the new directions in hagiographic research, by focusing on the new problems, and finally by offering new solutions. Geary identifies the four major trends in today's hagiographic studies as a focus away from saints and towards the society in which they were sanctified; a focus from *vitae* and *passiones* to others sorts of hagiographical texts; a tendency to study collectivities and serial records; and a growing recognition that none of these texts are transparent windows into the saints' lives and their society or its spirituality. In Geary's view, scholars have too often lost sight of the hagiographical text and its author and, therefore, the saints themselves have disappeared. He concluded that scholars should rediscover the meaning of hagiographical texts to their producers, the context of production, and should learn about the models of comportment and ideals of human existence that saints seem to offer.

In the first of the five papers that make up the initial section of this volume, saints in hagiographic texts, Jo Ann MacNamara examines the tradition of queenly sanctity, the *fama sanctitatis* of queenship within the confines of the established medieval concept of the *sanctitas regis* so frequent in medieval hagiographical literature. Starting with Helena, Constantine's mother, MacNamara shows how the diverse roles of queens as peacemakers, alms-givers, intercessors for the weak and intermediaries between the king's temporal power and the clergy's spiritual power, allowed them to practice sainthood as a function of their office—with one notable break in Carolingian times—until late in the eleventh century.

English hagiography represented, from the seventh century to the Middle English period, by a long-established popular tradition, provides the forum for T. Johnson-South who argues that the emphasis on St. Cuthberth's temporal power in the late-Saxon *Historia de Sancto Cuthberto*, compared to his humility and asceticism displayed in the early *Lives*, reflects an increase in the power of his community. As this power grew, St. Cuthbert himself became the symbol of the power. Land was given directly to the saint, new estates were purchased with his money, and the local inhabitants were described as his people. In particular, the persona of St. Cuthbert in the *Historia* reflects the values and needs of a powerful late-Saxon monastic community, rather than those of a seventh-century ascetic hermit.

Mary Lynn Rampolla focuses her attention in her reading of the *Vita Wulfstani* on the role played by one element in the saint's repertoire—his ability to cure the insane. She illustrates how, through the redactor's skillful manipulation of hagiographical conventions, the saint's ability to cure madmen becomes an important metaphor for sin, social disruption, and the loss of identity which threatened monks in the post-Norman Conquest period. Rampolla's analysis of the *Vita Wulfstani* demonstrates both the necessity of studying medieval hagiography as a genre whose conventions must be understood before it can be used as a source of historical information, and the importance of approaching each saint's life as a product of a particular time and situation.

Delving into the practice of adaptations in French vernacular hagiography, Laurie Postlewaite observes that just as clerical writers "translated" Latin lives into the vernaculars so too they brought to their works new ways of thinking about the spiritual life and a new understanding of the religious needs of laymen. By studying two adaptations in Old French of the life of St. Margaret of Antioch—Wace's *Vie de Sainte Marguerite* and Bozon's *Vie Seinte Margarete*—Postlewaite demonstrates that whereas in the former Wace used the imagery of love to depict the mystical union of Margaret and Christ, thus reflecting the influence of twelfth-century devotionalism and mystical theology, in the latter, Bozon, a Franciscan preacher of the early fourteenth-century, adapted his *Vie Seinte Margarete* to instruct the secular public in the practice of the Christian life by emphasizing those aspects of the saint's life that could be imitated by the laity, including poverty, celibacy, and prayer.

Within the field of Iberian vernacular hagiography, Roberto J. Gónzales-Casanovas studies Ramon Llull's Catalan prose romance *Blanquerna* (1283–85) and points out that it represents a fictional didactic narrative; in particular, it reflects Church renewal after the Fourth Lateran Council (1215) and the founding of the Dominican and Franciscan orders. He underscores the fact that Llull combines religious and secular genres—hagiography, quest, social mirror, utopia, and mystical allegory—into a modern novel-sermon in which he describes a prototype of the middle-class saint, gives a practical demonstration of urban preaching, and presents a complete image of the City of God into which Christendom is to be transformed *hic et nunc*.

Two papers make up the section on saints in liturgy and drama. In dealing with texts of late medieval offices of the saints, Andrew Hughes points out that traditional offices of the standard liturgy are exclusively in prose, that newly-composed offices of the centuries following the eleventh are usually in fully accented and rhymed poetry, and that in between the two are offices written in a variety of ways and with various kinds of structure including rhymed prose, the cursus, classical meters, and irregular poetical forms. Using only the texts, it is often not possible to know whether these structures are deliberate; but visible clues such as punctuations and capital letters in the manuscripts suggest that medieval scribes, at least, could distinguish artifice from accident. Hughes illustrates that repeated melodic motives in the chants confirm the structures.

Clifford Davidson examines the relationship between the English theater and saints' lives from the first record of a play dramatizing the life of a post-biblical saint at Dunstable around 1110, St. Catherine of Alexandria, and through a large number of plays down to those dramatizing the Virgin Mary at New Romney in 1512–13 and St. Martin at Colchester in 1527. Dramatic records from surviving sources strongly indicate that the miracle or saint play may have been the most important genre in the repertoire of the English medieval stage. The lives, legends, and miracles of saints became adapted to theatrical stage, for the playwrights catered to the people's desire to *see* the physical shape of the saint and the historical events associated with his life.

The publication in 1980 of Raoul Manselli's brilliant book, *Nos qui cum eo fuimus*, called by one critic "the most auspicious and distinguished contribution to the study of St. Francis to appear in many a year,"[15] established new foundations for studies on St. Francis as the section on this saint amply demonstrates. Of interest and relevance among these are studies that focus on hagiography and the visual arts, especially those concerned with pictorial illustration of episodes described in the earliest lives of St. Francis. Addressing this topic, Chiara Frugoni centers her paper on the iconography of the stigmata and its relationship to the early Franciscan sources in which the miraculous event is recorded, in particular Thomas of Celano's *Vita prima* and Bonaventure's *Legenda major*. Frugoni shows that a decisive shift in the iconography of the stigmata occurred soon after the Chapter of 1226 at which Bonaventure succeeded in ordering the destruction of all previous accounts of St. Francis's life, thus making of his own version the only official biography. Out of the close interaction between Bonaventure's biographical text and Giotto, the great painter who interpreted it and even improved on it, there developed an official and formal iconographical visualization of the stigmata that established a close identification of St. Francis with Christ.

Diane Cole Ahl, for her part, elucidates the iconography of the life of St. Francis at Montefalco (1451–52), one of the few fifteenth-century cycles of the saint's life. She investigates the patronage of these murals and explores the associations between Montefalco and Assisi, just thirty kilometers away. In her analysis of the narrative sequence within the cycle, Ahl shows how the deviations from the canonical chronology of St. Francis's life, including transpositions of sequence, can be explained within the context of Franciscan artistic, literary, and preaching traditions.

The final section of the volume groups papers dealing with the public, private, and popular cult of the saints. As the second most important Franciscan saint, St. Anthony of Padua was the object of one of the most vital and important cults of the late Middle Ages and early Renaissance, a fact that has been amply illustrated in Antonino's Pioppi's collection of critical essays on that saint.[16] Sarah Blake McHam

---

[15] Manselli: Bibliotheca Seraphico-Capuccina, vol. 28 (Rome: Istituto Storico dei Cappuccini, 1980); Rosalind B. Brooke, "Recent Work on St. Francis of Assisi," *Analecta Bollandiana* 100 (1982): 667.

[16] Antonino Pioppi, ed., *Liturgia, pietà e ministeri al santo di Padova fra il XIII e il XX secolo*, (Verona: Neri Pozza Editore, 1978).

explores in her paper how the joint sponsorship of the Franciscan Order and the city of Padua contributed to the development of the saint's cult through an analysis of the various *vitae* written between ca. 1232–1435, the different feasts and devotions instituted in his honor, and the sequence of increasingly large and grand shrines constructed to house his relics.

Venice, a city whose large number of sacred relics supported her claim to special favor with God, is the center of Patricia H. Labalme's investigation. Most treasured among its saintly patrons were the numina and bodies of St. Mark, St. Theodore, and St. Nicholas. Labalme clearly shows that the enhancement of the role of these three saints and their saintly certifications in the middle of the fifteenth century were related to a difficult period in Venice's interaction with other Italian powers and that the Venetian bishop's role in these events was crucial. At a time, between 1448 and 1451, when Venice found herself isolated and vilified, her bishop, Lorenzo Giustiniani (1433 to 1451), through his leadership and piety, was able to bridge the secular and the sacred with a renewed devotion to the saints' relics. In the process he earned for himself shortly after his death the title of "beato."

As the guardian angel to the young Tobias on his journey to collect money due to his father, the archangel Raphael came to be seen by the Florentine business community as the special protector of their children and junior partners. Konrad Eisenbichler examines the contribution brought to the cult of the archangel Raphael by the two Florentine confraternities specifically devoted to him: the *Compagnia dell'Arcangelo Raffaello detta Raffa* (for adult males) and the *Compagnia dell'Arcangelo Raffaello detta della Scala o della Natività* (for boys and youths). By drawing directly on the confraternities' archival records, Eisenbichler is able to show the special interest that the children's Confraternity of the Archangel Raphael holds for the history of drama by virtue of the short plays dealing with the archangel and the youth Tobias that were performed by the boys in their oratory.

Virginia Reinburg explores a variety of prayers to saints collected in French books of hours (ca. 1350–1550). Developing insights from the anthropology of religion, she treats prayers as a relationship between an individual devotee and a supernatural person. Reinburg explains that late medieval women and men understood this relationship as reciprocal: the devotee offered petitions, praise, and donations, and expected an answer or assistance from God or a saint. Widespread use of the concept "patron saint" suggests moreover that relationships between devotees and those to whom they prayed mirrored relationships in the secular world. By explicating prayers addressed to the plague saints Sebastian and Roch by individuals and communities, and penitential prayers addressed to St. Mary Magdalen, Reinburg offers a view of late medieval religious experience fuller than previous literature has suggested.

Martin W. Walsh offers a study of aspects of medieval popular culture surrounding the feast and figure of St. Martin of Tours. In particular, he attempts to explain the paradox of how a fourth-century ascetic monk and missionary bishop became associated with sexual humor, *fairie*, conspicuous feasting, and the grotesque in later medieval art, literature, and drama—how he indeed became the patron saint of a kind of shadow Carnival at the beginning rather than the end of the winter reveling season.

The papers that make up this volume, with their thematic variety, enrich current hagiographical studies and shed new light on the genre. In particular, they concern themselves with a systematic revaluation not only of traditional methods of investigation but with forgotten areas of hagiography, such as children saints, saints in the family (father and son; mother and daughter), royal saints (kings and queens), the saint play, and the much neglected topic of the rapport between saints and their families,[17] a provocative and original line of research especially in view of the fact that the saint's deliberate refusal of family affections was traditionally looked upon as an indispensable prerequisite to sainthood.

These new directions in hagiographical research have opened wider vistas for the careful student of hagiography, allowing him to distance himself from the historical-philological Bollandist school concerned primarily with the authenticity and veracity of the sources. While the contribution of the Bollandists to the study of hagiography remains a lasting and invaluable monument to which all scholars must refer, it is important that elements other than the liturgical, the historical, and the religious be considered in trying to understand the process of the sac-

---

[17] The recently published study by Alessandro Barbero, *Un santo in famiglia. Vocazione e resistenze sociali nell'agiografia latina medievale* (Turin: Rosenberg and Sellier, 1991), constitutes an auspicious beginning.

ralization of individuals in the Middle Ages and in the Renaissance. Looking beyond the image of perfection, the desire of perfectibility, the emblematic projection of a paragon that the saint's *vita* generates, one must consider the fullness of that hagiographical text in order to perceive the economic, social, political and religious power within which that *vita* is often articulated. One must understand the transformation of the concept of *sanctitas* and *sanctus* as it moved from the *contemplatio* of the early Middle Ages through the *imitatio* of the central medieval period to the *participatio* of the late Middle Ages where the saint participates fully in the complexity of the human and social condition.

Many areas need future elucidation: the collective memory, that oral transfiguration of the saint's reality which often contributed to confirm the written tradition; the context provided by social relationship and political structure; the relation between urban structure and the saint on the one hand and the *memoriae* and the *legendae* on the other; the vitality of local traditions; the contribution of the *illiterati*; the rapport between Latin and vernacular tradition; between autobiographies and diaries; the temporal distance between the saint and the moment of his sanctification; the encounter between the city and the desert in the life of the saint. These are some of the topics that await fuller investigation on the part of scholars who have made of the last decade one of the most fruitful in the history of hagiographical study.

SAINTS

Studies in Hagiography

Saints, Scholars, and Society: The Elusive Goal

PATRICK GEARY

round 1965, scholars began to turn to the legends of the saints with high hopes and enormous effort in an attempt to breathe new life into a long-ignored body of religious texts.[1] Hagiography seemed to promise a new window into medieval religious ideals and into the lives of ordinary people. New approaches and new questions have indeed generated a tremendous growth of interest in the cult of saints among scholars across a wide spectrum of disciplines. And yet the promise of such studies remains partly unfulfilled.

The old nineteenth-century debate between scientific free thinkers and pious defenders of the legends of the saints has largely ended. Those few who continue to write cynical, debunking comments about medieval credulity or who poke fun at the seven sacred foreskins or the various heads of St. John the Baptist venerated across Europe, seem as quaint as the pious defenders of the provençal legends of Mary Magdalene or the miraculous transport of St. James to Compostela. Likewise

---

[1] Comprehensive discussions of the literature of hagiography, something this paper does not aim to do, are the bibliographic essay by Sofia Boesch Gajano in her *Agiografica altomedioevale* (Bologna: Il Molino, 1976), 261–300, and the introduction and bibliography prepared by Stephen Wilson in his *Saints and their Cults: Studies in Religious Sociology, Folklore, and History* (Cambridge: Cambridge Univ. Press, 1983). I am grateful to Barbara Rosenwein for her criticisms of a preliminary draft of this paper.

the positivist concern to separate "fact" from "fiction" in hagiography, which gave birth to the great Bollandist undertaking, has largely taken a back seat in modern hagiographic studies. For decades it has simply not been accurate to begin a study of hagiography, as did Thomas Heffernan last year in an otherwise excellent book, with the rhetorical *planctus* that until very recently hagiography has "fallen through the net of scholarly research, avoided by the historians because it lacks 'documentary' evidential status and by the literary historians because saints' lives are rarely works of art."[2] Not only have hagiographic texts received frequent, close scrutiny from medievalists for years, but they have moved from the periphery to the center of the scholarly enterprise. Perhaps the most striking example of this trend can be seen in the two recent books by one of America's most outstanding medievalists, Caroline Walker Bynum. In the preface to her 1982 collection *Jesus as Mother*, she defended her concentration on formal treatises on spirituality in most of these essays in contrast to the growing attention to artifacts, charters, and rituals attended by the laity, saying:

> The new history of spirituality is therefore in a curious situation. It has abandoned detailed study of most of the material medieval people themselves produced on the subject of religion in favor of far more intractable sources. It has done this partly from the admirable desire to correct the concentration of earlier scholarship on mainline groups ... but partly, I suspect, from boredom and frustration with the interminable discussions of the soul's approach to God, which is the major subject of medieval religious writing. We cannot, however, afford to abandon what will always be the bulk of our information on medieval religion.[3]

Interestingly enough, her 1987 book, *Holy Feast and Holy Fast,* is based primarily on some of the most "intractable" of medieval sources, the

---

[2] Thomas J. Heffernan, *Sacred Biography: Saints and their Biographers in the Middle Ages* (New York: Oxford Univ. Press, 1988), 17.

[3] Caroline Walker Bynum, *Jesus as Mother: Studies in the Spirituality of the High Middle Ages* (Berkeley: Univ. of California Press, 1982), 5–6. Although Bynum includes saints' lives in her list of traditional sources, her sources for the essays in *Jesus as Mother*, in contrast to the works she characterizes as the "new approach," make little use of hagiography.

hagiographic dossiers of late medieval saints.[4] Bynum's growing interest in hagiographic sources may reflect a realization that hagiography, rather than formal treatises and commentaries, provides "what will always be the bulk of our information on medieval religion." As Heffernan accurately points out, "The sheer number of lives of saints which survived in manuscript"[5] is enormously impressive. If to the lives, one adds liturgical calendars, collections of miracles, accounts of translations, martyrologies, liturgies celebrating saints' feasts, and the like, it is obvious that "most of the material medieval people themselves produced on the subject of religion" is not "interminable discussions of the soul's approach to God," but innumerable biographies of saints approaching God.

It is perhaps the large number of hagiographic sources, as much as anything else, that has led historians, increasingly concerned with the representativeness of evidence and statistical approaches to the past, to turn to them. The volumes of the *Acta Sanctorum* lure scholars with the promise of a mass of evidence not simply about saints, but about their society, if only they can find a way to use it. Anyone who has suffered over the sparseness of historical, epistolary, theological, and legal sources from the Merovingian world, for example, can appreciate the temptation to dive into the five fat volumes of saints' lives that make up the bulk of literary production from that age. But it is not only the quantity of texts that is appealing. As historians turn increasingly from the history of events to that of perceptions and values, hagiography appears a kind of source superior to almost any other, because it seems to offer images of societies' ideal types. For both reasons we have thrown ourselves into the study of these texts. The results however have, quite frankly, been disappointing. Enormous efforts have been expended, but much of what we produce is somehow vaguely unsatisfying. We should stop and take stock of where we are, what has happened in hagiography since 1965, and what formal and conceptual problems have prevented us from achieving the great promise this material seems to offer. I put forward here an admittedly subjective review

---

[4] Caroline Walker Bynum, *Holy Feast and Holy Fast: The Religious Significance of Food to Medieval Women* (Berkeley: Univ. of California Press, 1987).

[5] Heffernan, vii.

of medieval Continental history focusing on hagiography, which makes no pretense to comprehensiveness.

New Directions

I would date the new historical interest in hagiography to 1965 because in that year appeared František Graus' magnificent *People, Lord, and Saint in the Kingdom of the Merovingians: Studies in the Hagiography of the Merovingian Period,* a work he had completed some three years earlier. Graus is one of the last representatives of a lost world: the Germanophone Jewish Prague of high culture and scholarship. In this book, dedicated to his grandfather, "murdered at Auschwitz," and his brother, "murdered during the evacuation of Buchenwald," Graus, fully in command of a century of scholarship in German, French, Russian, and English and informed by the Marxist critique of cultural production, focuses a perceptive mind on the hagiographic literature of the early Frankish period. Two methodological perspectives mark his work as a new departure. The first is his understanding of the importance of hagiography, for the study not simply of religion but of society: "For modern historiography the social function and the teaching of the legends are of particular interest. Thus the primary focus of this study concentrates especially on the attitude of the hagiographers toward the people and toward the rulers. This is a somewhat unusual point of departure for the study of hagiography. As far as I know, an exhaustive analysis of this sort has not been previously attempted, although the results will show that even the legends of the saints, and in many instances especially and only they, can become an important source of our knowledge."[6] In other words, not only can hagiography be used

---

[6] František Graus, *Volk, Herrscher und Heiliger im Reich der Merowinger: Studien zur Hagiographie der Merowingerzeit* (Prague: Nakladatelstvi Ceskoslovenske akademie ved, 1965), 11. "Für die moderne Historiographie sind besonders die gesellschaftliche Funktion und die Lehre der Legende von Interesse. Das Hauptaugenmerk der Untersuchung konzentriert sich also demgemäß besonders auf die Einstellung der Hagiographen zum Volk und zu den Herrschern. Das ist ein etwas ungewohnter Ausgangspunkt zur Untersuchung der Hagiographie; meines Wissens ist eine eingehendere Analyse dieser Art bisher noch nicht versucht worden, obzwar das Ergebnis lehren wird, daß auch die Legenden, und in manchen Fällen gerade und nur sie, eine wichtige Quelle unserer Kenntnisse werden können."

for incidental historical information, but it can and must be a privileged source for the study of social values. The second is his recognition that while investigating the social function of hagiography, one must never forget the essential literary nature of these texts. Understanding the formal components and traditions of this literary genre is an essential requirement for proper historical exploitation of hagiography. And a primary aspect of this literature is that it is, in part, consciously propaganda.[7] The implications of this second Grausian perspective are two. First, historians cannot avoid dealing with the formal literary tradition of the hagiographic texts with which they work; for these texts are anything but a transparent window into the everyday life of medieval people. Not only what they say about the virtues and miracles of the saints but even their presentation of ordinary people, even of the most mundane elements of the hagiographer's world, reflect other hagiographic texts and traditions that cannot be ignored. Historians thus must be formalists. But second and equally important, literary scholars cannot ignore propagandistic nature of this literature. Hagiography has an essential political dimension that escapes the intertextuality of the literary dimension. Formalists thus must be historians.

With these prolegomena in mind, I offer first my review of what I see as important trends in the literature since the appearance of Graus's book and then some suggestions for where we need to look to solve some of the problems this cascade of work has left us. I see four major trends in hagiographic scholarship. The first is a tendency to move from the study of saints to that of society. Here Graus is clearly the pioneer. Around the same time, Byzantinists such as François Halkin and Evelyne Patlagean were opening late classical and Byzantine hagiography to use by social historians.[8] The work that had the greatest impetus to the functionalist tradition of hagiographic research in the English-speaking world, however, was Peter Brown's "The Rise and Function of the Holy Man in Late Antiquity," which appeared in 1971.[9] By placing at the very center of late antique life figures whom political

---

[7] Graus, 39.

[8] F. Halkin, "L'Hagiographie byzantine au service de l'histoire," *XIIIth International Congress of Byzantine Studies* (Oxford: 1966), Main Papers, 11, 345–54; E. Patlagean, "A Byzance: Ancienne hagiographie et histoire sociale," *Annales: ESC* 23 (1968), 106–26.

[9] Brown, *Journal of Roman Studies* 61 (1971), 80–101.

and social historians had long dismissed as "marginal," by connecting their "religious" meaning to issues recognizable to the most secular twentieth-century intellectual, Brown not only invented "the world of late antiquity" as a fashionable area of study and inspired studies of holy men around the world, but he made the hagiography respectable to a generation of historians trained in the traditions of the social sciences.

Graus and Brown were able to use hagiography for social and political history because they broadened their perspective, examining, instead of a particular saint, many saints and their hagiographic dossiers. This move from individual to collective is the second, related phenomenon in hagiographic studies. It has near predecessors in the pioneering work of the Belgian Pierre Delooz which appeared in a series of publications between 1962 and 1969.[10] Excellent monographs on individual cults continue to be produced, such as David W. Rollason's *The Mildrith Legend*,[11] the essays on Elizabeth of Thuringia published by the University of Marburg in 1981,[12] and Dominique Iogna-Prat's studies on the hagiographic dossier of Saint Maïeul.[13] The trend toward broader documentary bases is clear, however, and is not an entirely new phenomenon. In 1908 Ludwig Zoepf published his study on tenth-century saints' lives in which he sought to understand the *Zeitideen* of the age through a systematic analysis of its hagiography.[14] Like Zoepf, some of these more recent historians are looking for social ideals in hagiographic production. Joseph-Claude Poulin, in his study of Carolingian hagiography in Aquitaine, puts it thus: "By their actual

---

[10] Pierre Delooz, "Pour une étude sociologique de la sainteté canonisée dans l'Eglise catholique," *Archives de sociologie des religions* 13 (1962), 17–43; "Notes sur les canonisations occitanes à l'époque de la croisade des Albigeois," *Annales de l'Institut d'études occitanes* 4 em. série 1 (1965), 106–12; *Sociologie et canonisations* (Liège-The Hague: Faulté de droit, 1969).

[11] D. W. Rollason, *The Mildrith Legend: A Study in Early Medieval Hagiography in England* (Leichester: Univ. of Leicester Press, 1982).

[12] *Sankt Elisabeth: Fürstin Dienerin Heilige Aufsätze Dokumentation Katalog* (Sigmaringen: Thorbecke, 1981). Other important studies of particular saints are found in Sofia Boesch Gajano and Lucia Sebastiani, eds. *Culto dei santi, Istituzioni e classi sociali in età preindustriali* (Aquila: L. U. Japadre, 1984).

[13] Dominique Iogna-Prat, *Agni immaculati. Recherches sur les sources hagiographiques relatives à Saint Maïeul de Cluny 954–994* (Paris: Editions du Cerf, 1988).

[14] Ludwig Zoepf, *Das Heiligen-Leben im 10. Jahrhundert* (Leipzig and Berlin: B. G. Teubner, 1908), esp. chap. 3, *Das Heiligen-Leben, ein Spiegel der Zeitideen*, 108.

life or by the deeds attributed to them, the saints incarnated the moral ideals of their epoch. Thus their lives can serve as an attempt to reconstitute the ideal model of a given society."[15] In his book of thirteenth-century saints, Michael Goodich sought the same kind of ideal: "The present study of thirteenth century sainthood, on the other hand, is more concerned with the saint himself as an ideal cultural type. While his character was presented to youth as an object worthy of emulation, whose life embodies the noblest ideals of his age, at the same time the saint's development reflects the social and political conflicts which engaged his contemporaries."[16] André Vauchez too was searching in his study of canonizations for the saint as "the person who is the eminent illustration of the ideas of sanctity that the Christians of a given time held."[17] In contrast, whereas Goodich and Vauchez announced the ideal as their focus, Donald Weinstein and Rudolf Bell attempted in 1982 to assess 864 saints spanning seven hundred years of Western Christian sanctity, asking who they were, how they came to pursue spiritual perfection, and how their society dealt with them.[18]

---

[15] Joseph-Claude Poulin, *L'idéal de sainteté dans l'Aquitaine carolingienne d'après les sources hagiographiques (750–950)* (Laval: Presses de l'Univ. de Laval, 1975), 3–4. "Par leur vie réelle ou par les hauts faits qu'on leur prête, les saints ont incarné l'idéal morale de leur époque. Leurs biographies peuvent donc servir à un essai de reconstitution du modèle idéal d'une société donnée; [elles représentent non plus des règles de conduite négatives, comme n'importe quel code pénal, mais une définition des règles de réussite, un portrait du juste—le 'méchant' n'apparaissant que secondairement, en manière de repoussoir.]"

[16] Michael Goodich, *Vita perfecta: The Ideal of Sainthood in the Thirteenth Century* (Stuttgart: A. Hiersemann, 1982), 3.

[17] André Vauchez, *La sainteté en Occident aux derniers siècles du Moyen Age d'après les procès de canonisation it les documents hagiographiques* (Rome: Ecole Française de Rome, 1981). "Selon l'heureuse formule de S. Bonnet, un saint, c'est d'abord un homme extraordinaire habité par Dieu. C'est aussi une réponse aux besoins spirituels d'une génération. C'est encore [un homme qui est l'illustration éminente des idées que les chrétiens d'un temps donné se sont fait de la sainteté.] Le premier aspect ne se prête guère à une étude historique; en tant qu'expérience individuelle vécue par un homme ou une femme en quête de perfection, la sainteté chrétienne est, dans son essence même, intemporelle et toujours identique. Aussi sa nature profonde échappe-t-elle nécessairement à une analyse qui ne prétend pas pénétrer le secret des consciences. Les deux derniers en revanche seront au centre de nos préoccupations puisque notre objectif est de dégager l'ensemble des raisons pour lesquelles les chrétiens des derniers siècles du Moyen Age, en Occident, ont accordé à certains de leurs contemporains le titre de saints."

[18] Donald Weinstein and Rudolf M. Bell, *Saints and Society: The Two Worlds of Western Christendom, 1000–1700* (Chicago: Univ. of Chicago Press, 1982), 1.

What distinguishes all these works from those of earlier scholars such as Zoepf is the prosopographic methodology these historians apply; their reliance, to at least some extent, on statistics; and their attempts to recover not simply religious, but social ideals.

Third, as historians have gone beyond research on individual saints, they have also gone beyond the study of *vitae* and *passiones*, what Heffernan, perhaps after Zoepf, terms "sacred biography." They now examine additionally, or even particularly, other kinds of texts such as collections of miracles; accounts of translations, *adventus*, and elevations; liturgies; and hymns, on the one hand, and sanctorales, martyrologies, legendaries, exempla collections, and other collective works on the other. As Martin Heinzelmann explains, the first group differs from *vitae* and *passiones* in that while "the rule of the *exemplum* of a life in accord with the standards of sanctity is at the center of hagiographic biography, the *testimonium* of miracles, that is, the glory of the patron in eternity, stands at the center of *translationes*."[19] Some of these works such as Benedicta Ward's *Miracles and the Medieval Mind* or the more comprehensive and enlightening work on some five thousand miracles by Pierre André Sigal, *Man and Miracle in Medieval France,* focus primarily on the meaning of miraculous in medieval society.[20] As Sigal expresses it, "To the study of the miraculous according to theoretical definitions, one must add a study of the miraculous in its daily reality through the testimony of those who were the object or the witness of a miracle...."[21] Henri Platelle has shown the ways miracle

---

[19] Martin Heinzelmann, *Translationsberichte und andere Quellen des Reliquienkultes,* Typologie des Sources du Moyen Âge occidental no. 33 (Turnhout: Brepols, 1979), 102.

[20] Benedicta Ward, *Miracles and the Medieval Mind: Theory, Record, and Event 1000–1215* (Philadelphia: Univ. of Pennsylvania Press, 1982); [Pierre-André Sigal, *L'homme et le miracle dans la France médiévale (XIe–XIIe Siècle)* (Paris: Editions du Cerf, 1985)].

[21] 10. Sigal, "A l'étude du miracle selon des définitions théoriques il faut donc ajouter une étude du miracle dans sa réalité quotidienne à travers les témoignages de ceux qui ont été l'objet ou le témoin d'un miracle. C'est ce miracle pratique que j'ai essayé d'étudier ici, pour la période médiévale, en recherchant les faits considérés comme miraculeux et en examinant comment ils se produisaient, qui en étaient les bénéficiaires, quels en étaient les types les plus courants. (15) ... Malgré l'écran de la composition hagiographique, l'attitude des hommes de l'époque vis-à-vis du miracle est suffisamment mise en lumière pour être observée et analysée et le crible même qui a servi à sélectionner les faits miraculeux peut être utilisé pour répondre à la question: qu'est-ce qu'un miracle au Moyen Age?"

collections reflect legal practice and disputing mechanisms.[22] Others, such as Michel Rouche and especially Ronald C. Finucane, have attempted to use miracle collections to study physical and psychological health in medieval society.[23] Vauchez's monumental work on sanctity is based largely on yet another kind of serial record, the inquisitions *de fama et sanctitate* or canonization cases conducted from the thirteenth through fifteenth centuries. Erika Laquer has drawn on the rich dossier compiled in the course of an extended legal process to examine the cult of Saint Eloi of Noyon during the thirteenth century.[24] William Christian's *Local Religion in Sixteenth-Century Spain,* perhaps the most successful examination of truly popular relationships between people and their patrons, is based entirely on the questionnaires sent by Philip II to the towns and villages of New Castille to investigate local religious and historical traditions.[25]

Just as these nonbiographical texts are receiving new attention, so too are collective texts, which are being analyzed not simply in terms of their components but as units. An outstanding example is Alain Boureau's *Golden Legend,* in which the author undertakes to examine a type of hagiographic genre, the vulgar Dominican legendary, which must be read, as he says, "both in its banality and in its singularity."[26] Boureau's systematic study of the *Golden Legend* from formal, structural,

---

[22] Henri Platelle, *Terre et ciel aux anciens Pays Bas: Recueil d'articles de . . . Platelle publié à l'occasion de son élection à l'Acatémie royale de Belgique* (Lille, 1991).

[23] Michel Rouche, "Miracles, maladies, et psychologie de la foi à l'époque carolingienne en Francie," *Hagiographie, cultures et sociétés IVe–XIIe siècles,* (Proceedings of a symposium at Nanterre and Paris, May 2–5, 1979) (Paris: Etudes augustiniennes, 1981), 319–37. Ronald C. Finucane, *Miracles and Pilgrims: Popular Beliefs in Medieval England* (London: Rowman and Littlefield, 1977).

[24] Erika J. Laquer, "Ritual, Literacy and Documentary Evidence: Archbishop Eudes Rigaud of St. Eloi," *Francia* 13 (1986), 625–37.

[25] (Princeton, Princeton Univ. Press, 1981). Other studies of hagiography in the context of local religion are Paolo Golinelli, *Culto dei santi e vita cittadina a Reggio Emilia, secoli IX–XII* (Modena: Aedes Muratoriana, 1980) and *Indiscreta sanctitas.* My own *Furta Sacra: Thefts of Relics in the Central Middle Ages* 2nd ed. (Princeton: Princeton Univ. Press, 1990) also focuses on non-biographical hagiography.

[26] Boureau, *La Légende dorée,* 12. Also showing appreciation of the importance of legendaries both in Latin and in the vernacular are the 1983 conference proceedings from Montréal: *Legenda aurea, sept siècles de diffusion actes du colloque international sur la Legenda aurea, texte latin et branches vernaculaires,* ed. Brenda Dunn-Lardeau and Sherry L. Reames, *The Legenda Aurea* (Madison: Univ. of Wisconsin Press, 1985).

and rhetorical perspectives brings us to the fourth trend in recent hagiographic work, the recognition of the critical problems of genre, of
rhetoric, and especially of intertextuality. As Gabrielle Spiegel points
out, the "linguistic turn" leads directly to the "prison house of language."[27] We should not pretend that Jacques Derrida has revealed
something radically new to us: that hagiography reproduces hagiography rather than some putative reality. Hippolyte Delehaye pointed this
out in 1905 in his *Legends of the Saints,*[28] although because he wrote
in plain, comprehensible language, his message was perhaps not as clear
as that of Derrida. Medievalists have returned to this warning with a
vengeance, deconstructing hagiographical texts into their constituent
literary and rhetorical echoes until little remains. Perhaps the most
thorough-going example of this is Friedrich Lotter's life of Severinus of
Noricum (†482).[29] Under his careful analysis the *Vita Severini,* long
considered the most important document for the history of late fifth-
century Noricum, proves a pure tissue of rhetorical topoi and textual
borrowings, incapable of telling us anything, not only about Severinus,
but about Noricum in the fifth century.

In brief, then, and with many omissions, this appears to be the general trajectory of work by historians on saints and society: a focus away
from the saints and toward the society in which they were sanctified;
a focus shifted from *vitae* to other sorts of hagiographic texts; a tendency to study collectivities and serial records; and a growing recognition
that these texts are not transparent windows into the saints' lives, their
society, or even the spirituality of their age.

New Problems

What has gone wrong, then, with this effort? Even as we have pursued the saints and their society, we have too often lost sight of what

---

[27] For a survey of the implications of the new historicism for medieval history, see
Gabrielle Spiegel, "History, Historicism, and the Social Logic of the Text in the Middle Ages" *Speculum* 65 (1990), 59–86.

[28] Hippolyte Delehaye, *Les légendes hagiographiques* (Brussels: Société des Bollandistes, 1905).

[29] Friedrich Lotter, *Severinus von Noricum: Legende und historische Wirklichkeit,* Monographien zur Geschichte des Mittelalters 12 (Stuttgart: A. Hiersemann, 1976).

a hagiographic text is, what an author is, and what the society—whose values the author is purportedly reflecting in his or her text—is. We have reconceived the hagiographical genre according to modern classifications and divisions. We have lumped hagiographers into a fairly homogeneous group of authors whose collective "mind" we purport to study, and we are seduced by our created text and invented author into thinking that they represent an equally fictitious society.[30]

To rediscover what a hagiographical text is, one begins not with the *Acta Sanctorum* or even the *Monumenta Germaniae Historica* but with the manuscript collections of major European libraries. Before we talk about the content of these texts or impose on them our own systems of classification and organization, we need to understand the systems of organization, use, and categorization of those who wrote, copied, and collected them. Let me offer a few examples from eighth-, ninth-, and tenth-century hagiographic manuscripts I have studied in Paris, Munich, and Brussels. A codicological examination of these manuscripts as artifacts suggests some important hypotheses about the diverse nature of hagiographical production and its meaning in the early Middle Ages.

Some, a minority, are prepared by a single hand or as a single program and contain interrelated texts: for example, the ninth-century Bibliothèque nationale MS lat. 5387, a manuscript of 191 folios containing, in order, *Sermones sancti patrum, Collectiones patrum* and the *Sententiae patrum*; or Bibliothèque royale (Brussels) MS. 8216–18, a copy of the *Vitae patrum* written in 819, begun "in hunia in exercitu anno d. 819" and finished in St. Florian. CLM (Munich) 1086, is an early ninth-century manuscript from the diocese of Eichstätt containing the lives of Bonifatius, Wynnebald, and Willibald. More common are manuscripts composed of miscellaneous portions of originally separate books or pamphlets bound together sometime between the ninth and eleventh centuries. For example CLM 18546b from Tegernsee is com-

---

[30] It is to reestablish the nature of hagiographical texts in their context of their production, use, and circulation, that Martin Heinzelmann, François Dolbeau, and Joseph-Claude Poulin have initiated the project Sources Hagiographiques de la Gaule (SHG). See their preliminary report, "Les sources hagiographiques narratives composées en Gaule avant l'an mil (SHG): Inventaire, examen critique, datation," *Francia* 15 (1987): 701–31. The first example of the results of this project is the remarkable study by Heinzelmann and Poulin, *Les vies anciennes de sainte Geneviève de Paris: Etudes critiques* (Paris: H. Champion, 1986).

posed of at least two manuscripts: the first, written in southern Germany in the ninth century, contains the *passio* of Cosmos and Damian, the *Visio Wettini*, the *Passio Viti Modesti et Crescentiae,* while folios 37 through 197 contain hagiographic texts written in Tegernsee in the eleventh century.[31] Bibliothèque nationale MS lat. 1796 contains, in its first 75 folios, Saint Jerome's *Adversus Jovinianum*; then two folios of a treatise on the seven deadly sins; followed by a *Vita Fulgentii* which, from its faded condition, obviously spent considerable time as the first folio of a different manuscript containing the *vita* and the epistles of Fulgentius. Bibliothèque nationale MS lat. 5596, although entirely of the ninth century, contains the life of Saint Remigius, the *Liber historiae Francorum*, and then a miscellaneous series of texts including excepts from Jerome, Augustine, Gregory the Great, and others. One could go on endlessly. The point is that hagiographic manuscripts were created in a wide variety of ways that suggest a spectrum of uses and purposes as well as modes of production. Passionaries and lectionaries, more or less connected to the development of the Roman martyrology or regional martyrologies, provide one kind of structure within which texts found their meaning. Some collections, such Bibliothèque nationale MS lat. 2204, contain hagiographical texts by a single author, in this case Gregory of Tours; or lives of types of saints, such as the lives of female saints in Bibliothèque nationale MS lat. 2994a, or single saints, such as Bibliothèque nationale MS lat. 13759, which concerns Martin of Tours. In his analysis of manuscript collections containing Merovingian saints' lives, Wilhelm Levison found still other principles of organization including regional collections and visions.[32] Still other hagiographic texts appear in manuscripts we would consider primarily historical or even medical. Bibliothèque nationale MS lat. 11218 begins with the "passions of Saints Cosmas and Damian, physicians," and announces, "The Lord will have mercy on whomever is ill and has this passion read above them." The passion is followed by a medical treatise

---

[31] C. E. Eder, "Die Schule des Klosters Tegernsee in frühen Mittelalter im Spiegel der Tegernseer Handschriften," *Studien und Mitteilungen zur Geschichte des Benediktinerordens und seine Zweige* 83 (1972), 8–155.

[32] Wilhelm Levison, "Conspectus codicum hagiographicorum," *MGH SSRM* (Hannover and Leipzig: Hahnsche Buchhandlung, 1920), 7:529–706.

attributed to the saints' mother.[33] Some manuscripts such as Bibliothèque nationale MS lat. 2832, which contains the *Translatio SS Cypriani Sperati, et Pantaleonis,* contain florilegia collected by individuals and intended for their own use. In this case, the *translatio* is one of a series of texts in a manuscript that belonged to Bishop Florus of Lyons.[34] Others, as indicated by the division of texts into readings, were obviously used for liturgical purposes, probably in chapter, although they would not be classified today as liturgical manuscripts.[35]

These associations, these contexts, within which hagiographic texts are embedded must be our points of departure for understanding one level of meaning of hagiography in medieval society. We cannot understand the "ideal of sanctity" purportedly espoused by such texts if we separate them from these specific contexts. If we want to understand values reflected in the hagiography of a period, texts must be seen in relation to the other texts with which they were associated, read, or gathered, not in relationship either to timeless views of Christian perfection or simply to other contemporary hagiographical texts. The meanings of texts change over time. The meaning, for example, of the lives of saints Euphrosyna and Pelagia preserved along with thirty-four other ascetic texts intended for a female monastic community of the ninth century is different from the meaning of these same *vitae* when contained within a lectionary. The *passio* of Cosmas and Damian means one thing at the head of a medical treatise, something else in Bibliothèque nationale MS lat. 10861, an Anglo-Saxon passionary.

What can be said about specific texts and their various meanings is also true of groups of texts. Poulin, Goodich, Vauchez, and others look for ideals of sanctity at different epochs by examining texts produced during the periods that they study. But an examination of the manuscript traditions within which these texts are embedded as well as the process of copying, reordering, and revising texts suggests that to ap-

---

[33] E. Wickersheimer, "Une vie des saints Côme et Damien dans un manuscrit médical du IXe siècle suivie d'une recette collyre attribuée à la mère des deux saints," *Centaurus* 1 (1950), 38–42.

[34] Célestin Charlier, "Les manuscrits personnels de Florus de Lyon et son activité littéraire," *Mélanges E. Podechard* (Lyon: Facultés catholiques, 1945), 71–84, esp. 83.

[35] For example, Paris, BN MS lat. 13760, composed of various ninth- and tenth-century manuscripts including one containing a *Translatio S. Vincentii* divided into twelve readings.

preciate the ideals of an epoch, we must take all of the hagiographic texts of the time into account. When meaning changes with context, the difference between author and copyist disappears, for copying, excerpting, and rearranging old texts is just as significant as composing new ones. Poulin's study of the ideal of sanctity in Carolingian Aquitaine should perhaps have examined not only the lives of saints written in Aquitaine by Aquitainians during this period but also those recopied, abridged, organized into lectionaries and passionaries, and inserted into martyrologies. Is it fair to consider Michael Goodich's list of 518 "thirteenth century saints" as reflective of the ideal of sanctity of that century when the *Golden Legend* of Jacques de Voragine, by far the most popular hagiographic text of the late thirteenth and fourteenth centuries, contains only the lives of four of these saints? Can we study the changing spiritual values of the later Middle Ages through the processes of canonization in the manner of André Vauchez if the *Golden Legend* includes only 6 percent of the saints canonized between 993 and its redaction around 1265? I think not. Such studies are not really of the values of "their contemporaries" (Bynum), or "their societies" (Poulin), or "their age" (Goodich), and still less of the "medieval mind" (Heffernan). If such abstractions exist at all, they can be approached only through the total production and consumption of the hagiography of their day, not through an artificially designated "creation." The author of original texts has no privileged position as interpreter of the values of his or her age. The notion, dear to Mikhail Bakhtin and Aaron Gurevich, that somehow the ideals of the audience, the listener, are invisibly present "in the utterance itself,"[36] can be asserted but not demonstrated. As Roger Chartier has argued, Bakhtin's world can be turned upside down because listener or reader can take fragments (in our case, texts) and give them new meaning by embedding them within other systems of meaning.[37]

What then are the images presented in such selective bodies of hagiography? Although scholars may organize them according to mod-

---

[36] Mikhail Bakhtin "Problema teksta," *Voprosy literatury* 10 (1976), 122–50, cited by Aaron Gurevich, *Medieval Popular Culture: Problems of Belief and Perception* (Cambridge: Cambridge Univ. Press, 1988), 35.

[37] Roger Chartier in "Intellectual History and the History of Mentalités: a Dual Re-evaluation," in *Cultural History* (Ithaca: Cornell Univ. Press, 1988), 39–40.

ern criteria, such as texts written within a particular period or lives of saints who lived within certain chronological boundaries, they are, as Graus reminded us a quarter of a century ago, propaganda: they are not simply reflective but programmatic. The production of hagiography, that is, not only the authoring of texts but also their copying and dissemination, was intentional action, even if its consequences, the uses to which these texts were put, were not intended by the producers. Nor was this intention essentially, or sometimes even incidentally, "designed to teach the faithful to imitate actions which the community had decided were paradigmatic," as Hefferman has suggested.[38] *Imitatio* is not a constant goal of hagiography, and the example of a life in conformity with that of Christ is not necessarily the message of the hagiographer. As Chiara Frugoni reminds us for Bonaventura, even Saint Francis was to be venerated, not imitated.[39] This purpose is especially true of much early medieval hagiography and of the lives selected for insertion into the popular edifices of later medieval legendaries such as the *Golden Legend*. The saint begins perfect, his or her perfection inherited from a saintly family, as is often the case in Merovingian hagiography, or predestined, in Carolingian.[40] Thus the virtues of the saint appear even before birth, and difficulties, temptations, and conflicts serve not to perfect but only to manifest a perfection already present. These are not lives to be emulated but rather to be admired. They glorify God; they do not provide models for mortals.

A better sense of the intentionality behind hagiographic production can be gained by examining, instead of the "ideals of a society," the particular situation in which the producers—meaning authors, copyists, and compilers—functioned. In a sense, the answer to the question "why did they write," is simple: they sought to glorify God. But in glorifying God, they also glorify the individual saint, the place he or she lived or was buried, the community where God chose to be glorified through his saints. Glorification is one of the major propagandistic roles of hagiographical production, and it too can be seen both in the writing of hagiographic texts and in their dissemination as evidenced by the codicological tradition.

---

[38] Hefferman, 5.

[39] Chiara Frugoni, "Saint Francis: A Saint in the Progress," 161–77.

[40] On inheritance and predestination see Poulin, 101–2 and notes 8 and 9.

Hagiography was always occasional literature. The production of *vitae, translationes* and the like was always precipitated by some specific need external to the life of the saint or the simple continuation of his or her cult, a need external to the intertextuality of the work itself but which would render the text comprehensible. These occasions varied enormously. As Brown has suggested in the case of Merovingian *passiones*, composition might be necessitated by challenges to the importance of particular saints.[41] In the Carolingian period, veneration of saints lacking *vitae* or *passiones* was condemned by regional councils; and of course, as papal involvement in canonization grew, official recognition of cults demanded appropriate dossiers. But other factors also influenced hagiographical production and provided occasions for hagiographic writing, occasions that affected the text itself. To understand a hagiographic work, we must consider the hagiographic tradition within which it was produced; but also the other texts copied, adapted, or read, or composed by the hagiographer; and the specific circumstances which brought him or her to focus this tradition on a particular work. The text stands at a three-fold intersection of genre, total textual production, and historical circumstance. Without any one of the three it is not fully comprehensible.

The hagiographical production of Otloh of St. Emmeram illustrates this intersection. One of the most remarkable monastic figures of the eleventh century, Otloh was born in the area of Freising and educated in Tegernsee but spent most of his life at Saint Emmeram in Regensburg, a career interrupted by a dispute which led him to Fulda for some years.[42] Through his long career he was constantly involved in writing, pausing, as he says, but rarely, only on feast days or at other appropriate times. In his autobiographical *Liber de tentationibus suis et scriptis* he discusses his writings, using the same verb, *scribere,* to describe

---

[41] Peter Brown, *The Cult of the Saints: Its Rise and Function in Latin Christianity* (Chicago: Univ. of Chicago Press, 1981), 82.

[42] On Otloh see Bernhard Bischoff, "Otloh," in *Die Deutsche Literatur des Mittelalters. Verfasserlexikon* ed. Karl Langosch, vol. 3 (1943), cols. 658–670; and "Literarisches und künstlerisches Leben in St. Emmeram," *Studien und Mitteilungen zur Geschichte des Benediktiner-ordens* 51 (1933): 102–42, repr. in *Mittelalterliche Studien, Ausgewählte Aufsätze zur Schriftkunde und Literaturgeschichte* (Stuttgart, 1966–81), 2: 77–115; and Helga Schauwecker, *Otloh von St. Emmeram. Ein Beitrag zur Bildungs- und Frömmigkeitsgeschichte des 11. Jahrhunderts* (Munich: Verlag der Bayer. Benediktiner-Akademie, 1965).

both composing and copying.[43] The distinctions among composing (*dictare*), revising (*emendare*), and copying, although clear, are not radical. He lists not only his compositions but also the most important books he has copied through his life time: one less than twenty missals, three Gospel books, two lectionaries, and four *matutinales*. His writings include sermons, a book on visions, a guide to the spiritual understanding of the material world, a sort of personal autobiography, and at least five *vitae* and a *translatio*. While listing his writings, he states explicitly when and why he wrote many of them.[44] The lives of saints Nicholas and Wolfgang he wrote at the request of brothers of Saint Emmeram before his departure. During this same period he wrote a life of Saint Alto as well as various poems dedicated to this saint. At Fulda, he reworked the life of Saint Boniface at the request of his hosts. Back at Saint Emmeram, he was encouraged by a member of his community and also by Adalham, a monk of the monastery of St. Magnus, to write a life of St. Magnus.

Otloh's *Vita S. Altonis*, described by Max Manitius as "in itself entirely worthless" and "devoid of content,"[45] illustrates the relationship between such occasional writing and the main stream of the producer's thought. Alto was thought to be an Irish monk who established his monastery at Altenmünster early in the eighth century. Aside from a tradition that Pepin the Short granted him the land on which the monastery was built and that Saint Boniface had been present at the consecration, nothing was known of him or the history of his monastery. The *vita* was presumably written at the request of the nuns of Altenmünster to defend their right to draw water from a well at the monastery which, according to tradition, Boniface had insisted should only be used by men. A fundamental issue was probably a dispute over continuing rights to the monastery claimed by the monks of the Welf monastery of Weingarten. By insisting that the nuns were not allowed

---

[43] Although he does speak of three separate activities, which took all of his time: "legere, scribere, aut dictare."

[44] PL 146: 55d–56a. He does not claim authorship of the most famous hagiographic text attributed to him, the "Translatio S. Dionysii Areopagitae"; see Andreas Kraus, *Die Translatio S. Dionysii Areopagitae von St. Emmeram in Regensburg* (Munich, 1972).

[45] Max Manitius, *Geschichte der lateinische Literatur des Mittelalters* 2 (Munich: Beck, 1928), 101.

to draw water, the monks perpetuated their claims to possession of the monastery.

Otloh's *vita* presents Alto as an archetypical monastic founder on the model of Columbanus, Gallus, Permin, and others. Boniface, apprised of the foundation by a vision, rushed to participate in the consecration and, requested by Alto not to exclude women altogether from the site, forbade them to visit or draw water from the well.[46] Later, after the monastery had fallen into decay Alto appeared to a venerable layman demanding that he tell Count Welf II (d. 1030) to reestablish the monastery. This was done, but later Irminda, the count's widow, replaced the community of men with one of women.[47] In 1056 the nuns petitioned for permission to use the well, and the culmination of the *vita* is an argument in their favor addressed directly to the nuns. Boniface had intended the prohibition so that monks and women would not mingle. Now that there were no men present, the prohibition should be understood differently. In scripture, *vir* applied not only to males, but to all who practiced "virile virtue." Thus, for example, the psalmist speaks to all humans when he says, "act manfully (*viriliter agite*) and your heart will be comforted, all you who hope in the Lord."

Here we see, first, a hagiographical tradition, that of the Irish monastic founder. Second, the account of Boniface's being admonished to hurry to the consecration of the monastery is echoed in Otloh's own life of Boniface, where Boniface is told by a vision of Saint Michael to proceed to the consecration of the monastery of Ordorf in Thuringia. The two texts thus reflect each other in the consistent manner in which the one common figure, Boniface, is presented. Third, the vision by which Welf is instructed to rededicate the monastery parallels Otloh's interest in visions elsewhere in his writings, particularly in his *Liber visionum*.[48] This collection in turn reflects back to both the *Vita Bonifacii* and the *Vita Altonis* by including Boniface's letter to Eadburga

---

[46] *MGH SS* 15.2: 843–46.

[47] The actual origins of the monastery and the role of the Welf family are unclear; see Karl Schmid, "Welfisches Selbstverständnis," *Gebetsgedenken und adliges Selbstverständnis im Mittelalter. Ausgewählte Beiträge* (Sigmaringen: Thorbecke, 1983), 430, for the competing tradition of the transfer of the monks.

[48] PL 146: 343–88.

which describes a vision seen by a monk of Wenlock.[49] The inclusion of Boniface's letter in the *Liber visionum* reflects Otloh's use of his letters in the saint's life, for there he stated that one finds no greater "*auctoritas*" of the saint than in the letters written or received by him,[50] and his primary addition to the life of Boniface was the inclusion of such letters within the *vita*. Finally, the solution to the question of how the saint's prohibition was to be understood reflects directly Otloh's writings on the interpretation of scripture, for example, his *Liber de cursu spirituali*. The psalmist's injunction to "act manfully" appears among the texts Otloh singles out in his *Liber proverbiorum*.[51] All of these traditions are thus brought to bear on the occasion of a defense of the rights of Altenmünster, an occasion without which the text would not merely lose much of its meaning but never have existed at all.

Thus far, this analysis connects only the hagiographic texts composed by Otloh, but these connections are far from complete. To understand Otloh's hagiographical horizons, we must look at the other saints who formed part of his cultic world in Regensburg. The first set of these appear in an Old High German prayer attributed to Otloh, which appeals to fifty-five saints, beginning with Mary, the archangel Michael, and then listing apostles, martyrs, confessors, and virgins.[52] Among these we find most but not all of the saints whose lives he had written, the Roman martyrs, the patrons of St. Emmeram, and saints as-

---

[49] Ibid., cols. 375–80.

[50] See Wilhelm Wattenbach, Robert Holtzmann, *Deutschlands Geschichtsquellen im Mittelalter: Die Zeit der Sachsen und Salier*. Part I was revised by Franz-Josef Schmale (Darmstadt: Cologne-Graz: Böhlau, 1967), 273. This is not the place to discuss the problem of Otloh's apparent forgery of some letters of Boniface.

[51] PL 146: col. 335: "Viriliter agite, et confortetur cor vestrum omnes qui speratis in Domino."

[52] PL 146: 428. Mary, Saint Michael, John the Baptist; the apostles: Peter, Paul, Andrew, James, John; the holy innocents; the martyrs: Stephan, Laurence, Vitus, Pancratius, Georgius, Mauritius, Dionysius, Gereonis, Kylianus, Bonifacius and Januarius, Hippolytus, Cyriacus, Sixtus; the confessors: Emmerammus, Sebastianus, Fabianus, Quirinus Vincentius, Castulus, Blasius, Albanus, Antoninus, Sylvestrus, Martinus, Remigius Gregorius, Nicolaus, Benedictus, Basilius, Patricius, Antonius, Hilarion, Ambrosius, Augustinus, Hieronymus, Wolfkangus, Zenon, Simeon, Bardus, Udalricus, Leo; the virgins: Petronella, Caecilia, Scholastica, Margareta. On this prayer see Eckhard Friese, "Kalendarische und annalistische Grundformen der Memoria," *Memoria: Der geschichtliche Zeugniswert des liturgischen Gedenkens im Mittelalter,* ed. Karl Schmid and Joachim Wollasch (Munich: W. Fink, 1984), 469–70, and for the literature notes 125–27.

sociated with Bavaria. The second set is that of the saints venerated at Saint Emmeram who appear in the monastery's martyrology, today Augsburg Codex I.2.2°.[53] Here we find those saints whose feasts marked the course of the monks' year, a combination, like that of the prayer, of Roman martyrs and Bavarian saints. As in the prayer, Saint Alto is conspicuously absent. This circle of sanctity, rather than some abstraction such as eleventh century saints or those particular saints for whom occasions presented themselves for him to write their *vitae*, must be seen as the matrix within which to understand the ideal of sanctity for Otloh. Finally, we must go one step further and place this group of saints within the communal network of Otloh's monastery. This is possible by comparing the saints of his prayer to the martyrology of St. Emmeram in the preparation of which Otloh was personally involved.[54] Thus we finally determine the horizons of sanctity which formed part of the daily liturgical and spiritual world of the Regensburg monk.

New Solutions

Otloh's case is but one small example of how we might better approach the question of the relationship between hagiographical production and society. We must rediscover the meaning of hagiographic texts to their producers, the interrelationships among modes of hagiographic production, the contexts of their production and distribution, and the uses of the texts, and this is being done. If one were to point to where saints, scholars, and society are heading, one might single out two scholars whose approaches exemplify the best of the new hagiography. Thomas Head, in his work on the saints of the Orléanais, begins with Bishop Walter of Orléans's 871 definition of the patrons of the region, and follows the interactions between these saints and the mortals in the diocese from the ninth through the twelfth centuries.[55] By making the hagiographic and liturgical production of the diocese as

---

[53] Recently edited and reproduced in *MGH Libri memoriales et necrologia* n. s. 3. *Das Martyrolog-Necrolog von St. Emmeram zu Regensburg*, ed. Eckhard Friese, Dieter Geuenich and Joachim Wollasch (Hannover: Hahnsche Buchhandlung, 1986).

[54] *Das Martyrolog-Necrolog von St. Emmeram*, 255–89.

[55] Thomas Head, *Hagiography and the Cult of the Saints in the Diocese of Orléans, 800–1200* (Cambridge: Cambridge Univ. Press, 1990).

well as what is known of its churches and altars the focus of his investigation, Head is able to avoid the anachronistic selection of texts, misunderstanding of authorship, and invention of public which have plagued other scholars. The second scholar is Sharon Farmer, who, like Head, focuses on a specific region and its hagiography.[56] She takes a single saint, Saint Martin of Tours, and in what she terms a "carefully contextualized local study" examines his function and utility in the different religious communities of the Tours area between the eleventh and thirteenth centuries. Saint Martin meant different things to each community: the bishop and cathedral chapter, the monks of Marmoutier, and the canons of the Basilica of Saint Martin. Drawing on a tradition of early modern scholarship particularly associated with Richard Trexler's work on Florence,[57] she concentrates not simply on the language of monastic piety and spirituality or on the saint as "ideal type" but on the particular historical contexts in which liturgical and hagiographic practices developed as these communities turned to Martin for very particular purposes. Her analysis extends beyond the internal life of the religious communities and examines the relationships among these communities and between them and lay society.

Both of these scholars recognize and confront the problems outlined above. By concentrating on a specific locale, by examining the codicological tradition, by going beyond classical hagiographic texts to look at liturgy, miracle collections, devotional literature, and even the evidence of archives, they avoid artificial constructs of author and ideal. By remaining sensitive to the context in which hagiographic production took place, they are able to understand for whom and, often against whom, these texts were produced. Finally, in their close readings of their texts, they find not a "medieval mind," but a variety of minds, a spectrum of people reacting to the living tradition of the saints within their midst.

---

[56] Sharon Farmer, *Communities of Saint Martin: and Ritual Legend in Medieval Tours* (Ithaca: Cornell Univ. Press, 1991).

[57] Among them "Florentine Religious Experience: The Sacred Image," *Studies in the Renaissance* 19 (1972), 7–41; "Ritual in Florence: Adolescence and Salvation in the Renaissance," in C. Trinkaus and H. A. Oberman, *The Pursuit of Holiness in Late Medieval and Renaissance Religion* (Leiden: Brill, 1974), 200–264; and *Public Life in Renaissance Florence* (New York: Academic Press, 1980).

And yet, even while recognizing the importance of these two fine books, I realize that something is lost. First, we have narrowed our scope to the point that the broader meaning of medieval hagiography cannot be answered until we have dozens of such microstudies. Second, while our texts have become valuable tools for understanding local ecclesiastical politics and monastic history, we are less well informed about the relationship between ordinary laity and their local saints. Third, we have learned little about the models of comportment and ideals of human existence that saints seem to offer. Finally, the saints themselves have disappeared. We have no better understanding of Martin, Lifardis, Maximinus, or Evurtius. These losses are perhaps necessary. And yet it is difficult not to feel some regret that the work of scholars since 1965 has not brought in a more perfect union of saints and their society.

Literary Transformation in Post-Carolingian Saints' Offices: Using all the Evidence[1]

ANDREW HUGHES

 e tend to regard the texts of the Roman Rite as traditional, mostly scriptural, and unchanged since their institution in the early Christian era. The repertory that makes this view possible is the result of Tridentine reforms of the late sixteenth century, which eliminated almost every liturgical text other than that central core of largely scriptural texts. Printing enabled that sanitized repertory to be made virtually universal.

Largely unknown is a much larger repertory of liturgical texts of the late Middle Ages. Most of this repertory is still unpublished or lies in long out-of-print editions of the late nineteenth century. As a consequence it has received very little systematic attention. Helping to keep this repertory from wider recognition, perhaps, are assumptions about the general anonymity of medieval authorship, a belief that liturgical composition in particular is likely to be anonymous, and the suspicion that anonymous composition is undistinguished and uninteresting.

---

[1] This paper was first read at the *Twenty-third Annual Conference of the Center for Medieval and Early Renaissance Studies*, Binghamton, 1989. In the text below, AH refers to *Analecta Hymnica*. CAO refers to Hesbert's *Corpus antiphonalium officii*, the monumental reference work for office texts. The manuscript sources may be sought in this publication.

By far the greater number of liturgical texts of the later Middle Ages were newly composed. They were sung, like nearly all of the texts of the medieval liturgy, and the chant that accompanies them was also newly composed. In many cases, the author can be identified and is known also to be the composer of the chant. These texts are literature, moulded by narrative esthetics as well as by liturgical and doctrinal considerations, constrained by their poetic forms, and shaped by the requirements of the chant.

When sung to melodies rather than to simple reciting tones, such texts, whether new or traditional, offer the scholar many opportunities for additional information. Although here I shall not deal with the chant in detail, some such information can be assessed even without musical knowledge. I shall describe some texts in conjunction with their chants, mostly by considering easily observable features of the musical notation.

These liturgical texts are part of the corpus known loosely as Gregorian chant. It is not necessary here to question this generally understood name, other than to say that it is not entirely appropriate either for the central core of liturgical texts with which I began this paper, or for the later repertory. Plainsong or its synonyms, plainchant and chant, may be preferred.

Of the two principal kinds of services in which plainchants were sung, the Mass and Offices, only the latter is of concern here.

At the one extreme is the standard repertory of prose texts—the antiphons, responsories, and their verses sung in the Office Hours, chiefly matins, lauds, and vespers. These are texts essentially drawn from the scriptures, and the sole element of structure sometimes to be found in them is the parallel half-verses typical of the psalms. For the most part surviving the sixteenth century, these texts are still sung, and had been sung for centuries before the Carolingians codified them and wrote down their chants.

At the other extreme is the huge repertory of rhymed offices, with antiphons, responsories, and verses whose liturgical functions are identical to those of the prose repertory, but whose texts are rhymed. We can often identify the composer-poets of these literary narratives. I estimate there are extant some 40,000 texts and chants, about which almost nothing is known.[2] Typical of this repertory are a) the goliardic metre, as in this matins antiphon from one of the offices for Thomas Becket of Canterbury:

Ex. 1a (AH 13 #94)

[the accentual and rhyme scheme is shown:
p paroxytone lines (accent on penultimate syllable: *adoremus*)
pp proparoxytone lines (accent on antepenultimate syllable: *Dominus*)]

Iustus pro iusticia	7pp a
stare non vitavit	6p b
equitatem Dominus	7pp c
eius approbavit.	6p b

and b) the metre typical of the Victorine sequence, as in a matins responsory from the offices for St. Francis of Assisi:

Ex. 1b (AH 5 #61)

Franciscus ut in publicum	8pp a
cessat negotiari	7p b
in agrum mox dominicum	8pp a
secedit meditari	7p b
inventum evangelicum	8pp a
thesaurum vult mercari.	7p b

The regularity makes it entirely possible to read such poems quite mechanically, pausing line by line. There is rarely enjambement, for example: each line is a complete thought, phrase or clause. This kind of poetry, then, has few subtleties of formal layout.

Regularly rhymed and accented verse occurs in earlier periods, but it emerges prominently in the first half of the twelfth century. It is

---

[2] See my report in the *Journal of the Plainsong and Mediaeval Music Society* 8 (1985): 33–49. The complete repertory of texts of some 1500 late medieval offices is now available on discs supplied with my recent publication, *Late Medieval Liturgical Offices: Resources for Electronic Research: Texts* [LMLO] *Subsidia Mediaevalia* 23 (Pontifical Institute for Mediaeval Studies, Toronto, 1994). The offices are formatted so that they can be searched by any wordprocessor, and so that word-lists and concordances can be produced by commercial programs and by the software released with LMLO.

partly defined by the use of bisyllabic rhyme, which is clearly deliberate. Given the inflections of Latin, monosyllabic rhyme may be purely
accidental. Ascertaining whether such ambiguous devices are intentional or otherwise is a chief topic of this study.

Existing concurrently with both standard and rhymed repertories are
hymns, whose texts are fully poetic in one form or another, from iam-
bic dimeters to more modern styles of rhymed and accentual poetry.
Somewhat surprisingly, classical metres too remain in use for the composition of antiphons and responsories. All of these repertories are formally well-defined, and are only the backdrop for the investigations.

The material central to this study falls stylistically between the two
extremes of prose and regular or classical poetry described. To establish
any kind of chronology would require years of liturgical, hagiographical, and paleographical work. It is not possible therefore to show a
continuous evolution from prose to poetry, but merely to explore the
other kinds of texts that occur, some of which indeed continue long
after truly poetic forms have been established as the norm.

The study of stylistically intermediate texts, for which we have no
terms other than conventional ones such as "rhyme", "accent", and
"metre", requires careful attention to terminology. All terms need
more careful usage than is often the case: one term and its relatives
must be discarded. Many of the words used to describe poetry have
everyday meanings with implications that we almost never remember.
When we speak of accentual poetry, for example, we usually mean that
the accents are placed in a manner regular enough to be clearly deliberate, thus incorporating what some would call "metrical" or "rhythmic" within the adjective "accentual". But "metrical" and "rhythmic"
may carry other meanings. And in everyday English, even when
accent, metre, and syllable count are not explicitly mentioned, the
unqualified word "rhyme" carries with it the implication of regular
accentuation and a regular syllable count for the lines.

The term that has become simply too ambiguous for scholarly use
is "rhythm", and its adjective "rhythmic". Already in the 4th century,
one writer refers to half a dozen different meanings for rhythm, and
more recently, some fifty usages have been identified.[3] Other than

---

[3] Allen W. Sidney *"Accent and rhythm: prosodic features of Latin and Greek."* Cambridge Studies in Linguistics 12 (Cambridge, 1973), xii.

those writers concerned with accentuation and rhythm per se, does one exist who, when discussing medieval poetry, states what he intends rhythmic to mean? Possible senses are:

i) writing or declamation characterized by general periodicity and proportion. This everyday understanding of the word perhaps stems from the etymological identity of rhythm and rhyme, because in order for the latter to be apparent it must appear with periodic regularity. The foreign terms for the fully rhymed repertory described above exemplify the difficulty. Rhymed office in German is *Reimoffizien*, in French *office rimé* or *office rythmé* or *rythmique*, and in Italian *uffizio ritmico*. *Reim* and *rime* can be translated perfectly adequately as rhyme: *rythme* and *ritmo* MUST NOT be translated as rhythm nor their adjectival forms as rhythmic.

ii) writing or declamation characterized by an accentual structure. This seems to be what is usually meant by writers who use the term in a technical context. Indeed, accentual poetry in the Middle Ages is called *ritmus*. But rather than referring to the rhythm, whatever that is, this term probably refers to the rhymed aspects of such poetry.

iii) composition that depends strictly on juxtaposition of long and short values. Perhaps even more common than i), this is surely the most likely casual meaning for the word. It is certainly the meaning understood by the musician, who would use metre to refer to the overall accentual layout in which individual rhythms occur. For the literary scholar the reverse is true: metrical describes poetry characterised by long and short quantities, whereas rhythmic seemingly is applied to the general character of the line or verse, loosely combining i) and ii) above. Poetry is frequently set to, and its structure indeed often determined by, music. It is all the more remarkable therefore how scholars in each field continue to use conflicting terminology, and how little each discipline knows of the other.

By bringing metre, accent, and rhythm together in this last description, we have merely recognised that they are exceedingly difficult topics to discuss, having, as they do, profound emotional, physical, and psychological implications. The most comprehensive accounts are those of Ernst Pulgram and W. S. Allen. The latter scholar discusses not only these elements but also stress, pitch, and delivery in the context of linguistics, phonetics, orthography, and physiology. His single most important conclusion is that duration, or metre or rhythm, and accent or stress are not separable. The length of the syllable is not a simple matter of duration, and the correlation between syllable length and rhythm is not direct. We are all aware of this when we use the well-known rule that the accent in Latin is on the penultimate syllable *unless it is short.*

Despite this interaction, we should try to isolate the individual elements when discussing the structure of verse as an abstract issue. Rhythm and rhythmic should be rejected in all literary commentary, as simply too ambiguous for scholarly use: proportional, symmetrical, or accentual are normally adequate. The word rhythm should be used only in its technical musical sense: long and short syllables should be subsumed within a metre, a term that is itself appropriate only for texts that can be scanned according to classical principles.

All of these matters make it taxing to analyze poetry that is not quite regularly poetic, or prose that seems to be structured in some indefinable way. The difficulty is compounded when we learn that, for the medievals, even in the performance of church texts accentuation was often wrong. Different ecclesiastical orders may even have had distinct methods of pronunciation.[4] Sometimes words that should be regarded as separate for the purposes of accentuation were run together, thus changing the position of the accent. Such concatenations were quite often needed for the rhyme to correspond. Thus, *nomen habet a re* was pronounced as *nomen habetare* to agree with *papare*, and, from a sequence and the Carmina Burana respectively:[5]

Ex. 2a

Causa cur occiderit
cunctis patet et erit
    semper clara

Ex. 2b

Venus que est et erat
tela sua proferat
    in amantes puellas.

---

    [4] *Analecta sacri ordinis Cisterciensis* 7 (1951): 68–70.
    [5] Dag Norberg, "*L'accentuation des mots dans le vers latin du Moyen Age,*" Filologiskt Arkiv 32 (Stockholm, 1985), 39–50. In the rhymed office repertory, an example is *Adalberte* and *per te.*

To make matters worse, authorities are uncertain as to whether there was any such thing as a secondary accent within long words or concatenations of words. One learns also that accent in verse may have differed from that in everyday speech.[6] The possibility of elision, as in Ex. 4 below, offers yet another area for different interpretation. Given all these uncertainties, in which anarchy seems to be the order of the day, any conclusions may be challenged: keeping a sense of perspective is very hard.

The most convenient source of office texts from the post-Carolingian period up to the twelfth/thirteenth century is Hesbert's monumental *Corpus Antiphonalium Officii*, a catalogue of twelve manuscripts of the era: six of these sources are secular, and six monastic. Of some 12,000 antiphons, responsories, and verses listed by Hesbert, a sampling of several hundred reveals some distinct tendencies that must be confirmed by further analysis. Offices cited in this study include many not catalogued by Hesbert. Even though it is a monumental and universally consulted reference tool, his catalogue gives a vastly incomplete picture of late medieval Office texts.

The repertory indexed by Hesbert, however, remains an excellent starting point. Let us consider what kinds, other than purely prose, of liturgical texts for antiphons and responsories and their verses do exist before the strictly rhymed form became usual, then let us explore how we might determine whether they are deliberately structured.

The cursus

One of the most difficult things to determine is whether chant texts that are at first glance clearly prose, without even accidental rhymes, are actually structured by means of the cursus. This literary feature is often described by terminology such as "a rhythmical cadence used to end lines of literary composition". Only in loose everyday parlance is there anything rhythmic about the cursus. For its original form, probably quantitative (i.e., metrical), the musical term referring to long and short might be remotely appropriate. But by the late Middle Ages the cursus was accentual. It consists of various arrangements of two accents

---

[6] Dag Norberg, "*Les vers latins iambiques et trochaïques au moyen âge et leurs répliques rythmiques.*" Filologiskt Arkiv 35 (Stockholm, 1988), 5, 15.

within the final syllables of the line. Ex. 3 shows the chief categories of cursus, and the appropriate caesura, with a mnemonic device.

Ex. 3

planus	xo oxo	he is PLAINLY . UNSEEMLY
tardus	xo oxoo	and a TARDY . INCOMPETENT
trispondaicus	xo ooxo	THREEFOLD . IN HIS SPENDING
velox	xoo ooxo	he goes SPEEDILY . TO HIS ENDING

Given the natural accentuation of Latin, the cursus can arise quite accidentally. In letters, or other lengthy documents, the frequency and regularity of occurrence make deliberate use virtually certain. Although antiphons, responsories, and verses are quite short texts, we must apply the same requirements—frequency and regularity—but with even more stringent restrictions. We cannot allow, as the Solesmes scholars and others have done, all the theoretical variants and subcategories of cursus. I allow only the *planus, tardus, trispondaicus,* and the *velox,* as above, and in short liturgical items only when the caesura or word breaks are in the correct position. Ex. 4 gives a fairly typical example, found in most of the manuscripts used for *Corpus Antiphonalium Officii.*

Ex. 4 (CAO 6061)

Matins responsory for St. Agatha

Agatha letissima	tardus?
et glorianter ibat ad carcerem	tardus
et quasi ad epulas invitata	velox
agonem suum Domino precibus	
commendabat.	velox

Responsory verse

Mens mea solidata (e)st	trispondaicus?
et a Christo fundata	planus

(the *agonem* following this verse, and similar cues after verses cited later, points to the word in the responsory from which the repeat is made)

another verse

Nobilissimus orta natalibus	tardus
ab ignorabili gaudens trahebatur ad	
carcerem	tardus

If such texts are laid out as prose or as in a manuscript, deciding where the phrases end is not always easy, and one must rely on the grammar and syntax, and on the location of words like *et* and *ab*. Although this example was meant to be one of the cursus in an unrhymed context, it is clear that there are two–syllable assonances between *invitata*, and *commendabat*, and in the first verse *fundata*, and, if the elision of *est* is allowed, also with *solidata* (is this assonance an echo of the name *Agatha* itself?). In this case, there can surely be no doubt that the cursus, strictly applied at all phrase ends and confirmed by assonance, was deliberate. In other cases, we may not be so certain. Other than an obvious layout in poetic lines in the original manuscript, are there other factors that would help us to determine more clearly the author's intention?

There are at least four. All are paleographical in nature, and therefore we would find them reliable only in well-written and carefully corrected sources. This kind of literary analysis cannot be done adequately without using the manuscripts. In the original we must look at least for punctuation, capital letters, highlights, and several pieces of information possibly conveyed by the musical notation. Whether a relationship exists between the musical notation and the cursus is a matter of considerable controversy, and far too complex for discussion here.[7] In fact, none of the six manuscript sources for this piece seems to be of any help in this respect, partly because they are not paleographically superior, and partly because it is very hard for a scribe to observe the cursus, since it depends on accent, which is not displayed graphically. Scribes ignored the cursus when punctuating their liturgical books. However, the musical notation is of help in emphasising where the ends of textual lines and assonances occur. It is not necessary to understand what the musical symbols mean in order to observe similarities.

---

[7] See Ruth Steiner "Cursus" in *The New Grove Dictionary of Music and Musicians*, and *Codex 121 de la bibliothèque d'Einsiedeln*, ed. by the monks of Solesmes, *Paléographie musicale* ser. 1:4 (Tournai, 1984), introduction; and John G. Johnstone, "In search of a musical grammar: musical inflection at St. Gall" paper delivered at the annual meeting of the American Musicological Society, November 9, 1985.

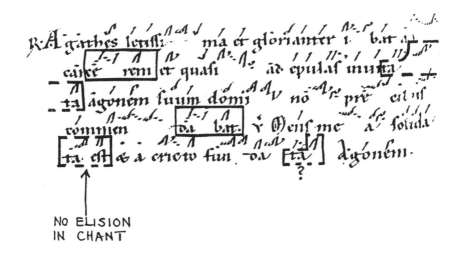

NO ELISION
IN CHANT

Plate 1: Bibliothèque nationale, Ms 17296
(with permission: *Phot. Bibl. Nat. Paris*)

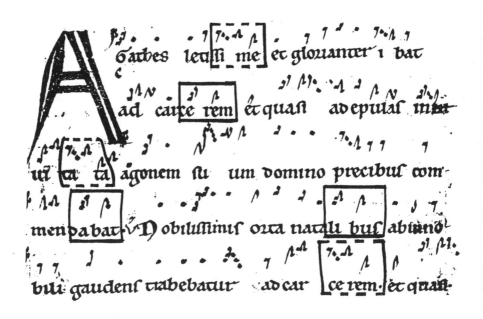

Plate 2: Staatsbibliothek Bamberg, Ms lit. 23

Describing the circumstances is inevitably complex. Let us first state what can be observed, and then summarize the findings. In plate 1, the symbols above car*cerem* and commen*dabat* are identical (motive 1). Those above invi*tata* and soli*data est* (where elision is clearly avoided) are very similar to each other (motive 2), and end with the symbol that concludes motive 1 and that also appears above the final assonance on fun*data*. The notation of the other source is squarer and aligned more accurately within the writing area for the chant. The tune is essentially the same as before, but its structure is even more evident. Set to a melodic variant, and emphasizing the structure at an additional point, the word let*issime* (for *letissima*) is made to rhyme musically with invi*tata* (motive 2). The end of the alternative verse, at car*cerem*, rhymes with motive 2 rather than with the *carcerem* in the responsory, whereas at the mid-point of the verse, nata*libus*, is a rhyme with motive 1 at car*cerem* and commen*dabat* rather than, as in the other source, with motive 2.

Accepting for the moment that *Agatha* is in fact accented on its penultimate syllable, we can assert immediately that each of the words of the preceding paragraph, emphasised by the echoing of musical motives, falls at the end of one of the cursus patterns. Even if *Agatha* should be accented, as in English, on its first syllable, we can assume that *letissima* is musically emphasised because it represents the end of the solo intonation that conventionally begins these choral pieces. Musical rhyme thus emphasises important structural points in the text, independent of the textual assonance/rhyme, and indeed including points like *natalibus* that have no textual echoes at all.

In fact, where the latter are accompanied by one of the musical rhymes, the musical and textual echoes may conflict. Thus, in plate 2 the two schemes are:

text echo		musical rhyme	
none		a	
-*erem*	a	b	
-*ata*	b	a	
-*abat*	b	b	end of responsory
none		b	
-*erem*	a	a	end of verse

Thus a triple counterpoint of accentual cadences, musical rhymes, and textual echoes is imposed on the alternation of solo and choral performance to create a sophisticated soundscape. All but the accentual nature of the textual cadences would be audible. Finality is asserted by the coincidence of musical and textual echoes. Is it extravagant to claim that organisation of this kind is a deliberate compositional device? Much more work will be necessary before we can confidently assert such a conclusion. Subsequent examples in this study contribute other evidence, but will not be examined so closely.

In other texts the cursus is strengthened, made more obviously deliberate, by the presence of more complete rhyme. Here is a responsory and verse for Mary Magdalen:

Ex. 5 (CAO 6034)

responsory
Adest testis divine misericordia
   beata Maria   planus
que lavans lacrimis maculas criminis   (no cursus)
susceptoris sui tetigit vestigia   tardus
ac prava sua derelinquens itinera   tardus
huic post hec assidebat   trispondaicus?
verbumque illius audiebat   velox
viventi adheserat   tardus
mortuum querebat   (no cursus)
viventem reperit quem mortuum quesivit   (no cursus)

verse
Tantumque apud eum locum gracie invenit
ut hunc ipsis quoque apostoli   trispondaicus
verax cius apostola   trispondaicus
resurrexisse nuntiaret.   trispondaicus

Paleographical evidence is little help in this case, so we shall pass to other kinds of structures.

Numerical or accentual structure

The term numerical also needs to be carefully handled in this kind of discussion.[8] Here, I use it to mean a structure in which the regularity of line length is determined by the number of syllables. It is hard to see how such a structure could be observed unless some regularity of accent was also involved. This structure is quite rare, perhaps because of the difficulty in observing it. Example 6 shows an invitatory made up of 8 paroxytone lines of 8 syllables each, alternating three and two accents. It is thus strictly regular accentually and numerically. But it has no rhyme or assonance:

Ex. 6 (CAO 1162)

invitatory for St. Mary Magdalen
Stellam Christum matutinam
cum Maria prestolantes
ne sola stet foris plorans
nos cum ea vigilemus
ut per noctem quem in somnis
queritando dilexerat
hunc inventum simul una
procidentes adoremus

Let us pass to a more interesting item. Consider this responsory for St. Findan:

Ex. 7a (CAO 6062)

responsory

Aggressus adhuc districcionis viam excellentio*rem*	18 a
contulit ad reclusionis pugnam singula*rem*	15 a
ubi tamdiu contra spiritales nequicias dimic*avit*	18 b
quo a Deo se confortante de inimico triumph*avit*.	18 b

verse

Super aspidem et basiliscum ambulabis et conculcabis leonem et draconem.

---

[8] See the reviews of Stevens, *Words and music* . . .

In addition, having undertaken the more excellent way of severe restriction, he faced the singular battle of the recluse, and as long as he struggled against spiritual excesses, by which means and by God comforting him, he triumphed over the enemy. V. You will trample on the asp and the basilisk, and will crush the lion and the dragon.

In CAO, Hesbert lays out the text as in Ex. 7a. Is this layout an appropriate editorial solution? The number of syllables is clearly almost regular, and the lines might be considered balanced, and the whole piece might be described by some as "rhythmic"! Four accents per line typify the responsory, and three typify the verse. Each line of verse is a self-contained part of the sentence, although line 1 has no verb. The syntax, accents, and general layout help to confirm that the rhyming is deliberate, even though the first rhyme is monosyllabic. But can we go further? Are there bisyllabic internal rhymes, at *districcionis* and *reclusionis*, and similar assonances at *spiritales* and *confortante*? The former anticipate the syllable that ends the first clause of the verse, at *ambulabis*. Is the verse then also part of the structure? Many verses are set in prose even when their parent responsory is clearly in poetic form: in Ex. 7a the editor seems not to think that the *-em* and *-is* are deliberate echoes of the responsory. If the responsory is spoken so that the accents fall at regular intervals, pauses must occur after the words referred to above, because there the accents fall close together, thus:

Ex. 7b

> x   x   x   x
> Aggressus adhuc districc*ionis* | viam excellenti*orem*
>
> x   x   x   x
> contulit ad reclus*ionis* | pugnam singula*rem*
>
> x   x   x   x
> ubi tamdiu contra spirit*ales* | nequicias dimic*avit*
>
> x   x   x   x
> quo a Deo se confort*ante* | de inimico triumph*avit*.

This might be described as a structure determined by a regular number of accents between the rhymes. The four lines would certainly look a lot better laid out as eight, each with an accent close to the beginning and a second accent close to the end. The number of syllables would then be 10, 8, 9, 6, 10, 8, 9, 9. The similarity of the two halves surely confirms the structure. But this arrangement makes for very poor syntax, especially where *ad* would be separated from the words it qualifies by an unacceptable pause. On the basis of the literary evidence, accentual structure, and syntax, one could certainly print the verse, *Super aspidem*, in two lines, allowing *ambulabis* to echo the *-is* of the responsory. What is the paleographical information in this case? Here is the original:

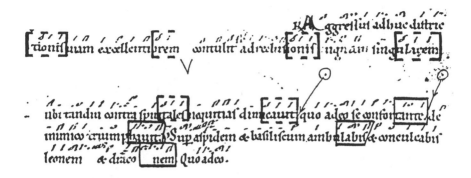

Plate 3: Zentralbibliothek Zürich, Ms Rheinau 28, f.592

There are no internal capital letters to help us. But there is a larger than normal space after *excellentiorem*, and a turn of the page after *singularem*, and dots after *dimicavit*, *triumphavit*, and *confortante*. No particular textual features, however, help us in the verse. Now let us examine the neumes. We would expect the end of the chant to have some kind of formulaic termination, so at that point a match with the preceding rhyme may not occur: draco*nem* does not rhyme musically with ambu*labis*, nor triumph*avit* with dimic*avit*. But at the end of the verse, draco*nem* does rhyme musically with the end of the responsory, triumph*avit* (motive 1). The other musical rhyme (motive 2) occurs at districc*ionis*, reclus*ionis*, sing*ularem*, spir*itales*, and dimic*avit*, and shortened at excellenc*iorem*. If anything, motive 2, occurring six times, emphasises the positions in the text where we might be *uncertain* about the intentional structure. And both motives, associated with the *certain* textual rhymes, link the **a** rhyme *-em* with the **b** rhyme *-avit*. In the verse, nothing in the notation confirms that internal rhymes are intended. We can conclude that quite probably the person who organised the chant—usually with such offices the same as the poet—recognized a structure that incorporated more than just the obvious rhymes.

Mixed structures

The previous text may date from as late as the thirteenth century. The office for St. Mildred of Thanet, near Canterbury, probably dates from 1091 or thereabouts. One or two of the texts in this office are regular and rhymed. Many others seem to have no structure and many might call them prose. Here is the long monastic Canticle antiphon of matins, printed without formatting.

Ex. 8a (unpublished[9])
Pacem et sanctimoniam inter vos habete et Deus pacis et dileccionis maneat cum omnibus vobis sic melliflua Mildretha in Christo valedicens omnibus aromaticam animam in odorem suavitatis Domino thurificavit.

Have peace and holiness amongst you, and may the God of peace and love remain with you all; thus sweet Mildred, saying farewell to you all in Christ sacrificed her scented soul to the Lord in the odour of sweetness.

Is it prose? How might we analyze this text? It divides quite neatly by sense into four lines, the third of which needs the verb of the fourth for completion:

Ex. 8b

Pacem et sanctimoniam inter vos habete	14p
et Deus pacis et dileccionis maneat cum omnibus vobis	20p
sic melliflua Mildretha in Christo valedicens omnibus	18pp
aromaticam animam in odorem suavitatis Domino	
thurificavit.	24p

But with lines of 14, 20, 18, and 24 syllables, this could hardly be said to be rhymed and regular. The main thoughts of lines 1 and 2 are separated by the *et*, and the thought of the remainder is separated from what precedes by *sic*. Small words of this kind that separate thoughts

---

[9] British Library Ms Harley 3098 fol. 47. See my article, "Word painting in a 12th-century office" in *Beyond the Moon: Festschrift Luther Dittmer*, ed. Bryan Gillingham and Paul Merkley, Musicological Studies LIII (The Institute of Medieval Music, Ottawa, 1990): 16–27.

are extremely important. Let us subdivide the text further, by using other similar separative words—that is, not conjunctive words such as the *et* between *pacem* and *sanctimoniam*, or between *pacis* and *dileccionis*.

Ex. 8c

Pacem et sanctimoniam	8pp
inter vos habete	6p
et Deus pacis et dileccionis maneat cum omnibus vobis	20p
sic melliflua Mildretha	8pp
in Christo valedicens omnibus	10pp
aromaticam animam	8pp
in odorem suavitatis Domino thurificavit.	16p

Three of the lines now have 8–syllable proparoxytone lines, and they turn out to be the lines with very important words: "peace and holiness," "Mildred," "sweetly-scented spirit". *Sanctimoniam* and *animam* in these lines rhyme with each other, and *Mildretha* in the third has the same vowel. In addition, the opening two lines make a catalectic pair, not un-like goliardic or Victorine verse. The last line, with 16 syllables, can easily be split into two lines of 8 syllables—*in odorem suavitatis/ Domino thurifi-cavit*—in which we have three-syllable assonance -*itatis*, and -*icavit*.

Now let us look at the paleographical evidence.

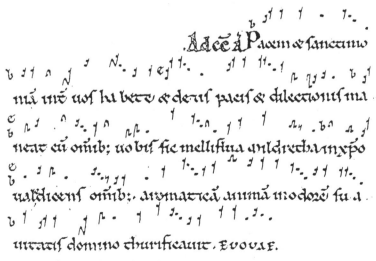

Plate 4: British Library, Ms Harley 3908, f.47
(by permission of the British Library)

Except at the beginning of the saint's name, there are no capital letters. But there is punctuation after the second *omnibus,* the end of one line in Ex. 8c. As before, it is not necessary to understand what the musical symbols mean in order to make some observations. Even amongst those who think themselves musically illiterate it will be generally common knowledge that symbols at the beginning of musical lines have a special significance. Here, we have two; they are the letters e and b. These letter-shapes are clearly distinct from the symbols within the line. But they also appear sometimes within the line, acting like textual punctuation—after *habete* and *Mildretha,* which are ends of lines in Ex. 8c. Another occurs after *dileccionis,* dividing that long line into two parts. Now consider some other symbols within the line. One need only observe patterns: the two symbols above the -*niam* of *sanctimoniam* occur also at the end of *habete,* of the second *omnibus,* of *animam,* of *odorem,* and of *thurificavit.* Observing also the height at which such formulas occur within the writing area for the chant gives other information. Other than the one at *odorem,* all are at the ends of the lines of our semi-poetic layout. All confirm and expand a more detailed formatting.

So this piece is obviously not entirely prose. It has some aspects of regular poetry. In this case surely the poet, Goscelin the precentor of Canterbury, was also the composer of the chant: it was part of the precentor's duties to arrange suitable music for the services. Even if he did not intend a semi-poetic result, he observed and emphasised the poetic qualities, not only in the script and musical notation, but also in the musical sound, with repeated formulas strengthening the rhymes, and on some occasions bringing out rhymes we would not otherwise have suspected.

Now let us move to an item in which a rather more sophisticated use of musical information is helpful. Nothing is required beyond ordinary powers of observation. Ex. 9 shows a responsory and verse for St. Wulstan:

Ex. 9a (unpublished[10])

responsory
Regis iram non formidans baculum non tradidit   15pp a

---

[10] In the Worcester Antiphonal, *Antiphonaire monastique, XIIe siècle, Codex F.160 de la Bibliothèque de la cathédrale de Worcester,* ed. by the monks of Solesmes, *Paléographie musicale* ser. 1:12 (Tournai, 1922), plate 248.

apud regem sed defunctum baculum deposuit   15pp a

quam iacentis virtus servat redit ut Wulstanus   17pp a
    voluit

verse

Viri usque gloria meritum   10pp b

et gracia cunctis hinc innotuit   11pp a

With lines of 15, 17, 10, and 11 syllables, this could hardly be said to be rhymed and regular. But the verse is simply laid out incorrectly: misled by the *-um* echo of the responsory, by the accentuation (two lines with four accents), and by usual division of responsory verses into two halves, like psalm verses, one might divide it into two equal halves at *et*. But this *et* is conjunctive rather than separative, linking *gloria* and *gracia*. The verse really consists of three balanced lines, a structure more typical of these offices of non-standard repertories and later composition. It should really be *Viri usque gloria/ meritum et gracia/ cunctis hinc innotuit*—three lines of seven syllables, in which the first two lines rhyme with each other, and the last rhymes with the responsory. The verse is clearly poetry. Many would dismiss the responsory as rhymed (or "rhythmical" !) prose at most, with balanced lines of almost equal length. But once the influence of the heavily accented *baculum* and the misleading concatenation of *defunctum* and *baculum* can be set aside, the natural punctuation of the first two lines allows a subdivision of each into 8 and 7 syllables, the Victorine verse. Line 1, in addition, allows for a subdivision into 4 and 4 syllables, perhaps emphasizing the solo intonation, with 2-syllable assonance. In line 3, *redit* is hypermetric, sitting between an 8- and a 7-syllable line like the others, making it parenthetic, and deliberately emphasised. The return of the dead king's virtue is thus made the main point of the narrative. But is this arrangement deliberate? A glance at the original will confirm that the end of every line is set off in the chant by musical formulas, incises, and clefs, circled or boxed in the plate (this is a diplomatic transcription):

Plate 5: redrawn from the *Worcester Antiphonal*
(facsimile, plate 251). Worcester Cathedral Libary, Ms F. 160

Even the hypermetric word is set off by pitch—all of its notes are higher than the surrounding ones, with a large leap before and after. The proper layout of the text, then, should be as in Ex. 9b:

Ex. 9b

responsory

Regis iram non formidans	8pp a or 4 + 4 with assonant "-i-a"	
baculum non tradidit	7pp b	
apud regem sed defunctum	8pp c	
baculum deposuit	7pp b	
quam iacentis virtus servat	8p d	
redit	b	hypermetric
ut Wulstanus voluit	7pp b	

verse

Viri usque gloria	7pp e
meritum et gracia	7pp e
cunctis hinc innotuit	7pp b

Not fearing the wrath of the king, he did not hand over the sceptre, but placed it near the dead king. The virtue of the dead king, which he protects, *returns*, as Wulstan wished. V. After this, the worth of the man became known continually to all because of his glory and grace.

The influence of Classical metres

Finally, although earlier rejected for discussion, classical metres must be introduced. Many offices use classical metres consistently throughout: they are therefore regular. Sometimes, however, a single item in a office is in a classical metre, when the others are prose, or loosely structured in some way already mentioned. Occasionally a single line in the middle of an accentual poem is in a classical metre. The discovery of a single classical metre makes one scramble to examine the other items more carefully for some structure difficult to perceive. And spotting such isolated items themselves is very hard. Plate 6 shows two manuscripts[11] transmitting the beginning of Stephen of Liège's office

---

[11] Left column: from Walter H. Frere's facsimile of the 13th-century Sarum Anti-

for Trinity Sunday.[12] The single item that consists of a Sapphic stanza hardly stands out. Even less would it be evident in the context of the whole page or manuscript. In order to allow the reader to work through this small section of the manuscript, the item is identified in the final footnote of this study. Paleographical and notational clues do not help to determine that the item is Sapphic, but do help to identify caesuras and rhymes. In the manuscript on the left, only the musical notation can help, since there are no clues in the text itself: in the other manuscript, punctuation (by dots) confirms the musical clues. Interestingly, in the latter source, at the point where a variant renders one of the classical lines defective, the punctuation is omitted.

Goscelin, the composer-poet of the office for St. Mildred mentioned earlier (Ex. 8), was skilled in classical metres. The first two lines of the first antiphon of first vespers make up a pentameter slightly defective in a manner perhaps allowed in the later Middle Ages: the double letter "-s s" counts as a single letter, keeping the previous syllable short. The remainder of the stanza shows only assonance, without metre or accentual regularity. An isolated pentameter is, of course, quite unclassical. Is it deliberate? By itself, we can hardly know. But the next item, the second antiphon of the service, also begins with a "near" pentameter, in this case defective only because of a hypermetric syllable. And the remaining lines of that item are almost regularly accentual, with rhymes matching the assonance of the previous item. Musical cadences, but not in this case the paleographical evidence, confirm nearly all of the rhymes and caesuras. One must therefore take into account not only the possible structure of individual texts in an office, but their relationship to each in a larger poetic form.

---

phonal, *Antiphonale Sarisburiense* (London: Plainsong and Mediaeval Music Society, 1901-24: repr. 1966) plate 286. Right column: f.8 of a 13th-century Franciscan Antiphonal, Bodleian Library Ms Canon. liturg. 379. See Stephen J. P. Van Dijk, *Handlist of the Latin liturgical manuscripts in the Bodleian Library, Oxford* (typescript in the Bodleian Library, no date) II, 234.

[12] Auda, Antoine *L'école musicale liégeoise au Xe siècle: Étienne de Liège* (Brussels, 1923).

Plate 6a: Cambridge University Library, Ms Mm.2.9,f.142 (by permission of the Syndics of Cambridge University Libary): *Sarum Antiphonal*, facsimile plate 286. Plate 6b: Bodleian Library, Ms Canon, liturg. 379, f.8 (by permission of the Bodleian Libary)

Ex. 9 (see Ex. 8)

first vespers, antiphons 1 & 2

Inter sidereos	6 a	rhymed pentameter ? NB
protoparentes suos	7 a	"-es s-" short syllable
Augustinum et socios eius	10 b	
fulget Mildretha	5 c	three-line
candida ut lilium inter rosas	11 c	assonance
aut rosa inter lilia.	8 c	"-ia"

Respondet meritis	6 a	rhymed pentameter ? NB
patribus (a)postolicis	8 a	hypermetric syllable
apostolica filia	8 b	"-ia"
respondet pudicicie	8 c	almost regular metre,
et certaminum palma	7 b	with some rhyme
et signorum potencia.	8 b	"-ia"

Finally, in Ex. 10, I show a responsory from the office for St. Lambert, also by Stephen of Liège[13]. As divided by caesuras and rhymes, emphasised by notation and cadence, the proportional (I almost wrote "rhythmical") balance of some of its lines suggests hexameters. But their quantities are quite wrong. Are they classical lines, dactyls characterised by accent rather than quantity? Once again, we can hardly know whether classical metres truly inspired the poetry. But we can state unequivocally that, because of the visual and musical reinforcement, the structure was recognised.

Ex. 10

second responsory for St. Lambert
Sanctus Lambertus

parvi pendebat presencia	xoo xo- xoo xoo xoo
veluti devoverat in puericia	—o xoo xoo xoo xoo
estimans pro nihilo omnia	xoo o xoo xoo
preter quod erat	
eterne salutis gracia.	xoo xoo xoo xo xoo

---

[13] Auda, *L'école musicale*. . . .

verse

Celestibus animo inherens	o xoo xoo o xo–
sese in holocaustum	xoo oo xo
(cursus velox)	
Domino mactabat.	xoo oxo

One could multiply examples indefinitely. A whole repertory of offices needs a major study. The later repertory of rhymed offices is already huge. And the number of offices that are neither prose nor strictly rhymed, but that are structured in some way, is probably equally large—and perhaps even more problematic.

The problem lies principally in the difficulty of knowing whether the structure is deliberate or accidental. Even more difficult is it to decide whether the structures that are enhanced are those of meaning, or of poetry. In other words, is it simply the meaning of the text that generates an attempt to reinforce it, to bring it more fully to the listener's or reader's attention? Or is it an attempt to write poetry per se? Probably enhancement of the text was the primary motive. But because such devices enhanced the acoustical properties of the text, they were perhaps eventually valued for themselves. A gradual increase in the use and significance of textual and musical devices perhaps brought about a recognition that the regular and predictable application of such devices created a much more powerful result than the haphazard application of them. Obviously structured texts occur apparently haphazardly within each office: unlike the fully rhymed office, where each and every item is regularly poetic, most items may be prose with only one or two structured items. Eventually poets recognised that consistent application of regular devices to every item was even more powerful. But an evolutionary concept of the development of literature and music—from prose to poetry in twenty-three easy steps—may not be appropriate and can be considered only very cautiously.

To summarize, whatever the primary concern of the poet, several textual devices are used independently or in combination: rhyme, regular accent, cursus, syllable count. And to these devices may be added isolated, defective, or accentual classical metres. Obligatory, then, is a comprehensive examination of the text and its immediate and symbolic meanings, its grammar and syntax, and its accentuation. But analysis by examining only the literary text, the words on the modern page, is incomplete. The original manuscript must be constantly in use. In carefully written sources, all structures tend to be reinforced by non-textual devices—by punctuation, and the use of capital letters; by the paleography, colour and highlighting; and by various musical techniques such as cadencing, the placing of incises or clefs, or abrupt changes of pitch. As with any repertory that is sung, then, also obligatory is a comprehensive examination of the musical notation and the melodic formulas.[14]

In conclusion, until many decades of work have been done, we shall know little about liturgical poetry for the offices, a huge hagiographical treasurechest of material on late medieval saints and feasts. At the moment we can only glean some hints about the origins, inspiration, and development of this important body of literature, and about how it was transformed in the post-Carolingian era.

Bibliography

Allen, W. Sidney, *Accent and Rhythm: Prosodic Features of Latin and Greek* Cambridge Studies in Linguistics, vol. 12. Cambridge: Cambridge Univ. Press, 1973.

Analecta Hymnica, vols. 5, 13, 14b, 17, 18, 24 (ed. Guido M. Dreves), 25 (ed. Clemens Blume), 26, 28, 45a (Blume and Dreves), 52 (Blume): Leipzig: R. Reisland, 1886–1922. (See Lütolf, below)

Auda, Antoine. *L'école musicale liégeoise au Xe siècle: Étienne de Liège*. Brussels: Maurice Lamertin, 1923.

Clemoes, Peter. "Liturgical influence on punctuation in late old English and early middle English manuscripts." *Old English Newsletter: subsidia* 4. Center for Medieval and Early Renaissance Studies, SUNY-Binghamton,

---

[14] This footnote identifies the Sapphic item in Plate 6. It is the fourth antiphon for first vespers. In the left-hand source: *Laus deo patri, geniteque proli/ et tibi sancte, studio perhenni/ spiritus, nostro resonet ab ore/ omne per evum*. In the other source: ... *paritque* [recte: *parilique*] *proli/ et tibi compar laude perhenni/ spiritui* ... Above *laude* are three pitches, not necessarily a safe indication of the number of syllables. If *laude* has the usual two syllables, the line is defective. Perhaps not coincidentally, the punctuation is omitted at this point.

1980; originally printed as Occasional Papers: Number 1, for the Department of Anglo-Saxon. Cambridge, 1952.

Fassler, Margot. "Accent, Meter, and Rhythm in Medieval Treatises *De Rithmis*." *Journal of Musicology* 5 (1987): 164–90.

Frere, Walter H. ed. *Antiphonale Sarisburiense*. London: Plainsong and Mediaeval Music Society, 1901–24: repr. 1966.

Hesbert, René-Jean, ed. *Antiphonale Missarum Sextuplex*. Brussels: Vromant, 1935.

———. *Corpus antiphonalium officii* I: *Manuscripti 'Cursus romanus'* II: *Manuscripti 'Cursus monasticus'* III: *Invitatoria et antiphonae* IV: *Responsoria, versus, hymni et varia* V: *Fontes earumque prima ordinatio. Rerum ecclesiasticarum documenta, ser. major, Fontes* 7–11. Rome: Herder, 1963–75.

Hughes, Andrew. "Research Report: Late Medieval Rhymed Offices." *Journal of the Plainsong and Mediaeval Music Society* 8 (1985): 33–49.

———. "Word Painting in a 12th-Century Office" in *Beyond the Moon: Festschrift Luther Dittmer*, edited by Bryan Gillingham and Paul Merkley, 16–27. Musicological Studies, vol. 53. Ottawa: The Institute of Medieval Music, 1990.

———. *Late Medieval Liturgical Offices: Resources for Electronic Research: Texts* [LMLO] Subsidia mediaevalia, vol. 23. Toronto: Pontifical Institute for Mediaeval Studies, 1994.

Johnstone, John G. "In Search of a Musical Grammar: Musical Inflection at St. Gall." Paper delivered at the annual meeting of the American Musicological Society, November 9, 1985.

Lütolf, Max, ed. *Analecta Hymnica: Register* 2 vols. in 3. Bern: Francke, 1978.

Monks of Solesmes, eds. *Antiphonaire monastique, XIIe siècle, Codex F.160 de la bibliothèque de la cathédrale de Worcester*. Paléographie musicale, ser. 1, vol. 12. Tournai: Société de Saint Jean l'Evangeliste, 1922.

Monks of Solesmes, eds. *Codex 121 de la bibliothèque d'Einseideln*. Paléographie musicale, ser. 1, vol. 4. Solesmes: Imprimerie Saint-Pierre, 1984.

Norberg, Dag. *L'accentuation des mots dans le vers latin du Moyen Age*. Filologiskt Arkiv, vol. 32. Stockholm: Almqvist & Wiksell International, 1985.

———. *Les vers latins iambiques et trochaïques au Moyen Age et leurs répliques rythmiques*. Filologiskt Arkiv, vol. 35. Stockholm: Almqvist & Wiksell International, 1988.

Pulgram, Ernst. *Latin-Romance Phonology: Prosodics and Metrics*. Ars grammatica, vol. 4. Munich: W. Fink, 1975.

Stevens, John. *Words and Music in the Middle Ages: Song, Narrative, Dance and Drama, 1050–1350*. Cambridge Studies in Music. Cambridge: Cambridge Univ. Press, 1986.

Uguccione da Pisa. *De dubio accentu*. Edited by Giuseppe Cremascoli. Biblioteca degli Studi medievali, vol. 10. Spoleto: Centro Italiano di Studi sull-'Alto Medioevo, 1978.

Van Dijk, Stephen J. P. *Handlist of the Latin Liturgical Manuscripts in the Bodleian Library, Oxford* (typescript in the Bodleian Library, no date), 2:234.

Imitatio Helenae: Sainthood as an
Attribute of Queenship

JO ANN MCNAMARA

ueenship is inherently ambiguous, unsteadily poised between royal rule and wifely subjection. Early medieval
queens made creative use of this ambiguity, collaborating
with clerical hagiographers to establish sanctity as an attribute of their office.[1] In the public sphere, often in highly ritualized
ceremonies, they were instrumental in converting the ruling class to
Christianity. They played a peace-making role between the warrior
king and his conquered subjects, pleading with him to have mercy on
his enemies. They used their husbands' gifts to bestow charity on the
poor. They acted as intermediaries between the king's temporal power

---

[1] Throughout this paper, I take the position that the hagiography I have used as
source material is a reasonably reliable testimony to actual behavior. Of course, this is
not always so, even in some portions of the *vitae* that I have not cited. However,
except where I have indicated otherwise, each of the pieces I have employed is contemporary to the subject and the hagiographer is generally accepted as a person nearly
acquainted with the subject or with her familiars. Moreover, the subjects themselves
were famous women whose public activities were widely publicized and in most
instances it would be highly unlikely that their biographers would fabricate their material too outrageously. It is far more likely that the exemplary character of the material
had its intended effect: queens behaved publicly as they were exhorted and expected
to do and thus, in turn, provided examples for their successors. In this sense, I feel that
the work cited here, barring the exaggeration and flattery we expect to find in authorized biographies, was produced in collaboration between subject and author.

and the clergy's spiritual power, building churches, collecting relics, going on pilgrimages and establishing the monastic life. In short, they practised sainthood as a logical and self-conscious division of royal labor with their warrior husbands.

Constantine's mother, Helena, was the original model for the saintly queen. Following his victories over his pagan rivals, the Emperor had her proclaimed Augusta and issued coins with her effigy upon them, indicating that she was to be treated as a participant in the imperial power. In 326, Helena undertook a pilgrimage to the Holy Land. As Constantine's deputy, she founded churches on the sacred sites associated with Jesus' life, tying sacred history to the success of the new Christian dynasty.[2] The watching public may have seen an expiative quality in these charities and services to the church following the scandals which shook the imperial household and forced the execution of Constantine's son and his wife's suicide, but Helena's piety spared the emperor any sign of humiliation.[3] As her son's surrogate, the devout old woman enacted the role of servant to the consecrated virgins of Jerusalem who represented the newly developing ascetic community.[4] She used her authority over the royal treasury to give generously to the poor and exercised the imperial power to free criminals condemned to servitude in the mines.[5] She thus transformed the power she derived from Constantine into a "womanly" model of Christian monarchy

---

[2] Socrates, *Ecclesiastical History*, Library of Nicene and Post-Nicene Fathers, ser. 2, vol. 2 (Grand Rapids, Mich.: Eerdmans, 1979), 1:17.

[3] Eusebius, *Life of Constantine* translated by John H. Bernard, in *The Churches of Constantine at Jerusalem* (London: Palestine Pilgrims Text Society, 1896), 3:42: "For she, having purposed to pay the due meed of a pious disposition to God the ruler of all, thought it right to make thank offerings by means of prayers for her son, now so great an emperor, and for his sons, her own descendants, the Caesars beloved by God." Timothy D. Barnes, in *Constantine and Eusebius* (Cambridge, Mass.: Harvard Univ. Press, 1981), 221, ties the pilgrimage to the scandal and therefore suggests a penitential element to Helena's efforts.

[4] Jan Willem Drijvers, *Helena Augusta: The Mother of Constantine the Great and the Legend of Her Finding the True Cross* (Leiden: Brill, 1991), 3; and E. D. Hunt, *Holy Land Pilgrimage in the Later Roman Empire, AD 312–460* (Oxford: Clarendon Press, 1982), 44, question the presence of a community of virgins in Jerusalem at that early date. Along with the finding of the cross, however, this incident was added to the Helena legend during the subsequent half-century and was thus firmly attached to the exemplary tradition taken up by the Theodosians.

[5] Eusebius, *Life of Constantine*, 3:44–45.

connected to piety, charity and mercy, royal qualities hard to reconcile with the warlike and coercive aspect of masculine rule.[6]

In pagan Rome, religion and public power had been joined: the emperor's coercive power substantiated his claim to divinity, which in turn justified his might. Only the empress shared that divinity with him, acting out a public role as his alter ego.[7] In that capacity, she shared in the ceremonies associated with the imperial cult and exercised extensive power in the administration of the imperial household. But if she used womanly wiles and blandishments to pursue her own policies, it was a private matter. Indeed, imperial excesses were frequently blamed on the secret, incalculable influence of the marriage bed.[8]

Christianity separated church and state and placed them in uneasy opposition. Ambrose of Milan's dramatic confrontation with the Emperor Theodosius over the massacre of the Thessalonians demonstrated conclusively how difficult it was to negotiate the relationship of a Christian emperor and an independent church without lowering imperial prestige or exposing the church to violent reprisals. However, in the first generations of the Christian Empire, the empresses still remained on Caesar's side of the great divide, while the emperor's loss of personal divinity somewhat loosened the tightly exclusive bond between the imperial couple by linking each individually to the church. This gave empresses freedom to play an intermediary role between the emperor and the episcopate.

Opponents of the imperial policy of toleration for Arians and pagans sometimes identified the empress as the vulnerable point in the imperial flank. Reluctant, perhaps, to confront the emperor too directly, Athanasius blamed Constantine's mother, Helena, for her son's deposition of

---

[6] By extending her mediative role downward to the emperor's subjects she encouraged their "willingness to obey" which was essential to his continuing power, see Kenneth Holum, *Theodosian Empresses: Women and Imperial Dominion in Late Antiquity* (Berkley: Univ. of California Press, 1982), 3.

[7] J.P.V.D. Balsdon, *Roman Women* (New York: John Day Co., 1963) in his chapters on the pagan empire.

[8] This aspect of the empress as "Jezebel" reasserted itself in the early Middle Ages whenever a queen failed in her bid for the role of saint, particularly among the wives of the Carolingian monarchs as elaborated by Pauline Stafford, *Queens, Concubines and Dowagers* (Athens: Georgia Univ. Press, 1983).

an anti-Arian bishop.[9] A generation later, Ambrose characterized the empress Justina as a "Jezebel" when she attempted to protect Arian freedom of worship.[10] The defeat for imperial policy was partially disguised by deflecting the responsibility to the empresses for the Theodosian decision to enforce Catholic orthodoxy against Arians and pagans. Gregory of Nyssa praised Theodosius' wife, Flaccilla, for her hostility to Arianism.[11] Arcadius' empress, Eudoxia, was also a champion of orthodoxy against Arianism, insistently "nagging" her husband to persecute his non-Catholic subjects. While he rejoiced over the birth of their son, she persuaded him to allow the bishop of Gaza to proceed against pagans. As the boundaries crystallized, a sort of public ritual was formulated in which the empress enacted the role of suppliant for the church and its constituency before her husband whose natural firmness could appropriately yield to family sentiment.[12]

Kenneth Holum depicted the empresses of the Theodosian dynasty as exercising reflective power, satellite moons to the royal sun. Like the moon, however, the queenly office had its own mystique and complemented the emperor's military might with softer Christian virtues. The legend of Helena's miraculous discovery of the instruments of Christ's passion gradually came to symbolize a new sanctification of imperial power. Eusebius credited Constantine with the decision to build a church on the site where Hadrian had contemptuously erected a temple to Venus, describing the consequent appearance of the Holy Sepulchre without involving an active agent.[13] A generation later, historians claimed that Helena, not her son, built the church after di-

---

[9] Athanasius, *History of the Arians*, cited in J. Stephenson, *A New Eusebius* (London: SPCK, 1957), 360.

[10] Ambrose, *Epistola* 20, *Patrologia Latina* 16.

[11] Kenneth Holum, *Theodosian Empresses: Women and Imperial Dominion in Late Antiquity* (Berkeley: Univ. of California Press, 1982), 23, citing Gregory, *Oratio funebris in Flacillam Imperatricem*, ed. Spira, 478–88 (Jaeger-Langerbeck, vol. 9).

[12] Holum, *Theodosian Empresses*, 54.

[13] Eusebius, *Life of Constantine*, 3:28, When the pagan temple had been demolished and the polluted earth which covered the sepulchre had been carted away, "contrary to all expectation, the venerable and hallowed monument of our Savior's resurrection became visible. . . ," with no explicit mention of the cross or the nails. Drijver, *Helena Augusta*, 85, agrees with Borgehammar that the cross was probably found at the time of Helena's journey but rejects his argument that Helena was the discoverer.

vine revelation led her to the appropriate site.[14] When Ambrose of Milan eulogized Theodosius, he elaborated the tale of the divine revelation which led Helena to destroy the pagan temple and uncover the cross and nails on the site of the crucifixion.[15] By then it was common belief that after miracles had verified the relics' authenticity, she had inserted pieces of the nails in Constantine's helmet and bridle and had ceremoniously conveyed the better part of the cross itself to the imperial palace. Thus queenly piety became a vehicle for restoring divine sanctions to imperial might. Attended by miraculous cures, the True Cross became an agent for healing political as well as physical injuries to his subjects and, as we shall see, an enduring symbol of queenly power.

The Theodosian empresses modelled their own conduct on Helena's, associating themselves with the cult of relics and with the ascetic movement.[16] The ritual of interceding for the poor, for the church (its monks and its bishops) and for prisoners was enhanced by hagiographical traditions that tended to isolate the empresses from their partners and from the secular politics of the palace. Helena's status as a foreigner and a repudiated wife, her "otherness," her alienation from the Roman ruling class and its political forces were grossly exaggerated by

---

[14] Eusebius, *Life of Constantine* 3:25, ascribed the building of a church on the site of the holy sepulchre to Constantine, quoting his letter to Macarius, 3:30. The letter makes reference to "that token of the Holy Passion . . . long ago buried which had been brought to light." It makes no reference to Helena but simply orders a church built on the spot. S. Borgehammar, *How the Holy Cross was Found. From Event to Medieval Legend* (Ph.D. diss., Univ. of Stockholm, 1991) argues strenuously that Eusebius's silence does not indicate that Helena did not find the cross but that Eusebius himself had theological reservations about adding to the prestige of a relic of Jesus's death. Socrates and Sozomen, a generation later, relate the traditional story of Helena's dream which led her to the site of the crucifixion and the miracles which guided her in deciding which of the three crosses she found was the true cross. Theodoret, *Ecclesiastical History*, trans. B. Jackson, vol., 3 of *Nicene and Post-Nicene Fathers* (Grand Rapids, Mich.: Wm. B. Eeerdmans, 1979), 1:16 copied the emperor's letter to the bishop of Jerusalem and added that it was carried by Helena, though he sets her discovery of the cross after her arrival with the letters.

[15] Mary Dolorosa Mannix, *Sancti Ambrosii Oratio de Obitu Theodosii* (Washington, D.C.: Catholic Univ. of America Press, 1925).

[16] Holum, 23. Gregory of Nyssa, *Oratio funebris in Flacillam Imperatricem*, praised Flaccilla as the archetype of philanthropy. He called her a pillar of the church, because of her hostility to Arianism, a stark contrast with her predecessors and her contemporary Justina.

Ambrose of Milan.[17] Eudoxia, who was also a foreign barbarian, secured the removal of the unpopular eunuch Eutropius from office by publicly pleading with her husband as the representative of his oppressed subjects.[18] Eudoxia went on foot in a procession to accompany a set of relics to a new shrine, humbly joining herself to the worshippers. Meanwhile, the Emperor Arcadius avoided the procession and the implicit humiliation of attending the relic altogether, claiming that his mounted guard might hurt people in the crowd and upset the proceedings. This was a powerful bit of image-making. The empress brought with her the accoutrements of power humbled before God and joined with the people while the emperor rode with the army in undiminished might.[19]

Such ritual displays enabled queens to form a sort of bridge between their all-powerful husbands and their subjects. Kneeling in supplication, sometimes with their children in their arms, they could readily personify the virtues of humility, mercy, charity, and reconciliation. Theodosius' wife, Flaccilla, acting as God's instrument, secured commutation of a prisoner's death sentence when he appealed for mercy at the altar.[20] She also cared for the sick, feeding them and washing their bowls with her own hands.[21]

This space between the two powers was difficult to define. As the ecclesiastical hierarchy grew stronger, it contested portions of the charitable ground. Widows, for example, were often wealthy and powerful but by longstanding custom they were counted among the weak who required protection. Eudoxia attempted to put widows and their prop-

---

[17] Ambrose in 395 exaggerated her humble background with the suggestion that she came from Britain and was a concubine rather than the divorced wife of Constantius, Sr. Mary Dolorosa Mannix, *Sancti Ambrosii Oratio de Obitu Theodosii*, 42ff., (Washington Catholic Univ. Press 1925), 59. He calls her a *stabularia*, tavern girl (literally, stable girl) whom Constantius raised from dung to the kingdom.

[18] Holum, *Theodosian Empresses*, 62. Ibid., 71, she used the same technique on Chrysostom to make him reconcile with a bishop he had exiled in 401.

[19] Holum, *Theodosian Empresses*, 57.

[20] Ibid, 27.

[21] Theodoret, *Ecclesiastical History*, 5:18, 2–3. Compare Ambrose *De Obitu Theod.* 41 (CSEL 73, 393) on Helena and Rufinus Tyrannus, *Historia monachorum in Aegypto*, *Patrologia Latina* 21, 387–462, 10:8, who described her as serving consecrated virgins with her own hands, copying the earlier version of Gelasius as established by Drijver, 81ff.

erty under crown control as part of her patronage of the poor while
the redoubtable bishop, John Chrysostom, was anxious to subject their
charitable activities to clerical supervision. Chrysostom discouraged his
wealthy friend Olympias from going out among the poor personally
and ultimately solved the "problem" by ordaining her as a deaconess,
thereby securing ecclesiastical exemption for her property and putting
it under episcopal control.[22] When Eudoxia's silver statue was raised
in a public square, he called it an idol and compared the empress not
only to Jezebel but to Herodias seeking the head of a new John on a
platter.[23] Eudoxia, refusing to recognize episcopal authority over her
charitable patronage, retaliated by exiling the bishop. Many contemporaries rejoiced at the downfall of a troublesome demagogue but others
recognized divine punishment when Eudoxia died shortly thereafter.[24]

Clearly, existing between the two powers of church and state yet
fully belonging to neither, was not always comfortable. But this growing conception of queenship was tough and soon took on a life of its
own. Friction with the emperor and even hostile separation from him
did not touch the queenly office. The empress Eudocia was estranged
from her husband, Theodosius II, and effectively exiled from the royal
court. But her continued disposal of wealth from the royal treasury
enabled her to transform her exile into a drama of pilgrimage to the
Holy Land.[25] Collecting relics and praying at the holy places, she was
acclaimed as a new Helena. Acting as patroness and advocate of the
"poor," she built monasteries and supported many desert hermits.[26]
Later she instituted public rituals of intercession to gain imperial mercy
for the defiant ascetics who had been condemned to death for their
violent demonstrations against the Bishop of Jerusalem.

---

[22] Peter Brown, *The Body and Society: Men, Women and Sexual Renunciation in Early Christianity* (New York: Columbia Univ. Press, 1988), 283. Elizabeth A. Clark, *Jerome, Chrysostom and Friends* (New York: Edwin Mellen Press, 1979), notes that Olympia's destruction of houses and workshops to make room for her convent suggests a certain lack of sympathy for the actual plight of the poor.

[23] Socrates, *Ecclesiastical History* 1:18; Sozomen, *Ecclesiastical History*, trans. C. D. Hartranft, vol. 2 of *Nicene and Post-Nicene Fathers* (Grand Rapids, Mich.: Wm. B. Eerdmans, 1976), 8:27.

[24] Holum, *Theodosian Empresses*, 72.

[25] Hunt, *Holy Land Pilgrimage*, devotes the whole of chapter 10 to this aspect of her career.

[26] Holum, *Theodosian Empresses*, 184.

In part, Eudocia's difficulties sprang from the fact that another Augusta had already pre-empted her role at court. Theodosius' sister, Pulcheria, had long played a queenly role during his minority. She avoided wifely subordination by vowing perpetual virginity and she refused ordination as a deaconess to maintain her independence from episcopal authority.[27] In Constantinople, her charity secured her a strong clientèle among ascetics who had previously been unremittingly hostile to the established order.[28] She protected them from her brother's government and from a more docile bishop than Chrysostom, who often allowed himself to be guided by the imperious lady. When Theodosius went to war against pagan Persia, Pulcheria supported the army with public appeals to the power of the True Cross. Completing her identification with Helena, she located other relics in her dreams and enshrined them in the palace. Like Eudocia, her rival, she used her robes as altar coverings, a ritual gesture that would remain a dramatic part of the queenly repertory for centuries.[29] As a virgin queen, she enlisted the prayers of all holy women in defense of the cult of the Virgin Mary. As the personal representative of Pope Leo I, she organized the defeat of monophysitism at the Council of Chalcedon which officially proclaimed her the "new Helena."[30]

At the same time, in the Western Empire, Galla Placidia was the first woman to be proclaimed Augusta. Redoubtable as she was in her old age as imperial regent, she found no opening for an intercessory role with the barbarian king who captured and married her in the wake of the sack of Rome in 410. His power was at once too raw and too vulnerable for softening. In the dying empire itself, she found more scope for her masculine powers than for queenly virtues.[31] According

---

[27] Sozomen, *Ecclesiastical History*, 9:1.

[28] Holum, *Theodosian Empresses*, 134.

[29] Pulcheria built the first church dedicated to the Virgin Mary and promoted her cult. She maintained her role as virgin queen and saint even after her brother's death, though she married a soldier-emperor to complement her queenship.

[30] In appealing for support to a wealthy leader of a women's community in Jerusalem, she presented herself as the leader of "all the women dedicated to God," Holum, *Theodosian Empresses*, 157–63. For the importance of these councils see W. H. C. Frend, *The Rise of Christianity* (Philadelphia: Fortress Press, 1984), 741–85.

[31] For a full account of her dramatic life see Stewart I. Oost, *Galla Placidia Augusta* (Chicago: Univ. of Chicago Press, 1968).

to legend, Pope Leo took over the queenly role of intercessor for the people of Rome before the Huns. This was not a durable division of labor, however. The humility which adorned a suppliant queen ill-fitted the prelates who wielded the spiritual sword. The warlords who swept the Empire away were Arian Christians who perceived Catholicism as a Roman, and therefore hostile, religion. Bishops who had freed themselves from the Catholic emperors could not shift their allegiance to heretic kings. Fifth- and early sixth-century hagiography is filled with stories of prelates accused of treason, attempting to protect their churches and their own lives through miracles designed to impress these warriors with the power of the Catholic God. At best, these confrontations produced a stand-off. At worst, they pointed toward a new age of martyrs.

But again in Gaul, as the pagan Franks settled into control of the conquered population, feminine sanctity offered a face-saving compromise. In the absence of a Christian queen, Saint Genovefa's spectacular reputation as a wonder-worker combined with womanly humility made it possible for her to negotiate for her conquered Gallo-Roman clientèle without threatening the king's reputation as a fierce warrior or compromising the integrity of her church.[32] Her most famous miracle is actually quite devoid of any magical element. Like her contemporary, Pulcheria, she organized a group of matrons to defend Paris from the advancing Huns with their prayers. The Huns went elsewhere. It was convenient for everyone concerned to regard it as a miracle. Her consequent prestige recommended her to the Frankish Childeric who allowed her to go out of the city while he had it under siege and collect grain to feed the starving people within. Similarly, the supernatural element in her later confrontations with Childeric was modest. He pretended to be so awed by her charismatic power that he took his prisoners outside the walls when he wanted to execute them and locked the city gates to keep her inside. Genovefa is said to have

---

[32] The *Vita sanctae Genovefae virginis Parisiis in Gallia, Acta Sanctorum,* 3 January, 137–53 was written shortly after her death. It contains some wildly miraculous material, and has provoked strong scholarly scepticism, outlined in the notes to the translation by Jo Ann McNamara and John E. Halborg, with Gordon Whatley, *Sainted Women of the Dark Ages* (Durham: Duke Univ. Press, 1992). Despite the difficulties, however, the widespread recognition of her intercessory activities by contemporaries confirms her exemplary value.

opened the gates by a miracle, after which Childeric felt able to grant her humble petition and pardon them without loss of face.[33] Clearly, these were people well-versed in the symbolism of power.

Conversion to the religion of the conquered was a greater risk for a warlord who could afford no sign of weakness. Where an intelligent king like Clovis probably recognized the political advantages of sharing the religion of his new subjects, his own people might have balked from embracing a religion whose God had not prevented the defeat of his worshippers. Legend long had it that when Clovis and his men were baptized they kept their sword arms out of the debilitating baptismal water. Gregory of Tours spared the "new Constantine" any appearance of weakness by ascribing his conversion first to his generosity toward his charming apostolic queen, Clothild, and secondly to her God's power to give him victory over his non-Catholic enemies.[34]

Unfortunately, Clothild's apostolate, which set the pattern for so many later queens, was ill-served by contemporary observers. Gregory's is the first detailed account of the conversion of a barbarian nation and it was written a full generation or more after the event. Though apparently based on popular traditions which probably reflect a basic truth, his account is clumsy and often implausible. Later re-castings are even less persuasive. Clothild's relationships with the Roman nobleman who acted as Clovis' envoy in plucking her from an unwilling and hostile Arian uncle, who allegedly murdered her parents, grew more muddled in every subsequent account.[35] Gregory introduces the Roman bishop Remi abruptly into the story only after the queen had apparently succeeded single-handedly in converting her husband. Then, he says, she summoned him secretly to come and instruct her husband. It seems impossible that so shrewd and ferocious a king as Clovis could have

---

[33] *Vita sanctae Genovefae*, 6:25.

[34] *Historia Francorum*, 2:30, ed. W. Arndt, vol. 1 of *Monumenta Germaniae Historica Scriptores Rerum Merovingicarum* 1 (Hannover: 1885). In later traditions, the political significance of Clothild's role became more prominent. Particularly, she was credited with a dream investing the fleur-de-lis with the same mystical significance that the cross bore in Constantine's vision.

[35] See Godefroid Kurth, *Sainte Clotilde*, 2d ed. (Paris: 1897) for the probable survival of her mother. The story of the envoy who noticed Clothild at the Arian court and helped Clovis to win her in marriage became more complicated and contradictory with each successive telling into the late Carolingian or Saxonian period.

been the dupe of his seductive queen and her Catholic backers. The elaborate scenario, however, provides a palatable justification for the proud warrior's capitulation to his wife's God, while Remi's unimpressive arrival robs the event of any appearance of triumph for him and his church.

Once the strategy proved successful it was repeated by a series of apostolic queens.[36] Clothild's granddaughter, Theodelind, was pressed by the pope himself to follow her grandmother's example and secure the conversion of the Lombards. Another descendant, Bertha, opened Kent to Roman missionaries. Her daughter married the king of East Anglia and their daughters brought Christianity to Wessex and Northumbria. In the tenth century, the widowed Queen Olga of Russia, having safely retired from a spectacularly murderous regency, was baptized and re-named Helena and completed the conversion of her grandson.[37] This association with conversion distinguished queenly saints as late as the twelfth and thirteenth centuries when Margaret of Scotland and Hedwig of Poland were still pushing the frontiers of Christianity forward against the pagan fringes of Europe. In every case, the apostolic queen was recognized as a saint but not the warrior king, unless he died as a martyr in battle.[38] This was, I think, a matter of role-playing, a mutual division of authority, for it only worked when the king was inherently willing to be converted. Though a genuine martyr for her faith, Clothild's daughter never received the honors of sainthood. It is highly likely that the Arian king she married perceived all too

---

[36] I have discussed this in detail in "Living Sermons: Consecrated Women and the Conversion of Gaul," in *Peaceweavers: Medieval Religious Women,* vol. 2, ed. Lillian Thomas Shank and John A. Nichols (Kalamazoo, Mich.: Cistercian Publications, 1987), 19–38.

[37] Unpublished paper by Marcelle Thiébaux, presented to the New York Hagiography group in the spring of 1989.

[38] This pattern holds true also for Anglo-Saxon England. Susan Ridyard, *Royal Saints of Anglo-Saxon England* (Cambridge: 1988) contests W.A. Chaney, *The Cult of Kingship in Anglo-Saxon England* (Manchester: 1970) who saw royal sainthood as a continuation of pagan sacral kingship by pointing out that sainthood was not an intrinsic attribute of Christian kings. Chaney himself, on p. 77, characterized them as "many kings who died unjust and violent deaths." Ridyard, p. 236, effectively proves that their cults were not popular in origin but were the result of patronage by the ecclesiastical and political elite. She also notes that the kings who achieved cults were always martyrs, whereas the women at least achieved a reputation for piety which satisfied the monastic standards of their time, 238.

clearly that the young Clothild was in his bed as a representative of her powerful and ambitious brothers. When she tried to advance her faith, her Visigothic husband so abused her that she ultimately died of it.[39] Rather than appealing to his royal clemency for his own oppressed Catholic population, she was a compelling threat that that population and its church might well help her Catholic brothers against him.

Queenship became prominently associated with church building, which in turn became a peculiarly public way for Catholic women to enlist God on the side of their husband's arms. When Clovis went to war, his queen devoted herself to constructing monasteries and cathedrals in Paris, Tours and other episcopal centers. Gregory of Tours frankly admits that this put a heavy burden on the fisc, but implies that the profitable victories of the Franks over their Arian enemies made the exchange worthwhile. The widowed Clothild retained her power to dispose of the royal treasury. She gave lavishly to monastic institutions and her sons did not intervene despite the heavy drain, though later accounts enhance Clothild's virtue in contrast to their complaints of her extravagance. But her son Clothar did not stop his queen Radegund from introducing churchmen into the palace regularly to shower them with gifts. To expand the sphere of royal influence, she customarily undertook small pilgrimages to bring gifts to local hermits and monasteries. In effect, just as the king distributed gifts to his warrior peers which assured their continued support in his looting expeditions, the queen's donations to the church and gifts to the poor assured God's continued blessing on Frankish arms and the continued willingness of his representatives to encourage popular obedience.[40]

Gregory of Tours took great pains to present Clothild as a friendless orphan, wholly dependent upon her magnanimous husband. Frankish kings were isolated figures in deadly competition with their closest relatives. Their queens had to be equally isolated. As long as the Merovingian monarchy was a successful one, no queen was associated with a powerful family. Hagiographers present successful apostolic queens as aliens, "others" who were essentially lonely and beleaguered figures, ap-

---

[39] Gregory of Tours, *Historia Francorum*, 3:9.

[40] For this effect of charity in barbarian economies see Georges Duby, *The Early Growth of the European Economy: Warrior and Peasants, 7th to 12th Centuries* (Ithaca: Cornell Univ. Press, 1974).

parently free of the encumbrance of family interests and influences. Thus the elder Clothild could do nothing to prevent her sons' murder of her grandsons. But once her political powerlessness was confirmed, she could assert herself as a peacemaker between her warring sons.[41] Her successor, Radegund, lost most of her family when her future husband slaughtered them in battle, and she could not save her surviving brother from her husband's murderous impulses. Yet she was respected as a peacemaker among his warring sons and recognized as an advocate for prisoners, customarily humbling herself to her violent husband to mitigate his wrath. Symbolically powerless women, with their wiles and their softness could act out a role designed to bring peace without detracting from the masterful and warlike countenance of men.

Their perilous position between powerful husbands and powerless people may have fitted them peculiarly well to share the uniqueness of royal power and exercise it in certain unwarlike activities, which could be characterized as "woman's work." Dependent upon their royal husbands for all their influence and wealth, queens made it their public office to secure forgiveness of enemies, charity to the poor, and protection for the church. Radegund practiced sainthood from early childhood, reading and imitating as many holy practices as she could encompass.[42] She may have derived some of her ideas from her one surviving relative who had taken service in Byzantium.[43] In any case, her broad concept of sainthood as an instrument of queenship would ultimately gain her praise as a new Helena.[44] Somehow she learned the vital trick of secur-

---

[41] Even to the point of commanding a miracle with her prayers, Gregory of Tours, *Historia Francorum* 3:28.

[42] Venantius Fortunatus, *Vita sanctae Radegundis, Liber I*, c. 2, ed. B. Krusch, *Monumenta Germaniae Historica, Scriptores Rerum Merovingicarum*, 2 (Hannover: 1888), translated in Jo Ann McNamara, and John E Halborg, with Gordon Whatley, *Sainted Women of the Dark Ages* (Durham: Duke Univ. Press 1992). Stafford, *Queens, Concubines and Dowagers*, 3–12, surveys hagiography as a source for queens' lives with a view to exposing the biases of the biographers, but does not address the influence of the subject upon the author.

[43] Radegund, "The Thuringian War," a letter in verse form published with the poems of Fortunatus, *Monumenta Germaniae Historica Auctores Antiquiores appendix 1*, 271–75. Nisard, the French editor of Fortunatus' *Opera Poetica* has attributed this work to Radegund and it at least bears the marks of her opinions and sentiments. Marcelle Thiébaux, *The Writings of Medieval Women*, (New York: Garland Publishing, 1987), includes Radegund as an author on the strength of the poem.

[44] Baudonivia, *Vita sanctae Radegundis, Liber II*, c. 16, ed. B. Krusch, *Monumenta*

ing her brutal husband's cooperation, which was perhaps not the least of the miracles attributed to her by her three biographers. But Clothar was, after all, the son of Clovis and Clothild and may have had his own clear sense of a queenly role. Even though he had a number of other wives, Radegund was his "public queen."[45] He had gone to some trouble to get her as his share of the Thuringian loot and to bring her up to her royal destiny. He married her with ceremony and expected her to share his public life. When she left his banquets singing a hymn to pour out charity to the poor at the gates, he complained that he had married a nun rather than a wife, but none of her persistent ascetic habits could influence him to give her up. Even when she fled from him and took refuge in a monastery, he recognized her as his lawful wife and tried to get her back. But he did not employ force against her and he continued to support her handsomely, which suggests that he continued to see her queenship as a valuable counterpart to his kingship.

Radegund's flight from her husband turned into a royal progress. Like Eudocia and Pulcheria before her, she entered the principal shrines along her route stripping herself of gold and jewels and precious fabrics which she laid as gifts upon the altars. As a pilgrim, attended by a crowd so great that the streets could not hold them, she retired into an imposing convent endowed by her husband.[46] In Poitiers, she became a more public queen than she had ever been before, pouring out an unbelievable stream of wealth in daily banquets for the poor, medical supplies and bathing facilities for the sick, new clothes and money for anyone who came to the door. Like Clothild, she never became a nun, and though she demanded the diaconate, she did not allow her ordination to prejudice her control of power and property.

After Clothar died, she maintained close contact with his royal sons, trying to act as a peacemaker among them. She brought a part of the True Cross with an impressive escort of saints' relics from the east to Frankland in concert with King Sigebert who was eager to gain this symbol of imperial Byzantium. We might better understand the undig-

---

Germaniae Historica, Scriptores Rerum Merovingicarum, 2 (Hannover: 1888) which includes a short synopsis of the Legend of the Cross as well. It is interesting to note that throughout the history I am recounting, no queen was compared to Esther.

[45] Fortunatus, c. 12.

[46] Fortunatus, c. 13.

nified resistance of the bishop of Poitiers to the reception of the mighty relic into Radegund's convent if we saw it for the potent symbol of her queenship that it was.[47] The public processions and ceremonies that accompanied the relic's progress toward Poitiers served to enhance Radegund's independence of episcopal authority—her queenly space between the temporal and spiritual powers. In centuries to come, the sainted empress Cunegund in Germany would bestow fragments of the cross upon her subjects to the north.[48] Wulfthryth, the repudiated wife or concubine of Edgar of Wessex brought a fragment of one of the nails of the crucifixion to Wilton from Trier.[49] Lacking a certified relic, Margaret of Scotland would ceremoniously erect a great cross of gold as a standard for her half-pagan subjects.

By the third generation of Frankish Christianity, when Gregory of Tours was chronicling the public careers of Clothild and Radegund, the queenly role was well established. The queens who married Clothar's sons, the proud Visigothic princess Brunhild and the ruthless slave Fredegund, who murdered her rival for the royal bed, were not meek or humble women by nature, but both were celebrated for piety and charity in their youth. Even Fredegund publicly knelt and persuaded her husband to burn the old Roman tax records claiming that the plague which threatened her children was God's revenge for their oppression of the poor.[50] Had one of the brothers lived and triumphed over the other, his queen was positioned to play her saintly role, but when both princes were slain, their widows evolved not into saints but into kings, waging war fiercely and brutally. In that fratricidal epoch, sainthood could only flourish far from the royal sphere.[51]

---

[47] Gregory of Tours, *Historia Francorum* 9:40, emphasizes the support of King Sigebert in the project. His version, in contrast with that of Baudonivia, puts less emphasis on the *imitatio Helenae*, whose role in the original *inventio* he takes from Eusebius, not the later historians of the fourth century (1:36).

[48] Unhappily, the author of her Vita, writing around 1200, does not say where the fragment came from.

[49] Ridyard, 146.

[50] Gregory of Tours, *Historia Francorum* 5:34.

[51] Beginning in this period with Jonas of Bobbio, *Vita Columbani Abbatis disciplinorumque eius, Liber II*, ed. B. Krusch, vol. 7 of *Monumenta Germaniae Historica Scriptores rerum merovingicarum*, hagiography turns in the direction of the great noble families who produced the courtiers, bishops and noble ladies who extended the monastic movement into the peripheries of Frankland. Those families began seriously to contest the

There is obvious interface between hagiographic texts and the activity of queens who read the texts as a guide to their own offices. Once the kingdoms were unified again, Clovis II's queen Balthild resumed the role of saintly queen. Her *Vita* was written soon after her death in the convent of Chelles where she spent her last years. It is a strange document, provocatively luring the reader to spy out quite another tale of an ambitious and possibly quite ruthless woman whose imitation of Radegund seems chilly and calculated. She had been an Anglo-Saxon captive in the household of the major-domo, Erconwald, who helped her to the throne and perhaps acted as her mentor. Her husband had an evil reputation for drunkenness and brutality, but he gave her the customary queenly powers over the royal fisc. In cooperation with Bishop Genesius, she founded monasteries and built new churches on a lavish scale. She distinguished herself for her charity, notably her fight against the slave trade and her wholesale redemption of prisoners brought into her kingdom. She was active in the governance of the church, presiding over an important reforming council. As a widow, she might have preferred to cultivate the qualities of the "Jezebel queens" of the more recent past.[52] But her political ambitions were frustrated and, not altogether willingly, she retired into a convent she had endowed at Chelles.[53]

At Chelles, Balthild re-shaped her history and her public image to reinforce the idea of sanctity as a suitable role for royal women, particularly one who was not welcome at the center of power. Her biographer drew freely on the lives of Radegund as a model for Balthild's continuing charity and her demonstrations of humility in doing kitchen work. She even had a god-daughter named Radegund in the convent

---

central powers of the monarchy. This is the theory persuasively set forth in a celebrated article by Friedrich Prinz, "Heiligenkult und Adelsherrschaft im Spiegel merowingischen Hagiographie," *Historische Zeitschrift* 204 (1967) 532. For further discussion and examples, see McNamara and Halborg, *Sainted Women*.

[52] Where at least one contemporary had already placed her, see Janet Nelson, "Queens as Jezebels: The Careers of Brunhild and Balthild in Merovingian History," in Derek Baker, ed., *Medieval Women* (Oxford: Basil Blackwell, 1978), 31–78.

[53] *Vita sanctae Balthildis*, ed. Bruno Krusch, vol. 2 of *Monumenta Germaniae Historica, Scriptores rerum merovingicarum* 2, 477–508, translated in McNamara and Halborg, *Sainted Women*. The biographer, a nun at Chelles, goes so far as to hint that the community itself, despite its financial dependence on the queen, was reluctant to welcome her into the house, presumably because of her bad political reputation.

with her as a protegée. With her secular career cut short, this saintly behavior transformed her retirement from demeaning exile into an acceptable form of queenship and it justified her continued intervention in public affairs.

At the end of Balthild's *vita*, the author appended a litany of saintly queens of Frankland, urging all her successors to emulate them. Under Balthild's guidance, Chelles linked the queenship of Frankland to that of Anglo-Saxon England, which was converting during her lifetime, by training nuns from her native land to strengthen the missionary activities of Anglo-Saxon queens. Though England only produced a developed hagiographical tradition in later times, the activities of its saintly queens in Bede's *History* suggests that they also drew their models of queenship from Frankland and the tradition known to the author of Balthild's life.[54] The Anglo-Saxon royal women appear to have practiced an *imitatio Radegundis*, if we can believe their later hagiographers. Osbert of Clare stresses Edburga's humility, cleaning the shoes of other nuns. Edith of Wilton devoted herself to the poor and sick and treated criminals as brothers. Sexburga and Eormenilda were both described as maintaining a monastic demeanor in the royal court and retired to religion as widows.[55] The Anglo-Saxon princesses of East Anglia massively turned the wealth of husbands and fathers over to the church and its charitable projects. Queen Etheldreda repeated Radegund's pattern of flight, accompanied by miracles from a raging husband and ultimately a powerful old age as monastic patroness. She turned her first husband's estates into a great monastery at Ely where she died in the same year as Balthild and was succeeded by her widowed sister in 680 and then by her virgin niece, Werburg.[56]

Balthild was the last effective Merovingian monarch. The political reality of Frankland and with it the hagiographical tradition changed in

---

[54] Bede, *A History of the English Church and People*, trans. Leo Sherley-Price (Baltimore: Penguin Books, 1968), 3:8; 4:19.

[55] Ridyard, *Royal Saints*, 86–92, analyzes these texts but without reference to Fortunatus.

[56] It is interesting to note that the Anglo-Saxon poem, *The Dream of the Rood*, describing the discovery of the True Cross, was composed in Northumbria about the time of Etheldreda's reign there. *Elene*, which explicitly credits Helena with the discovery, is unfortunately undatable, Peter Hunter Blair, *Anglo-Saxon England*, 2d ed. (Cambridge: Cambridge Univ. Press, 1977), 338.

the late seventh century. The great noble families began to claim the church as a field for their ambition and to compete with the monarchy for divine favors. The numerous saints associated with the monastic tradition of Luxeuil and the families surrounding King Dagobert took on the characteristics of "family saints" who acted as advocates for their noble kindred.[57] Bishops, abbots and noble women defined their sainthood in opposition to the king's ambitions, founding monasteries to divert their family wealth away from the crown and its adherents. Erconwald may well have promoted Balthild herself as a counter to Dagobert's ambitions. Her fall from power coincided with the monarchy's decline. As saints, queens fell out of sight to be replaced by women who refused marriage.

The Carolingian family in particular based much of its prestige on its saintly lineage, which included a number of nuns who had refused marriage.[58] Once they had attained power, they systematically bypassed their queens as mediators. Charlemagne viewed his relationship to the church as one of sovereign to subject and prided himself on being unsusceptible to favoritism. He once went so far as to stage a demonstration of his ability to withstand the wiles of Hildegard, his favorite queen.[59] He himself and his son Louis the Pious may have wanted to experiment with saintliness in their own right but their cults proved abortive. Charlemagne's own apostolic mission was in the crusading military tradition. He wanted his daughters to act neither as peace-weavers with other men nor with God, keeping them unmarried and at his court as secular women. In this atmosphere, the queenship took on the negative qualities of a scapegoat. Charlemagne's quasi-saintly qualities were balanced by the unpopularity of his wife Fastrada who was blamed for the mistakes of his later years. Nobles and bishops who opposed Louis the Pious justified their treason by blaming his wife, the beautiful Judith of Bavaria, for his unpopular actions. She was even accused of using magical spells to keep him under her control. Yet in

---

[57] Friedrich Prinz, "Heiligenkult und Adelsherrschaft im Spiegel merowingischen Hagiopraphie." *Historische Zeitschrift* 204 (1967): 532.

[58] Arnulf of Metz, Glodesind, Gertrude of Nivelles and her mother Ida, as well as assorted nuns like Modesta and Ora.

[59] Notker the Stammerer (The Monk of Saint Gall), *Charlemagne*, trans. Lewis Thorpe (Penguin Books: 1971) 1:4–6.

her first days at court, Judith had been celebrated with the customary praises of piety and virtue. Carolingian queens like Judith of Bavaria and Tetberga were well-connected women with powerful relatives. They clearly represented too much power of their own to confront their husbands as saints, while the husbands' direct intervention in church affairs displaced them from that queenly role.[60]

After the collapse of the Carolingians, the Saxon dynasty revived saintly queenship. Apparently unaware of Holum's work, Patrick Corbet has recently argued that the Ottonian empresses of the tenth century represented a unique pattern of royal sainthood, assigned specifically to the female half of the royal couple which does not fit into the pattern of family saints established by Prinz.[61] If I am correct in locating the tradition of family saints in the area of noble competition with monarchical claims, the revival of the queenly tradition must fit with a new dynastic response from the crown. None of the Saxon or Salian queens drew their saintly qualities from their blood relatives nor were their relatives active in establishing their cults.[62] Nor did they promote sainthood in their own lineage. Important as she was, Mathilda the abbess of Quedlinburg, who ruled Germany as regent for her brother and enjoyed the unique designation of *metropolitana,* did not get a cult, though her monastery promoted the sainthood of her royal mother.[63]

Like their predecessors stretching back to Helena, these new queenly saints were fully integrated only into their husband's lives. The life of Henry the Fowler's queen, Mathilda, describes their marriage as a hasty, disorderly affair, arranged by her abbess aunt without consulting her parents.[64] Otto I married successively princesses of high degree

---

[60] Stafford, 15–20 and passim explores the scapegoating of queens.

[61] Patrick Corbet, *Les saints ottoniens sainteté dynastique, saintete royalé et sainteté féminine autour de l'an Mil,* (Sigmaringen: Thorbecke Verlag, 1986), 239.

[62] In all, the Ottonian family between 866 and 1033 produced eight persons reputed to be saints, six of them women. See C. Erdmann, "Beiträge zur Geschichte Heinrichs I," *Ottonische Studien* (Darmstadt: 1968).

[63] *Annales Quedlinburgensis,* vol. 3 of *Monumenta Germaniae Historica Scriptores,* ed. G. H. Pertz, 22–69; 72–90.

[64] Corbet notes that the first biography of Mathilda almost depicts her headlong marriage as an elopement, possibly even a rape. Cf. the union of the Anglo-Saxon Edgar with the mother of Edith of Wilton, in C. Horstmann, ed., *S. Editha sive Chronicon Vilodunense im Wiltshire, dialekt aus ms. Cotton. Faustina B III,* (Heilbronn: Hinninger Verlag, 1883).

but far from their families left behind in distant lands. Edith was an English princess, dependent on personal charm and piety for acceptance among foreigners. She too was an orphan, living at the court of her half-brother. Hroswitha calls her the "hope of the people" whom she nurtured rather than ruled.[65] She died young, however, and her saintly reputation was ultimately overshadowed by the fame of Otto's second wife, the Empress Adelheid, a Burgundian princess whom Otto rescued from the greedy lords of Italy and elevated to imperial honors. Thus, despite the nobility of their background, Otto I plainly made himself the dominant partner in his marriages, keeping his wives firmly distanced from their relatives and therefore securely placed to enact the queenly role. Otto presumably expected a similar result when he arranged the marriage of his son Otto II to Theophanu, a Byzantine princess. She, however, never transferred her interests from her own family to her husband. Odilo of Cluny, Adelheid's hagiographer, blamed Theophanu's Byzantine outlook for Otto II's fatal adventure in Italy. In becoming regent over the German empire, she, like Brunhild and Fredegond before her, became too manly for the queenly role, in stark contrast to the widowed Adelheid who exercised her power under the guise of humble religion.

In the Christianized Germany of the tenth century, the dynamics of the couple had clearly changed from the confrontational quality of Merovingian marriage. As Corbet took particular pains to demonstrate, the royal Saxon and Salian couples formed a tight consortium. Mathilda's hagiographer emphasized her link with Widukind, who was the first Saxon to become a Christian, but virtually ignored her noble parents.[66] Similarly, Hroswitha noted that Edith sprang from the martyr king Oswald.[67] Though the days of conversion were long over and the Kings of the Saxon dynasty were not the brutal Merovingians, all the traditional elements of peace-making, charity, pleas for prisoners, attention to relics, are present in the lives of their queens. The royal division of labor was clearly accepted as a proper and normal means of

---

[65] Hroswitha, *De Gestis Ottonis I*, lines 411; 400–405, in *Hrotswithae Opera*, ed. Paulus de Winterfeld (Berlin: Weidmann, 1902), 215–16.

[66] *Vita Mathildis reginae*, vol. 4 of *Monumenta Germaniae Historica Scriptores*, c. 2, p. 285.

[67] Hroswitha, *Carmen* 320; see Bede, *Historia*, 3:2–9.

conducting the government. The king still stood for military strength and stern justice while the queen represented charity to the church and to the poor and mercy to the condemned. There is strong intertextual play between the *Vita Mathildis* and the contemporary *Vita Chrotildis* as well as the Merovingian biographies of Radegund.[68] But Mathilda's hagiographer makes it very plain that the similarities do not emerge from literary borrowing but from Mathilda's own self-conscious activity. She excelled in the ritual postures of her office. Even when she was experiencing the first grief of widowhood, she took care to present herself as a model of royal propriety. Moreover, her role-playing was plainly accepted and supported by her consort. Like Radegund, Mathilda rose from the king's bed to pray during the night.[69] But her biographer notes that the king only pretended to be asleep to help her in her pious intention, thus distinguishing Henry from the brutal Clothar and enhancing the sense of partnership which distinguished Saxon royalty.

In this spirit, Mathilda was energetic in pleading the cause of prisoners. Her biographer adds that many prisoners gained mercy through Mathilda's intercession when her husband was expected to pronounce the sentence of death demanded by customary law. Even when she was not in court her memory sweetened his internal deliberations.[70] On his deathbed, the king's formal leavetaking of praise and thanksgiving to his queen emphasized that she never failed in her duty of appealing to his mercy.[71]

The Saxon queens, like their Merovingian models, were associated with the enhancement of ecclesiastical power through the monastic movement. Magdeburg was founded in 937 from Edith's dower. Quedlinburg, founded by the Empress Mathilda on her dower lands, became a center of an imperial cult, celebrating her husband's death day with lavish charity. Toward the end of her own life, she installed her granddaughter as abbess who acted with the powers of a bishop. Adelheid enlisted the support of the powerful new reforming congre-

---

[68] *Vita Sanctae Chrothildis*, ed. B. Krusch, vol. 2 of *Monumenta Germaniae Historica SS rer. mer.* (1888), 341–48.

[69] *Vita Mathildis*, 5, p. 286.

[70] *Vita Mathildis*, 5, p. 287.

[71] *Vita Mathildis*, 8, p. 288.

gation of Cluny for her dynasty. Mathilda's alms, like Clothild's, were linked to Otto's spectacular successes in war.[72] In a highly elaborate ritual performance, perhaps drawn directly from Radegund or even the early Byzantine queens, Adelheid bestowed a portion of Otto's cloak on Saint Martin's altar, tying the emperor to the most popular of the Frankish saints in her public prayers.[73] Unlike her aggressive daughter-in-law who was blamed for drawing Otto II into southern Italy, she acted as peacemaker among her own relatives in Burgundy and again in Switzerland.[74] Through her marriage to Otto she also brought peace to the Italians torn by civil strife. Though Adelheid was unable to help her son, she was "rewarded" with a vision of his death during a long vigil undertaken to support his campaign in Italy.

Mathilda imitated Radegund in giving banquets lavishly to the poor and bathing them with her own hands.[75] Nor was hers a simple private act of devotion. Her greatest charities were deliberately organized in commemoration of her husband's death. She was still playing the saving saint to his worldly warrior. On one occasion, she is credited with a wonderful variation of Jesus' multiplication of the loaves and fishes from the mountain near her monastery.[76] Like Clothild, she had access to the royal treasury. Eventually she fell into strife with her sons over her charity. They deprived her of her dower lands and tried to force her to take the veil to protect the royal treasury from her depredations.[77] But like the queenly saints who were her models, she refused to be placed under the direct authority of the church, thus retaining her own mediating position.[78] Fortunately, the pious queen, Otto's wife Edith, "at the request of all the nobles and priests" who clearly understood the diplomatic protocol involved, made it possible for the emperor to seek reconciliation with his mother.[79] This abortive saint quickly undertook the proper propitiatory rituals of female

---

[72] *Vita Mathildis*, 21, p. 297.

[73] Odilo of Cluny, *Epitaphium Adalheidae imperatricis* 18, *Patrologia Latina* 142, 974–75.

[74] *Epitaphium* 13; 17 for Switzerland.

[75] *Vita Mathildis*, 17, p. 195.

[76] *Vita Mathildis*, 18, p. 296.

[77] *Vita Mathildis*, 11, p. 290. This too may be an *imitatio* of the *Vita Chrotildis*.

[78] *Vita Mathildis*, 10, p. 290.

[79] *Vita Mathildis*, 12, p. 291.

royalty to bring the two together. Later, when she was near death, Mathilda did not hesitate to prostrate herself before her mighty son to gain his public recognition of the wealth and privileges he and his father had bestowed on her monasteries.

Adelheid, like Radegund, made a practice of sitting at the royal feasts and only pretending to eat the sumptuous fare she served to others.[80] She founded many monasteries, including a major portion of Cluny's endowment, giving the jewels and clothes she was wearing to the poor or churches, again in emulation of Radegund.[81] Like Helena, she made pilgrimages to the sites of famous relics which she adorned with her own jewels. These journeys were particularly marked with extravagant charity and were enhanced in her biography by a food multiplication miracle.[82] All this activity was explicitly tied to her duties as queen dowager. Odilo describes her as giving "donatives" to the poor on the feasts of the royal kindred.[83]

Early in the eleventh century, Cnut, the Danish conqueror of England, sent for his conquered predecessor's Norman queen, Emma and married her. His motives were never recorded but in her later years, Emma commissioned a biography which strains to place her in the ranks of saintly queens.[84] This authorized description of her public life suggests that she and Cnut agreed that she should enact that traditional role. First of all, the author of the *Encomium* says that her marriage was welcomed by the English because it reconciled them with their Danish conqueror. This attribution of a peace-making role is particularly peculiar because the author makes no mention of the fact that she had previously been Queen of England as the wife of Ethelred. The *Encomium* goes so far as to suggest that her sons Alfred and Edward (the Confessor) were fathered by Cnut though it was common knowledge that they were the children of Ethelred. This reconciliative role of queens may explain why Cnut went out of his way to bring the

---

[80] Corbet, 68, notes that generosity is the outstanding characteristic of Adelheid, with humility modelled on the hagiography of abbots, but tailored for her worldly position.

[81] *Epitaphium*, 11.

[82] *Epitaphium*, 15.

[83] *Epitaphium*, 21.

[84] *Encomium Emmae Reginae*, ed. Alistair Campbell, Camden Society, Third Series, 72 (London: Royal Historical Society, 1949).

former king's widow to his own court. The obscure treatment of her children may have been intended to blur the fact that her child by Cnut took precedence in inheriting the kingdom. In a later generation, when a new style of government was being established, William of Malmesbury cuttingly suggested that her fame for charity and reconciliation was bought at the expense of Ethelred's sons, whom she kept in a state of poverty and whom she attempted to keep from their father's throne.[85]

With the eleventh century, saintly queenship began to give way to the claims of kings themselves to religious authority. One hagiographer even attempted to argue the case for Robert the Pious of France, best known for his scandalous marital adventures.[86] Edward the Confessor in England, along with the Emperor Henry II who shared the honors with his wife Cunegund, laid more successful claims to sacral qualities.[87] Henry II's biographer claimed that his noble councillors forced the reluctant emperor to marry, despite his desire for chastity. Though his wife, Cunegund, came from an outstanding aristocratic line with some royal connections of their own, her biographer stresses that she was an orphan.[88] The bond that was subsequently forged between the

---

[85] William of Malmesbury, *Gesta Regum Anglorum* (London: Camden Society, 1846), 2:13.

[86] Helgaud of Fleury, *Epitome Vitae Regis Rotberti Pii*, ed. and trans. R.-H. Bautier and Gillette Labory (Paris: Sources d'histoire médiévale, 1955) gives Robert the qualities I have attributed to queens: collecting and caring for relics; almsgiving and healing; mercy and humility. These qualities had little relationship to the real events of his life. His marital difficulties form a central chapter in Georges Duby, *The Knight, the Lady and the Priest: The making of modern marriage in Medieval France*, trans. Barbara Bray (New York: Pantheon, 1985).

[87] Though Corbet, 105, thinks it was at the expense of their kingly qualities. Helgaud wrote ca. 1040 and the *Vita Aedwardi Regis qui apud Westmonasterium requiescit: S. Bertini ascripta*, ed. and trans. Frank Barlow (London: Nelson's Texts, 1962) was produced around 1070. Joel T. Rosenthal, "Edward the Confessor and Robert the Pious: 11th Century Kingship and Biography," *Mediaeval Studies* 33 (1971) 7–20, places them in an early medieval context of Kingship which changes thereafter. I would argue that sacral kingship was unique to the eleventh century. *Adalberti vita Heinrici II Imperatoris, Monumenta Germaniae Historica Scriptores* 4, III, was written in the mid-twelfth century and the *Vita sanctae Cunegundis: Imperatricis, virginis, coniugis, viduis, demum sanctimonialis Benedictina, Confugiae et Bambergae in Germania, Acta Sanctorum* 3 March I, 265–80, belongs to the turn of the thirteenth century.

[88] Her own biographer says little about the conditions of her marriage but Adalbert took great pains to explain away the marriage itself and its subsequent lack of

royal partners is attributed to their extraordinary vow of mutual chastity which enabled them to thwart the designs of her noble backers.[89]
Similarly, a few years later in England, the childless Edward the Confessor and his queen Edith were said to have taken vows of perpetual
virginity.[90] William of Malmesbury frankly says that no one ever
knew whether they acted from love of chastity or hatred of the bride's
family who had imposed the marriage upon Edward.[91]

Almost as though to prove that both partners on the throne could
not easily be saints, the Empress and Queen Edith were both accused
during their lifetimes of unchastity and adultery. Henry II's biographer,
late in the twelfth century, relates a popular story that Cunegund had
voluntarily undergone an ordeal—walking barefoot over red-hot plow-
shares—to prove that tales that she had given up her virginity to a

---

progeny, directly denying the nobles' stated reasons for forcing the marriage. Additamentum, 816.

[89] This story appears in both Adalbert and Cunegund's biography as well as Raoul
Glaber's *Chronicon*, MGH SS 7, 62. Hugo Koch, *Die Ehe Kaiser Heinrichs II mit
Kunigunde* (Köln: 1908), argued that Henry hoped to have children and only gradually
came to accept that he would not, based on his interpretation of a letter to the bishop
of Wurzburg, Jaffé, *Biblioteca Rerum Germanicarum* 5:478, and of a remark in the
Chronicon of Thietmar von Merseburg, ed. Kurze, MGH 3/1, 152. The evidence is,
however, highly equivocal and at most shows that Henry wanted to avoid discussing
the disposition of his inheritance. Whether he and Cunegund really avoided consum-
mation or whether they later let the idea take root to explain their lack of children is
unknowable, but it is worth noting that only in the late eleventh and early twelfth centuries would such behavior be considered praiseworthy in a royal couple.

[90] The first source of the story is the *Vita Aedwardi*, written after Edward's death
at the request of Edith. There it appears only in coy references to their father/daughter
relationship. The account in general is complicated by a confusion of focus on the
author's part, which is discussed in detail by the editor, Frank Barlow, in his *Edward
the Confessor* (Berkeley: Univ. of California Press, 1970), appendix A. Some of that
confusion arises from the author's failure to determine the object of his account. I
would suggest that one difficulty may have been the failure of the queenly hagiographical tradition at about this time and the failure of the kingly tradition to take clear
shape. Barlow, 81, is positively scornful of the whole thesis of the chaste marriage.
Whatever the private accommodations of the royal pair, however, contemporaries apparently linked perpetual chastity to Edward's growing reputation for sanctity. Certainly the story fits comfortably into the atmosphere of nervous sexuality which sur-
rounds the age of the Gregorian conflict and the subsequent re-structuring of the
gender system which I have explored in "The Herrenfrage: The Restructuring of the
Gender System, 1050–1150," ed. Claire Lees, *Medieval Masculinities*, (St. Paul, Minn.:
Univ. of Minnesota Press, 1994), 3–30.

[91] William of Malmesbury, *Gesta Regum Anglorum* (London: Camden Society,
1846), 2:13.

knightly lover were false.[92] Thus Cunegund, slandered by malicious courtiers, was dependent on her generous husband and the miraculous power of God for her continued security. Edith voluntarily took an oath on her deathbed that her virginity had never been sullied.[93]

Henry II acted in consort with his empress Cunegund to benefit the church, a melding of the activities of queen and king that seems to have grown out of the increasingly sacral elements in eleventh-century kingship. As a widow, however, Cunegund could act more traditionally, lavishing her widow's fortune on the diocese of Bamberg where her cult still flourishes and retiring to her own convent of Kaufungen.[94] Cunegund endowed other monastic foundations, providing massive charities and procuring the head of Saint Valentine and the body of Saint Ouen to bless her German foundations. On the anniversary of her husband's death she presided over the dedication of her convent church in Kaufungen, "most fittingly bedecked in the imperial cult ornaments."[95] At the offertory of the mass, she advanced to the altar, like Helena, consecrating the northern Empire with that incomparably queenly relic, wood from the True Cross. During the reading of the gospel, she deposited her purple gown and ornaments before the altar to take a monastic habit. Through such ceremonial activities, the childless widow retained her queenship without posing a threat to the claims of her husband's elected successor.

The last of our sainted queens lived on the far frontiers of Christendom. Margaret of Scotland was famed for her charity, her church building, her monastic foundations and for her use of royal power to combat heresy and secure reform in the Scottish church. Margaret fol-

---

[92] *Adalberti vita Heinrici II Imperatoris*, Additamentum 3:3, *Monumenta Germaniae Historica Scriptores* 4. This story fits into a larger tradition of scapegoating queens and is virtually identical to the story of the suspect Carolingian queen Richardis recounted by Stafford. See *Queens*, 94.

[93] William of Malmesbury, *Gesta*, 2:13.

[94] Cunegund's husband, Henry II, is the only emperor to gain a cult of his own. They are worshipped in twin tombs in Bamberg. This may conceivably stem from the belief that the couple had never consummated their marriage which might blur the gender division of labor between them, making her more powerful and him weaker, an effect noted throughout Dyan Elliott's *Spiritual Marriage* (Princeton: Princeton Univ. Press, 1993).

[95] *Vita sanctae Cunegundis: Imperatricis, virginis, coniugis, viduis, demum sanctimonialis Benedictina, Confugiae et Bambergae in Germania* c. 5, *Acta Sanctorum* 3 March I, 265–80.

lowed the established models in rising from her bed to pray, wearing her royal garments over a humble heart. She always maintained two dozen paupers at her court whom she served personally and exhibited massive charity on public occasions. Hedwig of Poland, a country newly Christianized in the twelfth century, patronized monasticism as an instrument for conversion and established Cistercian nuns devoted to the education of noble girls. Within marriage, she practiced abstinence when child-bearing and turned completely to chastity after three children. With her husband she established and maintained a leper house at Neumarkt, personally attending to the leprous women by sending them money, food and clothing. Her sister Gertrude of Hungary and her daughter-in-law Anne of Bohemia were all involved in the struggle to impose Christianity in the east and to resist the Tartar invasions. This whole family of royal women actively patronized monasticism and engaged in charitable efforts for the poor.

Their daughters saw the end of the tradition. Margaret of Scotland's life was commissioned by her daughter, Edith/Mathilda, Henry I of England's queen, who provides a final example of the role of queens in making peace with a conquered population. Daughter of the conquered Saxon dynasty, she was "rescued" from a convent by the gallant Norman king. She was famous for personally tending to lepers and she founded a hospital for them in 1101. But though he praises her merits, Malmesbury complains of her as he had done of Cnut's queen Emma, that this ostentatious charity was at the expense of her tenants.[96] Throughout her life as queen, wearing a hair shirt and going to church barefoot in Lent, she was seen as the agent for mercy and reconciliation between her people and their conquerors as well as between her husband and his quarrelsome brother.[97] But though she tried to intervene with her husband in favor of priests who had been the victims of a royal campaign of extortion, her courage gave way.[98] In the end it

---

[96] William of Malmesbury, 454.

[97] Malmesbury, 453. There is a distant echo of the *imitatio Radegundis* in her indifference to the threat that her husband might not wish to kiss her after she had kissed lepers, in Marcelle Thiébaux, *The Writings of Medieval Women*, 2d ed. (New York: Garland Publishing, 1994), 297.

[98] Eadmer, *History of Recent Events in England*, trans. G. Bosanquet, (London: Cresset Press, 1964), 184–85.

was left to Bishop Anselm, the intractible representative of the Gregorian church to brave the king's anger. During his consequent exile, however, Mathilda's supportive intervention with the king and even with the pope helped restore the bishop to England.[99] Thereafter, however, the Gregorian revolution established an ecclesiastical monopoly over the oppositional role to kingly power and gradually bishops displaced queens.[100]

Cunegund's successor, Agnes of Poitou, was drawn ultimately too far from the imperial into the ecclesiastical orbit to be effective in her intermediary role. Her pursuit of sainthood recommended her to the increasingly aggressive papacy in its struggle against the theocratic claims of the empire but neither she nor the other women who upheld the papacy with manly vigor against the Empire were rewarded with canonization. As the church redefined itself as an autonomous competitive power, its rulers no longer sought alliances with women. Indeed, as the church strengthened its boundaries against the laity, its highest priority was the creation of a womanless space. Similarly, the state sought a clearer definition of its own sphere, withdrawing from the old theocratic models represented by the saintly queen. The secular state began to emerge with an ungendered (but male) bureaucracy doing much of the work previously assigned to the royal persons themselves and their retainers. The emergence of monarchy from the royal household meant that it also emerged from the queen's housekeeping.

The tragic saint Elisabeth of Thuringia was the last offshoot of the remarkable queens of the Slavic frontiers.[101] Elisabeth and her husband, the Landgrave of Thuringia, were already generous contributors to charitable causes before his death on crusade. She opened a hospital at Eisenach and another at Gotha, bringing the order of Lazarus into the country.[102] After her husband died, his brother withheld the

---

[99] Ibid., 196. She wrote to Anselm assuring him that she had prudently determined the king's spirit had softened toward him, in Thiébaux, *Writings of Medieval Women*, 307, and to the pope, pleading for his support in restoring Anselm, ibid., 309.

[100] Marion F. Facinger, "A Study of Medieval Queenship: Capetian France 987–1237," *Nebraska Studies in Medieval and Renaissance History* 5 (1968), 1–48.

[101] Lina Eckenstein, *Women Under Monasticism* (New York: Russell & Russell, 1963) 290ff.

[102] The popular tale of Elisabeth's bread turning to roses in midwinter when her husband sought to catch her stealing royal supplies for the poor might well have its

dower land and incomes which she held in life use, unwilling to allow her to give away goods of which she only had the use. Like William of Malmesbury, he clearly had a broader view of the consequences of unlimited charity. Elizabeth clearly still thought, as her predecessors had, that the revenues of the state were an evil to be purged only by their charitable dispersion. Her own maids testified that she was so convinced the royal revenues should be classed as ill-gotten gains that she refused to eat anything that might have been purchased with tax money, "to avoid participating in the exploitation of the poor too often practiced at princely courts."[103]

Solidification of coherent national identities buttressed the relative stability of the feudal system. This ensured that the marriages and vocations of women would be subjected to the ruler's own designs of domestic peace with little room for their own initiative. The indiscriminate mercy characteristic of early saints was being replaced with a more systematic ideal of justice. Charity was gradually becoming less admirable than enterprise and humility was giving way to the hope of upward mobility. It is ironic that the very power to seal alliances usually associated with royal marriages in modern times tends to negate the queen's personal power within the marriage. Indeed by the dawn of early modern times, the royal mistress was beginning to take over much of the public role that had once distinguished queenship. Blanche of Castile was the last of the great old queens and with her the saintly attributes of queenship were, for the first and only time, incorporated into a mystique of kingship. She raised Saint Louis to be a peacemaker among his people by asserting royal rights over church offices and by personally befriending the poor. Blanche never received the formal canonization that was her due and she energetically intervened between her son and his wife so as to renew the image of negative queenship against Marguerite of Provence, one of the first Europe-

---

roots in her genuine enmity for his brother and successor.

[103] Werner Moritz, "Das Hospital der heiligen Elisabeth," from *Elisabeth von Thuringia*, 112–40. Elizabeth of Thuringia is a particularly valuable example because sources were assembled for her canonization within a year after her death in 1231 by Conrad of Marburg. The most precious testimony is the testimony from two of her ladies in waiting and two servants who worked with her in the hospital of Marburg, 1228–31, in A. Huyskens, ed., *Der sog. Libellus de dictis quatuor ancillarum s. Elisabeth confectus* (Kempten und München: Jos. Kösel'schen Buchhandlung, 1911).

an queens to suffer from the unpopularity of being a foreigner in an increasingly self-conscious nation. Louis was the first king successfully to join the warrior to the peacemaker and charitable image of ruler-ship. Indeed, one was enough to establish a tradition in which men performed the roles formerly allotted to women.[104] St. Louis, who fought like Constantine under the sign of the cross, absorbed into himself the *imitatio Helenae* when he solemnly installed the crown of thorns in his royal palace.

---

[104] Gabrielle M. Spiegel, "The Cult of St. Denis and Capetian Kingship," in *Saints and Their Cults*, ed. Stephen Wilson, (Cambridge: Cambridge Univ. Press, 1983), 141–68.

Changing Images of Sainthood:
St. Cuthbert in the
Historia de Sancto Cuthberto

TED JOHNSON-SOUTH

y purpose in this paper is to examine the portrayal of St. Cuthbert in the late-Saxon *Historia de Sancto Cuthberto,* and to compare that portrayal with the presentation of the saint in earlier biographies. In doing this I will be examining hagiographical material from the perspective of a social historian; my aim is not to reconstruct the facts of St. Cuthbert's life, but rather to examine how the story and character of St. Cuthbert developed over time, and to see what that can tell us about changes in the popular perception of a medieval patron-saint.[1]

---

[1] From this perspective, the widespread scholarly dispute over whether hagiographical authors like Bede believed in the miracles they described—whether "Bede's words are not intended for material interpretation" (C. W. Jones, *Saints' Lives and Chronicles in Early England* [Ithaca: Cornell Univ. Press, 1947], 83) or "Bede and other writers who record miracles believed they were recording facts about events" (B. Ward, "Miracles and History: A Reconsideration of the Miracle Stories Used by Bede" in G. Bonner, ed., *Famulus Christi* [London: S.P.C.K., 1976], 71)—is beside the point. I agree instead with recent scholars like R. C. Finucane, who states that "the question of whether 'miracles really happened' is an artificial problem" (R. C. Finucane, "The Use and Abuse of Medieval Miracles," *History* 60 [1975]: 2). However, even Finucane cannot resist the urge to enter the debate on the objective reality of miracles; he concerns himself specifically with posthumous "miracle cures," and states that "if the medieval, rather than the modern, view of health and illness be considered,

Two authors wrote biographies of Cuthbert in the generation following his death. The first was an unknown monk of Lindisfarne who wrote the *Anonymous Life of St. Cuthbert* between the years 699 and 705. The second was Bede, who wrote his own *Life of St. Cuthbert,* based in large part on the *Anonymous Life,* around the year 721. Bede also inserted additional material concerning Cuthbert into his *Ecclesiastical History,* written in 731. These three works all paint essentially the same picture of the saint, especially when compared to the later *Historia de Sancto Cuthberto,* and throughout this paper I shall refer to them collectively as the "early Lives."

The life-story of St. Cuthbert is similar in all three early Lives. Even as a youth, his life contained signs of sanctity to come. The most important of these took place when young Cuthbert was tending sheep at night. He saw a vision of a soul ascending to heaven, accompanied by angels. The next morning he learned that Bishop Aidan, the man who had founded the monastery of Lindisfarne and spearheaded the conversion of Northumbria, had died during the night. Prompted by this vision, according to Bede, Cuthbert himself decided to enter a monastery.[2] As a monk, first at Melrose (or Ripon, according to the *Anonymous Life*) and later at Lindisfarne, he provided those around him with an example of holy life. Bede in particular characterizes him both as a man of intense ascetic and contemplative devotion, and as an active minister of the word of God who would travel for weeks on foot through the countryside to preach.

Eventually Cuthbert left the monastery at Lindisfarne to live as a hermit on the nearby island of Farne. It was only with difficulty that he was later persuaded to leave his island and become bishop of Lindisfarne. After two years as bishop Cuthbert returned again to Farne island to live in solitude and prepare for death. This is a fitting conclu-

---

then there is nothing supernatural about these events" (Finucane, "Medieval Miracles," 2). For me here the point is that, whether or not they "really happened," and whether they were viewed as fact or fiction by either their authors or their audiences, medieval miracle stories constitute a traditional mode of expression through which social attitudes and moral values were transmitted and reinforced.

[2] *Anonymous Life* 1, 5 and 2, 1–2; *Bede's Life* 4. (The texts used throughout this paper are *Vita Sancti Cuthberti auctore anonymo* and *Vita Sancti Cuthberti auctore Bede,* in B. Colgrave, ed. and trans., *Two Lives of St. Cuthbert* [Cambridge: Cambridge Univ. Press, 1940].)

sion to his story; throughout the early Lives St. Cuthbert emerges as a model of Christian humility and ascetic life who turns his back on temporal riches and earthly glory, at last fleeing his cathedral to return to a life of holy contemplation.[3]

Miracles play an important part in the early Lives, and their use follows a similar pattern in each work. Chapters concerning Cuthbert's life as a monk and hermit are dominated by nature-miracles, in which the elements themselves, as well as the birds of the air and the fish of the sea, do the saint's bidding or act in accordance with his prophecies. An example: when Cuthbert visits a neighboring monastery, one of the monks notices that the saint disappears every evening, and one night secretly follows him. Cuthbert goes down to the ocean and walks into the waves. He stands there in the North Sea with water up to his neck, singing and praying until dawn. Then he returns to the beach and kneels there, still praying. Two otters emerge from the sea, approach the saint, and proceed to warm his feet with their breath and dry him with their fur. When they are finished, Cuthbert blesses them and they return to the sea.[4]

When Cuthbert becomes Bishop of Lindisfarne, these nature-miracles are replaced by a series of healing miracles, in which men, women and children suffering from various illnesses are brought back from the point of death. Throughout his life Cuthbert is also gifted with visions; the most important of these are his visions of St. Aidan's soul being carried off to heaven, and of Northumbrian king Ecgfrith's death in battle against the Picts. Finally, each *Life* concludes with a small number of posthumous miracles, in which supplicants who come to the saint's tomb are cured of demonic possession, illness and paralysis.

We come now to the *Historia de Sancto Cuthberto,* a brief (c. 6,500 word) Latin work produced within the Community of St. Cuthbert between the mid-tenth and mid-eleventh centuries.[5] The *Historia* is

---

[3] In this Cuthbert has frequently been contrasted with his more secularly minded contemporary, Wilfred. See, e.g., Colgrave, *Two Lives,* vii, and J. Campbell, "Bede I," in *Essays in Anglo-Saxon History* (London: Hambledon Press, 1986), 16–17.

[4] *Anonymous Life,* 2, 3; *Bede's Life,* 10.

[5] For discussions of the date of composition of the *Historia* see E. Craster, "The Patrimony of St. Cuthbert," *English Historical Review* 271 (1954); L. Simpson, "The King Alfred / St. Cuthbert Episode in the *Historia de Sancto Cuthberto;* Its Significance for Mid-Tenth Century English History," in G. Bonner, D. Rollason, and C. Stanclife, eds., *St. Cuthbert, His Cult and his Community to AD 1200* (Woodbridge:

significant as the earliest surviving source for descriptions of a number of
events in the history of the Community, including its translation from
Lindisfarne to Chester-le-Street, and for a number of miracle stories
which became part of the later medieval Cuthbertine tradition.[6] It also
contains a detailed record of land-holdings which is unique for pre-Con-
quest Northumbria. In fact, the *Historia* is more the history of a monastic
community than a traditional saint's life, and it bears the significant sub-
title "A History of St. Cuthbert and a Record of the Places and Regions
of his Ancient Patrimony from the Beginning up to the Present Time."
A. Grandsen has characterized it as "institutional history" rather than strict
hagiography, citing it as a precocious example of a type of saint's life
which began to appear with some frequency in England in the later eleventh century, in which the text is characterized by "the authors's anxiety
to define the rights and possessions of the saint's see or monastery."[7]

Boydell and Brewer, 1989), esp. 397–98; and T. Johnson-South, *The "Historia de
Sancto Cuthberto": A New Edition and Translation, with Discussions of Surviving Manuscripts, the Text, and Northumbrian Estate Structure* (Ph.D. diss., Cornell Univ., 1990).
    Craster, whose opinion on the date of the *Historia* is generally accepted, assumes
that the text was written in three distinct stages; A) §§1–13 + 19b–28, written in the
reign of Edmund, c. 945; B) §§29–32, written in the reign of Cnut, c. 1030; C)
§§14–19a + 33, written at the end of the eleventh century. This scheme is based on
the fact that one manuscript omits B and ends with §28, which describes Edmund's
visit to Cuthbert's shrine. However, this same manuscript also includes C (except for
§33), which is assumed to be a later addition to the text, since it contains an anachronistic reference to the battle of Ashingdon (1016) in §16. If Craster is right and this
manuscript does preserve an early version of the text which was made shortly after
945, before B and C were written, then it is difficult to explain the presence of C in
the middle of the text. Furthermore, the second half of A, which deals with the reigns
of Ethelred and Edmund, contains references to events from Alfred's time that are only
described in C. This suggests that A cannot have been written before C, which would
mean that the entire text was written after 1016. Thus, Craster's scheme will need to
be revised if we wish to prove that the earlier portions of the *Historia* date from the
tenth century.
    Although the actual text of the *Historia* is presented without any internal divisions
in all three surviving manuscripts, for the sake of convenience I have adopted the sec-
tion-numbers introduced by Arnold, adding a final section (§34) to include a colophon
in one of the manuscripts overlooked by Arnold.
    [6] For a discussion of the *Historia's* miracles and their impact on the later hagiogra-
phy of the saint, see B. Colgrave, "The Post-Bedan Miracles and Translations of St.
Cuthbert," in C. Fox and B. Dickens, eds., *The Early Cultures of North-West Europe*
(Cambridge: Cambridge Univ. Press, 1950), 305–322.
    [7] A. Grandsen, *Historical Writing in England c. 550 to 1307* (Ithaca: Cornell Univ.
Press, 1974), 69; see also ibid., 76–77, 88.

In presenting its version of St. Cuthbert's earthly life, the *Historia* compresses and combines information from the three early Lives described above. At various points the *Historia's* version of the story incorporates details unique to each of these three sources.[8] There is, moreover, nothing in the *Historia's* brief outline of Cuthbert's life to suggest an unknown source beyond these three early works. All departures in the *Historia* originate either in misunderstandings of the historical sequence of events,[9] or in misinterpretations of one of our three source-texts.[10] The *Historia* is in fact a late-Saxon digest of these earlier sources, and so can demonstrate for us the relative values that a late-Saxon audience placed on various aspects of the saint's life-story.

The author of the *Historia* compresses all of St. Cuthbert's life into his first few pages; the rest of the work is dominated by later grants of property to the saint and the posthumous miracles performed by him. Only two incidents from the saint's lifetime are described in any detail; these are the miraculous vision of St. Aidan being carried up to heaven, which prompted Cuthbert to become a monk, and the sequence of events which led to Cuthbert being consecrated bishop of Lindisfarne. The author also deals quite briefly with St. Cuthbert's spiritual life. As a monk Cuthbert "faithfully observed both the contemplative and the active ways of living to the end of his own life";[11] as abbot of Mel-

---

[8] The setting of Cuthbert's vision of St. Aidan (near the River Leader) is unique to the *Anonymous Life (Anonymous Life,* 1, 5); Boisil's ahistorical description of Cuthbert's sanctity to King Oswin seems based on a similar incident in *Bede's Life,* in which Boisil speaks instead to abbot Eata (*Bede's Life* 6); the sequence of events surrounding Cuthbert's consecration as bishop is drawn from the *Ecclesiastical History (Ecclesiastical History* 4, 28). (The text used throughout this paper is B. Colgrave and R. A. B. Mynors, eds. and trans., *Bede's Ecclesiastical History of the English People* [Oxford: Oxford Univ. Press, 1969].)

[9] E.g., King Oswin makes a gift to Cuthbert after learning of Cuthbert's vision of St. Aiden's death, although Bede states Oswin died twelve days before Aidan (see *Ecclesiastical History* 3, 14), and Cedd and Chad are described as being among the seven bishops celebrating Cuthbert's ordination at York although, as Colgrave has pointed out, they would have been dead for 21 and 14 years respectively—see Colgrave, "Post-Bedan Miracles," 307.

[10] E.g., the author confuses the village of Alne in North Yorkshire with the River Alne in Northumberland; Bede states that the synod which named Cuthbert as bishop took place on the Alne in the vill of *Adtuifyrdi* (*Ecclesiastical History* 4, 28).

[11] Historia §3. (The translation used throughout this paper is Johnson-South, *The "Historia de Sancto Cuthberto."*) The most commonly used edition of the text is in T. Arnold, *Symeonis Monachi Opera,* Rolls Series vol. 75 (London, 1882), 1:196–214.

rose he "spread the word of God and baptized a great multitude";[12] and in later years he "took himself to a certain remote island called Farne, and for nine years enclosed himself there as in a prison, fighting against the enemy of human-kind."[13] Finally, miracle stories from Cuthbert's lifetime are also scarce. Apart from Cuthbert's vision of Aidan, there is only one oblique reference to the time when he "revived a boy from the dead at the vill which is called *Exanforda*."[14] This miracle probably derives from one recorded in both early sources, in which Cuthbert comes to preach in a village during a plague and is shown a woman whose son is at the point of death; he kisses the boy and reassures his mother that the boy will live.[15]

As we can see, the *Historia's* author deletes much of the detail from his three sources. What remains highlighted are the two key events which best serve as credentials of Cuthbert's sainthood. The first of these, Cuthbert's vision of St. Aidan, is the miracle by which God first marks Cuthbert's holiness. The second is the episcopal consecration with which that holiness was acknowledged by the temporal authorities, namely King Ecfrid and Archbishop Theodore. The character of Cuthbert's spiritual life, and the many miracles which help define that spirituality, remain secondary.

While the events of the saint's lifetime receive short shrift in the *Historia*, his posthumous miracles get considerably more attention. Since it is these which provide us with our chief impressions of St. Cuthbert's changing character, they are worth reviewing in detail.

1) The Destruction of Kings Osberht and Ælle (§10). The first posthumous miracle in the *Historia* describes how two ninth-century kings of York, Osberht and Ælle, broke their oaths and seized several estates from Cuthbert's patrimony. Because of this the wrath of God and St. Cuthbert descended upon them. Ubba, duke of the Frisians, led a Danish army against York, killing the two kings in battle. The episode ends with a stern warning: "Therefore let all kings and princes beware

---

[12] *Historia* §3.

[13] *Historia* §3.

[14] *Historia* §6.

[15] See *Anonymous Life,* 4, 6, and *Bede's Life,* 33. Bede does not mention the location of this miracle; in the *Anonymous Life* the village is called *Medilwong*.

lest they lie, and lest they take anything from St. Cuthbert, or consent to others taking."[16]

2) The Destruction of King Halfdene (§12). After the conquest of York, the Danish King Halfdene took an army north and sailed up the Tyne, "devastating everything and cruelly sinning against St. Cuthbert. But soon the wrath of God and of the holy confessor fell upon him, for he began to rave and to reek, so that his whole army drove him from its midst, and he fled far across the sea and never reappeared."[17]

3) The election of King Guthred (§13). This miracle, set in the later ninth century some years after the Danish conquest of York, describes how St. Cuthbert appeared at night to abbot Eaddred of Carlisle, and instructed him to go to the Danes of York and arrange the election of Guthred, son of Hardacnut, as their new king. In return the new king was to give to Saint Cuthbert "all the land between the Tyne and the Wear, and [to grant] that whoever shall flee to [him], whether for homicide or for any other necessity, may have peace for thirty-seven days and nights."[18] The saint's wishes were carried out, and King Guthred and the Danish host swore an oath of peace and fidelity over the body of St. Cuthbert.

4) King Alfred's Dream (§§14–18). This miracle takes us back to the mid-ninth century, during the initial Viking attacks on the south of England. King Alfred of Wessex had taken refuge from the Danes in the marshes around Glastonbury, and one day he generously shared his meager supply of food with a poor wanderer. The wanderer disappeared into the marsh and Alfred's household returned from fishing with three boatfuls of fish, the biggest load they had ever caught. That night, as Alfred lay awake marveling over these events, the wanderer returned and identified himself as St. Cuthbert. The saint told Alfred to arise at dawn and gather his troops, promising him victory over the Danes at *Assandune* (Ashingdon).[19] He then admonished the king:

---

[16] *Historia* §10.

[17] *Historia* §12.

[18] *Historia* §13.

[19] The author of the *Historia* has apparently confused Alfred's victory over the Danes at Edington in 878 with Cnut's victory over Edmund at Ashington in 1016; this suggests that this portion of the *Historia* cannot have been written before the early eleventh century.

"Be faithful to me and to my people, for all Albion has been given to you and your sons. Be just, for you are chosen king of all Britain. May God be merciful to you, and I will be your friend, so that no adversary may prevail against you."[20] This miracle is used to explain Alfred's special reverence for St. Cuthbert, which later led his descendants Athelstan and Edmund to make pilgrimages to St. Cuthbert's shrine.

5) The Waves of Blood (§20). This miracle again involves abbot Eadred of Carlisle and describes how he and bishop Eardulf took St. Cuthbert's body and fled Lindisfarne, wandering from place to place for seven years accompanied by all the saints people (*omnis populis eius*). When Eadred and Eardulf placed the saint's body in a boat and attempted to sail to Ireland without the saint's people, God intervened with a miracle. "A horrible storm arose on the sea, three tremendous waves fell on the ship, and at once, marvelous to say, the water was turned to blood. When the bishop and the abbot saw this, they fell at the feet of the saint and, terrified with fear, they returned to the shore as quickly as possible, and carried the holy body to Crayke [near York]."[21]

6) The Destruction of Onalafball (§23). This miracle takes place in the early tenth century, after the Norse king Rægnald invaded Northumbria. Considerable property belonging to the Community of St. Cuthbert passed into Rægnald's hands after the battle of Corbridge, some of which he gave to his lieutenant Onalafball. One day Onalafball burst into St. Cuthbert's church and confronted the bishop and his monks: "'What can this dead man Cuthbert do, whose threats are set against me every day? I swear by my powerful gods Thor and Odin that from this hour I will be the bitterest enemy of you all.'" The congregation knelt and prayed to God and St. Cuthbert for vengeance, and when Onalafball attempted to leave the church, he was struck down. "With pain transfixing his diabolical heart, he fell, and the devil thrust his sinful soul into Hell. St. Cuthbert, as was just, regained his land."[22]

7) King Guthred's Victory (§33). This final miracle, which is clearly out of chronological order and which may well have been added to

---

[20] *Historia* §16.

[21] *Historia* §20.

[22] *Historia* §23.

the *Historia* a few decades after its initial composition, refers back to the time of King Guthred. An army of Scots had crossed the Tweed, devastating the lands of St. Cuthbert and despoiling the monastery of Lindisfarne. King Guthred hastened to avenge the saint, but by nightfall he found himself trapped at the place called *Mundingedene* by a superior force of Scots. That night, St. Cuthbert appeared to Guthred in a dream and promised him victory; the next day, as the attack began, the earth opened up beneath the Scots and dropped them alive into Hell.[23]

In all, the *Historia* contains nine miracles: Cuthbert's vision of St. Aidan, his cure of the boy at Exanforda, and the seven posthumous miracles just described. Taken together, these miracles portray a saint quite different from the Cuthbert of the early Lives. Not only are Cuthbert's acts as a living man deemphasized in comparison with his posthumous miracles, but the details of Cuthbert's life that remain show a remarkable change in emphasis. Cuthbert's spirituality is passed over relatively quickly, and while single miracles still demonstrate his visionary gifts and healing powers, there are no longer any nature-miracles at all, despite the fact that these are quite prominent in the early Lives. Instead of using miracles to protect, nurture and heal, the saint now uses his power to punish and avenge. And while the early Lives portray the saint as turning his back upon the temporal life and political entanglements (although he is shown to have had contact with abbess Ælfflæd, sister of King Ecgfirth),[24] the posthumous Cuthbert in the *Historia* is quite active politically, acting as king-maker on behalf of both Guthred the Dane and Alfred of Wessex.

These changes in St. Cuthbert's character share a common motive. If we examine those episodes in which Cuthbert is portrayed as a punishing or avenging force, we find that in each instance the saint is responding to injuries done to the Community of St. Cuthbert, and in each case the injury involves the destruction or confiscation of the Community's property. Onalafball, Osbehrt and Ælle each seize the Community estates, while Halfdane and the Scots both ravage the lands of St. Cuthbert. This preoccupation with Community property also

---

[23] *Historia* §33.
[24] See *Anonymous Life*, 3, 6, and *Bede's Life*, 23–24.

helps explain St. Cuthbert's political role as king-maker in the *Historia*. Guthred and Alfred both promise fidelity to the saint and his people, and both of their royal houses make important grants of land to the Community and commit themselves to uphold its property rights. In death, St. Cuthbert has been transformed from an unworldly ascetic into a powerful temporal patron capable of protecting the rights of his Community, both by threatening potential transgressors with violent retribution and by securing political protection in the form of royal patronage.[25]

This surprising transformation reflects related changes in the social and political role of the Anglo-Saxon monastery between the seventh and tenth centuries. Even in the seventh century, as several scholars have noted, Anglo-Saxon monasticism was shaped by the values of the noble culture from which it sprang, and this secular influence became stronger in succeeding centuries.[26] Ironically, the very popularity of ascetic saints like Cuthbert drew their monasteries further into secular entanglements. Cuthbert's spirituality attracted great royal patronage, with the result that the *Historia* is devoted less to the details of the saint's life than to the estates granted to him and his successors by Northumbrian kings and nobles. The *Historia* names over one hundred vills belonging to the Community, each of which would have comprised a number of individual farmsteads. A conservative estimate based on the *Historia* suggests that in the tenth century the Community of St. Cuthbert controlled some 200,000–300,000 acres of land, most of it between the rivers Tyne and Tees.[27] As its holdings grew, the monas-

---

[25] This transformation is not unique to St. Cuthbert; for a discussion of the same pattern in the lives of other saints see note 35 below.

[26] Thus J. Campbell describes Cuthbert's contemporary Wilfrid as "very much part of a noble society which cared greatly for power and show, the possession of a loyal *comitatus* and the opportunity to exchange rich gifts" (Campbell, "Bede I," 17). For secular impact on early English monasticism see also E. John, "The Social and Political Problems of the Early English Church," in J. Thirsk, ed., *Land, Church and People* (supplement of *Agricultural History Review* 18 [1970]).

[27] The holdings ascribed to the tenth-century Community of St. Cuthbert by the *Historia* include the major estates of Norhamshire, Islandshire, Jedburgh, Bedlington, Chester-le-Street, Bishop Wearmouth, Easington, Bishop Auckland, Staindrop, and Gainford. All of these can be fairly accurately mapped: Norhamshire and Islandshire were retained by the bishopric of Durham after the Conquest, and are described in later medieval sources, including *Boldon Book;* the bounds of Jedburgh and Chester-le-Street are listed in the *Historia,* and the remaining estates are all accompanied by lists

tic community would have been drawn ever further into temporal pre-occupations, and into the political life of the kingdom.

As the temporal power of the monasteries increased, that of the Northumbrian kings began to decline. Some contemporaries, at least, perceived a link between these two changes. In his letter to Egbert, Bede observed that "there is a complete lack of places where the sons of nobles or of veteran thegns can receive an estate [from the king]."[28] Bede felt that the alienation of royal lands to monasteries was directly responsible for this problem, although he blamed only those lay foundations which were "allowed the name of monasteries by a most foolish manner of speaking, but having nothing at all of a monastic way of life."[29] While there is still debate concerning the relative power of the Northumbrian kings in the later eighth centu-ry,[30] it is clear that by the middle of the ninth century whatever royal authority there was had been overwhelmed by the Viking invasions. In particular, the capture of York by the Danes in 866 seems to have left

---

of *appendicii* (dependent vills), showing that each estate actually consists of twelve indi-vidual vills (except for the half-estate of Bedlington, and Gainford which contains and extra vill). These listed vills almost always correspond with later parishes, and can be mapped using the earliest recorded parish boundaries. Each twelve-vill estate or "shire" makes up a discrete block of territory between 7,500 and 10,000 hectares (approx. 20,000 acres) in size. When the larger territories of Islandshire and Chester-le-Street are added in, the resulting territory is a minimum of 200,000 acres in size. The *Historia* also claims several earlier estates which may still have belonged to the Community during the tenth century, including Carham, Bowmont Water, Melrose, Whitingham, Edlingham, and *Wudacestre* (Woodhorn?); if one includes these estates, assuming that each was roughly the same size as the shires described above, the estimate rises to over 300,000 acres.

[28] "Letter of the Bede to Egbert, archbishop of York" in D. Whitelock, ed., *English Historical Documents c. 500–1042* (London: Oxford Univ. Press, 1955), 1:741.

[29] "Letter of Bede to Egebert," 740. Since there was no established canon for monastic rules in England before the *Regularis Concordia* in the tenth century, the dis-tinction Bede makes between authentic and counterfeit monasteries is problematic.

[30] Given the dearth of post-Bedan historical evidence, the debate over the strength of Northumbrian kingship has focused primarily on the question of the size of Viking armies. If these were relatively small, as P. Sawyer suggests, they could only have con-quered an already fragmented kingdom. (See e.g., P. Sawyer, *The Age of the Vikings* [London: St. Martin's Press, 1962] 117–28.) N. P. Brooks, who defends the traditional view, argues for large Viking armies and implies that the kingdoms of East Anglia, Mercia, and Northumbria were still powerful on the eve of the invasion. (See N. P. Brooks, "England in the Ninth Century: The Crucible in the Ninth Century: The Crucible of Defeat," *Transactions of the Royal Historical Society* 5th ser., 29 [1978], 1–20.)

northern Northumbria in a power vacuum into which the community
of St. Cuthbert naturally moved. This would explain why in the 880's
it was the Community, rather than the high reeve at Bamburgh, which
came to terms with the Danes of York and secured the election of
King Guthred. Later, the pilgrimages to St. Cuthbert's shrine made by
kings Athelstan (c. 934) and Edmund (c. 944) suggest that the Community offered the kings a promising political alliance as they moved
to consolidate their power over Northumbria.[31] In fact, by the tenth
century the continued growth of their patrimony and the decline of
royal authority had left the monks of St. Cuthbert as the chief temporal
power in the region, leading W. Kapelle to describe them as "the most
powerful body of men in the North."[32]

With the growing power of the Community of St. Cuthbert, the
character of the saint began to change and the identities of the saint
and monastery began to merge. Throughout the *Historia,* grants of
property are regularly described as being made out not to the bishop or
the monks, but directly to St. Cuthbert. At one point the text describes
how in the early tenth century bishop Cutheard purchased a particular
estate *de pecunia sancti Cuthberti,* "with St. Cuthbert's own money."[33]
Similarly, the *Historia* twice mentions the *populus sancti Cuthberti,* the
"people of St. Cuthbert," for whom the saint is *pius eorum patronus,*
"their pious patron."[34] The people refered to are not merely the
monks of St. Cuthbert, but all the inhabitants of his lands; in later centuries inhabitants of the county of Durham were still called *haliwerfolc,*
"the saint's people." All these details demonstrate that, in the popular
perception, the central authority of the Community of St. Cuthbert

---

[31] For a discussion of the political advantages which monastic alliances offered the
house of Wessex in the later tenth century, see E. John, "The King and the Monks in
the Tenth-Century Reformation," in *Orbis Brittaniæ* (Leicester: Leicester Univ. Press,
1966), 177–80.

[32] W. E. Kapelle, *The Norman Conquest of the North* (Chapel Hill: Univ. of North
Carolina Press, 1979), 31. As I have discussed elsewhere, this contradicts the traditional
view, based on the twelfth-century *Historia Dunelmensis Ecclesiæ,* that the Community
of St. Cuthbert never recovered from the Viking raids of the eighth and ninth centuries. See T. Johnson-South, "The Norman Conquest of Durham: Norman Historians and the Anglo-Saxon Community of St. Cuthbert," *Haskins Society Journal* 4
(1991): 87–97.

[33] *Historia* §21.

[34] *Historia* §16, §20.

was the saint himself. The Community's lands belonged to him, its revenues became his money, its tenants were his people.

This transformation from a spiritual recluse into a powerful patron who regularly wields temporal power on behalf of his Community is not unique to St. Cuthbert, but is part of a pattern which has been observed in numerous saint's lives, and which seems to have reached its height in the eleventh and twelfth centuries.[35] The traditional explanation, as expressed by both Gaiffier and Segal, has been that the decline of royal authority in ninth and tenth centuries forced churches and monasteries to replace royal protection with the threat of divine retribution by powerful patron saints.[36] While this explanation seems workable for Carolingian Europe, it provides only part of the answer for Anglo-Saxon England, since English kings had never achieved such complete control over the Church as their Carolingian counterparts, and since even great kings like Alfred were sometimes known to confiscate Church lands rather than protect them.[37] In the *Historia,* kings represent potential threats to the Community who must either be won over by saintly aid (as with Guthred and Alfred) or destroyed (as with Osberht and Ælle).

---

[35] Recent discussions of this phenomenon include E. G. Whately, *The Saint of London: The Life and Miracles of Saint Erkenwald* Series (Binghamton, NY: Medieval & Renaissance Texts & Studies, 1989), esp. 82–83, which notes a similar change in the twelfth-century *Miracula sancti Erkenwaldi;* Ward, *Miracles and the Medieval Mind,* (Philadelphia: Univ. of Pennsylvania Press, 1982), esp. chap. 3, which discusses the changing characters of Ste. Foi, St. Benedict of Nursia, and St. Cuthbert; and P. A. Sigal, "Un aspect du culte des saints; le châtiment divin aux XIe et XIIe siècles d'après la littérature hagiographique du Midi de la France," *Cahiers de Fanjeaux* 11 (1976): 39–59, a comparative study of the lives of thirteen saints from Aquitane, Languedoc and Provence.

Ward's discussion of St. Cuthbert briefly mentions the *Historia,* noting that it characterizes Cuthbert "as a fierce and powerful protector of his own people and goods," (Ward, *Miracles,* 61), and generally suggesting that this change, like similar changes in the characters of Ste. Foi and St. Benedict, is due to the changing needs of the monastic community. I agree with this suggestion, and one of my goals in this paper has been to focus more precisely on what those changing needs might have been.

[36] B. Gaiffer, "Les revendications de biens dans quelques documents hagiographiques du XIe siècle," *Analecta Bollandiana* 50 (1932): 123–38 (esp. 126); Sigal, "Un aspecte du culte des saints," 52.

[37] For a comparison of Anglo-Saxon and Carolingian patronage of the Church see J. L. Nelson, " 'A King Across the Sea': Alfred in Continental Perspective," *Transactions of the Royal Historical Society* 5th ser., 36 (1986), 45–68 (esp. 65–66). For Alfred's confiscation of the lands of minster-churches in Kent and Mercia, see ibid., 58–61.

Beyond the disappearance of the patronage and protection of the Northumbrian kings, the *Historia de Sancto Cuthberto* shows us the increasing economic power of the Community of St. Cuthbert (demonstrated by its impressive land holdings), its growing political influence (shown by its influence over the election of King Guthred, and by the pilgrimages of Athelstan and Edmund), and the gradual identification of the earthly monastic community with its heavenly patron. All of these factors would have contributed to the saint's transformation from ascetic hermit to powerful lord and patron. As the community with which he was identified became an increasingly potent temporal power, it is easy to see how the saint's own character evolved to adapt to this new reality. If this evolution did violence to the saint's earlier persona, so much the worse for now-outdated Lives. The persona of St. Cuthbert in the *Historia* had come to reflect the values and needs of a powerful late-Saxon monastic community rather than those of a reclusive seventh-century saint.

"A Mirror of Sanctity":
Madness as Metaphor in the *Vita Wulfstani*

MARY LYNN RAMPOLLA

 s a result of the work of Hippolyte Delehaye and his followers, modern students of hagiography have become very much aware of the formulaic nature of the texts with which they work. Nevertheless, we are still grappling with several basic questions he first raised in 1905:[1] how should one read a traditional saint's life? How may the historian use such a text legitimately? And, having recognized them, how should one interpret the *topoi* and formulae which are scattered throughout the text? In a recent study of Anglo-Latin hagiography, David Townsend articulated the fundamental problem entailed in the study of the genre: "[The] stability of form, tone and function," he argues, "encourages approaches that focus either on the distinct historical realities which gave rise to the texts, or precisely on that sameness which substantially unites

---

[1] Delehaye outlined his aims in the introduction to his seminal work, *The Legends of the Saints*, as follows: "To indicate briefly the spirit in which hagiographic texts should be studied, to lay down the rules for discriminating between the materials that the historian can use and those that he should hand over as their natural property to artists and poets, to place people on their guard against the fascination of formulas. . . ." Hippolyte Delehaye, S. J., *The Legends of the Saints*, (Longmans, Green, and Co., 1907), trans. V. M. Crawford, (South Bend, Ind.: Univ. of Notre Dame Press, 1961), xii.

them. . . ."[2] Neither of these approaches is entirely satisfactory. A study aimed at determining the historical accuracy of a particular hagiographic text encourages the tendency "to view the *topoi* of hagiographical writing, more or less negatively, as a smokescreen to be penetrated," while "[p]ositive focus on the conventions themselves . . . cannot sufficiently emphasize the creativity of the individual text. . . ."[3] A more fruitful approach, Townsend suggests, entails a heightened awareness of "the dynamics of interaction between a text and its roughly contemporary readers."[4] The problems posed by hagiographic texts, then, might best be resolved by close studies of individual lives that are both textual and contextual, focusing not only on the author's choice and deployment of *topoi* but on the response he could expect those conventions to elicit in his audience. Few texts are as ideally suited to illustrate the value of this type of analysis as the *Vita Wulfstani*, a life of Bishop Wulfstan of Worcester composed between 1095 and 1113 by his chancellor, Coleman.[5] This paper focuses on the role that one

---

[2] David Townsend, "Anglo-Latin Hagiography and the Norman Transition," *Exemplaria* 3 (1991): 387.

[3] Ibid.

[4] Ibid., 390.

[5] *The Vita Wulfstani of William of Malmesbury*, ed. R. R. Darlington, Camden Society, 3rd series, 40, (London: Royal Historical Society, 1928). The *Vita* has been translated by J. H. F. Peile, *William of Malmesbury's Life of St. Wulfstan* (Oxford: Basil Blackwell, 1934), and by Michael Swanton, *Three Lives of the Last Englishmen*, vol. 10 of The Garland Library of Medieval Literature (New York: Garland Publishing, 1984), 89–148. Wulfstan died in 1095; Coleman's death is recorded by the Worcester chronicler under the entry for 1113 (Florence of Worcester, *Chronicon ex Chronicis*, ed. Benjamin Thorpe, [London: English Historical Society, 1849], 2: 66). According to a letter of Pope Innocent III (printed in Darlington, *Vita*, 149–50), dated 14 May 1203 and included in a collection of Wulfstan's miracles, a life of Wulfstan, which was written in English, was sent to Rome as part of the formal procedures to canonize Wulfstan. It is likely that this life was Coleman's *Vita*. (See Darlington, *Vita*, viii n. 4, xlvii.) At this point it was mislaid, and there is no known extant copy of the Old English life. The *Vita* survives only in a Latin translation made by William of Malmesbury during the priorate of Warin (1124–40). In the absence of the Old English text, it is impossible to establish with certainty the relative contributions of Coleman and William. However, the differences in content and tone between the *Vita*'s account of Wulfstan and that contained in William's *Gesta pontificum* (William of Malmesbury, *De gestis pontificum Anglorum*, ed. N. E. S. A. Hamilton, Rolls Series 90, [London: Public Record Office, 1870], 278–89), in addition to William's tendency to describe his own editing techniques in the text, indicate that credit for the bulk of the text as it now stands can be given to Coleman. For this view, see also Antonia Gransden, *Historical Writing in England c. 550 to c. 1307*, (Ithaca, New York: Cornell Univ. Press, 1974),

stock element in the saint's repertoire—his ability to cure the insane—plays in the overall structure of the text, and examines the ways in which the hagiographer used the image of madness to express the very immediate interests and concerns of both himself and his intended audience—the monks of Worcester cathedral priory.

The *Vita Wulfstani* holds a unique place in the literature of early post-Conquest England.[6] Although several lives of contemporary bishops and abbots were written in this period,[7] only Eadmer's life of Anselm and the *Vita Wulfstani* claimed to be biographies of contemporary saints. But Anselm, whatever his service to the English church, was not himself an Englishman; Wulfstan, on the other hand, was by 1075 the sole remaining Anglo-Saxon bishop in England, a position he retained until his death twenty years later. Thus, the *Vita Wulfstani* is the only contemporary account by an English monk of the last saint of the Anglo-Saxon period.

Just as the *Vita Wulfstani* holds a singular place in the hagiography of the period, so too is the history of Worcester cathedral priory distinctive. In the period immediately following the conquest, the pres-

---

87; Darlington, *Vita*, viii–ix; and Elizabeth E. A. McIntyre, "Early-Twelfth-Century Worcester Cathedral Priory, with special reference to the manuscripts written there" (D. Phil. thesis, Oxford Univ., 1978), 132–35. On the other hand, D. H. Farmer, "Two Biographies by William of Malmesbury," in *Latin Biography*, ed. T. A. Dorey (London: Routledge and Kegan Paul, 1967) 165–74, credits William with a greater influence on the current content and structure of the *Vita* as it now exists. For a recent biography of William of Malmesbury, see Rodney Thomson, *William of Malmesbury*, (Suffolk, England: The Boydell Press, 1987).

[6] During the late eleventh and early twelfth centuries, the monasteries of England produced an immense outpouring of historical writing, representing a wide variety of genres: chronicles, cartularies, local histories, and hagiography. Many modern historians, following the lead of Richard Southern, have seen a connection between the flurry of historical activity in this period—including hagiographic writing—and the Norman Conquest: English monks, they argue, recorded their past in an attempt to preserve it during a time of dramatic change. For this view of historical writing in England in the late eleventh and early twelfth centuries, see especially R. W. Southern, "Aspects of the European Tradition of Historical Writing: 4. The Sense of the Past," *Transactions of the Royal Historical Society*, 5th series, 23 (1973): 243–63; Gransden, *Historical Writing*, chaps. 6–8, passim; idem, "Cultural Transition at Worcester in the Anglo-Norman Period," *British Archaeological Association Conference Transactions*, vol. 1: *Medieval Art and Architecture at Worcester Cathedral* (1978): 1–14; idem, "Traditionalism and Continuity during the Last Century of Anglo-Saxon Monasticism," *Journal of Ecclesiastical History* 40 (1989): 159–207, passim.

[7] For a list, see Gransden, *Historical Writing*, 87–91.

ence of Wulfstan had eased the transition from English to Norman rule at Worcester.[8] Wulfstan had quickly made his peace with both the Conqueror and Lanfranc,[9] and was allowed to retain his see until his death in 1095. These years were not entirely untroubled: Worcester lost the revenues of several estates to Urse, the new Norman sheriff;[10] and Thomas, the Norman archbishop of York, not only held land which had been alienated from Worcester but even claimed the right to rule the see.[11] Nevertheless, Wulfstan's working relations with the Norman secular and ecclesiastical hierarchy were, on the whole, cordial, and Worcester cathedral priory was thus allowed to retain its Anglo-Saxon culture and traditions well into the third decade of Norman rule.[12]

Worcester's distinctive post-Conquest history, and the unique character of the *Vita Wulfstani*, have prompted historians to turn to the *Vita* for clues about the English reaction to the Norman Conquest; they have, on the whole, been disappointed. The *Vita Wulfstani* is firmly entrenched in the English hagiographical tradition. Frank Barlow says of it: "the *Vita Wulfstani* is as old-fashioned as the man it honoured.... Wulfstan appears as a monolithic survival, with all the rugged virtues of the Golden Age of English piety. There is no subtlety in the portrait,

---

[8] For a recent examination of the impact of the Norman conquest on Worcester, see Emma Mason, "Change and Continuity in Eleventh-Century Mercia: The Experience of St. Wulfstan of Worcester," in *Anglo-Norman Studies VIII: Proceedings of the Battle Conference 1985*, ed. R. Allen Brown, (Suffolk, England: The Boydell Press, 1986): 154–76. For the most recent biography of Wulfstan, see idem, *St. Wulfstan of Worcester, c. 1008–1095*, (Oxford: Basil Blackwell, 1990).

[9] Wulfstan was one of the first bishops to submit to William the Conqueror in 1066 (see Florence of Worcester, *Chronicon*, I, 228–29); in 1067, he received from William a grant of land (printed in Hemming, *Hemingi Chartularium ecclesiae Wigornensis*, ed. Thomas Hearne, 2 vols., [Oxford: Sheldonian Theatre, 1723], 2: 413). His early relationship with Lanfranc also seems to have been good; in ca. 1072 Wulfstan swore obedience to Lanfranc as "metropolitan of the holy church of Canterbury" (printed in Darlington, *Vita*, 190), and he sent his favorite, Nicholas, to study under Lanfranc at Canterbury (ibid., 57).

[10] See Hemming, *Chartularium*, 248–70, passim.

[11] Darlington, *Vita*, 24–26. According to the *Vita*, Thomas refused to return several disputed properties, and also claimed that the see of Worcester was subject to his jurisdiction (*Wigornensem ecclesiam sui iuris esse clamabat*), and that "control over it belonged to him by lawful succession" (*dominatum illius legitima successione sibi competere*).

[12] For a discussion of Wulfstan's role in easing Worcester's transition from English to Norman rule, see Gransden, "Cultural Transition."

and it seems that we have the picture of an old man, simplified into a type."[13] Indeed, as Barlow implies, the *Vita* follows all of the standard hagiographical conventions: in its general structure,[14] its use of *topoi*, and its extensive borrowings from the lives of other saints, it fulfilled the expectations of its monastic audience, demonstrating unchanging and immutable truths and providing, as its author states, "a kind of heavenly mirror in which was reflected the image of all sanctity."[15] Having recognized the author's extensive use of *topoi*, however, need we conclude that the *Vita* can tell us nothing about English reactions to the Norman Conquest? Quite the contrary; nuances of tone, recurrent images, even the use of those very conventions so often dismissed as irrelevant—all of these reflect the author's vision of the world. Given a new twist, traditional elements were used by Coleman to reflect contemporary anxieties and concerns in symbolic form.

One stock element of hagiography is the saint's ability to perform miraculous cures, and in conformity with the genre, the *Vita* describes 13 such miracles. What is unusual is that nearly half of these involve curing the insane, a fact that is particularly striking when we consider that Wulfstan was not especially revered as a patron of the insane, either in his lifetime or after his death.[16]

There are five miraculous cures of madmen described in Book II of the *Vita*; a sixth, posthumous, cure is recorded in Book III. The first

---

[13] Frank Barlow, *The English Church, 1000–1066*, 2d ed. (London: Longmans, 1979), 90–91.

[14] For example, although William ends his translation of Book 1 with the Norman Conquest, he notes that Coleman's version of the *Life* ends in the traditional place with Wulfstan's elevation to episcopate (Darlington, *Vita*, 23). For the traditional aspects of the *Vita*, see Gransden, *Historical Writing*, 87–89.

[15] Darlington, *Vita*, 49.

[16] A comparison of the *Vita Wulfstani* with other twelfth- and thirteenth-century accounts of Wulfstan's life makes this clear. In the *Gesta pontificum*, for example, William of Malmesbury only recounts the story of the brothers pursuing a blood feud; the cures of other madmen are left out, although William clearly relied on the *Vita* in composing his description of Wulfstan for this text. (See Darlington, *Vita*, ix.) The abbreviated life of Wulfstan, which was probably written around the year 1240, retains all but one of the stories (for the date of the abbreviated life, see Darlington, *Vita*, xx; for the text, see ibid., 68–114). But in the collection of miracles of St. Wulfstan compiled at about the same time (printed in ibid., 115–88), only five miraculous cures of madmen are listed amongst the dozens of cures of the blind, the deaf, the mute, paralytics, and many other sufferers.

three appear as a group, forming Chapters 4, 5, and 6 of Book II.

We are first introduced to a well-off woman from Evesham, who was driven insane by an evil spirit.[17] She lost her reason (*desapientem*), was driven to a violent frenzy, and finally became so disordered that "relinquishing the love of her parents and the bonds of kinship, she wandered through isolated fields, or wherever impulse drove her." [18] Her parents caught and bound her (binding was a traditional method of treatment in such cases) and spent most of their money hiring both physicians, to cure her by their medical arts, and priests to "recover her mind" [19] by exorcism—all to no avail. Finally, the prior of Evesham abbey brought her to Wulfstan who blessed her, and "immediately, she regained her lost senses and was aware of being healthy; she recognized her family, and blessed the bishop." [20]

The second madman is a husbandman of Gloucestershire, who was also possessed by an evil spirit which made him violent:[21] "He either tore apart with his hands or gnawed with his enormous teeth everything nearby; he ground his teeth at things that were farther away; he hurled abuse; he flung out spit." [22] His family and neighbors bound him with rawhide; when he bit through this, they tied him to a bedpost with iron fetters while he continued to utter frightening bellows which terrified all who heard him. Finally, his relatives called in Wulfstan. Although the madman insulted and spat at the saint, Wulfstan commanded the possessing demon to depart from "this image of God," [23] upon which the madman's sanity was immediately restored.

The third incident involves a squire, sent by Wulfstan's steward on a household errand, who was seized by a "restless spirit." [24] He lost his mind, fled from human company, and took up residence in a nearby wood. Although he was caught and bound by the country folk of the area, he escaped and fled to the wood once again. "So great" we

---

[17] Darlington, *Vita*, 27–28.
[18] Ibid., 27.
[19] Ibid., 28.
[20] Ibid., 28.
[21] Ibid., 28–29.
[22] Ibid., 29.
[23] Ibid.
[24] Ibid., 29–30.

are told, "was the terror of the inhabitants that they feared nothing so much as to come near the place where they knew him to be. This was either because of some harm he had done to one of them; or because it has been established by nature that men are horrified by those who have foresworn humanity."[25] Wulfstan and his household prayed for the squire, and on that very night, the young man's sanity was restored: "he returned to the village, without being called for. That same night, he joined his companions in the household, and never afterwards as long as he lived showed any sign of madness."[26]

The next two cures of insanity are also grouped together; they form Chapters 14 and 15 of Book II, and in these cases, explanations are offered about the onset of the illness: madness is the result of Divine vengeance. In the first instance, a crowd of children had been assembled at Gloucester in order to be confirmed.[27] Wulfstan, however, who was having a meal with the local monks, was slightly delayed, and in his absence, a young man began to ridicule both the bishop and the sacrament by executing mock confirmations. At first, the people found his performance entertaining, but their amusement turned to fear when he began to rave and fell into a frenzy, tearing his hair, grinning madly, and beating his head against a wall. Recognizing Divine punishment when they saw it, the people drove him away, whereupon the madman wandered aimlessly until he fell into a well or pit. Rescued by his kinsman, his sanity was restored by Wulfstan; nevertheless, he died shortly thereafter "because of what he had done or undergone"[28] at that time.

Chapter 15 once again finds Wulfstan in Gloucester, this time to dedicate a church. In the course of the ceremonies, he spent the better part of the day preaching on the subject of peace: and indeed, Coleman tells us, "many who had previously been at war with each other agreed to be recalled to peace on that day."[29] This was not, however, the case with five brothers who were so intent on pursuing a blood feud that they ignored all of Wulfstan's pleas for reconciliation, even

---

[25] Ibid., 30.
[26] Ibid.
[27] Ibid., 36–38.
[28] Ibid., 38.
[29] Ibid.

when he threw himself to the ground at their feet and begged. Faced with their recalcitrance, Wulfstan publicly declared that only children of the devil reject the call to peace. Wulfstan's speech was so moving that the people openly reproached the brothers, whereupon Divine vengeance struck: the most violent of the five suddenly became mad. The *Vita* describes his plight in graphic detail: "The wretched man rolled about on the ground, biting the earth, gouging with his fingers, and hurling spit violently; and, something that I have never heard on any other occasion, his limbs smoked, so that a horrible odor infested the air of the vicinity."[30] Understandably, the insolence of the other four was considerably diminished. Fearing that the same fate might overtake them—they were, after all, guilty of the same crime—they decided that it would be wise to reconsider their position and declare a truce. The feud settled, Wulfstan cured the madman.

The sole remaining miraculous cure of a madman is posthumous. When a lay servant of the church of Worcester found that a book which he had himself borrowed had been stolen, he prayed to the dead bishop for help.[31] Wulfstan complied by pointing out the perpetrator in a way which could not be mistaken: when the thief entered the church, he was "suddenly seized by a demoniacal madness,"[32] and screaming horribly, pulled the book from his clothing, declaring when and how he had stolen it. Luckily for the thief, his brother was a monk at Worcester. He called upon his brethren to intercede with Wulfstan for the madman, the saint relented, and the thief's sanity was restored.

None of these stories, by themselves, would be unusual entries in a saint's life; most hagiographies include some such incident, modelled on Jesus' cure of the demoniac in the synoptic gospels.[33] As a group, however, they possess several common features which shed an interesting light on the fears and attitudes of an English Benedictine in the early post-Conquest period.

The importance of madness as a metaphor in the *Vita* is elucidated

---

[30] Ibid., 39.

[31] Ibid., 65.

[32] Ibid.

[33] See Matthew 8:28–34; Mark 5:1–20; and Luke 8:26–39. Wulfstan refers to Jesus' cure of the demoniac during his exorcism of the husbandman of Gloucestershire (Darlington, *Vita*, 29).

when we consider what "madness" implied to a medieval audience in general, and Coleman in particular. In her study of medieval views of madness, Penelope Doob has demonstrated that "madness" was not simply seen as a medical problem; it was also thought to have a theological component. Indeed, madness and sin were closely linked in medieval thought.[34] In the first place, the madman and the sinner share a common condition; each has lost his reason, the image of God within him, and has thus been reduced to the level of the beasts. This is apparently Coleman's understanding of madness as it is represented in the *Vita*; the squire, for example, is described as someone who has "foresworn humanity,"[35] and the husbandman of Gloucester emits inhuman and bestial noises. In the case of the brothers pursuing a vendetta, Coleman notes that their anger was so great that "it had carried away all their humanity."[36] The madness inflicted upon the most violent brother as a punishment is simply an outward reflection of this inner lack of humanity: he gnaws at the ground and foams at the mouth. Secondly, it was generally believed that the ultimate cause of madness was sin. Madness could be inflicted by God, directly or through an angelic or demonic agent, as a punishment for sin. This, according to Coleman, is what happens to the young man who mocks Wulfstan. Madness could also be the direct physiological result of sin. Anger, for example, was thought to produce an excess of choler which could lead to madness;[37] this might be the origin of the insanity that overtakes the most violent of the five brothers. Sin was thought to be the underlying cause of madness even in cases where the victim seemed to be innocent, for it was generally believed that the devil could have no power over anyone unless that person had consented by sinning.

---

[34] Penelope B. R. Doob, *Nebuchadnezzar's Children: Conventions of Madness in Middle English Literature*, (New Haven: Yale Univ. Press, 1974). For other studies of madness in the Middle Ages, see Wilfrid Bonser, *The Medical Background of Anglo-Saxon England: A Study in History, Psychology, and Folklore*, (London: Wellcome Historical Medical Library, 1963); Judith S. Neaman, "The Distracted Knight: A Study of Insanity in the Arthurian Romances," (Ph.D. diss., Columbia Univ., 1968); and Charles Hugh Talbot, *Medicine in Medieval England*, (London: Oldbourne History of Science Library, 1967).

[35] Darlington, *Vita*, 30.

[36] Ibid., 39.

[37] Doob, *Nebuchadnezzar's Children*, 25–26.

Thus, although the squire appears to be blameless, Coleman describes him as one who has "foresworn humanity"[38] (note the active construction), and comments that he was afflicted "by the judgment of God which is sometimes hidden, never unjust."[39] Finally, sin, in one sense, *is* madness. When the young man smears mud on the foreheads of several children in mockery of the sacrament of confirmation, his sacrilegious actions are described as "madness;"[40] the insanity with which he is subsequently stricken is thus both an appropriate punishment and the concrete embodiment of his own actions.[41]

In the *Vita Wulfstani*, madness also seems to be a symbol for the disintegration of society. The young man who mocked Wulfstan overturns the social order by urging his fellows to criticize their bishop and mock the sacraments. The five brothers who refuse to relinquish their vendetta are clearly disruptive forces, resisting both secular and ecclesiastical authority. The thief has, of course, committed a crime against his brothers by stealing. And even though the woman of Evesham and Wulfstan's squire have not committed any obvious offense against society, they, too, can be seen as symbols of social disorder; they flee from their rightful place in the community—their families and neighbors—and wander in the wilderness.

Finally, madness in the *Vita* serves as a metaphor for the loss of identity. At the same time as they leave or are ejected from society, the madmen loose their sense of their own identity: they flee from their family and friends; they no longer know who they are or where they belong, or even that they are human beings.

Why did these images so fascinate Coleman that he repeats them again and again in the *Vita*? Biographical information about Coleman is limited; what exists, however, paints a portrait of a conservative English Benedictine who viewed the Norman regime with some trepidation. The Worcester monks' corporate identity had been tied to their

---

[38] Darlington, *Vita*, 30.

[39] Ibid.

[40] Ibid., 37.

[41] Insanity symbolized in an outward form the disorder of a sinful soul. According to Doob (*Nebuchadnezzar's Children*, 8), "ideally, all men's actions should be ruled by reason; to the extent that he departs from reason and its judgements of what is good, man is mad (seen physiologically) and sinful (seen morally)."

patron saints, their estates, and their traditional values and practices, all of which, in Coleman's view, were threatened in the post-Conquest period. He is concerned about the stability of the monastery's endowments, and spends a lengthy chapter describing the attempts of Thomas of York to attach several of Worcester's estates to the northern see.[42] It is significant that archbishop Thomas was the brother of Samson, Wulfstan's successor and the first Norman bishop of Worcester, who held the see at the time the *Vita* was written. Also important is Coleman's insistence that Thomas' plans to annex Worcester's estates were ultimately thwarted by Worcester's patron and founder, St. Oswald, aided by his successor, St. Dunstan.[43]

In addition, Coleman was deeply committed to the ideals of the English reform movement of the tenth century in which Oswald and Dunstan had been so instrumental. He was, for example, a staunch defender of the right of monks to preach to the laity. He was commissioned by Wulfstan to preach in his absence,[44] and his hand appears in several homily books and penitentials.[45] By the late eleventh and early twelfth centuries, however, this practice was increasingly called into question by proponents of the Gregorian reform movement.[46]

---

[42] Darlington, *Vita*, 24–25.

[43] Ibid.

[44] Ibid., 40. For the importance of the role of designated preacher, see Milton McCormick Gatch, *Preaching and Theology in Anglo-Saxon England: Ælfric and Wulfstan*, (Toronto: Univ. of Toronto Press, 1977), 56–57.

[45] See Neil Ker, "Old English Notes Signed 'Coleman'," *Medium Ævum* 18 (1949): 29–31.

[46] On the question of monastic involvement in preaching to the laity and other forms of pastoral care, see Thomas L. Amos, "Monks and Pastoral Care in the Early Middle Ages," in *Religion, Culture, and Society in the Early Middle Ages: Studies in Honor of Richard E. Sullivan*, eds. Thomas F. X. Noble and John J. Contreni (Kalamazoo, Michigan: Medieval Institute Publications, Western Michigan University, 1987), 165–80; Ursmer Berlière, "L'exercise du ministère paroissial par les moines dans le haut moyen-âge," *Revue Bénédictine* 39 (1927): 227–50; idem, "L'Exercise du ministère paroissial par les moines du XIIe au XVIIIe siècle," *Revue Bénédictine* 39 (1927): 340–64; Marjorie Chibnall, "Monks and Pastoral Work: A Problem in Anglo-Norman History," *Journal of Ecclesiastical History* 18 (1967): 165–72; Giles Constable, *Monastic Tithes*, (Cambridge: Cambridge Univ. Press, 1964); Sarah Foot, "Parochial Ministry in Early Anglo-Saxon England: The Role of Monastic Communities," in W. J. Sheils and D. Wood, *The Ministry: Clerical and Lay*, vol. 26 of *Studies in Church History*, (Oxford, 1989), 43–54; B. R. Kemp, "Monastic Possession of Parish Churches in England in the Twelfth Century," *Journal of Ecclesiastical History* 31 (1980): 144–45; Dom Jean

The *Vita* contains two stories in which monastic preaching is challenged. In the first, a foreign priest criticizes Wulfstan, then prior of Worcester, for "usurping the office of the bishop."[47] Preaching to the laity, he asserts, is contrary to the Rule. In the second, it is Coleman himself whose right to preach is challenged.[48]

Also in the tradition of the earlier English reform, Coleman was a strong advocate of clerical celibacy.[49] Worcester's copy of the *Old English Penitential* contains marginal headings in Coleman's hand; one points out a section on married priests.[50] In this, he was supported by the continental reform movement—but not by the lifestyle of his new bishop, who had been married and had fathered a clerical son. Nevertheless, Coleman was not hesitant to express his opinion of married priests. In the *Vita*, he makes much of Wulfstan's heroic efforts to resist assaults on his chastity.[51] He also includes a description of Wulfstan's rather harsh treatment of the married clergy in his diocese, who, according to Coleman, were forced to choose between their wives and their churches. Those who chose to stay with their families were driven from their parishes and wandered about until they either found some other benefice or starved to death.[52] This account of Wulfstan's treatment of married priests takes on added significance when we realize that it is probably exaggerated.[53]

Leclercq, "Prédicateurs bénédictins aux XIe et XIIe siècles," *Revue Mabillon* 33 (1943): 48–73; D. J. A. Matthew, *The Norman Monasteries and Their English Possessions*, (Oxford: Oxford Univ. Press, 1962), 59–61; and T. P. McLaughlin, "Le très ancien droit monastique de l'occident," *Archives de la France monastique*, 38 (Paris, 1935).

[47] Darlington, *Vita*, 14.

[48] Ibid., 39–40.

[49] For the ideal of celibacy in the tenth-century reform movement, see especially C. N. L. Brooke, "Gregorian Reform in Action: Clerical Marriage in England, 1050–1200," *Cambridge Historical Journal* 12 (1956): 1–21; R. R. Darlington, "Ecclesiastical Reform in the Late Old English Period," *English Historical Review* 51 (1936): 385–428; W. A. C. Sandford, "Medieval Clerical Celibacy in England," *The Genealogists' Magazine* 12 (1957): 371–73. According to Brooke, "the Norman clergy were by repute the most uxorious in Europe," and there is evidence for the existence of powerful ecclesiastical families, including that of Samson of Bayeux (11–13).

[50] The note appears in Corpus Christi College, Cambridge, MS 265. See Ker, "Old English Notes," 30.

[51] See Darlington, *Vita*, 6, 12.

[52] Ibid., 53–54.

[53] For this view, see Mary Lynn Rampolla, "'A Pious Legend': St. Oswald and the

In Wulfstan, Coleman served a bishop whose ideals mirrored his own, and who valued the service he gave. Coleman was Wulfstan's chaplain for fifteen years[54] and his name appears on the witness lists of several important Worcester charters.[55] Wulfstan entrusted him with the office of preaching during his absence; and when he refounded St. Oswald's priory of Westbury-on-Trym, Coleman became its first prior.[56]

Wulfstan's death, however, brought a different kind of bishop to Worcester. Samson had been a canon of Bayeux, and was in minor orders at the time of his election in 1096.[57] As noted above, his brother Thomas was archbishop of York;[58] in this capacity, he had attempted to gain control of the see of Worcester and its estates during Wulfstan's pontificate. Samson had been married, and his son, Thomas, would himself be elected to the northern archbishopric in 1108.[59] There is no record of overt hostility between the new bishop and his monks; in fact, Samson granted several estates to Worcester priory.[60] Nevertheless, Coleman could never have approved of his new bishop's marital status. Moreover, it is clear that Samson was appallingly insensitive to his chapter. Most telling is his decision to disband the newly refounded priory of Westbury-on-Trym.[61] Westbury had been Oswald's original

---

Foundation of Worcester Cathedral Priory," in *Oral Tradition in the Middle Ages*, ed. W. F. H. Nicolaisen (Binghamton, New York: Medieval and Renaissance Texts and Studies, 1995), 207–8. Mason, on the other hand, accepts the *Vita*'s account of Wulfstan's treatment of secular priests, (see Mason, *St. Wulfstan*, 38–41, 62–64, 163), as does Anne Llewellyn Barstow, *Married Priests and the Reforming Papacy: The Eleventh-Century Debates*, vol. 12 of *Texts and Studies in Religion*, (New York: Edwin Mellen Press, 1982), 87, 143.

[54] Darlington, *Vita*, 2.

[55] See, for example, the Alveston charter of 1089, printed in Hemming, *Chartularium*, 2: 420.

[56] Darlington, *Vita*, 52.

[57] For Samson's character and career, see V. H. Galbraith, "Notes on the career of Samson, bishop of Worcester (1096–1112)," *English Historical Review* 82 (1967): 86–101, and Barlow, *The English Church*, 71–72.

[58] Thomas I ruled the see of York from 1070 to 1100. See Sir F. Maurice Powicke and E. B. Fryde, *A Handbook of British Chronology*, 2nd ed. (London: Royal Historical Society, 1961), 264.

[59] Thomas II was nominated in May of 1108 and consecrated in 1109. He died in 1114. See Powicke and Fryde, *Handbook*, 264.

[60] See, for example, the charter granting Hartlebury to the monks, printed in Hemming, *Chartularium*, 2: 426–27.

[61] William of Malmesbury, *Gesta pontificum*, 290.

monastic foundation in Worcestershire, and its refoundation by Wulfstan had established a living link between the cathedral priory and its glorious past. In closing Westbury, Samson, whatever his intent,[62] must have shocked and offended the monks of Worcester, particularly Coleman, Westbury's prior. Samson died in 1112; Coleman followed the next year. It was thus sometime during the reign of Samson—a secular priest, married, foreign, and without respect for the ancient ties of Worcester to Oswald and Westbury—that Coleman wrote the *Vita Wulfstani*.

It is clear, moreover, that Coleman's intended audience shared his concerns. That Coleman wrote for the monks of Worcester is apparent. In a period when English was all but eclipsed as a scholarly language, Coleman chose to write his biography of Wulfstan in the vernacular,[63] a language he could expect neither his new bishop nor his *familia* to read. Moreover, he modelled the life on the traditional English saints' lives with which the monks of Worcester would probably be familiar.[64] In any case, the monastic community of Worcester had remained predominantly English into the reign of bishop Samson,[65] and

---

[62] Darlington has suggested that Samson intended to use the income from the church of Westbury to support the secular priests of his household, and that his grant of Wolverhampton to the monastic chapter may have been offered in compensation. See R. R. Darlington, *The Cartulary of Worcester Cathedral Priory (Register I)*, Publications of the Pipe Roll Society, n.s., 38 (London, 1968), xlvii–xlviii.

[63] It has been suggested that Coleman "wrote in English as a piece of conscious revivalism" (Gransden, *Historical Writing*, 88). A similar opinion has been expressed by McIntyre, "Early-Twelfth-Century Worcester," 137. This view overstates the case; it is more likely that Coleman simply wrote in the language in which he felt most comfortable. Other Worcester manuscripts also contain notes in English in Coleman's hand. See Ker, "Old English Notes"; William P. Stoneman, "Another Old English Note Signed 'Coleman'," *Medium Aevum* 56 (1987): 78–82; and McIntyre, "Early-Twelfth-Century Worcester," 40–45.

[64] For the traditional aspects of the *Vita*, see Gransden, *Historical Writing*, 87–89. In discussing the relationship of his translation to Coleman's original text, William of Malmesbury notes that he has eliminated some of these traditional elements, asserting that he is more interested in sketching a personal portrait of the man than in describing the typical saint (Darlington, *Vita*, 58). For a list of saints' lives that were probably available at Worcester in the early twelfth century, see McIntyre, "Early-Twelfth-Century Worcester" 85, 86, 90, and 200–215, passim.

[65] For example, an examination of the list of Worcester monks found in the Durham *Liber vitae*, compiled in ca. 1104, reveals a preponderance of English names. *Liber vitae ecclesiae Dunelmensis: A Collotype facsimile of the original manuscript*, introductory essay and notes by A. Hamilton Thompson, *Surtees Society*, vol. 163, (Durham: 1923), fol. 22r. For a discussion of this list and its date, see Sir Ivor Atkins, "The Church of

the same concerns found in the *Vita* are echoed in other Worcester sources from this period.

When we return to the descriptions of madmen in the *Vita* with Coleman's background and intended audience in mind, his preoccupation with this theme takes on new meaning. In the first place, as noted above, Coleman is preoccupied throughout the *Vita* with real or perceived threats to the monks' corporate identity. The madman's loss of identity parallels Coleman's concern, expressed throughout the *Vita*, to rediscover and redefine what it means to be an English monk in the post-Conquest period.

Secondly, the theme of social disruption, so apparent in the stories of the madmen, is also a motif which runs throughout the *Vita*. Tension between various groups in society is an ongoing refrain: rich vs. poor; priest vs. parishioners; secular vs. regular clergy; Norman vs. English. In each instance, one or both of the parties fails to fulfill his proper function in society, and not infrequently, tension erupts into outright violence. Here again, the stories of madmen, who so clearly disrupt the social order, parallel the condition of England; society is disordered and people do not fulfill their proper roles.

Social disorder is not, of course, a problem unique to post-Conquest England. However, the madmen of the *Vita* seem to represent a particular kind of social disorder: that which results from political upheaval. Although it is common for the madmen of medieval literature to wander in the forests,[66] the flight of the madman to the wilderness—an image present in two of the stories—was a symbol with political ramifications. An English audience would be reminded of Gildas' account of the Britons, who were forced to flee to the woods upon the coming of the Saxons. This event represented for Gildas an unnatural movement away from society, a breakdown of the social structure which is a punishment visited upon the Britons by God for their sins,[67] just as the Conquest, according to Coleman, is a punishment visited upon the English.

Worcester from the Eighth to the Twelfth Century," *The Antiquaries Journal* 20 (1940), 212–20. See also Darlington, *Vita*, xxxix, and Mason, *St. Wulfstan*, 222.

[66] Doob, *Nebuchadnezzar's Children*, 72–74, 138.

[67] See Robert W. Hanning, *The Vision of History in Early Britain From Gildas to Geoffrey of Monmouth*, (New York: Columbia Univ. Press, 1974), 158. The reference is to Gildas, *De exidio conquestu Britanniae*, MGH, *Auctores antiquissimi* 13, ii, 20, 25.

An anecdote found in two contemporary sources supports the notion that madness had special associations in the post-conquest period
with the social discord that follows the disruption of the established political order. In the *Miracles of St. Dunstan*, Osbern relates the story of
Aegelward, an English monk of Christchurch, who went mad while
serving Lanfranc at Mass. He shouted blasphemies and became violent,
and was only quieted after being brought to Dunstan's tomb. His cure
was only temporary, however, and madness overtook him once again.
When a second trip to the tomb failed to cure him, he was tied to his
bed in the infirmary, where visits from Lanfranc and a physician similarly failed to restore him to health. Ultimately, Dunstan's staff was laid
upon him and he was cured, this time forever. He gave thanks to
Dunstan, and lived a long and holy life.[68]

The dislocation of Dunstan's relics—they were temporarily housed
in the monastery's refectory while the new church was under construction—might, as Margaret Gibson has noted, have been the proximate
cause of Aegelward's madness, "but," as she says, "the crisis had originated elsewhere."[69] These events took place in the early years of
Lanfranc's episcopacy, when tensions between the English and Norman
members of the Christchurch community were high. Lanfranc's primary objective at this time was to establish "basic good order" at
Christchurch, which, Gibson argues, was an "unsettled and disorientat-
ed" community.[70] It is this disruption within the community that lies
at the root of Aegelward's madness.

The association between madness and political or social disruption
is even more apparent in Eadmer's version of the same event.[71] Eadmer based his *Miracles of St. Dunstan* on Osbern's text, but he adds two
important details to the story of Aegelward.[72] When he describes the

---

[68] Osbern, *Miraculi Sancti Dunstani*, in *Memorials of Saint Dunstan*, ed. William
Stubbs, Rolls Series 63 (London: Public Record Office, 1874), 144–51.

[69] Margaret Gibson, *Lanfranc of Bec*, (Oxford: Clarendon Press, 1978), 175.

[70] Ibid.

[71] Eadmer, *Miraculi Sancti Dunstani*, in *Memorials of Saint Dunstan*, ed. William
Stubbs, 234–38.

[72] The differences between Osbern's and Eadmer's accounts of this incident, and
the significance of those differences, have been discussed by R. W. Southern, *St.
Anselm and his Biographer: A Study of Monastic Life and Thought 1059–c. 1130* (Cambridge: Cambridge Univ. Press, 1963), 248.

members of the community who gathered around the afflicted man, he notes that many of the monks spoke French, which the madman could not understand, a fact which enraged him even further.[73] The association between madness and loss of identity seems clear here. In addition, Eadmer tells us that the English members of the community, dismayed by this event, ceased to resist Lanfranc's attempts to introduce reforms.[74] Thus, madness not only serves as a symbol for the social tensions within the monastery and the perceived loss of identity of the English monks, but also acts as a corrective, leading the English members of the community to remedy a disturbed situation by conforming to the new social order.

This brings us to the final aspect of madness that may have attracted Coleman's attention: the association of madness with sin. In the *Vita*, Coleman describes the Norman Conquest as a punishment for the sins of the English; all events, Coleman is convinced, have meaning, and punishment does not fall on the blameless. He is, however, rather at a loss when it comes to explaining what, exactly, the English have done to deserve such punishment, stating merely that the English led evil lives, that "excess flourished"[75] in the peaceful times before the Conquest, and that men wore their hair too long.[76]

In the image of the madmen, however, Coleman can find a parallel to the story of the English as a nation. In the madman, it is sin, perhaps even sin that is not readily apparent, as in the case of the squire, which leads to the destruction of the individual, just as the sins of English society, even if those sins are not easily identified, lead to the downfall of that society. The madmen thus serve as symbols for society at large. And indeed, in at least two instances, the individual madman is made to stand as a symbol for a larger group. The young man who mocks Wulfstan and the sacrament of confirmation, for example, is the only one punished, although he is originally spurred on by all the onlookers. Similarly, of the five brothers who refuse to give up their blood feud, only one is driven insane as a warning to the others. The stories of madmen thus reflect Coleman's belief that punishment, whether of an

---

[73] Eadmer, *Miraculi*, 236.

[74] Ibid., 238.

[75] Darlington, *Vita*, 23.

[76] Ibid., 22–23.

individual or of a whole group of people, comes by the just, if sometimes hidden, judgment of God.

Thus, while composing what is in many ways a very conventional
saint's life, Coleman apparently manipulated those conventions to reflect his own interests and concerns, with an awareness of the reso-
nances his choice of images would set up in the minds of his readers.
But he did more than this. If the portrait of the saint which emerges is
a timeless "mirror of sanctity," if Wulfstan is, indeed, a "type," he is
also, in Coleman's view, a saint for his own times, for Wulfstan provides the solution to the problems raised throughout the *Vita*.

If madness is a metaphor for social disruption and a symbol for the
loss of identity, it is Wulfstan who acts as a reintegrating force, healing
the madmen and restoring them to themselves and their families. Upon
receiving Wulfstan's blessing, the woman of Evesham recovers her sanity and recognizes her family, and at Wulfstan's command to "go in
peace,"[77] she becomes a nun, finding, in effect, a new sense of identity for herself. Similarly, Wulfstan's prayers effect the cure of the
squire, and enable him to return to the village and the society of his
fellow servants. And in the case of the brothers bent on a blood feud,
it is Wulfstan who acts as a mediator, healing the one stricken with
madness, reconciling all parties, and restoring peace. In all instances,
Wulfstan reintegrates the madman into society and gives him back a
sense of his own identity. Moreover, the posthumous cure makes it
clear that Wulfstan's death has not interfered with this function; in
telling the story of the thief, Coleman notes that the brethren continued to bring their problems to Wulfstan "just as if he were still living."[78]

Wulfstan's role in healing the madmen and restoring them to their
places in society reflects the role he plays throughout the *Vita*. He
helps the monks of Worcester to maintain their sense of identity by
fighting for their estates and defending their traditional values.[79] He

---

[77] Ibid., 28.

[78] Ibid., 65.

[79] For some examples, see ibid., 24–26 (Wulfstan defends Worcester's estates
against Thomas, Archbishop of York); 53–54 (Wulfstan insists upon celibacy for the
secular clergy); 13–15 (Wulfstan defends the practice of monastic preaching); 39–40
(Wulfstan assigns the office of preaching to a monk, Coleman).

is also a source of reunion and reintegration; of his episcopal functions, he is most often seen in the *Vita* hearing confessions, the sacrament which celebrates reunion and reconciliation,[80] and his favorite topic for preaching is peace and the reconciliation of those in conflict.[81] He is himself a bridge between Anglo-Saxon and Norman England; he is a confidant of both Harold and William the Conqueror,[82] and cures both Englishmen and Frenchmen.[83] Moreover, he is a link between the past, the present, and the uncertain future; Oswald and Dunstan, Worcester's ancient patrons, are present to him during his life,[84] just as he himself remains present to the monks of Worcester after his death.

The *Vita*'s portrait of Wulfstan contains all of the conventions and *topoi* consecrated by tradition. This is hardly surprising: one of the express aims of hagiography is to depict timeless and immutable truths. Nevertheless, the hagiographer's skillful manipulation of those conventions allowed him to express contemporary concerns and anxieties, and to suggest an answer to them. In the *Vita Wulfstani*, the saint's ability to cure madmen becomes an important metaphor. Madness stands for the sin, manifest or hidden, for which the Norman Conquest was punishment; for social disruption; and for the loss of identity which threatened the monks in the post-Conquest period. But the *Vita* not only presents these concerns; it also suggests a solution, for Wulfstan acts throughout as a unifying and integrating force. The ongoing veneration of Wulfstan, which the *Vita* was designed to foster, could provide for the monks of Worcester cathedral priory a new sense of identity and direction in the Norman world of which they were increasingly becoming a part.

Wulfstan was not formally canonized until the thirteenth century, and the Worcester monks of Coleman's time had little success in pro-

---

[80] The sacrament of Penance is mentioned several times in the *Vita*. On two occasions, Wulfstan's kindness towards penitents is emphasized (ibid., 49–50, 58).

[81] See, for example, ibid.: 38–39; 39–40; 45.

[82] For Wulfstan's relationship with Harold, see ibid., 13 (Wulfstan hears Harold's confession); 18 (Harold supports Wulfstan's election to the episcopate); 22 (Wulfstan helps Harold to pacify the North); and 34 (Wulfstan miraculously cures Harold's daughter of a tumor). For the Conqueror's high regard for Wulfstan, see ibid., 24.

[83] See, for example, ibid., 34–35.

[84] Ibid., 25.

moting his cult beyond the boundaries of the diocese.[85] Nevertheless, the veneration of Wulfstan was especially strong at Worcester in the years immediately following his death, for his cult served the same function for the monks of Worcester cathedral priory as the bishop's miraculous cures of madmen serve in the *Vita*. In venerating Wulfstan, an English Benedictine monk of their own times, the monks of Worcester could find a sense of their own identity in a time of great upheaval and social disruption, and reaffirm the value of their own traditions in the face of Norman criticism. For those of us reading his life almost 900 years later, the *Vita* illustrates the necessity of balancing a study of medieval hagiography as a literary genre, whose conventions must be identified and understood, with an historical approach that sees each individual saint's life as the product of a particular time and situation—always keeping in mind the ways in which the author deployed commonplaces and the other literary devices at his disposal to evoke a particular response from his contemporary audience.

---

[85] It was only after his formal canonization in 1203 that Wulfstan's cult finally spread beyond local boundaries, attracting a royal patron in King John, who requested to be buried at Worcester between Sts. Oswald and Wulfstan. See Peter Draper, "King John and St. Wulfstan," *Journal of Medieval History* 10 (1984): 41–50; Emma Mason, "St. Wulfstan's Staff: a Legend and Its Uses," *Medium Aevum* 53 (1984): 157–79; and idem, *St. Wulfstan*, 281–83.

Vernacular Hagiography and Lay Piety: Two Old French Adaptations of the Life of Saint Margaret of Antioch

LAURIE POSTLEWATE

tories about the saints have been told and retold by hundreds of writers, to readers and listeners from all walks of life, since the early Middle Ages. With respect to a particular saint, we can ask: is it the same story they retell? The saint's life is after all paradoxically both static and in constant flux: the central plot remains relatively fixed, yet the possibilities for variation in the way it is told, and even in details of the narrative, are endless.

Different kinds of retellings call for different kinds of adaptation. As clerical writers "translated" Latin lives into the vernaculars—and in particular into French beginning in the eleventh century—they brought to their works new ways of thinking about the spiritual life and a new understanding of the religious needs of the laymen.

I would like to examine here two such verse adaptations in Old French of the life of Saint Margaret of Antioch. The first of these is by Wace, a twelfth-century cleric in the court of Henry II,[1] the second by Nicholas Bozon, a Franciscan friar of the early fourteenth century.[2]

---

[1] Wace, *La Vie de Sainte Marguerite*, ed. Elizabeth A. Francis (Paris: Edouard Champion, 1932).

[2] Nicholas Bozon, *Three Saints' Lives by Nicholas Bozon*, ed. Sister Amelia Klenke, O.P. (Bonaventure, New York: The Franciscan Institute, 1947).

These two versions of Saint Margaret's story provide us with samples of vernacular adaptations of saints' lives as spiritual instruction for the secular audience. Both poets used Latin texts as the models for their versions: Wace's life of Saint Margaret is based on a tenth-century text known as the Mombritius version after its fifteenth-century editor;[3] Bozon's text is based on Jacobus de Voragine's version in the *Legenda Aurea*.[4] The authors were both clerics,[5] and in both cases members of the laity formed their audience.[6]

Wace, a writer in the court of Henry Plantagenêt, composed his *Vie de Sainte Marguerite* around 1150. Wace tells us in the *Roman de Rou* that he spent many years studying in France before returning to Caen where he was a *clerc lisant*, meaning that he was an educated man in Holy Orders, but not necessarily a priest.[7] Given his theological back-

---

[3] See Phyllis Johnson and Brigitte Cazelles, *Le Vain Siècle Guerpir: A Literary Approach to Sainthood through Old French Hagiography of the Twelfth Century*, North Carolina Studies in Romance Language and Literature (Chapel Hill, N.C., 1979), 271. The Mombritius version can be found in E. Francis's edition of Wace's *Vie de Sainte Marguerite*.

[4] While it is clear that Wace and Bozon based their versions of Saint Margaret's life on specific Latin models, this does not preclude the possibility that they knew of other versions—Latin and vernacular. Given the popularity of Saint Margaret in the Middle Ages and the number of extant *vitae* of this saint, it is indeed likely that our authors saw or heard more than one rendition of her story. In the present study, I am concerned not so much with the "originality" of the separate features of Wace's and Bozon's versions as with the way in which they chose and combined alterations to their Latin models in order to communicate a spiritual message to the lay public.

[5] See the introductions to the editions by E. Francis and Sister Amelia Klenke. Additional biographical information can be found for Wace in the review by Gaston Paris, *Romania* 9 (1880): 592–96; and for Bozon in an article by Antoine Thomas, "Nicole Bozon, Frère Mineur," *Histoire Littéraire de la France* 36 (1924): 400–424.

[6] My focus here is on how the changes that Wace and Bozon made to Saint Margaret's story reflect shifts in religious instruction for the secular public at large; a public composed of both men and women. Another interesting point of investigation which ultimately complements the present approach is that of the role of gender in vernacular lives of the virgin martyrs. See, for example, Brigitte Cazelles, trans. *The Lady as Saint: A Collection of French Hagiographic Romances of the Thirteenth Century* (Philadelphia: Univ. of Pennsylvania Press, 1991); Kathryn Gravdal, *Ravishing Maidens: Writing Rape in Medieval French Literature and Law* (Philadelphia: Univ. of Pennsylvania Press, 1991); Karl D. Uitti, "Women Saints, the Vernacular, and History in Early Medieval France" and Elizabeth Robertson, "The Corporeality of Female Sanctity in *The Life of Saint Margaret*" in *Images of Sainthood in Medieval Europe*, ed. Renate Blumenfeld-Kosinski and Timea Szell (Ithaca: Cornell Univ. Press, 1991), 247–87.

[7] For a more detailed discussion of the meaning of "clerc lisant," see M. Dominica Legge, "Clerc Lisant," *Modern Language Review* 47 (1952): 554–55.

ground, Wace certainly would have been familiar with the trend of "new devotionalism," which emerged from the monasteries of Western Europe in the late eleventh and twelfth centuries. This new spirituality, seen most clearly in the works of Anselm and Bernard of Clairvaux, emphasized the humanity of Christ and the union of God and Man through divine love.[8] Diane Mockridge has pointed to evidence of this new spirituality in Wace's version of the life of Saint Margaret.[9]

The most striking changes in Wace's adaptation from his Latin source are in the portrayal of God and in the relationship between Margaret and God.[10] The God of the Latin version is an omnipotent God—and he is to be feared. He makes the earth tremble, and the seas, winds, and creatures fear Him. Throughout Wace's version, on the other hand, He is portrayed as an accessible and *loving* God who cares for the faithful. The change in the characterization of God is evident in the first encounter between Margaret and the pagan prefect Olibrius. In the Latin version, Olibrius asks Margaret which gods she worships, and she replies that she loves the omnipotent God and his son Jesus Christ. Olibrius then questions her further to make sure she is speaking of Christ who was crucified by the Jews. Margaret's answer is concise and she insists on God's everlasting power:

> Prefectus dixit: "Ergo invocas nomen Christi quem Iudei cruci-fixerunt?" Sancta Margarita respondit: "Patres tui eum crucifixe-runt, ideo perierunt. Ipse autem permanet in eternum et regni eius non erit finis."   (ll. 92–96)

> The Prefect said, "So you call on the name of Christ whom the Jews crucified?" Saint Margaret answered, "Your fathers cruci-fied him, therefore they perished. He, however, remains into eternity and His reign will have no end."[11]

---

[8] See R. W. Southern, *The Making of the Middle Ages* (London: Century Hutchinson Ltd., 1988), 221–25.

[9] Diane Mockridge, "From Christ's Soldier to His Bride: Changes in the Portrayal of Women Saints in Medieval Hagiography" (Ph.D. diss., Duke Univ., 1984). Ms. Mockridge's well-documented exposition deals with twelfth-century lives in Middle English and French of Saints Juliana, Margaret, and Katherine.

[10] See Mockridge, 109–11 and 121–25.

[11] Translations from Latin and French, unless otherwise indicated, are my own.

In Wace's version, Olibrius presses Margaret on this point, because he wants to know how Christ can help her if he was crucified. Margaret's response makes it clear that Christ allowed himself to be crucified for a reason, to save his people:

"Comment, dist il, te puet aidier
Qui se laissa crucefier?"
La virge dist: "Se il volsist,
Ja nul sers mal ne li feïst,
Mais il l'estuet ensi morir
Por son pople d'enfer garir."   (ll.141–46)

How, he said, can he help you
Who allowed himself to be crucified?
The virgin said: If He had desired it,
No one would have done Him harm,
But it was necessary that He die in this
     way
To save His people from hell.

The bond between Margaret and God—which in the Latin version was that of the imperiled soul and her protector—becomes in Wace's text that of Bride and Bridegroom. Margaret repeatedly speaks of her love for God in Wace's version, and she is Christ's *espouse* and *amie*.[12] The Latin Margaret was a fighter who refused to surrender to evil—she asked God several times to allow her to meet her adversaries *facie ad faciem*, face to face. Wace's Margaret is the lover who prays that she may resist the threatening *felons* so that she may continue to love God, and be loved by him:

Aies merci, Sire, de moi!
Maintien moi, dist ele, a ta loi,
Ne perde m'ame o les felons
Qui font les persecutions.
Fai moi, biaus sire, delivrer,
Que tostans te puisse aourer....   (ll.109–114)

---

[12] Additional examples of the love motif in Wace's version can be found in lines 15–17, 32, 57–62, 655, and 671–72.

Have mercy, Lord, on me!
Keep me, she said, in your law,
Do not lose my soul with the cruel people
Who carry out the persecutions.
Allow me, Sweet Lord, to be delivered,
So that I may always adore You. . . .

De moi, biaus sire, aies merci:
Tol moi des mains al anemi
Que jo ne face por paor
Cose dont jo perde t'amor.   (ll.183–86)

Have mercy, Sweet Lord, on me:
Deliver me from the hands of the enemies,
So that I not do, out of fear,
Anything that would cause me to lose your
    love.

The topos of love is peculiar to the vernacular version; it is found nowhere in the Latin source.

In this portrayal of the saint's mystical union with her loving God we see the influence of the new spirituality of Wace's age.[13] We are not at all surprised that a cleric like Wace has incorporated the theology of the day into his reinterpretation of the saint's life. Of greater significance is the way he uses the imagery of love to communicate this theology to the lay audience, drawing them into participation in the story. His version of Saint Margaret's life makes the new spiritual thinking of the theologians conceptually accessible to a popular public—a public which had been for some centuries already Christian, but which had been hardly influenced at all by mystical thought. In the final lines of Wace's version the narrator warmly invites his public to join him in praying to God in the name of Saint Margaret's love:

Or prions Deus qui est e fu
E a sur tote rien vertu,
Por l'amor sainte Marguerite

---

[13] Diane Mockridge gives a full exposition of this in the final chapter of her dissertation quoted above.

Dont nos avons la vie dite,
Si voirement cum Deus l'ama
E en sa fin molt l'enora.   (ll.729–34)

Now let us pray to God who is and was
And who has power over everything,
For the love of Saint Margaret
Whose life we have told,
As God truly loved her
And in her death greatly honored her.

The loving relationship between Margaret and God is thus presented as a paradigm of spiritual union which the audience is invited to
imitate. This is another change from the Latin text which commands
its audience, in the second person imperative, to worship God and to
keep the memory of the saint: "Dominum adorate in unitate et trinitate, facite beate virginis memoriam, . . ." (Worship the Lord, Three in
One, keep willingly the memory of the virgin.) Wace wants his public
to be inspired by Margaret not only because she can act as an intercessor on their behalf, but also because she has demonstrated that the human soul is capable of intimate union with God. Wace has shown his
audience, through the example of Margaret, the possibility of an interior religious life which they had never before been encouraged to experience.

Wace's version gives us an early example of the ideas and language
of mystical theology, derived from monastic sources, then directed
toward a lay audience. André Vauchez[14] and Etienne Delaruelle[15]
have shown that in the tenth and eleventh centuries the religious understanding of the clergy hardly trickled down to the masses at all.
Moreover, the lay population was not only culturally but also spiritually inferior to the educated clergy. To be "spiritual" meant to be *not* a

---

[14] André Vauchez, *La spiritualité du Moyen Age occidental VIIIe–XIIe siècles* (France:
Presses Universitaires Françaises, 1975); idem, *Les laïcs au Moyen Age* (Paris: Les Editions du Cerf, 1987); idem, "Lay People's Sanctity in Western Europe: Evolution of
a Pattern (Twelfth and Thirteenth Centuries)," in Blumenfeld-Kosinski and Szell,
Images of Sainthood, 21–32.

[15] Etienne Delaruelle, *La piété populaire au Moyen Age* (Turin: Bottega d'Erasmo,
1975).

layman; to be removed from the concerns of the material world and to conquer human weakness by being chaste, which at the time implied celibacy. These conditions necessarily excluded the laity.

But Wace was writing at the threshold of a new era in lay piety. Beginning in the twelfth century, the Christian laity began to experience the kind of interiorized spirituality previously reserved to the cloister. The gradual religious enlightenment of the secular public would eventually have important consequences on their perception and practice of piety. It is not until the thirteenth century that one can see a clear transformation in the spiritual consciousness of the laity at large, accompanied by an emphasis on the practice of chastity, and by numbers of non-monastic Christians choosing to live in religious communities. But already in his vernacular hagiography Wace is a forerunner in the new attitude toward the lay audience. We have seen here only two examples of the new spirituality that permeates Wace's version of the life of Saint Margaret. He makes important alterations in Margaret's story in favor of a spiritual message which, at the midpoint of the twelfth century, is still very new for a secular audience.

Wace's innovative presentation of Saint Margaret's life is fully intelligible in the context of the specific audience for which he was writing. The Plantagenêt court was not just any secular milieu. Henry II and his entourage were, through their patronage of writers, somewhat self-consciously in the literary and religious avant-garde. A court writer such as Wace would aim first of all to please his patrons with his work; adapting his material to conform to the literary tastes of his audience.[16] But he would also have the opportunity to introduce to his secular audience ideas originating in the more purely intellectual and spiritual circles. Indeed, in a court such as that of the Plantagenêts, he would even be encouraged to do so. In Wace's case this meant recasting the story of Saint Margaret to reflect the new spiritual theology of the day.

Through his adaptation of the saint's life, Wace was able to represent figuratively a spiritual message that would have otherwise been difficult for a lay audience to grasp. This was not the only time Wace presented new theological ideas to a lay audience by means of a saint's

---

[16] Certain details of Margaret's vita as adapted by Wace are indeed "courtly," e.g., the emphasis on Margaret's nobility as well as her physical beauty, and the transformation of the ministers accompanying Olibrius into a band of "chevaliers."

life. In *La Conception Nostre Dame*, Wace also used hagiographical material to argue, to laymen, that there should be a feast in honor of the
Immaculate Conception—a controversial issue in the twelfth century.[17]

Wace's version of the life of Saint Margaret is the earliest of the extant French versions.[18] Almost all of the later versions in French retain his mystical message and emphasis on love. This is not to say that
Wace was necessarily the source of the more spiritual interpretation of
Margaret's life, for he may have seen or heard other non-extant inter-
pretations of the life. But judging from the manuscripts we have today,
it seems certain that from the mid-twelfth century on, as clerical writers such as Wace translated the story into the vernacular, they modified
its message to the audience.

I would now like to examine one of the later French versions,
by Nicholas Bozon, a Franciscan friar of the early fourteenth century
who was associated with the mendicant preaching movement in England. Bozon was a prolific writer, leaving us nine verse sermons,[19] the
Proverbes de Bon Enseignement,[20] the *Contes Moralisés*,[21] eleven verse
saints' lives,[22] as well as a number of free-standing poems.[23] Bozon's
work is addressed largely to a secular audience, and his focus is the
moral and religious instruction of the lay public.[24] His use of Anglo-

---

[17] Wace, *The Conception Nostre Dame of Wace*, ed. William Ray Ashford (Chicago:
Univ. of Chicago Press, 1933).

[18] A list of these versions can be found in E. Francis's introduction to her edition
of Wace's version, pp. ix–x, and in Paul Meyer's bibliography in *Histoire Littéraire de la
France* 33 (1906): 362–63.

[19] *Nine Verse Sermons by Nicholas Bozon*, ed. Brian J. Levy, Medium Aevum
Monographs New Series, vol. 11 (Oxford, 1981).

[20] *Les Proverbes de Bon Enseignement de Nicole Bozon*, ed. A. Chr. Thorn, Lunds
Universitets Arsskrift (Lund: C. W. K. Gleerup, 1921).

[21] *Les Contes Moralisés de Nicole Bozon*, eds. Lucy Toulmin Smith and Paul Meyer
(1889; Paris: Johnson Reprint Corp., 1968).

[22] *Three Saints' Lives by Nicholas Bozon*, ed. Sister Amelia Klenke (St. Bonaventure:
The Franciscan Institute, 1947); *Seven More Poems by Nicholas Bozon*, ed. Sister Amelia
Klenke (St. Bonaventure: The Franciscan Institute, 1951); *Vie de Saint Panuce*, ed. A.
T. Baker, *Romania* 38 (1909): 418–24; *An Anglo-Norman Life of Saint Paul the Hermit*,
ed. A. T. Baker, *Modern Language Review* 4 (1909): 491–504.

[23] Bozon's various verse works are described in Brian J. Levy's introduction to the
Nine Verse Sermons.

[24] On Franciscan preaching to the secular public, and in particular on Bozon's audience, see John Fleming, *An Introduction to the Franciscan Literature of the Middle Ages* (Chicago: Franciscan Herald Press, 1977), 110–52; Victor Green, *The Franciscans in Medieval*

Norman French has lead scholars to conclude that he intended his works to be read by members of the upper class of secular society (perhaps by the clergy as well), since he would have used Latin if his audience had been strictly clerical, and he would have been obliged to use English to address the masses directly.

Bozon's *oeuvre* can be situated in the larger program of religious instruction of the secular public as decreed by the Fourth Lateran Council in 1215 and put into practice on a wide scale by the preaching orders.[25] Bozon uses a distinctly Franciscan approach to the edification of his public in emphasizing that mystical union with God is achieved by living a Christian life. For Bozon, this does not mean understanding religious doctrine, but imitating, in a practical way, the lives of the holy; including the practice of poverty, celibacy, and prayer.[26]

The principal source for Bozon's *La Vie Seinte Margarete* was Jacobus de Voragine's Latin version of Margaret's story in the *Legenda Aurea*. The Margaret of the *Legenda Aurea* closely resembles the saint in the tenth-century Mombritius version examined above. In the *Legenda Aurea* she is portrayed as a powerful fighter against evil, and her victory over the Devil is the salient feature of her character. God is again seen as omnipotent, causing great fear in all creatures and the elements of Nature. Jacobus does not speak at all of Margaret's love for God, or of God's love for her; the topos of love is completely absent from his version. Here, and throughout the *Legenda Aurea*, Jacobus favors depiction of the saints as wielders of miraculous power which, while provoking great awe in the common man, is seen to have very little practical application.[27] While it is clear that Jacobus's version was the principal source for Bozon's adaptation, it is also clear that Bozon was familiar either with Wace's version or with one of the thirteenth-century ver-

---

English Life (1224–1348) (Paterson, N.J.: Saint Anthony Guild Press, 1939), 30–37; Maurice Hewlett, "A Medieval Popular Preacher," *Nineteenth Century* 28 (1890): 471–77.

[25] E. Birge Vitz, "1215 The Fourth Lateran Council: The Impact of Christian Doctrine on Medieval Literature," in *A New History of French Literature*, ed. Denis Hollier (Cambridge: Harvard Univ. Press, 1989), 82–88.

[26] See Fleming, 16–17.

[27] See Sherry Reames's discussion of Jacobus's presentation of the saints' lives in her *The Legenda Aurea: A Reexamination of Its Paradoxical History* (Madison: Univ. of Wisconsin Press, 1985).

sions that resemble Wace's text. As we shall see, this is evidenced by
the interpretation he gives to Margaret's martyrdom.[28]

The first change that Bozon makes to his source is to reach out to
the audience by addressing them directly. From the very beginning the
narrator solicits the attention of his public and suggests that he will offer them something to help them spiritually:

> Vus qui avez desirance
> Des mals aver allegeance,
> Vus donez a lire volentiers
> Ou de oyer de bon quers
> La vie seinte Margarete   (ll.1–5)

> You who have a desire
> To have alleviation from sufferings,
> Give yourselves up to reading willingly
> Or to eagerly hearing
> The Life of Saint Margaret[29]

Bozon's call to listen to Saint Margaret's *vita* is a significant addition to
Jacobus's version. This kind of direct address to the audience is found
in many a Latin and vernacular saint's life (including the Mombritius
version of Margaret's life), and suggests that the texts were likely intended for voiced performance. As Evelyn Birge Vitz has pointed out,
Bozon's "translations" of the Latin text of Jacobus de Voragine are also
"re-oralizations," in verse, of the dry, impersonal prose of the *Legenda
Aurea*.[30] By casting his version in the form of a direct, vocalized communication with the public (whether it was actually performed or simply simulates performance is another matter), Bozon draws his readers
and listeners closer to Margaret's story.

As in Wace's version, we find that Margaret has a loving relation-

---

[28] It is, of course, possible that Bozon also knew the Mombritius or other Latin
versions. However, since Bozon follows closely the *Legenda Aurea* in each of his nine
saints' lives found in British Library Cotton Domitian XI, I have limited myself here
to comparison of Bozon's text with that of Jacobus de Voragine. It should be noted
that Jacobus himself cites Theotimus, the tenth-century author of the Mombritius
version, as a source for his vita of Saint Margaret.

[29] The translation of Bozon's work is by Sister Amelia Klenke.

[30] Evelyn Birge Vitz, "From the Oral to the Written in Medieval and Renaissance
Saints' Lives," in Blumenfeld-Kosinski and Szell, *Images of Sainthood*, 97–114.

ship with God in Bozon's text; a detail which Bozon had to add to his Latin source. When Olibrius tells Margaret that she must marry him or suffer, she tells Olibrius of her marriage to Christ:

> "Jeo su" dit ele "mariee
> A li qui pere n'ad en poësté.
> Pur sa amour jeo ne face
> Nule force de vostre manace."   (ll.99–102)

> Said she: I am married
> To Him who has no equal in might.
> Through His love, may I not be
> Terrified by your threat.

Although Bozon shows that Margaret acts out of love for God in her martyrdom, he does not emphasize the intimacy of her bond with Christ as Wace did in his version. The focus in Bozon's version is not on the relationship of the saint with God, but on the saint's actions. Here Margaret is an example for the audience because of how she lived and how she conquered evil. Bozon's task as a preacher was to show to his lay public how *they* could attain salvation: through the practice of piety in the acted-out manifestations of devotion, such as poverty, prayer, and making the sign of the cross on the body.

The emphasis on the praxis of the spiritual life reveals the Franciscan bent to Bozon's message. Bozon insists first of all on the saint's poverty and humility. In the prologue, he follows the *Legenda Aurea* in explaining the virtues attributed to Margaret—but with one important change. Jacobus had said that Margaret had the power of stanching her own blood through her constancy in martyrdom: "Sic beata Margareta habuit virtutem contra effusionem sui sanguinis per constantiam." (Thus Margaret had power, through her constancy, against the spilling of her blood.) Bozon completely changes the meaning of the word "blood" and uses it in the sense of Margaret's blood ties to her aristocratic, pagan family. Margaret cuts off the blood link with her family when she comes up against her father's will:

> Le sanc estanchea de parenté
> Kant fit encuntre lur volenté
> Le honur del secle ad despisé
> E fut pur Dieu martirizé.   (ll.21–24)

> She stanched the blood of her relations
> When she acted against their wishes.
> She held in scorn the honor of the world
> And was martyred for God.

Thus Bozon shows Margaret turning away from the honor and wealth of the material world. The rejection of worldly concerns in favor of poverty and charity, a recurring motif in all of Bozon's work, is one of the most prevalent themes in Franciscan preaching to the secular public. Nine out of eleven of the saints in Bozon's other hagiographic poems are noble women who abandon their wealth and live as servants of God, often giving away all they own to the poor.[31] It is possible, indeed likely, that there were noble, wealthy women in Bozon's audience.[32] Regardless of the gender of his public, Bozon's message here is consistent with the warning he addresses to the rich in his other works: money and a great name mean nothing in the eyes of the Lord—you must renounce these in order to be saved.

Bozon's Margaret further demonstrates her humility through her willingness to become the servant of her servant: "Par humblesce ne tint pas vice, De estre servante sa nurice" (ll.51–52). (Through humility she did not hold it a fault [wrong], To be the servant of her nurse.) Margaret also refuses to heed the pleas of the spectators who beg her to save herself because, she says, it is fitting for a Christian to suffer:

> Vus conseilez pur bref solace
> Ke jeo me mette en long allas.
> Ceo est dreite vie de cristiene
> En ceste vie endurer peyne.   (ll.115–18)

> You advise for a short respite
> That I commit myself to long tribulation.
> It is a fitting Christian life
> To endure pain in this life.

---

[31] The saints are Mary Magdalene, Martha, Margaret, Lucy, Elizabeth of Hungary, Agnes, Agatha, Juliana, and Christine.

[32] M. D. Legge mentions the additional possibility of an audience of nuns in her section on Bozon in *Anglo-Norman Literature and Its Background* (Edinburgh: Univ. Press, 1950), 231, 271–72.

Margaret's words stress that one must endure suffering in order to be a Christian. It is significant that her remarks are directed to the Christian public in general and not just to virgin martyrs. Bozon suggests to his secular audience that *they* too can lead a pious life, as exemplified by the saint. Moreover, the point made here on how a Christian must live is entirely an addition by Bozon to his source.

In his hagiography, as in all of his works, Bozon warns his readers and listeners of the forces of evil that surround them. Man is weak and in constant need of God's help to lead a pious life. Bozon stresses the power of prayer and of making the sign of the cross on the body as a means of protection against evil. It is by making the sign of the cross, of course, that Margaret causes the Devil, in the form of a fire-breathing dragon, to explode. The Devil, in his second form as a man, tells Margaret that he "afflicts people who go to sleep at night without placing the sign of the cross on their brow" (ll.181–82). One can imagine the effect this demonic revelation had on Bozon's audience!

Margaret also prays often in Bozon's version—seven times, in fact, as opposed to twice only in the *Legenda Aurea*. Prayer allows the soul to reach out to God in its time of need and, as Margaret demonstrates, the prayers of the pious *will* be answered swiftly. Margaret makes very specific requests in her prayers, and they are *always* granted immediately:

> Ou ele pria Nostre Segnour
> Mult tendrement de socour
> Ke par le enmy ne fu vencue
> Et sa requeste li fu tendue.   (ll.89–92)

> She prayed our Lord
> Very tenderly for help,
> That she not be overcome by the enemy,
> And her request was granted her.

> En orbeysoun fit oreyson
> E dit a Dieu: "Sir jeo vus pri,
> Mustrez moy mon enemi
> Ke vere le puse apertement
> Ke me procure tel tourment."
> Lors apparut en la prison
> Un trop hidus et fiers dragon.   (ll.120–26)

> In darkness she said her prayer,
> And said to God: "Sir, I beg you,
> Show me my enemy
> That I may see him openly
> Who procures such torment for me."
> Then there appeared in the prison
> An extremely hideous and fierce dragon.

Bozon shows prayer not as a moment of mystical contemplation, but as a way to initiate action, and as an essential part of the Christian life.

Shortly before she is beheaded, Margaret recites a long prayer in which she lists all those she wishes to receive protection in her name. This prayer is of special significance, and it provides a powerful conclusion to her story, because in it she asks God to protect all those who write, listen to, or read her story:

> Je vus pri pur celi e cele
> Ki en angusse a moy apele,
> Par vus seit allegee;
> Jeo le vus pri pur amisté.
> E cels ki escriverunt
> Ou oyrunt ou lirrunt
> Mes gestes en seint lyvre,
> De mal pechié seient delyvre.   (ll.247–54)

> And I pray for such and such
> Who call upon me in distress,
> That they be comforted by You;
> I beg it of You for friendship's sake.
> And those who shall write
> Or hear or read
> My deeds in the holy book,
> May they be freed from the evil of sin.

This is the crucial moment in the use of the saint's life as exemplum. The members of the audience, by the very act of reading and listening to the saint's story, discover that they are engaged in an act of devotion that will protect them. Margaret's listeners and readers have already taken the first step in the devout life, a life of which the saint has given a wonderful example. And they can be sure that Margaret's prayers on their behalf will get results. As Margaret finishes praying, a white dove with a cross descends to confirm that wherever the story of her life is read, the audience will receive protection from evil:

> Kant la virgine out parfet
> Sa priere descendu est
> Une blanche columbe o une croice
> Of li parla de aperte voyce: . . .
> "Dieu vus grante par ses dulceours
> Vos priers a tuz jours . . .
> Dieu vus maunde ke en chescun leu
> Ke de pechié n'est corrumpu,
> Si votre passion i seyt leu,
> En chescun mal lur ert escu."   (ll.273–90)

> When the virgin had finished
> Her prayer there descended
> A white dove with a cross.
> It spoke to her in an audible voice: . . .
> "God grants you through his mercy
> Your prayers for all time . . .
> God assures you that in each place
> Which is not corrupted by sin,
> If your passion be read there,
> In every evil it shall be their defence
> (buckler)."

The dove thus affirms the power of prayer and of reading the saint's story—both devout acts of the Christian life.

Bozon has presented to his public an inspiring story that offers concrete examples of behavior they can imitate—even if they are not virgin martyrs themselves. At the conclusion of the poem, Bozon is the first to follow Margaret's example by praying and translating her life:

> Margarete, ore pensez
> De moy, cheytif, ke ay translatez
> Vostre vie et vostre passion.
> Ke Dieu me grante sauvacion,
> E a touz cels ke cest escrit
> Orrunt ou lirrunt o delit;

Ceo est le covenant avant fet.
Ore seit gardé, si vus plet. Amen.   (ll.323–30)

Margaret, now think
Of me, poor wretch, who translated
Your life and your passion.
May God grant salvation to me
And to all those who this account
Shall hear or read with delight;
That is the covenant made before.
Now may it be kept, if you please. Amen.

Bozon reminds Margaret (and his audience) of the covenant she made
with God through her martyrdom: that all those who follow the example of the devout life will receive salvation. It was not necessary for the
narrator of the saint's life to tell his audience directly: "This is what
you must do to be a Christian, to be saved." The audience was able to
understand immediately the implied lesson of the story, in the same
way they grasped without difficulty the lesson of an exemplum, such
as those which Bozon related in his *Contes Moralisés*.[33] The point is
that piety is an affair of actions, charity, prayer, and the like, which the
saint practiced in her life, and which they too can perform.

We have seen in these two adaptations of the life of Saint Margaret
how vernacular hagiography promoted the piety of laymen. For Wace
in the twelfth century, this meant emphasizing the ability of the soul to
communicate directly and intimately with God. For Bozon in the early
fourteenth century it meant giving examples of the power of the ordinary practice of piety. The saint's life was a particularly effective vehicle
for shaping the religious consciousness of the secular audience because
it showed piety being *acted out* in ways that were real and imitable for
the popular public. It gave figurative life to theological abstractions and
brought spirituality within the grasp of all.

---

[33] On the implicit lessons of the thirteenth-century exemplum, see Claude
Brémond, Jacques Le Goff, and Jean-Claude Schmitt, "*L'Exemplum*: Typologie des
sources du Moyen Age," *Occidental* 40 (Turnhout, Belgium: Brepols, 1982): 33.

Ramon Llull's *Blanquerna* and the Type of the Urban Saint: Hagiographic Fiction in Relation to the Preaching of the Friars

ROBERTO J. GONZÁLEZ-CASANOVAS

 critical examination of the Catalan romance *Blanquerna*, written by Blessed Ramon Llull around 1283–1285 in Montpellier, shows the close relationship between the arts of preaching and didactic narrative that gave rise to the Romance novel, as well as to a special form of hagiographic fiction.[1]

These developments followed the renewal of the Church in the af-

---

[1] On the relation of preaching to literature in the thirteenth century, see: D. L. D'Avray, *The Preaching of the Friars* (Oxford: Clarendon Press, 1985); Alan Deyermond, "The Sermon and its Uses in Medieval Castilian Literature," *La Corónica* 8, 2 (1980): 127–45; Derek W. Lomax, "The Lateran Reforms and Spanish Literature," *Iberoromania* 1, 4 (1969): 299–309; Francisco Rico, *Predicación y literatura en la España medieval* (Cádiz: UNED, 1977); and Michel Zink, *La Prédication en langue romane avant 1300* (Paris: Honoré Champion, 1976).

On the development of popular hagiography, especially by Franciscans and Dominicans, see Bekker-Nielsen, ed., *Hagiography and Medieval Literature* (Odense: Odense Univ. Press, 1981); Stanislao da Campagnola, *Francesco d'Assisi nei suoi scritti e nelle sue biografie dei secoli XIII–XIV* (Assisi: Porziuncola, 1981); John Wayland Coakley, *The Representation of Sanctity in Late Medieval Hagiography* (Th.D. diss., Harvard Divinity School, 1980); John V. Fleming, *An Introduction to the Franciscan Literature of the Middle Ages* (Chicago: Franciscan Herald Press, 1977); Michael Goodich, *Vita Perfecta: The Ideal of Sainthood in the Thirteenth Century* (Stuttgart: A. Hiersemann, 1982); and Thomas J. Heffernan, *Sacred Biography: Saints and Their Biographers in the Middle Ages* (Oxford: Oxford Univ. Press, 1988).

termath of the Fourth Lateran Council of 1215, and the foundation of the Dominican and Franciscan orders.[2] They were further stimulated by the cultural renaissance in both of the Spanish kingdoms, Castile and Aragón, as a result of the dialogue and debate among the three "religions of the book" (Judaism, Christianity, and Islam).[3]

In *Blanquerna*, Llull combines several of the religious and secular literary genres of his day into a unique Christian novel-sermon comprised of exemplary biography, symbolic quest, social mirror, religious utopia, and mystical allegory.[4] Many traditions underlie the composi-

---

[2] This period witnessed significant attempts at the renewal of the Church and the reform of Christendom. See E. Randolph Daniel, *The Franciscan Concept of Mission in the High Middle Ages* (Lexington: Univ. Press of Kentucky, 1975); Alexander Murray, *Reason and Society in the Middle Ages* (Oxford: Clarendon Press, 1978); Steven Ozment, *The Age of Reform, 1250–1550* (New Haven: Yale Univ. Press, 1980); and André Vauchez, *Religion et société dans l'Occident médiéval* (Torino: Bottega d'Erasmo, 1980).

[3] The Spanish religious renaissance of the thirteenth century developed against a background of military crusades, theological disputes, and social controversies. See Américo Castro, *España en su historia* (Barcelona: Crítica, 1984); Robert Chazan, *Daggers of Faith* (Berkeley: Univ. of California Press, 1989); Jeremy Cohen, *The Friars and the Jews* (Ithaca: Cornell Univ. Press, 1982); Jocelyn N. Hillgarth, *The Spanish Kingdoms, 1250–1516* (Oxford: Clarendon, 1976), vol. 1; Benjamin Z. Kedar, *Crusade and Mission* (Princeton: Princeton Univ. Press, 1982); Angus Mackay, *Spain in the Middle Ages* (London: Macmillan, 1977); Joseph F. O'Callaghan, *A History of Medieval Spain* (Ithaca: Cornell Univ. Press, 1975); and W. Montgomery Watt and Pierre Cachia, *A History of Islamic Spain* (Edinburgh: Edinburgh Univ. Press, 1965).

[4] On Ramon Llull's theological and literary achievements, see Anthony Bonner and Lola Badia, *Ramon Llull: Vida, pensament i obra literària* (Barcelona: Empuries, 1988); Miguel Cruz Hernández, *El pensamiento de Ramón Llull* (Valencia: Castalia, 1977); Sebastián Garcías Palou, *Ramón Llull en la historia del ecumenismo* (Barcelona: Herder, 1986); idem, *Ramón Llull y el Islam* (Madrid: Gráficas Planisi, 1981); Jocelyn N. Hillgarth, *Ramon Llull and Lullism in Fourteenth-Century France* (Oxford: Clarendon, 1971); Mark D. Johnston, *The Spiritual Logic of Ramon Llull* (Oxford: Clarendon, 1987); Edgar Allison Peers, *Ramon Llull: A Biography* (London: Society for Promoting Christian Knowledge, 1929); and Jordi Rubió Balaguer, *Ramon Llull i el lul.lisme* (Montserrat: Publicacions de l'Abadia, 1985). Studies on *Blanquerna* have focused on the exemplarity of the narrative: M. Arbona Piza, "Los exemplis en el *Llibre de Evast e Blanquerna*," *Estudios Lulianos* 20 (1976): 53–70; Rudolph Brummer, "Sobre les fonts literàries del *Blanquerna* de Ramon Llull," *Iberoromania* 9 (1979): 1–11; Frank Pierce, "*Blanquerna* and *The Pilgrim's Progress* Compared," *Estudis Romànics* 3 (1951–52): 88–98; Martí de Riquer, *Història de la literatura catalana*, 6 vols. (Barcelona: Ariel, 1964), 1: 197–352; Arthur Terry, *Catalan Literature*, vol. 7 of *A Literary History of Spain* (London: Ernest Benn, 1972): 12–22; and David J. Viera, *Medieval Catalan Literature: Prose and Drama* (New York: Twayne, 1988): 4–24. Two monographs that address the issues of the homiletic contexts (of missionary reception) and techniques (of vernacular piety) of Llull's novel, respectively, are:

tion of this hagiographic romance: Latin and Hispano-Arabic didactic narratives, Catalan and Castilian compilations of traditional wisdom, French allegories of courtly love, and Italian popular preaching by the Franciscans.[5] But Llull's achievement was: (a) to transform these traditions in the light of his own religious experience and mission, (b) to convert his fiction-parable into an instrument for spiritual restoration and social reform, and (c) ultimately to transcend the limitations of literature and society by way of mystical love. *Blanquerna* emerges not only as Llull's literary masterpiece in Catalan, but also as a document which is central to understanding the religious renewal which followed the directives of Pope Innocent III, and the example of saints Dominic and Francis of Assisi. It must thus be read in the historical context of the new preachers, reformers, educators, and missionaries who flourished in the thirteenth century. With the exemplary history and teachings of the fictional saint Blanquerna, Ramon Llull in effect creates the modern Christian novel: he describes the prototype of the new middle-class saint, gives a practical demonstration of urban preaching, and represents the City of God into which Christendom is to be transformed *hic et nunc.* He offers a model hagiography for the formation of new saints in contemporary society.

In order to examine Llull's *Blanquerna* as a mode of popular religious fiction that both reflects and attempts to reform the culture of its day, it is important to establish the subgenre of sacred biography and to define the type of saint offered as a model. This study will therefore focus

---

Roberto J. González-Casanovas, *Predicación y narrativa en Ramón Llull: De imagen a semejanza en* Blanquerna (Ph.D. diss., Harvard Univ., 1990); and Wolfgang Schleicher, *Ramon Lulls* Libre de Evast e Blanquerna: *Eine Untersuchung über den Einfluss der Franziskanisch-Dominikanischen Predigt auf die Prosawerke des Katalanischen Dichters* (Genève: Librairie E. Droz, 1958), reviewed by Rudolf Brummer in *Estudios Lulianos* 7 (1963): 105–7 and 256.

[5] On the interaction of traditional forms of didactic literature and contemporary arts of preaching, see Claude Bremond, Jacques Le Goff, and Jean-Claude Schmitt, *L'Exemplum* (Turnhout: Brepols, 1982); Carolyn Walker Bynum, *Docere verbo et exemplo* (Missoula: Scholars Press, 1979); Ernst Robert Curtius, *European Literature and the Latin Middle Ages*, trans. W. R. Trask (Princeton: Princeton Univ. Press, Bollingen, 1973); María Jesús Lacarra, *Cuentística medieval en España* (Zaragoza: Univ. de Zaragoza, 1979); James J. Murphy, *Rhetoric in the Middle Ages* (Berkeley: Univ. of California Press, 1974); Rameline E. Marsan, *Itinéraire espagnol du conte médiéval* (Paris: Klincksieck, 1974); and Mark Silk, *Scientia Rerum: The Place of Example in Later Medieval Thought* (Ph.D. diss., Harvard Univ., 1982).

on (1) the hagiographic narrative in relation to its homiletic structure
and exemplary hermeneutics, (2) the saint's vocation and mission as it
evolves in interaction with his times, (3) the saint as reformer of church
and society, and (4) the saint himself as author of pious and homiletic
works.

A critical approach to the sacred, yet fictional narrative of *Blanquerna*
should begin with the devotional frame. Llull begins the work as if it
were a sermon: he addresses a prayer directly to God and states in the
prologue the theme of his preaching and purpose of the romance: for
this work "és fet per intenció que los hòmens agen de amar, entendre,
recordar e servir a vós com a ver Déu, senyor y creador que sóu de
totes coses" [is made with the intention that men love, understand, remember, and serve You as true God, who are Lord and Creator of all
things].[6] The whole novel, then, serves as an objective meditation and
extended sermon on the imitation of Christ in terms of both the interior life (the contemplation of the five wounds) and social experience
(the observation of the five "estates of people").

In the *Llibre de Evast e Blanquerna*, Llull narrates the religious adventures and spiritual experiences of the protagonist Blanquerna, his parents Evast and Aloma, and Natana (or Tana), the young woman who
would have become his wife. The novel therefore follows the linear
structure of the fictional hagiography or exemplary legend, which in
this case turns out to be a mixture of archetypal quest and authentic
Bildung. But this romance, as it reinterprets the message of the Gospels
and thus develops into a modern evangelical parable, also seeks to offer
to the reader/listener emblems of the Christian vocation and models
for the imitation of Christ that constitute cyclical motifs. These transcend the horizontal lines of the history of a holy life in contemporary
Catholic society and ultimately come to represent the spiral stages in
the soul's ascent towards and fulfillment in God.

The two formal characteristics of linearity and circularity reflect the
basic duality of the work. First, there exists the novel as exemplary life,
which the author divides into five books with the homiletic purpose

---

[6] Prol.; 1: 17–18. Quotations indicate book, chapter, volume, and page in Ramon
Llull's *Libre de Evast e Blanquerna*, 4 vols., eds. S. Galmés, A. Caimari, and R. Guilleumas (Barcelona: Els Nostres Clàssics, 1935–54); the translations are mine.

(Prologue) of recalling the five wounds of Christ and of reviewing all of the estates (or orders) of the society and church of the period. Secondly, the novel functions as a symbolic parable, which the author represents in three complementary parts: Blanquerna's hagiographic legend itself (chaps. 1–99 and 115), his mystical confessions (the 366 "moral verses" of the "Llibre d'Amic e Amat," or "Book of the Friend and the Beloved," contained in chap. 100), and his guide for ascetics (the "Art de contemplació," or "Art of Contemplation," in chaps. 101–14). These three different compositions that make up the novel reflect, in Llull's Trinitarian system,[7] man's pilgrimage as a creature made in God's image, the devotion centered on the likeness of Christ, and the illumination by the Spirit. But the duality of form and structure is transcended by the thematic and ideological unity of the novel, since all of the religious lessons and experiences of the author himself are recapitulated and exemplified by means of a character who is pseudohistorical, semiautobiographical, and prototypical. In this sense, it is necessary to incorporate the five books and three parts into a grand Trinitarian scheme of the Christian life, which would be simultaneously linear and cyclical, mutable and constant. This scheme consists of: (a) the evangelical vocation in the world and in "religion," or monasticism (bks. 1, 2A, and 2B); (b) the apostolic mission in the church and in its hierarchy (bks. 3 and 4); and (c) the spiritual way in the devotions of the ascetic and mystic (the "Book of the Friend and the Beloved" and the "Art of Contemplation" in bk. 5).

Turning to the hagiography itself, as the object of the fictional narrative and subject of the author's sermon, one notes that the work starts with the vocational fortunes of Evast, Aloma, Blanquerna, and Natana, who debate the states of matrimony and "religion" (monasticism). Llull goes beyond the conventional topics by means of vivid and emotional scenes (the interviews between the protagonist and his parents, and between the two young persons, in bk. 1, chaps. 5 and 6), which stand out for their psychological drama and social realism. The Christian vocation is here revealed through narrative monologues and dialogues, realized through pious practices and charitable deeds, and confirmed

---

[7] See R. D. F. Pring-Mill, "The Trinitarian World-Picture of Ramon Llull," *Romanistisches Jahrbuch* 7 (1955–56): 229–56.

through a series of tests and self-trials. When Llull comes to treat the religious vocation, in the strict sense in which he here understands it, he shows that it requires a complete formation of the individual as temporal and spiritual subject, which in the best of cases, as with Blanquerna, leads to a teaching role and apostolic ministry based on those of the divine Teacher and Servant of the Gospel.

Upon reaching adulthood, Blanquerna, like saint Francis of Assisi before him, rejects the plans his parents have made for him (the life of a Christian as merchant and spouse); he chooses instead to lead the ascetic and solitary life of a hermit according to the example of Elijah and saint John the Baptist.[8] In this resolve, he follows the fruit of his meditations on the cross, which serve as the basis of his Franciscan-like imitation of Christ: Blanquerna "començà a considerar e guardar en la creu, e remembrà la santa passió de nostre senyor Jesu Crist, e con era estat pobre in lo món, ell e sos apòstols, ni con hac menyspreats los béns temporals" [began to consider and to look upon the Cross, and he remembered the holy Passion of our Lord Jesus Christ, and how he was poor in the world, both he and his apostles, and how he had scorned temporal goods].[9] At eighteen, he thus decides to renounce the world "per ço que puscha pus perfetament contemplar, amar lo Fill de Déu, qui vench en est món per nosaltres peccadors" [in order more perfectly to contemplate and love the Son of God, who came into this world for us sinners].[10]

In Blanquerna's quest for a hermitage, he encounters the allegorical figures of the Ten Commandments, Faith, Truth, Understanding, Devotion, and Valor,[11] which, taken together, represent the very balance of scholastic learning and affective piety that characterize the preaching of the friars. As he discovers, what is needed by the Church is a missionary apostolate that will "convert" not only the minds and souls of the infidels, but also the schools and clergy of the Christians (symbolized by the philosophy and theology students at the feet of Understanding[12]). The new apostolate must be equally based on teaching

---

[8] Bk. 1: chap. 5; vol. 1: 56.
[9] Ibid., p. 55.
[10] Ibid., p. 56.
[11] Bk. 2: chaps. 43–45 and 48.
[12] Bk. 2: chap. 44; vol. 1: 220.

the "art" of theology (Llull's own *Ars magna*) and on exemplifying the life and Passion of Christ.[13]

It is significant that Evast sends Blanquerna to an urban center of learning, probably one of the new universities (such as that of Montpellier where the novel is written) with a curriculum based on the teaching of the friars, where he studies the liberal arts, medicine, and scholastic theology.[14] Later, when Blanquerna enters a monastery, it is his learning and wisdom, as well as his devotion, that serve to renew the spiritual life of the monks: as he explains the Scriptures to them, they recognize the importance for their community of the liberal and scholastic studies mastered by Blanquerna and the friars.[15] As the Abbot argues, "injúria fem a l'ànima con no li satisfem de viandes sperituals, per sermons e per paraules de Déu" [we do injury to the soul when we do not satisfy it with spiritual food, by sermons and the words of God].[16] The renovation of monastic learning and preaching by the scholasticism of the friars in the urban universities is thus manifested in Blanquerna's reforms as the new master of studies at the monastery.[17]

Once the author has described the saint's vocation and mission as it unfolds in a life of prayer and service (in the family and in the Church, in solitude and in society), he makes a transition from the individual's formation in piety to the conversion of the whole world to the true faith and to a good order. From the contemplation and imitation of Christ, Llull and Blanquerna pass on to the emulation and interpretation of the mission of the Apostles. For the Christian living in the thirteenth century who desires a return to the original fervor and commitment of the gospel, this means the reform of society through the reform of the Church. It is for this reason that Blanquerna's "religious" and "ecclesial" trajectory (each in the strict sense) is so significant: his original vocation to be a hermit providentially evolves into service as a monk, teacher, sacristan, abbot, bishop, and pope, before it can bear the inward fruit of the hermit and mystic.

As abbot, Blanquerna develops his reforms of the monastery and the

---

[13] Ibid., pp. 221 and 222.
[14] Bk. 1: chap. 2; vol. 1: 33.
[15] Bk. 2: chap. 53; vol. 1: 276.
[16] Ibid., p. 277.
[17] Bk. 2: chap. 56; vol. 1: 288–92.

surrounding countryside according to a rule of preaching that is based on the "Hail Mary."[18] This systematization of popular forms of prayer, as symbolic patterns for the transformation of institutions and for the conversion of the heart, reflects the new spirituality of the friars: in particular, the Franciscans' appeal to the common people through simple examples of piety, and the Dominicans' cultivation, among the clergy and populace, of devotions to the Virgin Mary. This Marian spirituality serves to focus on the human compassion and mediation of Christ himself. As Blanquerna explains to his monks, "Tot lo major honrament que creatura aja pugut reebre de son creador, fo fet en lo ventre de nostra Dona com lo Fill de Déu hi pres natura humana" [The greatest honor that a creature received from his Creator was done in the womb of our Lady when the Son of God there took upon himself human nature].[19]

When Abbot Blanquerna is elected bishop, he undertakes a renewal of his clergy and a reform of his city that is predicated on the return to the gospel teachings of Christ. As a "modern" pastor and urban preacher inspired by the new devotion and apostolate of the friars, he models his role on the evangelical example of the Beatitudes.[20] After singing the passage from the Sermon on the Mount during mass, Bishop Blanquerna convokes the canons so as to reorder the diocese: "Entès havets, senyors, con nostre senyor Déus Jesu Crist promet en l'avengeli VIII benauyrances. Ab consell e ab volentat de vosaltres, vulria ordenar aquest bisbat a tal regla e ordenament que les VIII benauyrances poguésem aver" [You have heard, my lords, how Our Lord Jesus Christ promises eight beatitudes in the Gospel. With your counsel and willingness, I would like to order this bishopric with such a rule and ordinance that we may enjoy the eight beatitudes].[21] Moreover, Blanquerna divides the canons themselves into three groups: those who serve the cathedral church, those who study theology and canon law, and those who preach by word and deed the Beatitudes (and by extension the whole Gospel itself) in the city streets and marketplaces. The scholastic preparation and evangelical responsibility of the priests as

---

[18] Bk. 1: chaps. 61–66.
[19] Bk. 2: chap. 61; vol. 2: 29.
[20] Bk. 3: chaps. 68–76.
[21] Bk. 3: chaps. 68; vol. 2: 75–76.

ministers of Christ's Word among his people are thereby restored to the clerical offices and functions of the Church. In this way, as one of the canons tells a group of pilgrim-preachers, the original order or rule of Christ's disciples would be reestablished:

> Si ells volien ésser en l'orde dels Apòstols, covenia que en les çiutats e en les viles e.ls castells per on passarien preycasen la paraula de Déu, e que reprenesen los hòmens dels peccats que.ls veurien fer, e que no duptasen mort ni trebaylls, e que la fe catòlicha anassen preycar als infeels per ço que mills fossen semblants als apòstols.

> [If they wished to enter the order of the Apostles, they should preach the word of God in the cities, towns, and castles through which they passed; reprimand persons for the sins which they saw them committing; not hesitate to suffer death or hardship; and go to the infidels to preach the Catholic faith so that they might be more like the apostles.][22]

By means of Blanquerna's episcopate, Llull unleashes a criticism of society that embraces all the sins and abuses of his age. He also engages in a clerical debate that examines, from theoretical (theological) and institutional (ecclesiological) points of view, all the urgent problems confronting contemporary Christianity. For both author and protagonist (as reformers), the preaching by the bishop should include moral denunciations and challenges, as well as scholastic questions and disputations. It is Bishop Blanquerna's concern with the renovation of theology, renewal of the clergy, and reform of the Church that leads him to draw up ten questions to be debated among the pope and cardinals in Rome, "per ço que ... ells les solvessen e les determenassen, e que feesen les obres qui.s covenria ab la solució e determinació" [so that they might solve and determine them, and perform the works that were proper to their solution and determination].[23] Once in the court of Rome, the pope dies and Bishop Blanquerna is elected to succeed him. As the "Apostle," he sees his role in the evangelical terms of pastor and teacher of the Church. He now undertakes the renewal of Catholic spirituality and the reform of

---

[22] Bk. 3: chap. 76; vol. 2: 124.
[23] Bk. 2: chap. 77; vol. 2: 127.

Christian society on the basis of the rule of the *Gloria in excelsis:*[24] that is, he applies the rule of prayer as adoration of God and action on behalf of one's neighbor. The ecclesiastical hierarchy must thus mirror both the order of God and responsibility for his people.

By means of Blanquerna's papacy, Llull establishes a vertical order which is to serve as a guarantee of church discipline and universal harmony; he thus projects a model of authority (doctrinal and moral) and responsibility (homiletic and pastoral) which is to promote not only the renewal of the clergy and people, but also the unification and pacification of the world under the kingdom of Christ. As pope, Blanquerna undertakes to fulfill, in the light of the gospel, the apostolic mission of the Church by preaching the reconversion of Christians in the cities of Europe and the conversion of infidels in foreign lands. To accomplish this double crusade of the word, he enlists not only the cardinals and their clerical assistants, but also a host of lay people as street criers, storytellers, theological disputants, and devout witnesses.[25] In effect, he revitalizes and recommissions the Church as the people of God engaged in the evangelization of the whole contemporary world. He is even willing to adopt the methods of preaching of the Muslim Sufis, whose affective way of devotion and broad popular appeal recalls that of the Franciscan friars who preach sermons in the vernacular to the urban masses: "era recomtat com los devots hòmens fahien cançons de Déu e d'amor, e com per amor de Déu lexaven lo món e anaven per lo món, pobretat sustinent" [they would tell of how devout men sang songs of God and of love, and how for the love of God, they would leave the world and go throughout the world suffering poverty]; indeed, "tan devotes paraules preycaven, que quaix tots aquells qui los scoltaven se ploraven" [they would preach such devoted words that almost all who heard them would weep].[26]

Once the temporal mission of the apostles to go throughout the world proclaiming, instructing, and baptizing in the Holy Name has been achieved, there remains the spiritual task of the Christian's self-fulfillment by divine grace and human effort. By means of Blanquerna's

---

[24] Bk. 3: chaps. 79–95.
[25] Bk. 4: chaps. 83, 85, 86, 88, and 93.
[26] Bk. 4: chap. 88; vol. 2: 216–17.

hermitage, Llull returns to the original inspiration of the protagonist when he undertook his symbolic quest and exemplary pilgrimage. His success in reforming the Church now allows him to dedicate himself entirely to the adoration of God and the salvation of his soul. As a result, he resigns from the papacy and becomes a hermit.[27]

Although Blanquerna finds a retreat in the country where he can meditate in the midst of nature, he cannot escape the needs of the urban Church. His hermitage is sought out by the hermits of Rome, minstrels from noble courts, a bishop who is a theologian, and the emperor himself, who has abdicated and now wishes to join Blanquerna in praying to God, conversing about God, and writing verses and guidebooks for those who seek God.[28] Just like the Franciscan and Dominican friars who combine mystical devotion with theological education and moral preaching, Blanquerna now discovers that his vocation consists of finding a balance between the inward withdrawal of the contemplative and the outward commitment of the active reformer and missionary. This balance is symbolized by the image of the minstrel of God, who sings of the love of Christ, Mary, and the saints with the fervor of the true mystic, but in the words of the popular poet of the palace courts and city squares: "l'ufiçi de juglaria fo atrobat per bona entenció, ço és a saber, per loar Déu e per donar solaç e consolació a aquells qui són treballats e turmentats en servir Déu" [the office of minstrel was created for a good intention, that is, to praise God and to give solace and consolation to those who suffer hardship and torment in serving God].[29] Like Saint Francis of Assisi, Blanquerna sees himself as God's minstrel. For in his life story, as it is to be recited in the city squares, palace courts, and monastery cloisters,[30] as well as in the de-

---

[27] Bk. 5: chap. 96; vol. 2: 252. History sometimes follows precedents established in fiction: in 1294, nine years after Llull wrote *Blanquerna*, Celestine V (Pietro de Morrone) resigned from the papacy after reigning for only six months. He was a hermit and "spiritual" reformer (founder of the Celestines) who was elected supreme pontiff in the hope of renewing the Church; he was canonized in 1313 by the Avignon pope Clement V. St. Celestine's act earned him the reprobation of Dante (*il gran rifiuto*). See Sebastián Garcías Palou, "El Papa Blanquerna de Ramón Llull y Celestino V," *Estudios Lulianos* 20 (1976): 71–86.

[28] Bk. 5: chaps. 99, 100, and 115.

[29] Bk. 5: chap. 115; vol. 3: 179.

[30] Ibid., p. 181.

vout verses composed by the emperor for the edification of the papal court of Rome, are to be found the mirror of "la vida dels Apòstols, en lo temps dels quals santedat de vida e devoció e valor vivien" [the life of the Apostles, in whose times sanctity of life and devotion and valor were alive].[31]

What is striking about Llull's fictional hagiography is the way in which it transforms novel into sermon and sermon into novel. The exemplary narrative of a modern saint as reformer and as contemplative in effect evolves into an example of how to write—as well as read and interpret—pious arts and fictions that will inspire others to convert themselves and their society. Once the papal court has been "restored" to an apostolic rule, Blanquerna attempts to reform the rule of the hermits of Rome; this in turn leads him to transform his own spiritual experience into forms of literature: a mystic's confession and a theologian's manual. Blanquerna, a character who acts out the life of a saint, is transformed into an author (of the "Llibre d'Amic e Amat," the "Art de contemplació," and even the romanç of Blanquerna itself[32]) who shows others how to become holy. The outer hagiography in the world of action is turned inside out to reveal the very process of sanctification in the saint's heart and mind; the exemplary legend of pious and charitable deeds is converted into autobiographical examples of the inward workings of grace and faith.

These two short works supposedly "written" by the saint constitute autonomous compositions, not only because they were in fact drafted by Llull years earlier (around 1275–1276), but also because they are different in content and form. Nevertheless, Llull manages to integrate them, in an organic and convincing way, into the overall structure of the novel and into the exemplarity of his hagiographic preaching. The "moral metaphors" of the "Amic e Amat" and the divine attributes or "virtues" of the "Art" show the author's lively interest in assimilating

---

[31] Ibid., p. 182.

[32] See bk. 5: chap. 115; vol. 3: 181. Here Blanquerna entrusts the exemplary book of his own life to a minstrel converted by him and given the penance of reciting it wherever he goes. Although this parallels the action of the emperor, who, after his abdication, composes pious verses to be sung by the Minstrel of Valor, it is a striking instance of a saint, albeit a fictional one, who redacts his *vita* and has it "interpreted" (performed and exemplified) in his lifetime for the benefit of others that may be converted by it.

the most apt and efficacious forms of devotional and doctrinal sermons, which in his day included both Christian (Dominican and Franciscan) and Muslim (Sufi) models.[33] At the same time, they illustrate, in dramatic and discursive ways, the concerns of his era for orthodoxy (the contemplative's praise of divine attributes) and orthopraxis (the Amic's or Friend of Christ's parables of love). Finally, they reflect the tradition of Augustinian contemplation preserved and renewed by the Franciscans, as well as Llull's own experience as ascetic and mystic.[34]

Through the hagiographic fiction of Blanquerna the character and the author, Llull orders and coordinates a series of exemplary sermons: the novelistic ones of a practical nature (*Blanquerna* proper, bks. 1–4); the poetic ones of an affective mode ("Amic e Amat"); and the theological ones of a discursive type ("Art de contemplació"). Llull thereby shows the double trajectory of the saint: on the one hand, the way in which divine grace animates human love in the various estates of society by the paths of piety, formation, charity, and reform; on the other hand, the manner in which the Passion of Christ invites the compassion of the Christian in the interior life by the paths of sacrifice, conformity, service, and transformation. In these ways, the fictional hagiographer concludes the linear narrative and rounds out the cyclical symbols of the life and teachings of Blanquerna, saint, sage, and witness of love.[35] For Ramon Llull, this is the role of the modern saint: to mirror society in such a way that the image of God is revealed in all and the likeness to Christ is approximated in the community.

---

[33] Bk. 5: chap. 99; vol. 3: 10.

[34] Cf. Llull's autobiographical writings: the early confessions and meditations in *Libre de contemplació* (1270–1272); the critical reevaluation and reaffirmation of the middle poems, *Desconhort* (1295–1296) and *Cant de Ramon* (1298–1299); and the spiritual and missionary witness of the late *Vida coetània* (1311) and *Phantasticus* (1311). All but the last one are included in Llull's *Obres essencials*, 2 vols., eds. M. Batllori, T. and J. Carreras Artau, and J. Rubió Balaguer (Barcelona: Selecta, 1957–1960); the *Phantasticus* (or *Disputa del clergue Pere i de Ramon, el Fantàstic*) exists in modern Catalan, trans. and ed. L. Badia (Barcelona: Stelle dell'Orsa, 1985).

[35] On the various models of sanctity found in medieval hagiographies, see: Peter Brown, *The Cult of the Saints* (Chicago: Univ. of Chicago Press, 1981); Edgar Allison Peers, *Studies of the Spanish Mystics* (London: Sheldon, 1927); Paul Szarmach, ed., *An Introduction to the Medieval Mystics of Europe* (Albany: State Univ. of New York Press, 1984); André Vauchez, *La sainteté en occident aux derniers siècles du Moyen Age* (Rome: École Française de Rome, 1981); and Donald Weinstein and Rudolph M. Bell, *Saints and Society* (Chicago: Univ. of Chicago Press, 1982).

Saints in Play:
English Theater and Saints' Lives

CLIFFORD DAVIDSON

n the earliest Easter drama, contained in the *Regularis Concordia* of ca. 970, three brethren ("fratres") vest themselves in copes and carry thuribles with incense "in imitation [ad imitationem] of . . . the women coming with spices to anoint the body of Jesus."[1] One of the women is Mary Magdalene, whose role is not yet distinguished from the roles of the other holy women who encounter the angel at the tomb of the resurrected Christ as if on the first Sunday morning following the Crucifixion. As a biblical saint whose life was regarded as a sign of the personal and spiritual renewal toward which all Christians should aspire, her function here not only hints at the surprise and wonder which accompany the recognition of the Resurrection, but also affirms for the members of the congregation that they can be touched by this event as if they were themselves living at that biblical moment.

While Christianity historically held to an understanding of saints—

---

[1] I quote from the translation by David Bevington, ed., *Medieval Drama* (Boston: Houghton Mifflin, 1975), 27; see also Karl Young, *The Drama of the Medieval Church*, 2 vols. (Oxford: Clarendon Press, 1933), 1: 249–50; and Pamela Sheingorn, *The Easter Sepulchre in England*, Early Drama, Art, and Music, Reference Series, No. 5 (Kalamazoo: Medieval Institute Publications, 1987), 20–22, who also publishes a facsimile of the manuscript in figs. 3–4.

biblical figures, including the apostles, Mary Magdalene, and the Virgin Mary, and also martyrs and confessors of the post-biblical period—as existing both in time and in the supra-temporal realm, they had come to provide focal points in the liturgical year long before the compilation of the *Regularis Concordia*. Celebrating the date on which a saint had died, the Church's concern was to harness his or her power to achieve an experience of transcendence. It is perhaps no accident that on Easter morning at Winchester in the final years of the tenth century the scene to be dramatized in the ceremony of the Visit to the Sepulchre (*Visitatio sepulchri*) was not the Resurrection itself but the coming of St. Mary Magdalene and two other saintly women to the empty tomb. The Resurrection event was to be made visible in the drama from the perspective of the early saints who witnessed the empty tomb.

The first record of a play dramatizing the life of a post-biblical saint in England was at Dunstable, Bedfordshire, in ca. 1110 when the choir copes borrowed from St. Albans Abbey for the production were lost in a fire. The play ("ludus"), on the subject of St. Catherine of Alexandria and perhaps intended for a royal audience, is not extant, but was described as a "miracle" play—terminology which was noted to be the popular designation for such drama.[2] The medieval legend of St. Catherine is well known, especially for its spectacular scene of the broken wheels which, fitted with knives, had been intended to tear the saint apart. The wheel is therefore her emblem, though in the end she was martyred by being put to the sword and her body taken off to Mount Sinai by angels. There she was allegedly buried, in a place regarded as holy after the discovery of a body attributed to her in the eighth century. In the wake of the crusades, her fame spread widely in England—more than sixty churches are dedicated to this saint[3]—and other plays and quasi-dramatic tableaux, all lost but probably requiring realistic costuming rather than liturgical vestments, are noted in records from London, Hereford, and Coventry.[4] At Coventry, the production

[2] C. B. C. Thomas, "The Miracle Play at Dunstable," *Modern Language Notes* 32 (1917): 337–44.

[3] Frances Arnold-Forster, *Studies in Church Dedications* (London: Skeffington and Son, 1899), 1:117–22, 2:344–45.

[4] See Clifford Davidson, "The Middle English Saint Play and Its Iconography," in *The Saint Play in Medieval Europe*, ed. Clifford Davidson, Early Drama, Art, and Music,

of the drama, recorded in the City Annals in 1491, has plausibly been linked to the guild associations, since St. Catherine was one of the patrons of the important Holy Trinity Guild.[5] Presumably the guild's effort to make the life of one of their patron saints seem more vivid to the people attending the play, staged in the Little Park,[6] was specifically calculated to bring the saint into the field of vision of the spectators. Because vision was held to provide the "window of the soul" and hence to place one's eyes in direct contact with an object such as a representation of the saint,[7] its goal was to achieve a participative closeness with the saint thus represented that would benefit the viewer.

Peter Brown indicates that already by the final years of the sixth century the places of burial of saints had been transformed into important centers of religious life.[8] Such holy men and women, though no longer among the living, nevertheless are dead and yet not dead; as it was said of St. Martin of Tours, his "soul is in the hand of God; but he is fully here, present, and made plain in miracles of every kind."[9] Much later, in 1527, the story of St. Martin seems to have been dramatized at Colchester, England,[10] presumably in a manner very different from the liturgical presentation of the *Visit to the Sepulchre*. The

---

Monograph Series, No. 8 (Kalamazoo: Medieval Institute Publications, 1986), 45–52.

[5] R. W. Ingram, ed., *Coventry*, Records of Early English Drama (Toronto: Univ. of Toronto Press, 1981), xx. See also Charles Phythian-Adams, *Desolation of a City: Coventry and the Urban Crisis of the Late Middle Ages* (Cambridge: Cambridge Univ. Press, 1979), 118–22.

[6] Ingram, *Coventry*, 74.

[7] Ellert Dahl, "Heavenly Images: The Statue of St. Foy of Conques and the Significance of the Medieval 'Cult-Image' in the West," *Acta ad archaeol. et artium hist. pertinentia* 8 (1978): 187; see also Margaret Miles, "Vision: The Eye of the Body and the Eye of the Mind in St. Augustine's *De trinitate* and *Confessions*," *Journal of Religion* 63 (1983): 127; and Sixten Ringbom, "Devotional Images and Imaginative Devotions," *Gazette-des-Beaux-Arts* 73 (1969): 159–70.

[8] Peter Brown, *The Cult of the Saints* (Chicago: Univ. of Chicago Press, 1981), 3.

[9] E. le Blant, *Les inscriptions chrétiennes de la Gaule* (Paris, 1856), 1:240; as quoted by Brown, *Cult of the Saints*, 4.

[10] W. G. B., " 'Seynt Martyns Pley' at Colchester," *Essex Review* 48 (1939): 83. The term 'play,' however, may in this context refer to *playing* in the sense of *game* rather than of drama; for a discussion of the ambiguity of this terminology, see John C. Coldewey, "Plays and 'Play' in Early English Drama," *Research Opportunities in Renaissance Drama* 28 (1985): 181–88. The Colchester St. Martin play is, however, accepted by Ian Lancashire, *Dramatic Texts and Records of Britain: A Chronological Topography to 1558* (Toronto: Univ. of Toronto Press, 1984), 114 (No. 553).

play at Colchester would have been presented in English rather than Latin, and would have been designed, we may assume, as a source of delight, edification, and devotion among the audience who looked upon the scenes of the life of this saint. Unfortunately, like most of the saint plays from the medieval English repertoire, no text of the Colchester *St. Martin* is extant, not implausibly lost among the accouterments of the "old religion" swept away so precipitously by the Reformation. Saints were soon to be no longer required for mediating between the time in which men lived and the eternity to which they aspired, and in Protestant England, curiously, they were to be seen as the objects of superstition rather than of faith, as factors alienating men from God rather than bringing them more near.

The closeness which Christians had traditionally felt with the holy dead—with the saints—was reflected in the relics which were deposited in their places of worship—relics that might on occasion be the object of their pilgrimages—and in the dedications of their churches. These phenomena are also mirrored in the desire to *see* the physical shape of the saint, who was thus frequently depicted in an image, either a painting or a three-dimensional carving. Images of saints could be deeply venerated even when no relic seems to have been present. In his will of 1458, John Dautre requested to be buried in the church of St. Michael Spurriergate in the city of York at the altar of the Holy Trinity before the image of St. John the Baptist, whom he had loved above all other saints since his childhood.[11] The document is unclear about whether his devotion was to the saint or to his image, but such a distinction was clearly much less significant in the fifteenth century than in the twentieth. The image provides access to the saint who has been depicted; there is no clear line of demarcation between the one and the other.

In the same city of York, two other wills from the middle of the fifteenth century refer to plays about saints, in neither case surviving. In 1446, William Revetour left a playbook of *St. James* "in six pageants" ("in sex paginis") to the St. Christopher Guild, which very likely produced the drama as part of its celebrations around the date of the Feast

---

[11] *Testamenta Eboracensia*, Part 2, ed. James Raine, Surtees Society, vol. 30 (Durham, 1855), 230–31.

of St. James on 25 July.[12] The other will, prepared in 1456 by Robert Lasingby of the parish of St. Denys, gives proof of a play on the life of St. Denis, a play associated with a church that contains a contemporary depiction of the saint in painted glass.[13] Both images and plays were popularly understood in terms of visualizing the scenes of events and persons of very great importance in sacred history. The oft-quoted Wycliffite *Tretise of Miraclis Pleyinge*, which is the most detailed piece of theatrical criticism available from the late fourteenth or early fifteenth century in spite of its hostility to the stage, nevertheless pronounces the position in defense of drama:

> Also sithen it is leveful to han the miraclis of God peintid, why is not as wel leveful to han the miraclis of God pleyed, sithen men mowen bettere reden the wille of God and his mervelous werkis in the pleyinge of hem than in the peintinge? And betere they ben holden in mennus minde and oftere rehersid by the pleyinge of hem than by the peintinge, for this is a deed bok, the tother a quick.[14]

Pictures, statues, and plays alike place the imitation of the historical events surrounding the biblical story or the life of the saint before the eyes of the people, who are thus able to *see* as if they were looking on the actual events themselves. But drama is a living art, in contrast to the static pictures of the painters and carvers.

In creating such a lively art around the lives of saints, medieval vernacular playwrights and players in England were actively responsible for theatrical displays that were designed to be deliberately popular. The evidence of the dramatic records is that the saint play genre was normal

---

[12] *York*, ed. Alexandra F. Johnston and Margaret Rogerson, Records of Early English Drama (Toronto: Univ. of Toronto Press, 1979), 1:68; see also Davidson, "The Middle English Saint Play," 32. The term *pagina* signifies both *pageant* and *page*, and hence there may be some ambiguity here, though generally it is believed that six *pageants* were implied in this record; on the term *pagina* see *Devon*, ed. John Wasson, Records of Early English Drama (Toronto: Univ. of Toronto Press, 1986), xxxi.

[13] Johnston and Rogerson, *York*, 1:88; Davidson, "The Middle English Saint Play," 33, fig. 2.

[14] *A Tretise of Miraclis Pleyinge*, ed. Clifford Davidson, Early Drama, Art, and Music, Monograph Series, No. 19 (Kalamazoo: Medieval Institute Publications, 1993), 98.

fare in England—more common, in all likelihood, than the liturgical drama or moralities, though probably less popular than the folk play or biblical drama, which includes the great cycle plays that we associate with cities like Coventry, York, and Chester.[15] The popular appeal of a play of St. Francis was one of the aspects of the drama that offended the author of the poem "On the Minorite Friars" in British Library, MS. Cotton Cleopatra B.ii, fol. 64ᵛ; this antitheatrical writer complains that Franciscans in their pride have failed to praise St. Paul and instead have staged lies about their founder. The play apparently involved some rather spectacular effects such as the appearance to St. Francis of the Seraphim in the form of a crucifix as well as the miraculous sight of the deceased saint, marked by the stigmata, to Gregory IX. The final portion of the play included as a property a "cart . . . made al of fire" with a "gray frer . . . ther-inne"—a dramatization of the appearance of St. Francis to those who were his followers at Rivo Torto.[16] Effects of this kind, which can be paralleled by those reported in connection with continental plays, have all the marks of the popular theater, as we might expect in the case of drama allegedly sponsored and directed by members of the order. Nothing about the staging of this English saint play, however, is perhaps as sensational as the effect achieved in the Majorca SS. *Crispin and Crispinian*: "They are to be beheaded. Where they are standing, there are to be two dead bodies which are to be dummies filled with straw, and the heads are to be made with masks with calm expressions. . . ."[17]

Yet the sufferings of saints as well as oftentimes their deaths, both implying the enlisting of the empathy of members of the audience, must have appeared vividly in other dramas in the saint play repertoire

---

[15] See John Wasson, "The Morality Play: Ancestor of Elizabethan Drama?" *Comparative Drama* 13 (1979): 210–21; Davidson, "Middle English Saint Play," 31; Alexandra F. Johnston, "What If No Texts Survived? External Evidence for Early English Drama," in *Contexts for Early English Drama*, ed. Marianne G. Briscoe and John C. Coldewey (Bloomington: Indiana Univ. Press, 1989), 6–7.

[16] For the text of this poem, see Davidson, *Tretise*, 12–13; for discussion, see Lawrence G. Craddock, "Franciscan Influences on Early English Drama," *Franciscan Studies* 10 (1950): 399–415.

[17] *The Staging of Religious Drama in Europe in the Later Middle Ages: Texts and Documents in English Translation*, ed. Peter Meredith and John Tailby, Early Drama, Art, and Music, Monograph Series, No. 4 (Kalamazoo: Medieval Institute Publications, 1983), 110.

in England, while in Perth, Scotland, there is record from 1518 of a play of St. Erasmus, a holy man whose symbol, the windlass, resulted in the mistaken belief that he had been martyred by having his intestines wound around such a mechanism. That such a martyrdom was included in the Scottish play is indicated by the existence of a record indicating payment of eight pence to "The cord drawer."[18] In the early sixteenth century before the suppression of his cult by Henry VIII,[19] the show of St. Thomas Becket at Canterbury apparently utilized a false head for the saint which required frequent painting.[20] The effects required in the lost play of St. Lawrence at Lincoln in 1441–1442 would, we might assume, require the gridiron for the saint's martyrdom, since this instrument of his torture inevitably appears in representations of him in the visual arts.[21]

Like most heroes of the Renaissance tragedies, which were successors to the medieval saint play in England, the martyr was someone about whom the members of the audience were encouraged to care a great deal. Audience response in such a drama is, to be sure, highly complex, but consciously the saint was the focal point for sympathy and, though we cannot verify it, tears. However, we do have the witness of the author of the Wycliffite *Tretise* concerning tears reportedly shed for Christ when the Passion was played; for this writer, "they ben reprovable that wepen for the pley of Cristis passioun" (they would be better off, he says, if they would weep for their own sins "and of theire children, as Crist bad the wymmen that wepten on him").[22] That tears were a characteristic of Northern piety at the end of the Middle Ages is implied by a sneering remark about Flemish painting attributed to Michelangelo;[23] in all likelihood weeping was considered an appropriate response to the conclusion of the life of a martyr in spite of the inevitable receipt of the saint's soul into heaven.

---

[18] Anna Jean Mill, *Mediaeval Plays in Scotland* (1924; reprint, New York: Benjamin Blom, 1969), 272.

[19] Davidson, "Middle English Saint Play," 55.

[20] Ibid., 54–55.

[21] *Records of Plays and Players in Lincolnshire, 1300–1585*, ed. Stanley Kahrl, Malone Society Collections, vol. 8 (1974 [for 1969]), 30.

[22] Davidson, *Tretise*, 102.

[23] Cited by Erwin Panofsky, *Early Netherlandish Painting* (Cambridge: Harvard Univ. Press, 1953), 1:2.

But all plays focusing on the lives of saints did not conclude in martyrdom, for in the fourth century a violent death at the hands of persecutors was found no longer to be essential for canonization among post-biblical saints. One such saint whose popularity extends to the present is St. Nicholas, whose life and miracles were dramatized in ca. 1250 at an unspecified location, possibly in ca. 1283 at Gloucester, and in 1473 at the Scottish court. Extant Latin play texts by Hilarius and in the Fleury Playbook suggest emphasis on miracles such as the resuscitation of the three clerks who had been murdered by the wicked inkeeper and his wife, or the gifts of money which saved the three daughters of a poor man from prostitution.[24] Middle English saint plays of such saints' miracles form the only variety that is available for study today; two dramas with similarly non-violent endings have been said to comprise the entire corpus of extant texts of pre-Reformation saint plays from this language area. These are the plays of *Mary Magdalene* and *Conversion of St. Paul* in Bodleian Library MS. Digby 133.[25]

Mary Magdalene is the longer of the two plays, and it is also the more interesting in spite of the introductory section that separately introduces the Roman emperor (Tiberius), Mary's father Cyrus, Herod, and Pilate, and then shows Cyrus mortally ill on stage in the presence of his children, who also include Lazarus and Martha. Thereafter, as a result of the successful siege of her Castle of Bethany by the troops of the World, Flesh, and Devil—i.e., the Seven Deadly Sins—she falls into the sinful life as a pupil of the gallant Curiositas (Pride) and becomes the prostitute who will later be converted by Christ, whereupon the seven devils which are in fact the Seven Deadly Sins are seen literally to escape from her body in a sensational scene.

Her sinful life is briefly depicted in an episode (ll. 470–546) in the

---

[24] Young, *Drama of the Medieval Church*, 2:306–60.

[25] *The Late Medieval Religious Plays of Bodleian MSS Digby 133 and e museo 160*, ed. Donald C. Baker, John L. Murphy, and Louis B. Hall, Jr., EETS, vol. 283 (Oxford, 1982); quotations from the Digby *Mary Magdalene* in my text are from this edition. For commentary on the 'Single Magdalene,' a composite of three biblical women, see Davidson, "Middle English Saint Play," 73; Helen Meredith Garth, *Saint Mary Magdalene in Mediaeval Literature*, Johns Hopkins Univ. Studies in Historical and Political Science, ser. 67, No. 3 (1950), 19; and Marjorie Malvern, *Venus in Sackcloth: The Magdalen's Origins and Metamorphosis* (Carbondale and Edwardsville: Southern Illinois Univ. Press, 1975).

tavern—a location which, if we are to believe Mirk, is the devil's church[26]—and as she awaits her "valentynys" in an arbor (ll. 564–87); it is a life characterized by self-indulgence and waywardness, which make her thrall to the powers of evil represented by the Bad Angel and his cohorts. What has happened to her has resulted in the forging of an alliance with the powers of death and hell—an alliance ultimately implying total alienation from the powers of good. She has been "onstabyll" and "veryabyll" (ll. 588, 590), as her guardian angel tells her in a vision while she is sleeping. She is required only to "Remembyr . . . on mercy" and to "make [her] sowle clyre" (l. 600). Such a vision of the perfect life is all that is required for her to come to a recognition of her alienated state, and she sets out to make herself close to the Second Person of the Trinity, whom she will encounter at Simon's house. When her separation from God has been overcome by Christ through his absolution of her sins, the Deadly Sins, along with the Bad Angel who tempted her, will "*dewoyde from the woman, and . . . entyr into hell wyth thondyr*" (l. 691).

As we might expect, neither the scene of the visit to the sepulchre nor the *hortulanus* scene (in which she mistakes the risen Christ for a gardener) is omitted. Also, selected from the period prior to Christ's Passion is the important episode of the death of Lazarus, which is present as a means of stressing the connection between earthly life and the need for a power over death which the world cannot provide. The miracle inspires belief in those who stand by and, as presented in play, is intended also to affect the lives of the members of the audience— i.e., those who *look* upon the drama. But transcendental goodness and power, now identified with Magdalene herself, are much more sensationally represented in the final part of the play which dramatizes the events following Pentecost.

The remainder of the play is divided first into her missionary work with the king and queen of Marseilles and then into a final segment in which she becomes a hermit devoted entirely to the contemplation. At Marseilles she successfully opposes the false rites of "Sent Mahownde" and also his "relykys brygth," which are responsible for diabolic "miracles"—e.g., being struck with permanent blindness (ll. 1232–41). When the king and queen return from their remarkable pilgrimage to

---

[26] John Mirk, *Festial*, ed. Theodor Erbe, EETS, extra series, vol. 96 (1905), 203.

Jerusalem, she will turn entirely from the active life of a missionary to the contemplative life in the deserts of Provence where she will abide with humility. Here she foregoes earthly food, and is fed each day by angels, who bring her the communion wafers which sustain her. Her participation in this heavenly Eucharist and her separation from the values represented by the World, Flesh, and Devil reconcile her to herself, and she achieves the peace which the world cannot give. At her death, her soul is received by angels as it ascends directly into heaven. This entire segment of the play provides opportunity for spectacular staging.

After her conversion, therefore, Mary Magdalene is a model of human behavior, and in the play she is a saint whom ordinary people were invited to look upon for their spiritual benefit. She was regarded as a link between the present and the historical past and also between the audience and the miraculous power released by the Resurrection event. In his final speech in the play, the priest who had been present at the Magdalene's death speaks directly to those who are looking at the play: "Sufferens of this processe, thus enddyth the sentens/ That we have playyd in yower syth." Then he continues: "Allemythty God, most of magnyfycens,/ Mote bryng yow to hys blysse so brygth,/ In presens of that King!" (ll. 2132–35).

More central to medieval Christianity than Mary Magdalene was another biblical St. Mary, the Blessed Virgin, who had been recognized as the Mother of God from the third century.[27] She was not only felt to be present at such shrines as Walsingham, but also her image and candles in her honor were seemingly to be found in every parish church. Her power was regarded as far greater than that of any apostle, and her intercession for the individual supplicant was often thought to be potentially crucial since the Son could not resist any reasonable request by the merciful mother. At the conclusion of the Chester banns of 1539–1540, she is invoked along with Christ:

> Iesu crist that syttys on hee
> And his blessyd mother marie/

---

[27] For convenience see *The Oxford Dictionary of the Christian Church*, 2d ed., s.v. *Theotokos*.

Saue all this goodely company
And kepe you nyght and day[28]

Often depicted standing at the right hand of Christ the Judge at the
Last Judgment, she shows her kindly nature by her love, interceding
for those who implore her help.

The Virgin Mary's very great popularity leads us to believe that
plays about her life would have been among the most common in
medieval England. Records of such dramas are not totally lost. We
know, for example, that a Mary play was performed at New Romney
in 1512–1513.[29] A portion of a drama about one of her miracles has
been identified in a fragment in the Durham Cathedal Library; the
Durham *Prologue* dramatized a miracle of the Virgin in her role as protector of a knight who, in spite of his denial of Christ as part of an
agreement to regain the riches he had lost through his profligacy, refused to relinquish worship of his Mother.[30] Another fragment, *Dux
Moraud*, has also been claimed as a possible segment of a miracle of the
Virgin drama, though there is considerable room for scepticism in this
instance.[31] At Chester in August 1499, a play of "the Assumption of
our Ladye," regularly sponsored as part of the Whitsun cycle by the
wives of the city, was presented for Prince Arthur.[32] On the feast of
Mary's mother, St. Anne, at Lincoln, a *visus* representing the Assumption and presumably the Coronation of the Virgin in the cathedral
nave was recorded between 1458 and 1469; later, these scenes were
apparently transferred to the St. Anne's Day procession.[33]

Recent study of the N-town manuscript has shown that the Marian

---

[28] *Chester*, ed. Lawrence M. Clopper, Records of Early English Drama (Toronto:
Univ. of Toronto Press, 1979), 39.

[29] *Records of Plays and Players in Kent, 1450–1642*, ed. Giles E. Dawson, Malone
Society Collections, No. 7 (Oxford, 1965), 130.

[30] See Stephen Wright, "The Durham Play of Mary and the Poor Knight: Sources
and Analogues of a Lost English Miracle Play," *Comparative Drama* 17 (1983): 254–65.
For the text of the fragment, see *Non-cycle Plays and Fragments*, ed. Norman Davis,
EETS, supplementary series, vol. 1 (Oxford, 1970), 118–19.

[31] Constance Hieatt, "A Case for *Duk Moraud* as a Play of the Miracles of the
Virgin," *Mediaeval Studies* 32 (1970): 345–51. For the text of this fragment, see Davis,
Non-Cycle Plays, 106–13.

[32] Clopper, *Chester*, 21, 23.

[33] Kahrl, *Plays and Players in Lincolnshire*, 32–62.

scenes depicting the events leading up to the birth of the Virgin and continuing through the Annunciation make up a unit that had been grafted into the main cycle.[34] Quite remarkably, therefore, we are able to see the emergence of the structure of a Marian cycle originally intended to stand alone as a dramatization of both biblical and extra-biblical material treating the early life of the Virgin Mary. Once it is separated from the larger cycle in which it is embedded—and here the recent edition by Peter Meredith is very useful[35]—the Mary play may be added to the list of extant saint plays in England.

The extent of this East Anglian play's dependence on biblical sources is, to be sure, much less than its use of the New Testament apocrypha[36] as filtered through the liturgy and such works as the *Golden Legend* and the *Meditations on the Life of Christ* (the latter well known in England through Nicholas Love's translation).[37] The purpose of the play was not merely to tell an interesting story in honor of the Virgin, but rather, in Meredith's words, "to make the audience visualise and feel emotionally how the events occurred."[38] The added scene of the Parliament of Heaven presents the reconciliation of Mercy

---

[34] The layers of composition in the N-town cycle have been studied by Stephen Spector, "The Composition and Development of an Eclectic Manuscript: Cotton Vespasian D. VIII," *Leeds Studies in English*, n.s. 9 (1977): 62–83; for the conclusion that "the Marian (Contemplacio) group (plays 8–11, 13) was a separate and self-contained composite Mary play," see *The N-Town Plays: A Facsimile of British Library MS Cotton Vespasian D VIII*, ed. Peter Meredith and Stanley J. Kahrl (Leeds: Univ. of Leeds School of English, 1977), VII. So too the *Assumption of the Virgin* in the same manuscript was undoubtedly a separate play about the life of the Virgin.

[35] *The Mary Play from the N. Town Manuscript*, ed. Peter Meredith (London: Longman, 1987); citations of this play in my text will be to this edition. See also Alan J. Fletcher, "Layers of Revision in the N-Town Marian Cycle," *Neophilologus* 66 (1982): 469–78.

[36] The ultimate source of the legend of the Immaculate Conception and episodes of Mary's early life is the *Protevangelium*, for which see M. R. James, trans., *The Apocryphal New Testament* (Oxford: Clarendon Press, 1924), 38–49. On the iconography, Mrs. [Anna] Jameson, *Legends of the Madonna as Represented in the Arts*, rev. ed. (London: Longmans, Green, 1890), 137–95, remains useful, though the focus is not on English art. The East Anglian context has, however, been studied by Gail McMurray Gibson in *The Theater of Devotion: East Anglian Drama and Society in the Late Middle Ages* (Chicago: Univ. of Chicago Press, 1989).

[37] Meredith, *Mary Play*, 14–15. Meredith notes that another work, *The Charter of the Holy Ghost*, also figured as a source for the author of this play (p. 15).

[38] Meredith, *Mary Play*, 14.

and Truth and of Justice and Peace within heaven itself as a necessary prelude to earthly reconciliation envisioned through the acts of the Son of Mary. The theology which is developed here, adapted from Psalm 84.11 (*AV*: 85.10), articulates a transcendent principle upon which subsequent earthly reconciliation may be based. The incarnation is a process that is dependent upon heaven, yet in its function of reconciliation will need to be extended to earth first of all through the miraculous birth of the Mother of Jesus, whose conception will take place without the physical sexual contact of her previously barren parents. So at their meeting at the East, or "Golden," Gate of Jerusalem, the parents of the Virgin exchange a "kusse of clennesse," and St. Anne remarks that "was nevyr joy sank in me so depe" (ll. 241, 243). The scene is one that received frequent illustration in the visual arts (e.g., the sculptural relief in the Lady Chapel at Ely[39]) and involved a devotional stance that was important for the medieval understanding of Mary, holy and blessed, the one who carried God within her womb and gave birth to him so that he could redeem the world.

The playwright's sources provided motivation for Mary's father's previous departure from the city. The first scene had shown the priest Ysakar during the Feast of Incense expelling Joachim from the temple (represented in the play by a separate platform) because "thu and thi wyff arn barrany and bare" (l. 101). Joachim's offering had been rejected. As a result, he fled to the countryside, where he was seen, temporarily alienated and ashamed, among his shepherds. But even while he was in such a state, an angel of heaven came from above as a messenger who abrogated the normal order of things to reveal to him that something remarkable will happen which will rescue mankind from its normally fallen condition.

Skipping over the birth of Mary, the playwright then focuses upon her presentation in the temple at the age of three. In the stage directions, we learn that Mary had been taken from the location of her parents' home to the scaffold representing the temple—surely the same scaffold that had been used for the rejection of Joachim's offering. The

---

[39] See M. R. James, *The Sculptures in the Lady Chapel at Ely* (London: D. Nutt, 1895), South Side, pl. XI; *Iconoclasm vs. Art and Drama*, ed. Clifford Davidson, Early Drama, Art, and Music, Monograph Series, No. 11 (Kalamazoo: Medieval Institute Publications, 1989), fig. 18. This sculpture is now severely mutilated.

core of the scene is the sight of the three-year-old toddler unsteadily walking up the fifteen steps to the temple as she recites a paraphrase of the gradual psalms. Again, this is a scene familiar in the visual arts, and, like the illustration of the meeting at the Golden Gate, is present in the famous relief sculptures in the Lady Chapel at Ely Cathedral.[40] Mary would stay in the temple until her fourteenth year among the priests and attendant virgins, the latter ultimately adapted from the vestal virgins of antiquity who had been introduced into her story but who now are allegorized into Meditacyon, Contryssyon, Compassyon, Clennes, and Fruyssyon (ll. 481–83). Following the account in the *Golden Legend*, Mary is told by a heavenly messenger that she will be fed heavenly food "day and nyght" by angels, who will also help her to learn more about "oure Lordys lawe" than she would otherwise be able to acquire (ll. 533–35). But the angel who comes to her with this message also declares her name to be holy and her power to extend to both heaven and hell—a strange and disturbing message to be received by a small girl.

At fourteen years of age, however, Mary will be married, and the man who is chosen through the miracle of the budding rod is Joseph, old and comic according to tradition established by the *Protevangelium*.[41] As such, he will be a guarantee of her virginity, which will be preserved even after her Child has been born. This play is intended to be a command performance throughout, with angels frequently coming down to announce words of prophecy and explanation to the human participants in the drama. Further, the play is one of the richest individual dramas in Middle English with regard to its use of music, which is entirely made up of appropriate liturgical items.[42]

Married and yet a virgin, Mary's famous encounter with the angel Gabriel allows the playwright to display her feelings for the audience to see and hear. After she has been saluted by Gabriel, who requires her "assent to the incarnacyon" (l. 1343), the Holy Spirit descends "*with*

---

[40] James, *Sculptures in the Lady Chapel*, South Side, pl. XIII; *Iconoclasm vs. Art and Drama*, ed. Davidson, fig. 19.

[41] James, *Apocryphal New Testament*, 43.

[42] See JoAnna Dutka, *Music in the English Mystery Plays*, Early Drama, Art, and Music, Reference Series, No. 2 (Kalamazoo: Medieval Institute Publications, 1980), 124 and *passim*.

thre bemys to Our Lady," followed by the Son "*with thre bemys to the Holy Gost,*" and then the Father "*with thre bemys to þe Sone, and so entre all thre to here bosom*" (l. 1355 *s.d.*). "A," Mary responds, "now I fele in my body .../ Parfyte God and parfyte man" (ll. 1356–57). There has, she insists, been no pain; her virginity is intact—a requirement if she is to be seen as the sinless God-bearer, the "trone and tabernakyl of the hygh Trinité" (l. 1549). Her pregnancy is a miracle, an abrogation of the normal laws of nature; so seeing and hearing the story of her miraculous birth and of the conception of Jesus are expected to involve visual and aural perception that will result in an appropriate cognitive experience with supra-natural dimensions for those attending the play. Through participation in such an imaginative experience, then, viewers may have their lives touched by the imitation of an original event that lies near the center of history itself. As Mary's cousin Elizabeth says in the final scene of the Visitation,

> A, ye modyr of God, ye shewe us here how
> We xulde be meke that wrecchis here be;
> All hefne and herthe wurcheppe yow mow,
> That are trone and tabernakyl of the hygh Trinité.
>
> (ll. 1546–49)

Finally, Contemplation, acting as epilogue, reminds the audience that a pardon of 10,800 years[43] will be given to anyone who faithfully says "Oure Ladyes sawtere dayly for a yer" (ll. 1567–68). He announces that the play will end with *Ave,* the word with which the angel had hailed Mary at the Annunciation in the biblical account and the word which traditionally was regarded as the reverse of *Eva*—Eve, through whom sin had come into the world. The word is then transformed into the incipit of the antiphon *Ave regina celorum,* which in this play is directed to Mary as an act of devotion. The drama hence needs to be seen not merely as a didactic or mimetic exercise to increase knowledge or enjoyment on the part of the viewers—a pageant which basically reflects the page (*pagina*) of a book brought to life on stage,[44] a

---

[43] This number is a multiple of 12, and hence surely represents a mathematical context prior to the introduction of the Eastern system of basing calculations on the number 10.

[44] On the term *pagina* see n. 12, above.

more vivid book for the unlettered—but also as a complex offering that repeats the pattern of the incarnation in bringing divinity into the womb of human experience.

Mary, even more than the other saints, was a visible presence in the parishes of medieval England, where saints' lives, legends, and miracles became adapted to the theatrical impulse which would represent them by means of living actors. Saints could even lend their names to characters in the folk drama, as in the case of St. George, whose legendary battle with the dragon had become a central myth in England that survived into Protestant times. But such folk expression was very different from the saint play with its mixture of the sensational, spectacular, and emotionally stimulating elements, all of which were tuned to the hearts of the spectactors.

Saint Francis, a Saint in Progress

CHIARA FRUGONI

t was friar Elias, the vicar of the Franciscans, who announced, a few days after the death of St. Francis in 1226, the news of that death. His letter, sent to all the provinces of the Order, included the startling news of the miracle of the stigmata:

> Annuncio vobis gaudium magnum et miraculi novitatem. A saeculo non est auditum tale signum, praeterquam in filio Dei.[1]

> (I want to announce to you a very great joy and an amazing miracle. This sign has never been heard of before, except in the Son of God.)

A little before the death of St. Francis, scars appeared, (the vicar wrote), as if he had been crucified with Christ. They really were the *stigmata Christi in corpore suo*,[2] the five wounds which Christ had in his crucified body. These wounds in his hands and feet were as punctures of nails, visible on the upper and lower parts of the hands and feet. And the breast appeared to have been wounded. Blood had seeped out of the flesh.

It should be noted that during his lifetime St. Francis never said a word about the stigmata, and none of the friars saw them. Even when

---

[1] Helias, *Epistola encyclica de transitu s. Francisci* (in *Analecta Franciscana* [1926–1941], 10:526; *Analecta Franciscana* hereafter cited as *AF*).

[2] Ibid.

one of the friars asked St. Francis about the origin of some of the wounds he saw in his hands and feet (as Thomas of Celano related in a much later account), St. Francis answered him very rudely, saying in the vernacular: "Mind your own business!"[3] In point of fact, his skin was very disfigured as a result of illnesses, some of which he had contracted in the Orient.[4]

Elias's identification of Francis with Christ was too bold, and his contemporaries did not accept it. However, over the next century there were nine papal bulls commanding painters to paint the signs of the stigmata in the frescoes and icons of St. Francis and also condemning people who were scratching away these signs.[5] Furthermore, there were many accounts which dealt with the problem of people not believing in the miracle of the stigmata. Given the fact that Pope Gregory IX did not mention the stigmata in the Bull of Canonization of St. Francis in 1228, it would appear that either he did not believe the story or he did not accept it for those first two years after Francis's death. However, he later espoused the idea of the miracle when he appreciated how much devotion it inspired, and found that it was useful politically.

When we think of the stigmata of St. Francis today, both the image and idea is of wounds received from the crucified Christ-seraph which appeared to him in a vision—wounds impressed into the flesh of a saint. This image comes to us from St. Bonaventure, who at that time was the head of the Order of Friars Minor, and from Giotto, who happened upon a happy formula to express pictorially the concept which Bonaventure put forth in his version of the life of St. Francis, the version which became the last official biography. The problem of the stigmata is complicated, since the versions of the stigmata in both written and iconographical sources vary considerably. It is therefore worthwhile to turn back to the earlier written sources. The image we have today may be considered a victory on the part of Bonaventure; when the chapter of 1266 met, Bonaventure ordered the destruction of

---

[3] Thomas of Celano, *Vita secunda S. Francisci Assisiensis*, cap. 98, 135 (in *AF*, 10:209): "Curam habe de facto tuo!"

[4] On this problem see my *Francesco, un'altra storia* (Genoa: Marietti, 1955), 21 ff.

[5] A. Vauchez, "Les stigmates de saint François et leurs détracteurs dans les derniers siècles du Moyen Âge," *Mélanges d'archéologie et d'histoire* 80 (1968): 595–625.

all previous official sources of the biography of St. Francis. This destruction was carried out so meticulously that only very rarely have unique copies of those early biographies been uncovered in distant monasteries.[6]

Thus, for many centuries Francis was the Francis of Bonaventure. It was Bonaventure who linked the vision of the seraph with the appearance of the stigmata, diverging from previous versions which separated the two events. I would like to demonstrate that Bonaventure's interpretation of the stigmata was quite different from that of St. Francis and his followers. For Bonaventure, Francis became physically another Christ, because Francis carried on his flesh the marks that Christ received on the cross. However, for Francis and for his companions, the meaning was something else entirely: the suffering of St. Francis and his identification with Christ was of a spiritual nature.

The first account of the stigmata is a commentary by friar Leo, Francis's closest friend, on a poem (*Laudes Dei*) composed by St. Francis and written by him in his own hand. Friar Leo states that two years before his death, St. Francis fasted on Mount Verna in honor of the Virgin Mary, the Mother of God, and of the Archangel St. Michael from the feast of the Assumption of Mary until the feast of St. Michael in September, a fast of forty days. Leo says that, after St. Francis had seen and spoken with the seraph, the marks of the stigmata appeared on his body. In the *Laudes Dei*,[7] St. Francis thanks God for the good he has received. Leo does not imply that it was the seraph who caused the stigmata; he clearly separates the two episodes.

Thomas of Celano, who wrote the first account of the life of St. Francis in 1228, also completely separates the vision from the occurrence of the stigmata.[8] He uses as his sources friar Leo's account and also the letter of friar Elias who speaks of the stigmata but not of the

---

[6] Frugoni, *Francesco*, 8–9.

[7] See the interesting comments of D. Lapanski, "The Autographs on the 'Chartula' of St. Francis of Assisi," *Archivum Franciscanum Historicum* 67 (1974): 18–37. For the text, see *S. Franciscus, Opuscola,* Analekten zur Geschichte des Franciscus von Assisi, 4, ed. H. Boehmen (Tübingen: J. Mohr, 1961), 47: "et facta est super eum manus Domini: post visionem et allocutionem Seraphym et impressionem stigmatum in corpore suo fecit has laudes. . . ."

[8] Thomas of Celano, *Vita prima S. Francisci Assisiensis et eiusdam legenda ad usum chori,* cap. 2, 94–95 (in *AF*, 10:72–73).

seraph. According to Thomas of Celano, after the man-seraph had vanished, St. Francis did not understand the meaning of the vision, and so God gave him understanding by manifesting a miracle in his flesh: the appearance on his own body of the nails which held Christ to the Cross. The miracle was that St. Francis saw in his own flesh the nails, the same nails with which Christ had been crucified on the cross.

But on this very important point Thomas of Celano corrects friar Elias: Elias had spoken only of *puncturas clavorum*, wounds made by the puncturing nails; Thomas of Celano says that it was

> non clavorum quidem puncturas sed ipsos clavos ex eius carne compositos

> [not nail punctures but the real nails in the form of raised flesh scars]

with the head of the nail on one side and the nail not only piercing the hand but the point of the nail hammered down and flattened against the back of the hand. This is a decisive shift, because Thomas wants to stress that these nails were not only made *in* the flesh of St. Francis, but that they were formed *of his very body*, coming from within St. Francis. What Elias tried to promote was exactly the reverse; Elias understood the stigmata to be received from outside of St. Francis. Thomas of Celano stressed that the marks came from within St. Francis just as if he had been crucified *with* Christ on the cross (*ac si in cruce cum Dei filio pendisset*)—not instead of Christ, but as a replica of Christ. Thomas means that he did not receive these wounds *by* Christ, but *with* Christ. The nails were a copy of the nails in Christ's flesh. Thomas sees the black nails as an outer manifestation of the inner suffering of St. Francis, suffering of a spiritual nature. Thomas emphasizes the idea that this apparition pointed the way from inner suffering to the presence of God. He gives a symbolical explanation of the seraph's wings: their meaning is the Christians' journey—the movement from a virtuous life of good deeds to God.[9] Thomas does not go so far as to say that the body of St. Francis has become divine as a result of the stigmata; he always speaks of a seraph and of a man, not conflating the figures of seraph and Christ.

---

[9] Thomas of Celano, *Vita prima*, pars 2, cap. 9, 114 (in *AF,* 10:89–90).

According to Thomas, St. Francis, just before the apparition of the man-seraph, wanted to know how his life would end. Pondering this, he opened the Bible three times,[10] and each time it opened to the same page in the Gospels where Christ is on the Mount of Olives before the crucifixion.[11] With this in mind as he shaped his account of the stigmata, Thomas pictured St. Francis as being like Christ, feeling very alone and suffering on the Mount of Olives as described in Luke 22.39–46. Christ asks: "Father, if thou art willing, remove this cup from me," and then comes to understand that he must accept the suffering of the coming crucifixion. After the vision of an angel, Christ is consoled, but nevertheless he goes on suffering, and blood comes out of his skin like perspiration—he "sweats blood."[12] Like Christ, St. Francis is on Mount Verna, he sees the seraph, and he understands that he must accept all the sufferings that are coming. As a result of his mental sufferings St. Francis receives the stigmata, and like Christ, he sweats blood. That is, after the vision of the seraph disappears, St. Francis's mental sufferings with Christ are manifested in the stigmata. Thus Thomas wants to stress the identification of St. Francis with Christ on

---

[10] This "superstitious" gesture—if the book opened three times at the same page, God was speaking—was called in the Middle Ages *sortes apostolorum*, because it was believed that in this way the Apostles chose another apostle to replace Judas. See R. Manselli, *San Francesco* (Rome: Bulzoni, 1980), 87ff.

[11] Thomas of Celano, *Vita prima*, pars 2, cap. 2, 92–93 (in *AF*, 10:70–71, and particularly p. 71): "Factum est autem, cum aperuisset librum, occurrit sibi primo Passio Domini nostri Jesu Christi, et id solum quod tribulationem eum passurum denuntiabat. Sed, ne hoc casu evenisse possit aliquatenus suspicari, bis et ter librum aperuit, et idem vel simile scriptum invenit. Intellexit tunc vir spiritu Dei plenus, quod per multas tribulationes, per multas angustias et per multas pugnas oporteret eum intrare in regnum Dei." [It happened that, when he had opened the book, what first met his eye was the Passion of our Lord Jesus Christ, and just that passage which foretold that he would suffer tribulation. However, lest it be thought this happened by chance, a second and a third time he opened the book, and again he found the very same passage. Full of the spirit of God, he understood then that only after many tribulations, many difficulties and many struggles could he enter God's kingdom.]

[12] Christ is shown sweating blood (while the angel is bringing him a chalice full of the symbols of the Passion), for example, in the frescoes of the Franciscan hermitage founded by Lord Niccolo della Corvaia (then a Franciscan tertiary) of Belverde near Cetona (Siena), about the end of the fourteenth century. The images of a few saints, among them St. Francis (who also appears in the eposode of the stigmata), accompany the Christological cycle. See E. Carli, *Gli affreschi di Belverde* (Florence: Edam, 1977), figs. 50–52 (Christ); fig. 15 (St. Francis); figs. 30–33 (St. Francis's stigmata).

the Mount of Olives, and the meaning of the vision, concentrating on the suffering of St. Francis as spiritual suffering.

A contrasting account is in the *Legend of the Three Companions*,[13] which perhaps even predates[14] the *Life* by Thomas of Celano. The *Legend* speaks of a very beautiful seraph, and stresses the burning love experienced by the saint in seeing the beautiful face of Christ in this seraph, rather than stressing the internal suffering of St. Francis.[15] It is thus this burning love which produces the nails.

I want to underline the great resistance to thinking of Francis as a parallel to the crucified Christ, even if Thomas of Celano had spoken of a beautiful seraph and of a man (not Christ!) crucified. Describing the vision, Thomas does not stress the hands and feet of the crucified man, as Bonaventure does, but speaks always of spiritual sufferings. As a consequence, there would have been a faint possibility of painting a crucified seraph, but the painters before Bonaventure preferred to retain just the image of the seraph, without the stigmata. In this detail they are in agreement with the *Legend of the Three Companions*. In the *Legenda maior* of Bonaventure, which is a mosaic of quotations from previous sources, Thomas's account is repeated also, but with a very important, though small, difference: Francis opens the Gospel three times not to the announced Passion but to the culminating moment of the Crucifixion.[16] In this way, the accent shifts from a spiritual, mental suffering, to a physical one. St. Francis, in order to be able to feel in his body the sharp pain of the torturing nails, has to *receive the pain from*

---

[13] *Legenda trium sociorum*, critical edition by Th. Desbonnet in *Archivum Franciscanum Historicum* 67 (1974): 38–144, esp. pp. 141–43.

[14] Chiara Frugoni, "La giovinezza di Francesco nelle fonti (testi e immagini)," *Studi medioevali* 25 (1984): 115–43.

[15] For the stigmata seen as the result of an inner flame of divine love see E. Gilson, "L'Interprétation traditionnelle des stigmates," *Revue d'histoire franciscaine* 2 (1925): 467–79.

[16] St. Bonaventure, *Legenda maior S. Francisci Assisiensis*, cap. 13, 2 (in *AF*, 10:616): "Sane cum in trina libri apertione Domini passio occurreret, intellexit vir Deo plenus, quod sicut Christum fuerat imitatus in actibus vitae, sic conformis ei esse deberet in afflictionibus et doloribus passionis, antequam ex hoc mundo transire." [Therefore as the book opened for the third time on the Passion of the Lord, the man full of God understood, that just as he had imitated Christ in the actions of life, so he would have to conform to Him in the afflictions and sorrows of the passion, before he could pass from this world.]

the outside and, in this manner, he is ready to become another Christ not only in his soul, but even in the flesh.

It seems that later painted representations are very different from earlier ones, and that the *turning point* is the writing of Bonaventure, and the painting of Giotto. To illustrate this I will survey some paintings which reveal the progression of thought. In a miniature from the early thirteenth century (fig. 1), neither the seraph nor Francis has the stigmata; in this example the two events of the vision and the stigmata do not coincide.[17] The earliest preserved image of St. Francis and the seraph occurs in the panel by Bonaventure Berlinghieri, dated 1235 (fig. 2).[18] Francis is kneeling at the base of La Verna, with his hands in prayer. The seraph is completely enveloped in its own wings, only its hands and feet exposed. Though the cross itself is absent, the position of the exposed hands and feet serve to suggest it. As described in the *Legend of the Three Companions*, the seraph is extremely beautiful. The iconography here corresponds to the account of St. Francis given by Thomas of Celano in the first version of his *Life*. Further, compare the Berlinghieri panel with the depiction of Christ on the Mount of Olives, as rendered on the earlier bronze doors of the cathedral of Benevento, dating from the late twelfth century (fig. 3):[19] in the St. Francis panel, the praying figure of Francis kneels at the base of La Verna, while the seraph occupies the section of blue sky above; in the detail from the bronze doors, Christ is represented kneeling on the Mount of Olives, with the angel leaning out of his sphere in the sky above as from a window.

The same iconography is seen in a much later but related panel painting[20] by Roberto d'Oderisio, a Neapolitan painter of the second

---

[17] Fitzwilliam Museum, Cambridge, MS. 300, fol. 24v. The miniature is published and discussed by J. Gardner, "The Louvre Stigmatization and the Problem of the Narrative Altarpiece," *Zeitschrift Für Kunstgeschichte* 45 (1982): 226. As for the iconography, the miniature follows that of the panel painted by Bonaventure Berlinghieri in 1235 (fig. 2). This miniature is not an exception; I have gathered a good number of examples which I am planning to publish in a book on St. Francis.

[18] *Francesco d'Assisi. Storia e Arte*, Catalogue of the Franciscan Exhibitions of 1982 in Assisi (Milan: Electa), 116.

[19] Gertrude Schiller, *Ikonographie der christlichen Kunst* (Gutersloh: Gutersloher Verlagshaus G. Mohn, 1966), fig. 145, 2:55ff.

[20] Printed in *La pittura in Italia. Le origini* (Milan: Electa, 1985), fig. 663, p. 427.

half of the fourteenth century (fig. 4), in which the angel is a red seraph. In the panel by Bonaventure Berlinghieri the angel is connected with St. Francis by a golden river which seems to divide the mountain into two halves.

We have also the painting by the Master of St. Francis (fig. 5), which is kept in the Bardi Chapel in Santa Croce in Florence.[21] I date this work to about the year 1243. The painter is following the first account of Thomas of Celano. Here the seraph, still without any cross, is looking toward St. Francis and seems to serve only as a link between earth and sky; the beams originate in the sky behind the seraph, curve from behind him and lead directly to the face of St. Francis. The beams of gold suggest the idea of divine communication as seen in other contexts: there are three beams here, recalling the Trinity, and very often three beams of gold connect the Virgin with God during the episode of the Annunciation; further, golden beams often connect the divine Fatherhood of God with Christ, as seen, for example, in the mosaic of San Marco in Venice (fig. 6).[22]

In a somewhat later work now preserved in the museum of Orte (fig. 7),[23] St. Francis is again seen in the praying position (fig. 8). The

---

[21] Frugoni, *Francesco*, fig. 12, pp. 26–28. For the first time the arms of St. Francis are open in the ancient gesture of prayer. There is a very similar panel at the Galleria degli Uffizi, Florence (half of a diptych), attributed to an anonymous painter of the thirteenth century (or to the Master of the Bardi St. Francis, active between 1240–1270: Gli Uffizi, *Catalogo Generale* [Florence: Centro Di, 198], p. 353, N. p. 948). Just the episode of the stigmata, however, is represented and, because of the influence of Bonaventure, the seraph is shown crucified (fig. 13). In the Lower Church of San Francesco of Assisi, where, for the first time, a cycle of the life of St. Francis was painted in fresco around 1260 by an anonymous painter called the Master of St. Francis, the seraph is without a cross—the figure of the saint is destroyed; on this see G. Lobrichon, *Les fresques de la Basilique inférieure* (Paris: Cerf, 1985), 68. We find the same iconography in the slightly later stained glass window in the nave of the Upper Church, attributed to the same master: the seraph is now affixed to the cross and St. Francis, with open arms, is in an ambiguous position is he falling down or rising up?—and for the first time the wound of the breast is visible; the painter is now obliged to follow the *Legenda maior* (see *Corpus vitrearum medii aevi*, Italia, 1, of *L'Umbria. Le Vetrate dell'Umbria* by G. Mancini [Rome: De Luca, 1973], 66–67); and for the reproduction of St. Francis only, *Giotto e i Giotteschi in Assisi*, D.A.C.A., fig. 26.

[22] O. Demus, *The Mosaics of San Marco in Venice* (Chicago: Univ. of Chicago Press, 1984), vol. 2, 2, *The Thirteenth Century*, pl. 17: west arm, south wall: *Kneeling Christ on the Mount of Olives*. Demus attributes this part of the mosaic to the "third master," around 1220 (ibid., vol. 2, 1, pp. 16 and 20).

[23] *Francesco d'Assisi. Storia e Arte*, 120.

seraph, who is now fixed to the cross, is still without signs linking him bodily to St. Francis; the connection of the seraph with the saint is, however, indicated by three golden beams starting from the mouth of the angel, and going to the mouth of the saint. This detail is based on friar Leo's account which said that the seraph appeared and spoke with St. Francis. This iconography of divine communication through the breath of God may also be seen in another context in Perugia, in the Sala dei Notari (Hall of Notaries); a golden beam starting from the mouth of Christ and arriving at the mouth of Adam was the device used to express the divine breath which forms Adam in the image of God and like God (fig. 9).[24]

In the image at Orte only four episodes are represented: two from the life of St. Francis (the stigmata and the preaching to the birds), and two which relate miracles (one of the chicken and fish, and one of the vanishing stigmata).[25] The miracle of the vanishing stigmata is related by Thomas of Celano in his *Treatise on Miracles*, written in 1253. The story tells of a lady who asked a painter to paint for her an image of St. Francis to keep in the room where she prayed. To her great disappointment the painter omitted the stigmata. However, one day the stigmata miraculously appeared and the woman called her daughter, who confirmed the miracle. After the daughter's confirmation the sign disappeared again. With some embarrassment, Thomas of Celano concludes that God sent this second miracle to affirm the first miracle of the stigmata. In the depiction of this story (fig. 10) we see the image of St. Francis bearing the stigmata, and in front of it a crowd led by the lady and her daughter. The crowd is the painter's invention to make the miracle better attested to, and to inspire more devotion. This indicates to us that by 1282 it was still so difficult to accept the miracle at La Verna that it needed another miracle to reinforce its authenticity. However, the second miracle was ephemeral, indeed.

The final source of this story is Bonaventure, who changed it completely. He ordered the destruction of all the early accounts of the life

---

[24] Follower of Pietro Cavallini, Perugia, Palazzo del Cambio, reproduced by R. Longhi, *La pittura umbra della prima metà del Trecento* (Florence: Sansoni, 1973), fig. 32.

[25] On the miracle of the chicken and fish, see Thomas of Celano, *Vita secunda*, cap. 48 (in *AF*, 10:177–78); on the miracle of the vanishing stigmata, see Thomas of Celano, *Tractatus de miraculis S. Francisci Assisiensis* (in *AF*, 10:275–77).

of St. Francis, and, cleverly forming a mosaic of the various ideas, he issued his own version which enabled him to restore peace to his factious Order. For example, he writes that from a distance the vision looked like a seraph, but as it came closer, St. Francis saw that it was Christ. And while retaining the concept of the stigmata coming from within St. Francis, Bonaventure indicates that these wounds began to appear *at the same moment* that the vision disappeared. Thus he makes the two events so close together in time that they almost overlap. In doing so he offers the painters another possibility: they can illustrate the vision of the seraph as Christ with the stigmata already appearing.

A new iconography of the stigmata is exemplified by a late thirteenth-century work (fig. 11) which is kept in the Pinacoteca of Siena.[26] The text followed by the painter is that of Bonaventure, since the four miracles used for the canonization of St. Francis, always represented in the earlier works, are here missing. These are the miracles which St. Bonaventure suppressed in his text. The painter chose the moment, described by Bonaventure, of the vanishing vision. When the vision was very near it resembled a crucified man, when it was far away it looked like a seraph.[27] In fact here the seraph is not like Christ at all, and the saint is not kneeling; he is just standing with his arms stretching up as if to hold on to the vanishing vision. These are details which Bonaventure took from the *Legend of the Three Companions*, which says that St. Francis, just before the stigmata, felt himself rising up toward God attracted by a burning seraphic desire. Also from the *Legend* comes the tale that, while St. Francis was praying on the feast of the exaltation of the Cross on Mount Verna, the seraph appeared with six wings. When the vision disappeared, the soul of Francis was like a red-hot iron, and the stigmata of Christ were generated in his flesh.[28]

The same pattern is followed in a diptych of about the same time or

---

[26] The panel comes from the church of San Francesco at Colle Val d'Elsa near Siena and is attributed to a follower of Guido da Siena (toward the end of the thirteenth century): F. Torriti, *La pinacoteca nazionale di Siena* (Genoa: Sagep, 1977), 39. The right hand of St. Francis is still without stigmata.

[27] *Legenda maior*, cap. 13, 23 (in *AF*, 10:617).

[28] *Legenda trium sociorum*, cap. 17, 69 (in *AF*, 10:142–43).

perhaps a little later (fig. 12).[29] The only difference is that the seraph is crucified—in this case the painter put together the two aspects of the vision by Bonaventure—and the three beams of gold go *from the mouth of the seraph* to the mouth of St. Francis. This is a detail taken from Leo's account on St. Francis, which still maintained the idea that the stigmata are coming from within the flesh of St. Francis. The lines are of gold or a dark color, and they do not cross. In later works the beams change color: they are blood red, and they cross from Christ like arrows, to pierce the flesh of St. Francis from Christ's own wounds. In the earlier depictions, the Christ is like a mirror for St. Francis. Only St. Francis is real, while the vision is like St. Francis's own image in a mirror. I will show this more clearly as I discuss the paintings.

Giotto is the painter of great genius who interpreted the text and even improved on it, as we see in the Assisi fresco (fig. 13) which he painted around 1290. It is very similar to the painting from the church of San Francesco in Pisa, also by Giotto, which was painted and signed around 1300 (fig. 14) and so I will describe the Pisa one in more detail.[30] In the Assisi fresco Giotto introduced the companion holding the Gospel opened at the Passion, following Bonaventure's text: Francis *Evangeliorum . . . librum aperiri fecit per socium, virum utique Deo devotum et sanctum.*[31] Since the cycle is the official representation of the life of St. Francis, it was necessary to depict the witness to the event. In the painting at Pisa this detail was no longer necessary, and Giotto suppressed it. As in the Assisi fresco, the seraph is Christ, but now has a black beard and a halo with a cross within it. In addition, Giotto lowers the wings of the seraph so that we can see the wound in the breast of Christ. Giotto links St. Francis and Christ by beams, which,

---

[29] Diptych of St. Clare, attributed to a follower of Guido da Siena and kept in the pinacoteca of Siena: see Torriti, *La pinacoteca,* 37, who dates it about 1280. Since St. Clare was canonized in the year 1255, the diptych must be after this date. A repetition of the detail of the stigmata in the work at Colle Val d'Elsa is seen in a diptych painted by Andrea Gallerani. It is kept in the Pinacoteca in Siena and dated around 1270 (see Torriti, *La pinacoteca,* 35). It is obviously attributed to a follower of Guido da Siena: the seraph is attached to the cross, there are no beams, and the left hand of the rising Francis is still without stigmata.

[30] See Gardner, "The Louvre Stigmatization," 234, whom I follow also for the sequence of Giotto's work: Assisi fresco, Pisa icon, Bardi chapel fresco (see later in the main text).

[31] *Legenda maior,* cap. 13, 2–3 (in *AF,* 10:616).

as in the Assisi fresco, go to the hands, feet, and breast of St. Francis.[32] Further suggesting that the vision appeared during the Feast of the Exaltation of the Cross, as Bonaventure wrote, Giotto shows a great cross in the little chapel at the right hand side of the composition. On this arm of that great cross we see the Virgin mourning her Son. Even though by the end of the thirteenth century the feet of Christ are usually shown as one on top of the other, Giotto retains the older iconography of keeping the feet apart, making it easier to illustrate the connection of the beams from Christ to St. Francis. It is important to remember that, for Bonaventure, the stigmata coming from the flesh of St. Francis are a consequence of his burning love of God, engendered by his vision. For this reason the beams proceed directly as if being reflected in a mirror, and not diagonally as if coming from the corresponding sides of the person in the vision. The identification of St. Francis with Christ is very close.

Yet Giotto further improves this iconography in the following fresco, in the Bardi Chapel in Santa Croce in Florence (fig. 15). In this fresco he overlaps the feet of Christ, making it easier to cross the beams, for the first time, as they go from Christ to St. Francis to the hands and feet.

The final version of the stigmata, which goes beyond the bounds of this paper, is a complete change of both representation and meaning. In this version the stigmata come from Christ, the beams are blood red, and like arrows which pierce the flesh of St. Francis. With this seal, with this branding, St. Francis becomes divine. The source of power is outside of St. Francis and the vision is not a mirror-like reflection, but rather the generating power is going on from outside inside St. Francis's skin. The beams from the Bardi fresco do not go forward directly but transversely (fig. 16).

This idea, so new and bold, is wonderfully expressed in a cross by Margaritone of Arezzo (fig. 17).[33] Francis has substituted himself for

---

[32] The beams are golden in the Assisi fresco, and black in the Pisa work (now kept in the Louvre).

[33] For the description of this cross, I follow the analysis of G. Didi-Huberman, "Un sang d'images," *Nouvelle Revue de Psychoanalyse* 32 (1985): 137–38, who speaks from a completely different point of view of the problem of the "reality" or not of the blood in the image, and, with regard to the cross of Margaritone, says (p. 137): "la relation de saint François à l'image du Christ en croix se présente-t-elle souvent, des

the Magdalene, and he is embracing the right foot of Christ. He kisses the nail from which the blood is spilling. The rivulet of blood substitutes for the device of the beams. The blood drips down to the hands of the saint; one hand has already formed a mark. Then the blood falls on the feet of St. Francis and crosses, so that the blood spilled by the right foot of Christ drips on to the right foot of St. Francis and vice versa. The foot on the much larger figure of Christ reaches the breast of St. Francis, the clothing is open, and we see the wound in St. Francis's side.

In the words of Dante, "Francis has taken from Christ his final seal."

---

le XIIIᵉ siècle, comme une relation d'*incorporation* plutôt que de face-à-face spéculaire." [The relation of St. Francis to the image of Christ on the cross presents itself often, from the thirteenth century, as a relation of *incorporation* rather than of a specular face to face.] The author has also noticed that in some images of St. Francis's stigmata the beams cross, and in some others they do not, but the explanation he gives comes from a psychoanalytical, not a historical, point of view; for this reason he completely ignores the problem of the changing texts in relation to the changing official image of the founder of the Franciscan order.

Fig. 1. *The Vision of St. Francis*. Fitzwilliam Museum MS. 300, fol. 204v. Dated before 1270. Cambridge.

Fig. 2. Bonaventure Berlinghieri. *The Stigmatization of St. Francis. Detail from St. Francis and Scenes from His Legend.* 1235. Panel. San Francesco, Pescia.

Fig. 3. *Christ on Mount of Olives*. 12th century. Detail from bronze doors, Cathedral, Benevento.

Fig. 4. Roberto d'Oderisio. *Christ on Mount of Olives.* Second half of the 14th century. Panel. Fogg Art Museum, Harvard Univ., Cambridge, Mass.

Fig. 5. Master of the Bardi St. Francis. *The Stigmatization of St. Francis.* 1243. Detail from *The Life of St. Francis.* Bardi Chapel, Santa Croce, Florence.

Fig. 6. "Third Master". *Christ on Mount of Olives*. Around 1220. Mosaic. West arm, south wall, San Marco, Venice.

Fig. 7. *St. Francis*. Around 1282. Museum, Orte.

Fig. 8. *The Stigmatization of St. Francis*. Detail of Fig. 7, *St. Francis*.

Fig. 9. Follower of Pietro Cavallini. *The Creation of Adam*. Fresco. 14th century. Sala dei Notari, Perugia.

Fig. 10. *The Miracle of the Vanishing Stigmata.* Detail of Fig. 7, *St. Francis.*

Fig. 11. Follower of Guido da Siena. *The Stigmatization of St. Francis.*
Panel. Last quarter of the 13th century. Pinacoteca, Siena.

Fig. 12. Follower of Guido da Siena. *The Stigmatization of St. Francis.*
Detail from *St. Clare.* Around 1280. Pinacoteca, Siena.

Fig. 13. Giotto (?). *Stigmatization of St. Francis*. Around 1290. Upper Church of San Francesco, Assisi.

Fig. 14. Giotto. *Stigmatization of St. Francis*. Around 1300. Originally in the church of San Francesco in Pisa, now kept in the Louvre, Paris.

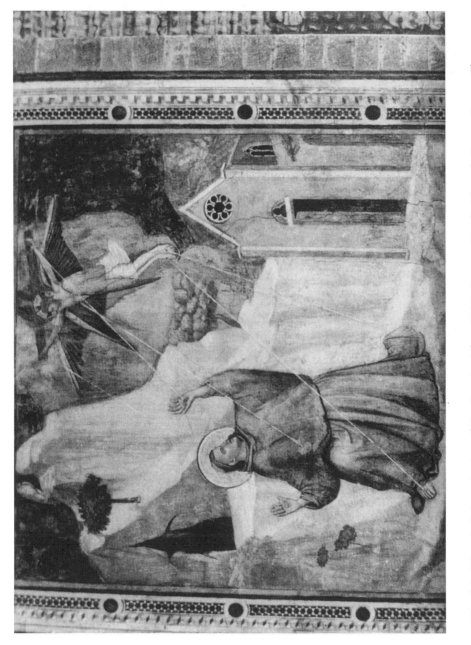

Fig. 15. Giotto. *Stigmatization of St. Francis.* After 1317. Fresco. Bardi Chapel, Santa Croce, Florence.

Fig. 16. Pietro Lorenzetti. *The Stigmatization of St. Francis.* Around 1319–1320. Fresco. Lower Church of San Francesco, Assisi.

Fig. 17. Margaritone of Arezzo. *St. Francis Kissing the Feet of Christ*. Detail
from *Crucifixion*. 13th century. San Francesco, Arezzo.

Benozzo Gozzoli's Cycle of the Life of Saint Francis in Montefalco: Hagiography and Homily*

DIANE COLE AHL

he frescoes of the life of Saint Francis in San Francesco, Montefalco constitute an important chapter in the history of sacred art (Fig. 1).[1] They were painted by Benozzo Gozzoli in 1452 in the choir of the town's major Franciscan church. As one of the few fifteenth-century cycles of the saint's

* I wish to express my deep gratitude to the *comune* of Montefalco and their *sindaco,* the Honorable Dott. Angelo Preziosi, as well as to Dott.ssa Maila Orazi for their extraordinary generosity and gracious hospitality during my visits to their beautiful town. My early research on the chapel was facilitated greatly by the resources of the Franciscan Institute at Saint Bonaventure University. Dott. Gino Corti kindly corroborated the accuracy of all the archival material to which I refer, access to which was obtained through the kind offices of Prof. Roberto Abbondanza. Prof. Howard Marblestone assisted my translation of the Latin inscriptions. Benozzo's other Franciscan commissions of the 1450s and their historic context are discussed at greater length in Chapter Two of my forthcoming monograph, *Benozzo Gozzoli,* to be published by Yale University Press.

[1] A bibliography through 1966 appears in Anna Padoa Rizzo, *Benozzo Gozzoli pittore fiorentino* (Florence: Editrice Edam, 1972). The most significant of these studies and recent publications include Raffaello Morghen, "Tradizione religiosa e Rinascimento nel ciclo degli affreschi francescani a Montefalco," *Atti del V Convegno internazionale di studi sul Rinascimento* (Palazzo Strozzi, Florence, 2–6 settembre 1956) (Florence: Sansoni, 1956), 149–56; Antonio Boschetto, *Benozzo Gozzoli nella chiesa di San Francesco di Montefalco* (Milan: Istituto Editoriale italiano, 1961); Silvestro Nessi, "La

life, these frescoes occupy a significant place in the history of Franciscan iconography.[2] But in spite of their uniqueness, they have been little studied. While proclaiming their influence on local painting, art historians have largely ignored the chapel's patronage and iconography.[3] The textual sources of the individual scenes have been identified,[4] but their meaning and relationship to contemporary Franciscan thought and history have not been fully elucidated. Questions about the historic context and patronage of the frescoes, their relationship to the order's literary and homiletic tradition, and the conception of the saint's life that they express have not been answered.

The cycle provides a unique opportunity to address such concerns. Throughout its history, Montefalco was affiliated closely with Assisi, just thirty kilometers away.[5] Francis performed many miracles in and

---

vita di San Francesco dipinta da Benozzo Gozzoli a Montefalco," *Miscellanea Francescana* 61 (1961): 467–92; Henk Van Os, "St. Francis of Assisi as a second Christ in Early Italian Painting," *Simiolus* 7 (1974): 115–32; Elisabeth Giese, *Benozzo Gozzolis Franziskuszyklus in Montefalco: Bildkomposition als Erzählung* (Frankfurt am Main: Lang, 1986); Bruno Toscano, ed., *Museo Comunale di San Francesco a Montefalco* (Perugia: Electa, 1990), 106–14.

[2] For Franciscan cycles, see George Kaftal, *Saint Francis in Italian Painting* (London: Allen and Unwin, 1950); idem, *Iconography of the Saints in Central and Southern Italian Schools of Painting* (Florence: Sansoni, 1965), 469–500; and idem, *Iconography of the Saints in the Painting of North West Italy* (Florence: Sansoni: 1985), 284–304; Pietro Scarpellini, "Iconografia francescana nei secoli XIII e XIV," in *Francesco d'Assisi. Storia e Arte* (Milan: Electa, 1982), 91–126; Dieter Blume, *Wandmalerei als Ordenspropaganda. Bildprogramme im Chorbereich franziskanische Konvente italiens bis zur Mittes des 14. Jahrhunderts* (Worms: Werner'sche Verlagsgesellschaft, 1983); and Mario Pavone, *Iconologia Francescana. Il Quattrocento* (Todi: Ediart, 1988).

[3] Typifying this approach are the monographs of G.-J. Hoogewerff, *Benozzo Gozzoli* (Paris: Collection Art et Esthétique, 1930), 12–15, and Marcel Lagaisse, *Benozzo Gozzoli* (Paris: Henri Laurens, 1934), 156–60.

[4] Nessi, "La vita di San Francesco," cites the texts for these scenes.

[5] Silvestro Nessi, "Storia e arte delle chiese francescane di Montefalco," *Miscellanea Francescana* 62 (1962): 232–332; and Giovanna Chiuini, "Montefalco," in Federico Zeri, ed., *Storia dell'arte italiana: inchieste su centri minori*, vol. 8 (Turin: Einaudi, 1980), 206–18. On the early history of the town, see Silvestro Nessi, *Le Origini del comune di Montefalco* (Spoleto: Arti Grafiche Panetto e Petrelli, 1977). On Francis's preaching to the birds, see Ewert Cousins, trans., *Bonaventure. The Soul's Journey into God. The Tree of Life. The Life of Saint Francis* (New York: Paulist Press, 1978), 12.3, 294–95. On the miraculous spring of water, see the account in Joannis Hyacinthi Sbaraleae, *Bullarium Franciscanum Romanorum pontificum, constitutiones, epistolas, ac diplomata continens Tribus Ordinibus Minorum, Clarissarum, et Poenitentium a S. Patre Francisco institutis concessa*, vol. 4 (Rome: Typis Sacrae Congregationis de Propaganda Fide, 1768), 253 n. 1.

around Montefalco. In the nearby town of Bevagna, he preached to the birds. Outside of San Rocco in Montefalco, the *poverello* caused a spring of fresh water to gush forth from the parched earth. As early as 1215, a Franciscan hermitage had been established outside the city walls,[6] and the order's strength never diminished there. Indeed, this small town and its environs supported no fewer than eleven Franciscan churches during the Middle Ages and Renaissance.[7]

Two centuries after the saint's death, chronicles and documents attest to the intimacy between the town and the Franciscan order. Documents from Assisi record friars from Montefalco serving in important capacities throughout the fifteenth century.[8] In 1425, San Bernardino of Siena preached at San Francesco in Montefalco.[9] Fra Antonio da Montefalco was appointed Provincial Vicar of the Reformed Franciscans in all of Umbria in 1442; fully committed to Observant ideals, he had begun the reform of the nunnery of Monteluce and Montefalco's own monastery of San Fortunato by decade's end.[10] A brilliant orator who fervently promoted the Crusades, he was nominated to the papacy after Nicholas V died, and he served as Vicar General of the Italian Observance in 1457. The first Chapters General of the Franciscan tertiaries *in virtute sanctae obedientiae* were celebrated in Montefalco's church of San Rocco in 1448 and 1451.[11] When Benozzo's frescoes in San

---

[6] Nessi, "La vita di San Francesco," 469.

[7] Nessi, "Storia e arte," 232.

[8] As may be deduced from Cesare Cenci, *Documentazione di vita assisiana, 1300–1530*, vol. 1 (Grottaferrata: Editiones Collegii S. Bonaventurae ad Claras Aquas, 1974), passim.

[9] On the dates of San Bernardino's presence in Montefalco, see Antonio Palmucci Genolini, "S. Bernardino da Siena a Montefalco," *Miscellanea Francescana* 1 (1886): 185–86.

[10] In Chapter Two of my forthcoming *Benozzo Gozzoli*, I reconstruct the life and artistic patronage of Fra Antonio, a luminary of the Franciscan Osservanza, who commissioned Benozzo's earliest works in Montefalco for the monastery of San Fortunato. Major sources for his life are collected in compendia of documents published by Antonio da Stroncone, "L'Umbria serafica," *Miscellanea Francescana* 4 (1889): 158–87; ibid. 5 (1890): 28, 69f., 86–90; Bonaventura Marinangeli, "Descrizione e memorie della Chiesa e del Convento di San Francesco a Montefalco," *Miscellanea Francescana* 14 (1913): 137–39, 142; Cenci, *Documentazione di vita assisiana*, 468, 569, 572; and Ugolino Nicolini, ed., *Memoriale di Monteluce* (Assisi: Casa Editrice Francescana, 1983), 4.

[11] Gabriele Andreozzi, "S. Rocco in Montefalco," *Analecta T.O.R.* 5–6 (1949–52): 81–89, 169–75, 345–47.

Francesco were completed in 1452,[12] the Franciscans dominated the town's spiritual life in virtually every sphere.

San Francesco was the major church in Montefalco.[13] It was founded in 1328 as the order's first monastery within the city walls, and soon became a focal point of artistic patronage. Though the church has been renovated extensively, fresco fragments and completely preserved chapels suggest that its interior once glowed with color.[14] The nave is dominated by its lofty, luminous choir, decorated with Benozzo's frescoes of the life of Saint Francis and the triumph of the order he founded. As the inscriptions on the north and south walls attest,[15] these frescoes were completed in 1452 at the behest of Fra Iacopo, one of the brethren.

The archives of San Francesco have been largely destroyed, and no contract for the frescoes is known to exist. However, documents not previously associated with this commission establish the patron's erudition and contacts with Assisi.[16] A notary from Assisi recorded Fra Iacopo as *lector sacri conventus* in 1437. Later that same year, the friar served as *magistro novitiorum pro predicazione*. In 1441, he was document-

---

[12] This is stated in the inscription on the south wall: IN NOMINE SANCTISSIME TRINITATIS HANC CAPELLAM PINSIT BENOTIUS FLORENTINUS SUB ANNIS DOMINI MILLESIMO QUADRINGENTESIMO QUINQUAGESIMO SECUNDO. QUALIS SIT PICTOR PREFATUS INSPICE LECTOR (This chapel of the most Holy Trinity was painted by Benozzo of Florence in the Year of our Lord One Thousand Four Hundred Fifty-Two. See for yourself, O reader, what sort of painter has made the preamble.). Without citing what is apparently an archival source, Silvestro Nessi, *Montefalco e il suo Territorio* (Spoleto: Arti Grafiche Panetto e Petrelli, 1980), 36, states that donations were made that year *pro coro magno fiendo* as well.

[13] On the history of the church, see Nessi, "Storia e arte," 252–68.

[14] Indeed, San Francesco is now a museum: see Silvestro Nessi and Pietro Scarpellini, *La Chiesa-museo di S. Francesco a Montefalco* (Spoleto: Arti Grafiche Panetto e Petrelli, 1972), and Toscano, *Museo Comunale.*

[15] The north wall inscription reads: AD LAUDEM OMNIPOTENTIS DEI AC BEATISSIME MATRIS EIUS ET BEATI FRANCISCI ANTONII LUDOVICI BERNARDINI CLARE ET HELZEARE ET [H]OC OPUS FECIT FIERI FRATER IACOBUS DE MONTE FALCONE ORDINIS MINORUM (In praise of Almighty God and of his Most Blessed Mother, as well as of Saints Francis, Anthony, Louis, Bernardino, Claire, and Eleazar. And this work was commissioned by Fra Iacopo da Montefalco of the Friars Minor.). For that of the south wall, see n. 12, above.

[16] The two notices from Assisi are published in Cenci, *Documentazione di vita assisiana*, 530 and 532, respectively.

ed as a *lector* in Bologna,[17] famed for its university's school of theology. By decade's end, Fra Iacopo had returned to Umbria. Along with the Observant reformer Fra Antonio da Montefalco, he joined the Perugian *confraternità di San Girolamo*, which was founded to promote the order's spiritual values.[18] Fra Iacopo must have been grounded thoroughly in Franciscan thought by the time he commissioned the choir frescoes in 1452. As its patron, he is likely to have composed its iconographic program. In contrast to the Saint Francis cycle at Assisi which depends on Bonaventure's authoritative *Legenda maior*,[19] the Montefalco cycle is inspired by several sources, attesting to Fra Iacopo's erudition.

The theme of the frescoes is the *leitmotif* of Franciscan thought: Francis as *alter Christus*.[20] In addition to its appearance in official as well as non-canonical Franciscan texts throughout the Middle Ages,[21] this fundamental doctrine is underscored in writings and sermons from the late thirteenth through early fifteenth centuries.[22] From Thomas

---

[17] Stroncone, "L'Umbria serafica," 157.

[18] On the confraternity, founded by the Observant preacher Fra Giacomo della Marca, see Silvestro Nessi, "La Confraternità di San Girolamo in Perugia," *Miscellanea Francescana* 67 (1967): 78–115. *Frate Antonio da Monte Falcho, vicario* and *Frate Giapeco [=Iacopo] da Monte Falco* are listed among the brethren who joined in 1448 and 1449.

[19] The literature on the cycle—its attribution, chronology, and iconography—is voluminous. Three recent studies are excellent. For its iconography, see Charles Mitchell, "The Imagery of the Upper Church at Assisi," in *Giotto e il suo tempo, Atti del Congresso internazionale per la celebrazione del VII centenario della nascita di Giotto*, 24 settembre–1 ottobre 1967 (Rome: De Luca, 1971), 113–34; and Gerhard Ruf *Franziskus und Bonaventura: die heilsgeschichtliche Deutung der Fresken im Langhaus der Oberkirche von San Francesco in Assisi aus der Theologie des Heiligen Bonaventura* (Assisi: Casa Editrice Francescana, 1974). Alastair Smart, *The Assisi Problem and the Art of Giotto* (Oxford: Clarendon Press, 1971), convincingly discusses the frescoes from a variety of perspectives.

[20] The first critic to identify the thematic unity of the cycle at Montefalco was Morghen, "Tradizione religiosa."

[21] Stanislao da Campagnola, *L'Angelo del sesto sigillo e "l'alter Christus"* (Rome: Ed. Antonianum, 1971), traces the origins and development of this fundamental theme of Franciscan theology through the fourteenth century.

[22] See San Bernardino, "De homine novo et peregrino cui beatus Franciscus vel alius sanctus potest appropriari" and "De stigmatibus gloriosi Francisci," *Opera omnia*, vol. 5, (Florence: Quaracchi, 1956), 191–203; 204–30, respectively. For Franciscan authors of the fifteenth century and major themes of their writings, see Atanasio G. Matanic, "Le Fonti francescane conosciute dagli storici del 1400," in Gerardo Cardaropoli and Martino Conti, eds., *Lettura delle fonti francescane attraverso i secoli: il 1400* (Rome: Ed. Antonianum, 1981), 107–18.

of Celano's assertion that *Christi et beati Francisci una persona foret*
through the later writings of Matthew of Acquasparta, Franciscans proclaimed the saint's perfect identification with the Savior.[23] The *pove-*
rello's likeness to the Lord is the subject of Bartholomew of Pisa's *De*
conformitate vitae B. Francisci ad vitam Domini Iesu (1385–90), a work
fundamental to Franciscan historiography.[24] It recurs in Saint Bernardino's discourse on the stigmatization, which reiterates at length Francis's similitude to Christ.[25] In nearby Foligno, unpublished sermons
on this theme are recorded from the fifteenth century.[26]

The San Francesco frescoes reveal an extraordinary vision immortal-
izing the saint and his order.[27] Thirteen scenes in three tiers recount
the life of Francis from birth to death. The narrative begins on the
lowest register and ascends to the vaults. It rests literally on a frieze of
twenty-three conservators of Franciscan faith, each a portrait identified
by inscription (Fig. 2). Standing in niches, six Franciscan saints, from
Claire to Anthony of Padua and Bernardino, flank the window; five
others appear in the firmament of the vaults. Along the entrance arch,
twelve of Francis's earliest followers—apostles of the *alter Christus*—
surround the *poverello*, who displays the stigmata and faces the congregation.

---

[23] For these authors, see Campagnola, *L'Angelo del sesto sigillo*, 49f. and 190f., respectively.

[24] Bartholomeus Pisanus, *Liber de conformitate vitae beati Francisci ad vitam domini Jesu*,
Analecta Francescana, vols. 4 and 5 (1906, 1912). On this treatise, see Carolly Erickson,
"Bartholomew of Pisa, Francis exalted: *De conformitate*," *Medieval Studies* 34 (1972):
253–74; and more recently, Antonio Blasucci, "Le Fonti francescane nel 'De Conformitate' di Fra' Bartolomeo da Pisa," in Cardaropoli and Conti, *Lettura delle fonti*
francescane, 301–23.

[25] See n. 22, above, for complete reference. Van Os, "St. Francis of Assisi as a
second Christ," 126–30, observes that Bernardino's preaching on this subject expands
themes already expressed in *De conformitate vitae*.

[26] These sermons were preserved in the Biblioteca Comunale, Foligno in C. 37
(A-IX-11-37) and C. 87 (A-IX-IV-87). Both collections of sermons originated from
the monastery of San Bartolomeo, Foligno. Their contents are described explicitly as
Latin and vulgate sermons in the library's inventory, and their subjects are identified
(i.e., "Saint Francis and the Birth of Christ"). Along with a number of other manuscripts, C. 37 and C. 87 were reported stolen from Foligno in 1971.

[27] See n. 20, above. This paragraph follows Morghen, "Tradizione religiosa," who
was the first critic to discern the theme of *Franciscus alter Christus* in the cycle. However, he focuses on the decoration of the intrados and friezes, and only in passing
mentions two of the scenes.

Aligned with this roundel and the altar itself is the saint in apotheosis (Fig. 3). He is seated on clouds and radiates light, calling to mind the description of Francis as *sol in Ecclesia Dei fulgens*, sent to save the world at its time of greatest need, *in ora undecima*.[28] He is dressed as a deacon and bears an open book with the inscription EGO ENIM STIGMATA DOMINI JESU IN CORPORE MEO PORTO (For I bear in my body the marks of the Lord Jesus). Taken from Galatians 6:17, these words are repeated in the chapter on the Sacred Stigmata by Bonaventure,[29] and signify Francis's identification with the Savior. The saint's severe stare, frontality, and attributes seem calculated to recall images of Christ as Pantocrator. Hands impressed with the Lord's wounds, Francis is here transformed into the apocalyptic angel who ushers in the Last Judgment; this, too, is a recurrent theme in the order's writings.[30] Sited above the very keystone of the entrance arch, this image proclaims Francis's role in initiating a new age of grace.

The arrangement and sequence of scenes in the cycle are distinctive, though they conform to a Franciscan narrative tradition.[31] In contrast to many fresco cycles that begin at the top, the early scenes in the saint's life occupy the bottom tier with later events depicted in the upper registers. This "ascending narrative" is a hallmark of Franciscan cycles, found in the Magdalen Chapel and Simone Martini's Saint Martin Chapel in the Lower Church, Assisi, among others.[32] As if to denote spiritual ascension, this narrative mode leads us from the unenlightened early life of the *poverello* to the upper register, in which the Lord's will is served and his sanctity proven.

---

[28] Quoted from the Bull of his canonization, *Mira circa nos*, as cited in Campagnola, *L'Angelo del sesto sigillo*, 127.

[29] Cousins, *Bonaventure*, 13.9, 312.

[30] Campagnola, *L'Angelo del sesto sigillo*; the theme of Francis as *alter Angelus* evidently was inspired by the millennial texts of Joachim of Fiore.

[31] On Franciscan narrative cycles, see Blume, *Wandmalerei als Ordenspropaganda*, and Marilyn Aronberg Lavin, *The Place of Narrative. Mural Decoration in Italian Churches, 431–1600* (Chicago: University of Chicago Press, 1989), 51–70.

[32] My thanks to Eve Borsook (communication of 4 September 1984) for responding to my initial queries on ascending narrative. Lavin, *Place of Narrative*, 7, identifies an "Apse pattern, up" as a distinctive mode of narration. In 1464–65, Benozzo employed an ascending narrative in the apse of Sant'Agostino in San Gimignano; see Diane Cole Ahl, "Benozzo Gozzoli's Frescoes of the Life of Saint Augustine in San Gimignano: Their Meaning in Context," *Artibus et historiae* 13 (1986): 35–53.

The theme of Francis as *alter Christus* is announced by the scene of
the saint's birth (Fig. 4). This episode is not included in early canonical
texts, but is based on apocryphal nativity legends.[33] With the haloed
infant bathed by midwives and attended by ox and ass, this scene
parallels depictions of the birth of Christ. At the same time, the arrest-
ing image of Francis's mother, supported by midwives as she suffers the
pangs of labor, contrasts the saint's mortal birth to the Savior's divine
one. The adjacent episode shows the visit to Francis's home of a
pilgrim who foretells the saint's greatness. The haloed figure resembles
Benozzo's images of Christ in the cycle for good reason: according to
the inscription beneath, this displays QUALITER.B.F.FUIT DEN-
UNTIATUS.A.XPO.INFORMA.PEREGRINI.QUOD.DEBEBEAT.
NASCI.SICUT.IPSE.IN.STABULO (This is how Saint Francis was
given an intimation by Christ, who took the form of a pilgrim. Why
he had to be born, just as Christ, in a manger).[34] To the right, the
youthful Francis and his suddenly wary companion encounter a simple-
ton. Recognizing Francis's future sanctity, he spreads his cloak before the
saint, paralleling Christ's entry into Jerusalem. In the next frame, it is
Francis, moved by charity, who gives *his* cloak to a poor knight (Fig.
5).[35] That night, he dreams of a castle hung with banners which he mis-
takenly construes as a prophecy of a military vocation. The Lord himself
enlightens Francis in a vision, informing him of his true ministry.[36]

The saint's conversion by the speaking crucifix of San Damiano
originally was represented next to this, as a nearly effaced inscription
below the window attests.[37] This critical episode was destroyed when
the window was enlarged in a later renovation.[38] It is no coincidence

---

[33] For these, see Giuseppe Abate, *La casa dove nacque Francesco d'Assisi nella sua
nuova documentazione storica* (Gubbio: Casa editrice Oderisi, 1941).

[34] Pisanus, *Liber de conformitate vitae*, 109, however, describes the visitor as an angel
dressed as a pilgrim, *angelus in specie peregrini*.

[35] Cousins, *Bonaventure*, 1.2, 187.

[36] Cousins, *Bonaventure*, 1.3, 187–88.

[37] QUALITER B. F. IN ECCLESIA SANCTI DAMIANI AUDIVIT CRUCI-
FIXUM TER DICENTEM SIBI FRANCISCE VADE REPARA DOMUM MEAM
ET QUIA IAM.CADIT.VERSA.QUANTITATEM.PECUNIE.IN QUANDAM.FE-
NESTRAM (How Saint Francis in the Church of San Damiano heard the Crucified
saying to him thrice, "Francis, come repair my church," and now a quantity of money
fell through a certain window.).

[38] Tentatively, I might propose that the appearance of this now-lost work may be

that this scene was placed behind the altar, aligned with the *Stigmatization* above, which it prefigured. In this *Stigmatization*, the winged, crucified Savior, rather than the seraph alone,[39] imprints his wounds on the kneeling saint in the adjacent lunette, his golden rays traversing the sacred, liturgical space (Fig. 6).[40] In no other extant cycle is the stigmatization represented in separate frames or this luminous epiphany placed above the window in allusion to the divine light that transfixed the *poverello*, sealing his perfect identification with the Lord.[41] San Bernardino, whose sermon on the stigmatization identified Francis as the apocalyptic angel, is painted against the starry firmament of the vault directly above, and aligned with the image of the saint as Pantocrator. Liturgical needs surely mandated the location of these scenes— in which the cross is the agent of transformation—behind the altar. A

---

reflected in a fresco Benozzo executed just a year after completing the Montefalco chapel. The work in question is *Santa Rosa da Viterbo and the Speaking Crucifix*, a scene from the fresco cycle for Santa Rosa, Viterbo, that Benozzo painted in 1453. Although the murals were destroyed in renovations to the church, watercolor copies in the Museo Civico, Viterbo, preserve their appearance. Benozzo often repeated compositions in his works; parallels between the lives of Francis and Rosa, a Franciscan tertiary, would have been particularly appropriate. Indeed, *Santa Rosa da Viterbo and the Speaking Crucifix* is markedly similar in composition to the Saint Francis Master's *Saint Francis Praying Before the Crucifix at San Damiano*, Upper Church, Assisi. For the Santa Rosa cycle, see Stefania Pasti, "Lo scomparso ciclo di affreschi di S. Rosa da Viterbo di Benozzo Gozzoli e la sua influenza nel Viterbese: Gli Affreschi dell'Isola Bisentina," *Il Quattrocento a Viterbo*, exhibition catalogue, Museo Civico, Viterbo, 11 giugno–10 settembre 1983 (Rome: De Luca, 1983), 159–78, fig. 138; and Diane Cole Ahl, "Benozzo Gozzoli's Santa Rosa da Viterbo Cycle: The Decorum of Saintly Narrative," Francis Ames-Lewis and Anka Bednarek, eds., *Decorum in Renaissance Narrative Art*, (London: Caldra House Ltd., 1992), 61–69, fig. 14.

[39] This suggests an emphasis on the liturgical rather than apocalyptic aspects of the stigmatization. On the latter, see Stefan Bihel, "S. Franciscus fuitne Angelus sexti sigilli?," *Antonianum* 2 (1927): 59–90.

[40] For Van Os, "St. Francis as a second Christ," 130, the sequence of the entire narrative cycle was configured to emphasize the stigmatization.

[41] There is, however, a precedent in stained glass in Assisi; see Lavin, *Place of Narrative*, 332f. n. 78. Benozzo also may have conflated Taddeo Gaddi's solution for the *Annunciation to the Virgin* and the *Stigmatization* on the window wall of the Baroncelli Chapel, Santa Croce, Florence, illustrated in Andrew Ladis, *Taddeo Gaddi. Critical Reappraisal and Catalogue Raisonné* (Columbia: University of Missouri Press, 1982), 98, 4b–1. Here, the Virgin awaits the radiant archangel, shown in flight in the narrow intrado above the chapel's stained glass window. In the window itself, the *Stigmatization*, identified with light, is shown with a winged, crucified Christ and Francis in two separate panes. Such creative adaptations reveal Benozzo's understanding of the order's art and its iconographic traditions.

monumental *sagomata Crucifix* originally was suspended above the altar table.[42] The *Crucifix* would have tangibly linked the scenes of conversion and stigmatization to the sacred space of the choir as an example to the brethren who lived in perpetuation of Francis's ideals.

The now-lost, solitary episode of the speaking cross would have contrasted to the next two scenes. In the adjacent frame, Francis publicly renounces his paternity (Fig. 7).[43] The civic square, towering buildings, and bystanders' reactions—from the uncomprehending anger of Francis's father to the sympathy of Assisi's bishop—serve as foils to the youth's serenity. The subsequent scene translates Gerard of Fracheto's account (1260) of the meeting of Saints Francis and Dominic in Rome (Fig. 8).[44] To the left, Dominic's millennial vision of Christ is portrayed: symbolized by the lances of judgment he brandishes, the Savior's wrath at humanity's sinfulness is mitigated by the Virgin's promise to send her servants, Francis and Dominic, to reform the world.[45] On the right, the two founders meet in Rome, where they have gone to seek approval of their orders from the pope. The public square of the previous scene has been replaced by the deserted piazza before Old Saint Peter's; the child with his flowing locks by the tonsured saint; the tale of worldly renunciation by apocalyptic and apostolic themes.

While the lowest register of scenes follows the accepted chronology of the saint's life, several episodes from the tiers above do not.[46] Pope

---

[42] On the *Crucifix*, attributable to a Giottesque master active in Umbria in the late thirteenth through early fourteenth century, see Toscano, *Museo comunale*, 176f.

[43] Cousins, *Bonaventure*, 2.4, 193–94.

[44] Michele Faloci Pulignani, "S. Francesco e S. Domenico," *Miscellanea Francescana* 9 (1902): 13–15, first described the source of this scene. See Christie F. Stephany, "The Meeting of Saints Francis and Dominic," *Franciscan Studies* 47 (1987): 218–33, for a thorough discussion of the history and interpretation of this theme. Given the homiletic concerns of this paper, it is worth observing that this theme was the subject of a famous sermon by the patron's contemporary, the Franciscan Roberto da Carraciolo da Lecce (1425–95), who urged unity in the order. On this influential preacher, see Raphael M. Huber, *A Documented History of the Franciscan Order (1182–1517)* (Milwaukee: Nowing Publishing Apostolate, 1944), 378, 381.

[45] Quoted from Gerard's *Vitae fratrum Ordinis Praedicatorum*, as cited in Stephany, "Meeting of Saints," 220.

[46] By accepted chronology, I mean the biographical sequence as presented in Bonaventure's canonical *Legenda maior*. The later events that Benozzo represents do not proceed in this order, as this listing of the registers, read bottom-to-top and left-to-right, reveals:

Innocent III's vision of Francis supporting the falling Lateran is conflated with the approval of the Rule by Honorius III, though the latter
occurred some fourteen years later. With Francis's own dream of the
palace diagonally below, these episodes must have been depicted
together to express the fulfillment of the saint's vocation. Following the
chronology of Bonaventure, the *Expulsion of the Demons from Arezzo* is
shown next, to the left of the choir's only window. On the other side
of the window, the *Preaching to the Birds* is represented with the apocryphal *Blessing of Montefalco*, in which Francis, venerated by the kneeling donor, among others, offers his benediction to the town.[47]

Contrary to the canonical sequence of the saint's life, the *Institution
of the Creche*, the *Trial by Fire before the Sultan*, and the *Story of the
Knight of Celano* follow the *Preaching to the Birds*. Such deliberate transpositions of chronology require explanation.[48] Did Benozzo place the
Preaching before these three episodes to balance the *Expulsion of the
Demons from Arezzo*, the only other landscape scene in the cycle, save
for the *Stigmatization*? Was the *Death of the Knight of Celano* placed
nonsequentially so it would serve as a foil to Francis's funeral above, in
which the saint's wounds are verified and his sanctity proven (Fig.
9)?[49] Were the scenes of the lunettes placed out of "historical" order

---

Innocent's Vision (3.10), *Honorius's Approval of the Order* (4.10), *Expulsion of the Demons from
Arezzo* (6.9), *Preaching to the Birds* (12.3), *Story of the Knight of Celano* (11.2), *Institution of the
Crèche at Greccio* (10.2), *Stigmatization of Saint Francis* (13.3), *Funeral of Saint Francis and
Doubting of Jerome* (14.6 and 15.4). *Francis Preaching before the Sultan and the Trial by Fire*,
inserted between the *Institution of the Crèche* and the *Stigmatization*, is not recorded in Bonaventure, but appears in Thomas of Celano, *Vita prima S. Francisci Assisensis et eiusdem
legenda ad usum chori*, *Analecta Franciscana* 10 (1926): 57, 60–62. For the *Blessing of Montefalco*, represented with the *Preaching to the Birds*, see n. 47.

[47] For the saint's purported visit to Montefalco, see Sbaraleae, *Bullarium Franciscanum Romanorum*, 253 n. 1, and Nessi, "La vita di San Francesco," 485–86, who also
proposes the identity of the kneeling men.

[48] See n. 40, and Lavin, *Place of Narrative*, 149–52, for different explanations of the
transposed narrative.

[49] Indeed, the inscription below—QUANDO.BEATUS.FRANCISCUS. MI-
GRAVIT.EX.HAC.VITA.AD.DOMINUM. (How Saint Francis passed from this life
to the Lord)—suggests that we misread the scene if we refer to it as the saint's death,
as have earlier critics; with his "migration" to God, Francis begins his true life. The
saint's identification as the new Elijah ascending to the heavens in a fiery chariot is
rendered in the frescoes at the Upper Church, San Francesco, Assisi. The *poverello* is
related to both Elijah and Enoch in Matthew of Acquasparta's *Commentarium super
Apocalypsim*, unpublished and preserved in Assisi; he is called *alter Enoch* in the sermon

to highlight major Franciscan devotions? Visible over the tall rood
screen that originally separated monks from laity, these episodes, because of their thematic importance, may have transcended the con-
straints of chronology.

While linear sequence may be central to our notion of storytelling,
a study of painted and written narrative from the Middle Ages and
Renaissance suggests that "historic" chronology often was sacrificed to
other interests. Non-linear narration seems entirely in keeping with the
Franciscan artistic and literary tradition. For example, the thirteenth-
century *Bardi Dossal* in Santa Croce, Florence, deviates dramatically
from the chronology of its source, Thomas of Celano's *Secunda Vita*.[50]
A strictly historic sequence is rejected by Bonaventure, who explicitly
states in his *Prologue* to the *Legenda maior* that "I did not always weave
the story together in chronological order. Rather, I strove to maintain
a more thematic order ... as seemed appropriate."[51] That this approach persisted beyond Bonaventure is revealed by Bartholomew of
Pisa's *De conformitate vitae*, eighteen chapters of which eschew chronology entirely to focus on the virtues shared by Christ and his imita-
tor.[52] Non-Franciscan authors abided by such conventions as well, as
The Golden Legend of the Dominican Jacopo da Voragine demonstrates.
The climactic stigmatization of Francis actually is recounted *before* the
meeting of Francis and Dominic, an event that occured early in the
saint's ministry.[53] We misunderstand the spirit of hagiographic writing
if we impose our own sense of order on it.

Franciscan sermons from the Renaissance adhered to similar conventions.[54] Studies of fifteenth-century preaching reveal that many

---

Enoch placuit Deo et translatus est in paradisum. For Matthew of Acquasparta's texts, see
Campagnola, *L'Angelo del sesto sigillo,* 190f.

[50] Most recently analyzed by Rona Goffen, *Spirituality in Conflict: Saint Francis and
Giotto's Bardi Chapel* (University Park: Pennsylvania State Univ. Press, 1988), 28–33.
Domenico del Ghirlandaio's Sassetti Chapel, Santa Trinita, Florence (1483–86) also
deviates from "accepted" chronology. See Eve Borsook and Johannes Offerhaus,
*Francesco Sassetti and Ghirlandaio at Santa Trinita, Florence. History and Legend in a
Renaissance Chapel* (Doornspijk: Davaco, 1981), 28.

[51] Cousins, *Bonaventure,* "Prologue," 4, 183.

[52] Erickson, "Bartholomew of Pisa," 262f.

[53] *The Golden Legend of Jacobus de Voragine,* trans. Granger Ryan and Helmut Ripperger (New York: Longmans, Green and Co., 1941), describes the stigmatization on
602f., and the meeting of the two saints on 603f.

[54] There is an extensive literature on Franciscan preaching. For a general overview,

homilies were organized thematically, not chronologically. That the Montefalco cycle was conceived specifically as painted preaching is suggested by the didactic inscriptions beneath each scene, similar to those originally visible in the Saint Francis cycle at Assisi.[55] They begin with QUALITER (This is how) and QUANDO (When), illustrating by example, exhorting as would spoken sermons. Unlike the Assisi cycle, however, the Montefalco choir excludes the *Vision of the Fiery Chariot* and the *Vision of the Thrones*, the *Apparition at Arles*, and the posthumous miracles. The emphasis on the *living* Francis and his deeds corresponds to conceptions expressed in contemporary sermons and writings.[56] Underlying all of this, the saint's critical role as *alter angelus* and *alter Christus*—implicit in every scene—resonates especially in the triumphal arch and the *Stigmatization*.

The Montefalco frescoes were painted at a time of great controversy within the order of the Friars Minor.[57] The debate over poverty between the Spiritual and Conventual Franciscans was never resolved sat-

---

see Anscar Zawart, "The History of Franciscan Preaching and of Franciscan Preachers (1209–1927)," *Franciscan Studies* 7 (1928). More specifically, see Johannes B. Schneyer, "Lateinische Sermones-Initien des Hochmittelalters für die Heiligenfeste des Franziskanerordens," *Archivum Franciscanum Historicum* 61 (1968): 3–78; Alberto Ghinato, "La predicazione francescana nella vita religiosa e sociale del Quattrocento," *Picenum seraphicum* 10 (1973): 24–98; and Carlo Delcorno, "Il racconto agiografico nella predicazione dei secoli XIII–XV," *Agiografia nell'occidente cristiano secoli XIII–XV*, Atti dei Convegni Lincei, 1–2 marzo 1979, Rome (Rome: Accademia Nazionale dei Lincei, 1980), 79–112.

[55] For the inscriptions, see Smart, *The Assisi Problem*, 263–93.

[56] Scholarship on Franciscan hagiographic preaching in the fifteenth century has focused on the sermons of San Bernardino. Specifically addressing the issue of his conception of Saint Francis are Mariano d'Alatri, "La figura di San Francesco nella predicazione di San Bernardino," in Cardaropoli and Conti, *Lettura delle fonti francescane*, 283–98; and Roberto Rusconi, "San Francesco nelle prediche volgari e nei sermoni latini di Bernardino da Siena," in Domenico Maffei and Paolo Nardi, eds., *Atti del simposio internazionale cateriniano-bernardiniano* 17–20 aprile 1980, Siena (Siena: Accademia Senese degli Intronati, 1982), 793–809. On Bernardino's sermon *In festo beati Francisci* during his visit to Perugia and Assisi in 1425, when his presence in Montefalco also is recorded, see Dionisio Pacetti, "La predicazione di S. Bernardino da Siena a Perugia e ad Assisi nel 1425," *Collectanea Franciscana* 10 (1940): 177f.

[57] The best general surveys of the controversy are Huber, *Documented History of the Franciscan Order*, 361–425, and John Moorman, *A History of the Franciscan Order from its Origins to the Year 1517* (Oxford: Clarendon Press, 1968), 441–585. See also Celestino Piana, "Scritti polemici fra Conventuali ed Osservanti a metà del 1400 con la partecipazione dei giuristi secolari," *Archivum Franciscanum Historicum* 72 (1979): 41–51, and Mario Fois's papers on the Franciscan *Osservanza* in Cardaropoli and Conti, *Lettura delle fonti francescane*, 53–106.

isfactorily, and was renewed by the *Osservanza*.[58] While traditional
histories of the order have focussed on the polarization between Conventual and Observant houses that led to their final rupture in 1517,
recent revisionist studies have challenged such an interpretation.[59]
Such research has emphasized the desire for reconciliation, rather than
division, among the brethren. It has argued for the continuity in Franciscan spirituality throughout these years, proposing that the central vocation of *imitatio Christi*, affectivity, and evangelism remained a constant
of monastic life. The Montefalco frescoes translate these themes that
were so fundamental to the order's identity.

Sanctioned by long tradition and supported by contemporary homily, the cycle's iconography proclaims the truth of the saint's ministry,
his humanity, and his imitation of Christ. The unprecedented presence
of Franciscan worthies, portrayed in the frieze above the choir stalls,
and of the twelve apostles of the *alter Christus* along the entrance arch,
establish the spiritual genealogy of the saint's followers, from the patron
of the frescoes to his fellow brethren seated below them in the choir.
Francis's role as apocalyptic angel and herald of the world's salvation is
proclaimed dramatically by the Pantocrator-like image of the entrance
arch. The frescoes unequivocally assert the authority, venerability, and
continuity of Francis's apostolate; that they were painted in Montefalco
attests the town's consciousness of its renewed importance within the
Order in the 1440s and 1450s. Unique to its moment in time and to
its location in the shadow of Assisi, the cycle glorifies a saint whose
ministry was and is eternal.

---

[58] On this question, see the fundamental Malcolm D. Lambert, *Franciscan Poverty,
The Doctrine of the Absolute Poverty of Christ and the Apostles in the Franciscan Order,
1210–1323* (London: SPCK, 1961).

[59] See n. 57, as well as Emmett R. Daniel, *The Franciscan Concept of Mission in the
High Middle Ages* (Lexington: Univ. Press of Kentucky, 1975); and David L. Jeffrey,
The Early English Lyric and Franciscan Spirituality (Lincoln: Univ. of Nebraska Press,
1975). In the absence of adequate documentation, it is of course impossible to
reconstruct the situation in Montefalco completely. However, as has been observed
earlier in n. 18, the town's most influential clerics—the Observant reformer Fra
Antonio da Montefalco and the cycle's patron, the Conventual Fra Iacopo—belonged
to the same confraternity in Perugia. While this might indicate no more than a shared
devotion to the sodality's ideals of faith and scholarship, it also appears to suggest that
the larger ideological conflicts of the order were not experienced universally. Although
much of the historical evidence for this period is lost, none of the surviving documents for Montefalco refer to discord among its Franciscan congregations.

Fig. 1. Benozzo Gozzoli. *Life of Saint Francis*. Choir, San Francesco, Montefalco. 1452. Soprintendenza ai Beni artistici, architettonici, ambientali e storici dell'Umbria, Perugia.

Fig. 2. Benozzo Gozzoli. *Conservators of Franciscan Faith*, from *Life of Saint Francis*. Soprintendenza ai Beni artistici, architettonici, ambientali e storici dell'Umbria, Perugia.

Fig. 3. Benozzo Gozzoli. *Saint Francis in Apotheosis*, from *Life of Saint Francis*. Soprintendenza ai Beni artistici, architettonici, ambientali e storici dell'Umbria, Perugia.

Fig. 4. Benozzo Gozzoli. *Birth of Saint Francis*, from *Life of Saint Francis*. Soprintendenza ai Beni artistici, architettonici, ambientali e storici dell'Umbria, Perugia.

Fig. 5. Benozzo Gozzoli. *Saint Francis giving his Cloak to a Poor Knight and the Vision of the Castle*, from *Life of Saint Francis*. Soprintendenza ai Beni artistici, architettonici, ambientali e storici dell'Umbria, Perugia.

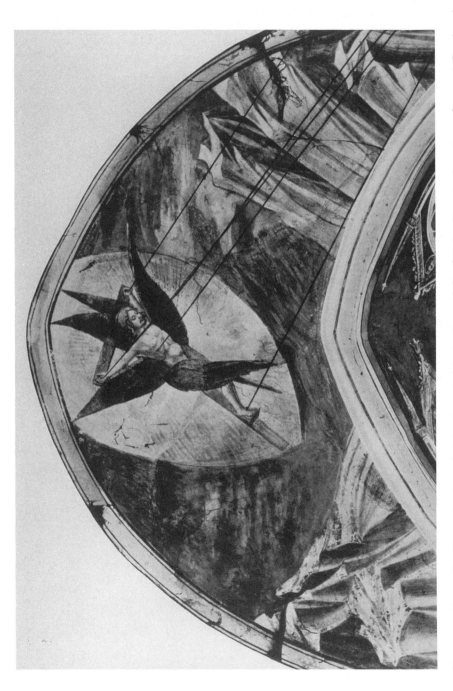

Fig. 6. Benozzo Gozzoli. *Stigmatization of Saint Francis* (det.), from *Life of Saint Francis*. Soprintendenza ai Beni artistici, architettonici, ambientali e storici dell'Umbria, Perugia.

Fig. 7. Benozzo Gozzoli. *Saint Francis renouncing his Paternity*, from *Life of Saint Francis*. Soprintendenza ai Beni artistici, architettonici, ambientali e storici dell'Umbria, Perugia.

Fig. 8. Benozzo Gozzoli. *Meeting of Saints Francis and Dominic,* from *Life of Saint Francis.* Soprintendenza ai Beni artistici, architettonici, ambientali e storici dell'Umbria, Perugia.

Fig. 9. Benozzo Gozzoli. *Funeral of Saint Francis*, from *Life of Saint Francis*. Soprintendenza ai Beni artistici, architettonici, ambientali e storici dell'Umbria, Perugia.

The Cult of St. Anthony of Padua

SARAH BLAKE MCHAM

t. Anthony of Padua was the object of one of the most vital and important cults of the late Middle Ages and early Renaissance—and his cult is still flourishing in the twentieth century. Anyone who has visited the Santo in Padua, where Anthony's relics are enshrined, can attest to the huge crowds who still make the journey to Padua to invoke the saint's protection.

Anthony, the second most important Franciscan saint, typifies the efflorescence of piety and surge in canonizations stimulated by the establishment of the mendicant orders in the thirteenth century. But, on the other hand, the veneration of Anthony is highly unusual. He is almost the only saint canonized in this period whose cult focused on the healing power of his miracle-working relics and generated such fervor that their site became a major center of international pilgrimage.[1] The

---

[1] This study is derived from my book on the cult of St. Anthony as it affected the Cappella dell'Arca di S. Antonio, where his relics are enshrined in the Santo (*The Chapel of St. Anthony at the Santo and the Development of Venetian Renaissance Sculpture* [Cambridge: Cambridge Univ. Press, 1994]).

For an analysis of late-medieval saints, see particularly André Vauchez, *La Sainteté en Occident aux derniers siècles du Moyen-Age d'après les procès de canonisation et les documents hagiographiques*, (Bibliothèque des Ecoles Françaises d'Athènes et de Rome, fasc. 241; Rome, 1981) and Michael Goodich, "The Dimensions of Thirteenth-Century Sainthood" (Ph.D. diss., Columbia University, 1972); and idem, *Vita Perfecta: The Ideal of Sainthood in the Thirteenth Century*, Monographien zur Geschichte des Mittelalters (Stuttgart: Anton Hiersemann, 1982).

veneration of Anthony signals furthermore three major shifts in Franciscan spirituality that had great consequences for the history of Christianity. Francis's approval of Anthony's teaching is the only evidence that Francis condoned learning, and hence is a primary justification for the order's institutionalization. Before becoming a Franciscan, Anthony had been in the Augustinian order, which meant that he had received a thorough theological training. His learned background was most unusual for a Franciscan in the very early days of the order. In a letter which is the unique evidence that St. Francis approved of learning, Francis asked Anthony to teach his fellow friars. The letter's authenticity as an autograph document has been questioned, but it is generally accepted that its contents at the least reflect Francis's instructions to Anthony.

Anthony's teaching in Bologna, and perhaps in Padua and southern France as well, are probably the first instances of a Franciscan friar instructing theology. In fact, Anthony has even been credited with having founded the Studium at the Santo convent.[2] The precedent set by Anthony marked a turning point in the history of the Franciscan order. It was an impetus to the development of Franciscan theology, and within a few decades of Anthony's pioneering example, learning became an integral part of Franciscanism. Increasing numbers of friars became cultured, educated priests, not simple laybrothers. Gradually the prestige of the order became vested in its clerics and priests. As early as 1240, it was decided that no laybrother could be chosen Provincial, Custos, or Superior, except in those regions where there were no priests. By the late thirteenth century, there were numbers of Franciscans teaching at the major universities of France, England, and Italy.[3]

Secondly, Anthony, who like Francis had been canonized primarily

---

[2] For a detailed analysis of St. Anthony's career as a teacher and its importance, see the study of Hilarin Felder, *Geschichte der wissenschaftlichen Studien im Franziskanordern bis um die Mitte des 13. Jahrhunderts* (Freiburg im Breisgau: Herdersche Verlagshandlung, 1904), 131–59. On Anthony's foundation of the Studium at the Santo, see Antonio Sartori, "La 'Ratio Studiorum' al Santo," in *La Storia e la cultura al Santo fra il XII e il XX secolo,* ed. Antonio Pioppi, Fonti e studi per la storia del Santo a Padova, Studi 3 (Vicenza: Neri Pozza, 1976), 120–21.

[3] On these developments, see Raphael M. Huber, *A Documented History of the Franciscan Order (1182–1517)* (Washington, D.C.: Catholic Univ. Press, The Nowiny Publishing Apostolate, 1944), 41, and 114–15.

because of his virtuous life, became the focus of an extraordinary cult after death.[4] The veneration of Anthony shifted the exclusive focus of the order from Francis and acknowledged the important role of miracles and relics, aspects of saintliness generally underplayed in the order's cult of the personality of Francis.[5] Finally, in an age—at least, in Italy—when miracle-working powers increasingly centered on images of the Virgin and Christ, and when images of Francis functioned to diffuse his cult (though none worked miracles), the cult of Anthony followed earlier medieval tradition in focusing on relics and pilgrimage.[6]

The cult of Anthony has important civic associations as well: the death of this non-Italian in Italy provided the ideal opportunity for the appropriation of his cult by Padua, whose authorities were eager to correct the city's lack of a charismatic patron saint.[7] It is the joint sponsorship of the city and the Franciscan order that explains the unusual history of Anthony's cult: their combined forces made Anthony an internationally venerated saint and his relics in Padua the primary locus of his power.

The increasing emphasis on his relics and their thaumaturgic power can be traced—in the growing crowds who made the pilgrimage to Padua; in a comparison of contemporary and later *vitae*, most sponsored

---

[4] See Vauchez, *La Sainteté*, 583–620, for the evaluation of sanctity through a virtuous life rather than through miracles. The relatively limited number of miracles presented for Anthony's canonization are recorded in chaps. 30–47 of Anthony's earliest biography, the *Vita prima*; see Giuseppe Abate, "Le Fonti biografiche di S. Antonio. I. La 'Vita Prima' di S. Antonio," *Il Santo* 8, fasc. 2–3 (May–Dec. 1968): 185–201. After Anthony's canonization, however, the ever-increasing emphasis on the thaumaturgic powers of his relics can be traced in the later *vitae*, for which see below, note 26. On this phenomenon, see Léon de Kerval, *L'Evolution et le développement du merveilleux dans les légendes de S. Antoine de Padoue* (Paris: Opuscules de Critique Historique, fascs. 12–14, April 1906).

[5] On the Franciscan order's cult of the personality of St. Francis, see Rosalind Brooke, "The Lives of St. Francis of Assisi," in *Latin Biography*, ed. T. A. Dorey (New York: Basic Books Publishers, 1967), 177–98.

[6] Beginning in the thirteenth century the faithful more and more often prayed to visual representations of saints, rather than making pilgrimages to their relic shrines; see Vauchez, *La Sainteté*, 519–52; and Jonathan Sumption, *Pilgrimage: An Image of Mediaeval Religion* (Totowa, N.J.: Rowman & Littlefield, 1976), 267–302. On the particular role of the images of St. Francis, see Rona Goffen, *Spirituality in Conflict: Saint Francis and Giotto's Bardi Chapel* (University Park: Penn State Press, 1988), 13–26.

[7] Anthony was born in Lisbon, according to Abate, "Vita prima," 139. Padua's other major patron saints are Daniel, Prosdocimus, and Giustina.

by the Franciscan order; in new feasts and devotions established by the order and the city; and in the sequence of increasingly large and grand shrines constructed to house Anthony's relics.

Our primary source concerning the life, canonization, and early veneration of St. Anthony is the *Vita prima*, a biography of the saint that seems to have been written between 1232–34, that is, just after his death in 1231 and canonization a year later. The author of the *Vita prima* (which is sometimes also called the "Assidua") is unknown. The biography is particularly rich in detail about Anthony's death, his translation to Padua, his canonization, and the miracles worked by his relics in the years immediately after his death. This focus has led historians to speculate that it was probably written by a Franciscan in Padua. Many suggestions about the author's possible identity have been advanced, including ones which attribute authorship to such eminent Franciscans as John Peckham and Bonaventura. The editor of the most recent edition of the *Vita prima* considered the equally eminent Celano, author of the first two biographies of St. Francis, the most likely candidate.[8] The so-called *Vita secunda*, written at about the same time, essentially retells the *Vita prima*, and thus corroborates its account.[9]

---

[8] On the internal evidence in the biography that dates it before March 1234 and the arguments about the author's identity, see Abate, "Vita prima," 128–30. Abate's edition of the *Vita prima* supersedes what had been the authoritative edition by Léon de Kerval, *Sancti Antonii de Padua Vitae duae quarum altera huiusque inedita*, Collection d'études et de documents sur l'histoire religieuse et littéraire du Moyen Age (Paris: Librairie Fischbacher, 1904). Abate's edition of the biography includes newly discovered manuscripts and additions, and takes into account recent scholarship on St. Anthony. Furthermore, Abate's edition of the *Vita prima* forms part of a comprehensive review of all the important thirteenth- to fifteenth-century *vitae* of Anthony. New editions of all the major early biographies, many of them by Abate, were published in *Il Santo* between 1967–75. Another series of editions of the *vitae*, called the Fonti agiografiche Antoniane and edited by Virgilio Gamboso, is underway.

[9] The *Legenda secunda*, which is also called the "Anonyma," is the work of a German minorite from Speyer known as Giuliano da Spira. He compiled it just after composing the liturgical office recited and sung by the Franciscan order on the Feast of Anthony. The most exhaustive study of the *Vita secunda* was written by Michele Bihl, "La leggenda antoniana di Fra Giuliano da Spira OFM, e il suo epilogo inedito," *Studi francescani*, 3d ser., 4 (1932): 429–53. A recent edition was edited by Giuseppe Abate, "Le fonti biografiche di S. Antonio (cont.). II. L'Ufficio ritmico di S. Antonio di Fra Giuliano da Spira, O. Min. c. 1235," *Il Santo* 9, fasc. 2 (May–Aug. 1969), 149–89, and again by Jacques Cambell, "Le Culte liturgique de Saint Antoine de Padoue," *Il Santo* 11, fasc. 2–3 (May–Dec. 1971): 3–70, 155–97; and ibid. 12 (1972): 19–63.

The *Vita prima* recounts the extraordinary celebrations surrounding the translation of Anthony's body to Santa Maria Mater Domini in Padua. The numbers of miracles worked by his relics spurred increasing crowds of visitors, the numbers of which overwhelmed the tiny church of Santa Maria Mater Domini, where his body was temporarily enshrined.[10] Popular fervor forced the decision to build a new, large church (the Santo) in Anthony's honor, thereby incorporating Santa Maria Mater Domini into the new church's fabric. The construction work, which must have begun almost immediately after Anthony's canonization, was financed by the Franciscan order and donations of the faithful.[11]

The city of Padua quickly asserted her special claim to the protection of Anthony. She attributed her liberation in 1256 from the dreaded tyrant Ezzelino da Romano to Anthony's intervention. Local legend affirms that on the saint's feastday in 1256 the Guardian of the Santo Convent prayed at Anthony's tomb for the freedom of Padua. Anthony answered, assuring him that the city would be delivered from Ezzelino on the eighth day of the celebration of his feast.[12] In some accounts, the Blessed Luca Belludi, a close associate of St. Anthony, is claimed to have experienced a similar vision of Anthony prophesying the liberation of Padua.[13] The pace of construction on Anthony's new church

---

[10] See Abate, "Vita prima," chaps. 25–46, 176–201.

[11] This is revealed by a will of August 9, 1238, which reads: "Dominus Buffonus de Bertholoto de hora Sancti Mathei ... Testamentum ... condidit ... reliquid ... Item solidos centum laborerio ecclesie Sancti Antonii et libras decem necessitati fratrum minorum ecclesie Sancte Marie Matris Domini." (Archivio Civico, Padua, Pergamene, 18 Testamenta I, perg. 14). The will is cited in *L'Edificio del Santo di Padova*, ed. Giovanni Lorenzoni, Fonti e studi per la storia del Santo a Padova (Vicenza: Neri Pozza, 1981), 7: 197. For the incorporation of Santa Maria Mater Domini into the new basilica, see Bernardo Gonzati, *La Basilica di S. Antonio di Padova* (Padua: A. Bianchi, 1852–53), I; 4–13; and Marcello Salvatori, "Costruzione della basilica dall'origine al secolo XIV," *L'Edificio*: 34–71.

[12] See the additions to the "Vita prima" found in the manuscript in the Biblioteca dei Cappuccini, Lucerne, XVI–F.6–4 A, fols. 127ff., known as the "Lucerne additions," under chap. 3, nn. 8–11. Scholars agree that the "Lucerne additions" date before 1337; see Kerval, *S. Antonii vitae duae*, 126–27; and Abate, "Vita Prima," 202–23.

[13] See Michele Savonarola, *Libellus de magnificis ornamentis regie civitatis Padue*, written in 1445–47, vol. 24 of *Rerum Italicarum Scriptores*, ed. Ludovico Antonio Muratori (Città di Castello: S. Lapi, 1902), book 1, chap. 2, lines 17–22, p. 16. This version originated much earlier; it is depicted in a fresco by Giusto de' Menabuoi dated 1382 in the Chapel of the Blessed Luca Belludi in the Santo; for a color illustration of the

accelerated because of increased donations from grateful citizens. The city established a two-week festival in Anthony's honor[14] and formally named him her protector (fig. 1).[15] Rolandino da Padova's account of Anthony's defeat of Ezzelino, in which he called Anthony the patron saint of the city, was read publicly on 13 April 1262.[16] Anthony's effigy was added to the *Carroccio* of Padua—the battle carriage that symbolized her status as an independent commune—and the rebuilt carriage was installed in the piazza next to the Palazzo della Ragione, the seat of government.[17]

Shortly thereafter, in 1263, the remains of St. Anthony were translated from Santa Maria Mater Domini to a site in front of the High Altar of the new church. The scaffolding necessary to complete the crossing blocked access to Santa Maria Mater Domini, which was being incorporated into the left transept. Rather than disrupt the worship of pilgrims who wanted to pray at the tomb of the saint, his relics were transferred from their burial place (apparently in the ground)[18] to a sarcophagus before the High Altar.

The saint's relics were translated into a marble sarcophagus elevated on columns so that, as the early sources tell us, the sick and lame could

---

newly restored fresco, see G. Bresciani Alvarez et al., *La Cappella del Beato Luca e Giusto de' Menabuoi nella Basilica di Sant'Antonio* (Padua: Messaggero, 1988), 70.

[14] Gonzati, doc. 11. As early as 1236, the government of the commune had ordered that all shops close on the Feast-day of St. Anthony—a mark of respect otherwise granted at that time in Padua only to the Virgin. See Angelo Portenari, *Felicità di Padova* (Padua: P. P. Tozzi, 1623), 409–10. For a complete description of the elaborate state ceremony marking his Feast, see P. Beda Kleinschmidt, *Antonius von Padua in Leben und Kunst, Kult und Volkstum*, vols. 6–8 of Forschungen zur Volkskunde, ed. Georg Schreiber (Düsseldorf: L. Schwann, 1931), 251.

[15] See Portenari, *Felicità di Padova*, 409.

[16] Rolandino da Padova, *Cronica in factis et circa facta Marchie Trivixiane (aa. 1200–c. 1262)*, ed. A. Bonardi, vol. 8, part 1 of *Rerum Italicarum Scriptores*, 1905 1908, book 2, chap. 5, p. 44. See Paolo Marangon, "Traslazioni e ricognizioni del corpo di S. Antonio nelle fonti storico-letterarie," *Il Santo* 21, fasc. 2 (May–August 1981): 15.

[17] Attilio Simioni, *Storia di Padova dalle origini alla fine del secolo XVIII* (Padua: Giuseppe e Pietro Randi Librai, 1968), 354.

[18] See Abate, "Vita Prima," Paris addition, 2–3, p. 224. Paris addition here refers to the manuscript of the *Vita prima* in the Bibliothèque de la Faculté Théologique Protestante in Paris, which has emendations dating from the late thirteenth century. For further arguments about the burial of Anthony's relics in the ground of Santa Maria Mater Domini, see Marangon, "Traslazioni," 16–18.

Fig. 1. Engraving of the celebrations of the Feast of St. Anthony outside the Santo (photo: Museo Civico, Padua).

be placed underneath it and healed.[19] At some point, stairs were added so that mass could be celebrated atop the sarcophagus.[20]

These practical reasons for the translation were secondary to the desire to place St. Anthony's relics in a more grandiose container and in
a more visually prominent location. Most importantly, their position
before the high altar meant that they dominated the devotional focus
of the new basilica.

The status accorded Anthony's relics by the Franciscan order is indicated by the presence of Bonaventure, its minister-general and leading
spokesman, who presided over the translation. During the ceremony,
the relic container was opened, revealing that the tongue of St. Anthony remained uncorrupted.[21] This further confirmation of Anthony's
sanctity spurred even greater devotion to the saint. The tongue was
separated from the rest of the relics and placed in its own reliquary,
which was moved into the main ambulatory chapel.

Two years after the translation, Padua consolidated her identification
with St. Anthony. She named Anthony her defender and prime patron,[22] and erected a gold statue of the saint in the Piazza della Signoria.[23] The city assumed financial responsibility for the new basilica
by agreeing to make a large annual contribution to speed its comple-

---

[19] The various early sources that record the appearance of St. Anthony's *arca* are
analyzed in *L'Edificio*, 258.

[20] The "Legenda Raymondina," a biography of St. Anthony written around 1293,
provided this information; see Antonio Maria Josa, *Legenda seu vita miracula S. Antonii
de Padua* (Bologna: Pontificia Mareggiani, 1883), 105, 110. On the "Raymondina," see
also Giuseppe Abate, "Le fonti biografiche di S. Antonio. V. La 'Vita Sancti Antonii'
di Fra Pietro Raymondina da San Romano, c. 1293," *Il Santo* 10, fasc. 1–2 (Jan.–Aug.
1970): 3–34.

[21] For an analysis of the 1263 translation of the relics, together with relevant documents, see Antonio Sartori, "Le Traslazioni del Santo alla luce della storia," *Il Santo* 2,
no. 1 (Jan.–Apr. 1962): 5–31. On the veneration of the tongue of St. Anthony, see
idem, "La Festa della traslazione di S. Antonio e il culto alla sua sacra lingua nel corso
dei secoli," *Il Santo* 3, no. 1 (Jan.–Apr. 1963): 67–98. The day of the translation of
Anthony's relics was celebrated as early as 1267; see the sermons of Luca of Padua
from that date edited by Virgilio Gamboso in *Il Santo* 9 (1969): 273–81.

[22] See the chronicle of Giovanni da Nono, *Visio Egidij regis Patavie*, edited and
annotated by Cesira Gasparotto, "Guide e illustrazioni della Basilica di Sant'Antonio in
Padova—I", *Il Santo* 2 (1962): 382. See also the discussion of this visionary chronicle
in *L'Edificio*, 249–52.

[23] Portenari, *Felicità di Padova*, 409.

tion and to maintain the finished structure.[24] As part of the deal, a board of governors charged with overseeing all aspects of the church's functioning was instituted. Since the board was comprised of two lay persons and one friar, control over the new church was, in effect, transferred from the Franciscan order to the city of Padua.[25]

The next major stage in the development of Anthony's cult occurred at the chapter meeting of the Franciscan order held in Padua in 1276, where it was decided that Anthony should be honored by the entire order as the second most important Franciscan saint.[26] It was probably at the same chapter meeting that a new biography of St. Anthony was commissioned. This *vita*, which is now known as the "Benignitas" because its prologue begins with that word, is fragmentary.[27] The new *vita* marks a fundamental change in the veneration of St. Anthony. It included the many miracles worked by Anthony's relics since his canonization, making it the first permanent record of the changed pattern of his cult: it traced how the thaumaturgic powers of Anthony's

---

[24] See *Statuti del comune di Padova dal secolo XII all'anno 1285*, ed. Andrea Gloria (Padua: F. Sacchetto, 1873), n. 1156, included in *L'Edificio*, 202. I am grateful to Prof. Benjamin Kohl for sending me a copy of the relevant statutes from Gloria, and for informing me that the donation was not continued under the Carrara dynasty's domination of the city, according to the *Codex statutorum carrariensis*, fols. 101v–104v, in the Biblioteca Civica, Padua (MS B.P. 1237).

[25] On the composition of the board of governors and their regulations, see Gonzati, *La Basilica* 1, pp. 22, 42–46. Giovanni Lorenzoni argued that the commune took on the financial and administrative responsibility for the Santo because it wanted to enlist the support of the people of Padua and the Franciscan order against the regular clergy in Padua; see his "Sulla fondazione della basilica del Santo a Padova," in *S. Antonio di Padova fra storia e pietà. Colloquio interdisciplinare su 'il fenomeno antoniano,'* *Il Santo* 16, fasc. 2–3 (May–Dec. 1976): 163. Contending that the Commune's regular contribution was what allowed the grand scale of the Santo, Lorenzoni also discerned that the Commune harbored a third goal, that of rivaling Venice's state church of S. Marco (p. 164).

[26] See the *Sources of the Modern Roman Liturgy: The Ordinals of Haymo of Faversham, and related documents (1243–1307)*, ed. S. J. P. Van Dijk, Studia et documenta Franciscana, vols. 1, 2 (Leiden: E. J. Brill, 1963), 2:443, statute 1, cited in Cambell, "Le Culte liturgique," 5. As noted by Cambell, the earlier chapter general at Metz in 1254 had prescribed the way in which Anthony's legend should be used; see Van Dijk, *Sources of the Modern Roman Liturgy*, 2:416, statute 27.

[27] On this *vita*, see Kerval, *S. Antonii vitae duae*, 159–235; Giuseppe Abate, "Le fonti biografiche di S. Antonio. VII. I frammenti della 'Benignitas' e la 'Vita S. Antonii' edita dal Surio, *Il Santo* 10, fasc. 3 (Sept.–Dec.1970): 223–72; 12, fasc. 1–2 (Jan.–Aug. 1977): 3–106; and Vergilio Gamboso, "Ricerche sulla leggenda antoniana 'Benignitas'," *Il Santo* 15 (1975): 13–89; 17 (1977): 3–106.

relics had become the primary reason for the saint's ever-growing popularity. Because the "Benignitas" was the most influential source for later biographies, it contributed to their emphasis on Anthony's reputation as a great miracle worker.[28]

The cult of Padua's patron saint surged once again in the fourteenth century. A second challenge to the independence of the commune, which had remained free since the expulsion of Ezzelino, occurred when Cangrande della Scala, ruler of Verona, seized Padua after 17 years of war. Just one year later, and apparently in the bloom of health, he died.[29] Paduans attributed this second deliverance from foreign domination to the miraculous intervention of St. Anthony.

Perhaps spurred by this reminder of the saint's protection, Giovanni da Nono soon thereafter (1330s) wrote a chronicle of Paduan history that emphasized St. Anthony's role as the city's patron saint. Da Nono reviewed the city statutes that outlined how the commune took financial and administrative control of the basilica because, as he made clear for the first time, the Santo was considered the state church of Padua.[30] It was no doubt important to the city that, like her increasingly powerful neighbor Venice, she, too, had a state church. This rivalry is also reflected in the multi-domed plan of the Santo, which is very like that of San Marco.

The final translation of St. Anthony's relics took place in 1350 when the sarcophagus was resituated in its final location, the left tran-

---

[28] Gamboso, "Ricerche," 14. The fourteenth- to sixteenth-century biographies, all of which stress the thaumaturgic capacities of St. Anthony, are as follows:

1. the "Vita Rigaldina" of the early fourteenth century, for which see Giuseppe Abate, "Le Fonti della biografia di S. Antonio. VI. Legenda Rigaldina," Il Santo 10, fasc. 1–2 (Jan.–Aug. 1970): 35–77.

2. the Liber miraculorum of c. 1370 (included in the Acta Sanctorum, 3:196–269 [under 13 June]).

3. Sicco Polentone, "La 'Sancti Antonii Confessoris de Padua Vita,'" of c. 1435, ed. Vergilio Gamboso, Il Santo 11, fasc. 2–3 (May–Dec. 1971): 198–283.

4. Paul Fridenperger, Vita e miracoli di Sant'Antonio da Padova (Verona: Paul Fridenperger, 1493/1495).

5. Ippolito da Ponte, trans., Compendio volgare della vita et opere (Venice: Guglielmo da Fontaneto, 1532). This includes an Italian translation of Polentone's biography.

6. Lorenzo Surio, "La 'Vita S. Antonii,'" of 1572, for which see Abate, "Le Fonti biografiche . . . 'Benignitas,'" 246–72.

[29] Simioni, Storia di Padova, 480–96.

[30] See Gasparotto's edition of Da Nono, "Guide e illustrazioni . . . I," 229–55.

sept chapel.[31] Several motives must have dictated this last transfer. Because the transept chapel incorporated the foundations of Santa Maria Mater Domini, the small church where St. Anthony had requested burial and where his relics were originally placed, it held intense devotional meaning. On a practical basis, the location was ideal: it was the largest available chapel in the church and near the entrance, so that it was easily accessible to the hordes of pilgrims who came to pray to the relics of St. Anthony. The sarcophagus was placed in the middle of the chapel, supported by four columns and preceded by steps. This original arrangement was retained because it allowed mass to be celebrated atop the tomb.

In honor of this final translation, the General Chapter of the Franciscan order held in Lyons the following year established a special feast. This decision was rescinded by the chapter held at Assisi two years later, once it was recognized that otherwise Anthony would have been honored with more feasts than Francis.[32]

In the 1370s, the new site of the arca of St. Anthony was grandly decorated with frescoes by the renowned north Italian painter, Stefano da Ferrara.[33] We know little about these frescoes, which were destroyed in the late fifteenth century when St. Anthony's chapel was redecorated, except that they were much admired for their lifelike fig-

---

[31] On this translation, see Giovanni Fabris, "Il Cardinal legato Guido d'Alvernia e l'ultima traslazione di S. Antonio (15 febbraio 1350)," in his *Scritti di arte e storia padovana* (Quarto d'Altino: Rebellato, 1977), 303–11.

[32] See Cambell, "Le Culte liturgique," 7–8.

[33] See Savonarola, *Libellus de magnificis ornamentis regie civitatis Padue*, book 1, chap. 2: "Sunt denique eo in loco molto plures [cappelle], e quibus due ita magnifice et ornate existunt, ut existimem paucas, immo fortasse nullas, eis pares reperiri. Estque prima Antonio nostro, suis cum pictis miraculis manu Stephani Ferrariensis dedicata." In book 1, chap. 3: "Postremo Stephano Ferrariensi non parvum honorem dabimus, qui stupendi miraculis gloriosi Antonii nostri cappellam figuris veluti se moventibus miro quodam modo configuravit." The text of Savonarola is analyzed by Cesira Gasparotto, "Guide e illustrazioni della Basilica di Sant'Antonio in Padova - I," *Il Santo* 2 (1962): 369–87. See also Marcantonio Michiel, *Der Anonimo Morelliano (Marcanton Michiel's "Notizie d'opere del disegno")*, ed. Theodor Frimmel, Quellenschriften für Kunstgeschichte und Kunsttechnik, n.s., vol. 1 (Vienna: Graeser, 1888), 10: ". . . questa cappella era dipinta, e la pittura, per essere vecchia, e caduta mezza: fu ruinata per refarla de sculpture de marmi. Dipinsela Stefano da Ferrara, bon maestro a quei tempi."

ures,[34] and that several of the frescoes represented miracles of St. Anthony.[35] In general terms, we can posit that the Chapel of the Arca of St. Anthony must have resembled the chapel dedicated to St. James opposite it in the right transept (fig. 2). The latter was frescoed with scenes of St. James's life by Altichiero and Avanzo just after Stefano da Ferrara completed the cycle of St. Anthony, and was never redecorated.[36]

The final stage in the development of the cult of St. Anthony which we shall trace in this paper occurred in the mid-fifteenth century. It was then that the Paduan cult of the saint was profoundly colored by the city's pride about her famous Roman past, a heritage kept alive through the antiquarian focus of the university and Paduan humanist tradition. In 1435, one of these humanists, Sicco Polentone, wrote another biography of St. Anthony.[37] The direct stimulus for the new *vita* must have been the spate of miracles worked by Anthony's relics between 1433 and 1434. Polentone included accounts of these miracles, along with a lengthy series of earlier miracles culled from the important thirteenth- and fourteenth-century biographies of the saint.[38]

Polentone donated a manuscript of his biography to the Santo,

---

[34] See the second quotation from Savonarola in note 33, above.

[35] From the contracts for the chapel's redecoration awarded between 1500–1502 to Tullio Lombardo, Antonio Lombardo, Giovanni Minello, and Antonio Minello, we learn that the miracles of the newborn child, the reattached leg, the miser's heart, the mule, and the death of St. Anthony, were all part of the fresco cycle. See the transcription and analysis of these contracts in Sarah Blake Wilk (McHam), "La Decorazione cinquecentesca della Cappella dell'Arca di S. Antonio," in *Le Sculture del Santo di Padova* (Vicenza: Fonti e studi per la storia del Santo a Padova, Neri Pozza, 1984), Studi 4, 110–11.

We know nothing more about the subjects of the remaining frescoes in the fourteenth-century decoration of the chapel. They could have represented the same scenes as the other marble reliefs that replaced them, but that is strictly a hypothesis.

[36] On the Chapel of St. James, see Giuseppe Fiocco and Antonio Sartori, "La Rivincita di Altichiero," *Il Santo* 3, fasc. 3 (1963): 284–326; Giuliano Bresciani Alvarez, "L'Architettura e l'arredo della cappella di S. Giacomo ora detto di S. Felice al Santo," ibid., 5, fasc. 2 (May–Aug. 1965), 131–41; Giuseppe Fiocco, "'Storia e storie' della Cappella di S. Giacomo," ibid., 6, fasc. 2–3 (May–Dec. 1966), 261–66; and Antonio Sartori, "La Cappella di S. Giacomo al Santo di Padova," ibid., 267–361.

[37] The authoritative critical edition is Vergilio Gamboso, "La 'Sancti Antonii Confessoris de Padua vita'," *Il Santo* 11, fasc. 2–3 (May–Dec. 1971): 199–283.

[38] For an analysis of his reliance on the earlier biographies, see ibid., 204–10.

Fig. 2. The Chapel of St. James in the Santo (photo: Art Resource).

where it was attached by a chain in the sacristy.[39] Polentone clearly intended his new biography to instruct pilgrims about St. Anthony. Making this sort of record of the saint's miracles available to the faithful who visited his shrine followed a longstanding precedent of other pilgrimage shrines. The record of miracles was consulted privately or read aloud to induce the proper spiritually-charged atmosphere for the saint's thaumaturgic powers to be re-activated.[40] Polentone's biography filled a significant gap: all the earlier *vitae* of Anthony had been written by Franciscans for a Franciscan audience, and were only available in a limited number of copies. Polentone's biography was accessible to any pilgrim.[41] Despite the intended audience, Polentone's life of Anthony was written in Latin, although in a more straightforward prose style than the learned humanist's earlier biographies of great Greek and Latin writers.

A decade later, Michele Savonarola, an eminent antiquarian and close friend of Polentone (he had encouraged Polentone to write a new life of Anthony), wrote an encomium of Padua.[42] Savonarola made the Santo the centerpiece of his native city. He argued that Padua's religious traditions and monuments were second only to those of Rome, and the greatest of these was the Santo.[43]

---

[39] The rubric on folio 39v of the manuscript, now in the Biblioteca Antoniana, Padua, cod. 559, reads: "Ad honorem et gloriam summi dei Intemerateque virginis Marie ac om[n]ium sanctorum. Anno nativitatis domini nostri ihesu xristi M.CCCC. XXXVIIIJ. liber iste, in quo scripte sunt vite ac miracula devotissimi sancti Antonij confessoris de padua ordinis fratrum minorum Conventus padue, per Sicconem Polentonem, et scriptum per me fratrem Jacobum de padua, atque ferrea cathena hic alligatus, ut ipsum libere ad commodum suum quisque legere possit ... sed aufferre nemo possit."

[40] See Peter Brown, *Relics and Social Status in the Age of Gregory of Tours* (Reading: Univ. of Reading, 1977), 6–7.

[41] See Gamboso, "S. Antonii vita," 202.

[42] See Polentone's letter to Savonarola: "Incitasti me exhortionibus tuis, nunc annus, ni fallor, est tertius; ut, que prope in oblivionem abierant, miracula et vitas sancti Antonii confessoris, beati Antonii Peregrini et beate Helene memorarem. Id enim existimasti equum ac dignum fore, si quemadmodum vitas scriptorum illustrium latine lingue seculares ad litteras memoravi, ita Dei ad laudem horum sanctorum miracula et vitas absolverem ..." (Gamboso, "S. Antonii vita," 200).

[43] "Quam itaque michi dabis, Antoni, urbem, que apud Regem Regemtot talesque intercessores habeat, queve tanta polleat dignitate...? Hoc tamen loco Romam excipio, que velut aceldama sanctorum habita est." from the *Libellus*, book I, chap. 2, lines 12ff., quoted in Gasparotto, "Guide e illustrazioni ... I," 373, n. 20.

In this way, her devotion to St. Anthony and her Roman heritage were made the twin glories of Padua, and when the Chapel of St. Anthony was lavishly redecorated at the end of the fifteenth century, the saint was honored in the artistic language of a classical hero. For the first time, a saint's chapel was entirely decorated with sculpture, the medium known to have been favored by the Greeks and Romans (fig. 3). Anthony's entry into the Franciscan order and his subsequent miracles were recounted in nine sixteen-foot reliefs. Not only the material, but the scale of these sculptures was virtually unprecedented.[44] Most earlier burial chapels of saints were either decorated with fresco cycles of the saint's life and death, or else an elevated sarcophagus with small-scale reliefs. The latter type was established in Italy with the Arca of St. Dominic by Nicola Pisano and his shop, and emulated in dozens of thirteenth- to sixteenth-century examples.[45] All the monumental reliefs concern heroic acts of Anthony (fig. 4), some even performed after his death. The only artistic precedents for this type of subject focus and artistic language are the relief cycles honoring the virtues of the emperor that decorated triumphal arches like that of Constantine, which were well known in the Renaissance. Similarly, the small-scale narratives and decorative motives carved all over the chapel's architecture, as well as its gilded and white stucco vault covered with grotesques, derive directly from pagan prototypes.[46]

The patronage of the chapel's redecoration demonstrates once again how the joint sponsorship of the city and the Franciscan order affected

---

[44] On the chapel's redecoration, see Wilk (McHam), "La redecorazione cinquecentesca," 109–72.

[45] On the Arca of St. Dominic, see John Pope-Hennessy, *Italian Gothic Sculpture, Introduction to Italian Sculpture*, vol. 1, (New York: Vintage Books, 3rd ed. rev. 1985), 180–81. On the influence of this type of *arca*, see Sarah Blake McHam, "Donatello and the High Altar in the Santo, Padua," in *IL60. Essays Honoring Irving Lavin on his Sixtieth Birthday*, ed. Marilyn Aronberg Lavin (New York: Italica Press, 1990): 73–96; and idem, "Donatello's High Altar in the Santo, Padua" in *Andrea del Verrocchio and late Quattrocento Sculpture: The Acts of Two International Symposia commemorating the 500th Anniversary of his Death*, ed. Steven Bule (Florence: Licosa-Sansoni, 1990).

[46] For a brief analysis of the chapel's relationship with ancient art, see Sarah Blake McHam, "La Decorazione della Cappella dell'Arca di Sant'Antonio nella Basilica del Santo, Padova, e sue relazioni coll'arte antica" in *Rivista di Archeologia. Supplementi 7. Congresso Internazionale Venezia e l'Archeologia*, ed. Gustavo Traversari (Venice: Giorgio Bretschneider, 1988) 195–98; a more complete analysis is found in idem, *The Chapel of St. Anthony at the Santo.*

Fig. 3. The Chapel of the Arca of St. Anthony, Santo.

Fig. 4. Reliefs of the Miracle of the Miser's Heart (left) and the Miracle of the Reattached Leg (right), both by Tullio Lombardo, Chapel of the Arca of St. Anthony, Santo.

the development of the cult of St. Anthony. The artistic language of the redecoration specifically speaks to Padua's patriotic association with her Roman past—an emphasis that civic control of the Santo's governing board could guarantee. Nevertheless, the redecoration was largely funded through a bequest of Francesco Sansone, the minister-general of the Franciscan order.[47] Another considerable sum of monies was derived from the donations of the faithful, whose pilgrimages to the Santo were in part spurred by indulgences promised them by Pope Sixtus IV, a Franciscan who had spent several years at the Santo convent.[48]

The city of Padua and the Franciscan order both promoted the cult of St. Anthony. Their devotion was inspired by Anthony's saintly character, the miracle-working power of his relics, and recognition that the tremendous popular appeal of the saint contributed to the reputation and economic health of each. Padua's interests were best served by the continuing focus on the Santo as the primary locus of the saint's miracle-working powers—the hordes of pilgrims who visited Padua were a major source of city revenues. The localization of the cult of St. Anthony at the Santo, where it centered on Anthony's miracle-working relics, was effective as well for the Franciscan order, which focused otherwise on universal devotion to the personality and model of St. Francis. The unusual circumstance of their joint promotion of the veneration of Anthony caused an equally unusual development of his cult.

---

[47] See Gonzati, La Basilica, 1:77–78 and pp. lvi–lvii, doc. 52.

[48] On Sixtus IV's devotion to St. Anthony and his connections with the Santo, see Dino Cortese, "Sisto Quarto Papa Antoniano," Il Santo 12, fasc. 3 (Sept.–Dec. 1972): 211–72.

Holy Patronage, Holy Promotion: The Cult of Saints in Fifteenth-Century Venice

h happy Venice! Oh blessed Venice! You have St. Mark the Evangelist to defend you in battle like a lion, and Nicholas, father of the Greeks, to guide your ships.... Therefore we pray to you, glorious protectors of Venice ... and to you also ... Theodore.... With your grace preceding and your intercession following, may we who venerate your holy remains deserve to share with you in the celebration of the angels.[1]

In the beginning of the fifteenth century, Venice was, and considered herself, a most miraculous city. Perched like the sea-birds of her

---

[1] "O felix Venetia! et o beata Venetia! quae beatum Marcum evangelistam, utpote leonem in bellis habes defensorem, et Nicolaum, patrem Graecorum, in navibus gubernatorem.... Rogamus ergo vos, gloriosissimi Venetiae protectores! ... et ... martyr Theodore ... quatenus, divina gratia praecedente, vestroque suffragio subsequente, qui festa vestra temporalia veneramur, festis angelorum vobiscum interesse mereamur." For the Venetian text of the *translatio* of St. Nicholas from which this excerpt is taken, see Biblioteca Nazionale Marciana Cod. Lat. IX, 28 (2798), fols. 208–20, published in Flaminio Corner, *Ecclesiae Venetae Antiquis Monumentis ... Illustratae* (Venice: Typis Jo. Baptistae Pasquali, 1749), 9:6–39; and *Receuil des Historiens des Croisades: Historiens Occidentaux* (Paris: Imprimerie Nationale, 1895; facsimile repr. Farnborough, Hants: Gregg Press Ltd., 1967), 5:281 for the Latin text cited above. The author was a twelfth-century monk at the monastery of St. Nicholas on the Lido.

skies upon her several islands, she regarded her very existence, as well as her extensive empire to the East, as the fruit of God's special favor,[2] mediated through the active presence of his saints. Three of these saints had especially important roles in the city: Mark, Theodore, and Nicholas of Myra, especially the first. When, from 1404 on, the Venetians turned their commercial and political ambitions toward a new empire of the *terraferma*, acquiring large parts of northeastern Italy, their hired armies conquered these lands to the battle cry of "Marco, Marco," their merchants traded in coins which bore Mark's image, Mark's symbolic lion was emblazoned on governmental buildings and marketplace wells throughout Venetian domains, and subject territories pledged their allegiance to the patronage of St. Mark.[3]

But by the middle of the fifteenth century, the holy patronage of these saints apparently required further certification. In 1449, there was an investigation and validation of the relics of St. Nicholas in his church on the Lido. In the same year, the bishop of Venice, together with the doge, proposed a formal recognition of St. Mark in his resting place. In the next year, 1450, the feast of St. Theodore was elevated to a holy day of obligation. What was the relation of these saints to Venice? Why, at this mid-century moment, was their holy protection pro-

---

[2] The proemium of a 1464 law reads: "Nos qui in huiusmodi salsis paludibus reducti tam amplam civitatem tantumque dominium adepti non nostrorum predecessorum neque nostra industriam vel potentiam sed solum Dei bonitate et gratia . . ." (Archivio di Stato di Venezia [hereafter ASV], Council of Ten, Misti, reg. 16, fol. 165v n.m. [for *numero moderno*], August 25, 1464).

[3] Paduan statutes spoke of that city as *filius* of St. Mark. The Trevisan College of Nobles, in its statutes of 1419–41, invoked the Trinity, St. Mark, and the local St. Liberale (Bianca Betto, *Il collegio dei notai, dei giudici, dei medici e dei nobili in Treviso (secc. XIII–XIV)* [Venice: Deputazione Veneta di Storia Patria Miscellanea di Studi e Memorie, 1981], 388). Bassano invoked St. Mark as patron in June 1404 in the articles of its submission to Venice (Giovanni Battista Verci, *Storia della Marca Trevigiana* [Venice: G. Storti, 1786–89], XVIII, appendix, doc. 2031) and the ambassadors of Cologna on a particular embassy to Venice recalled the moment "cum . . . Deus omnipotens . . . comunia et singulares personas villarum infrascriptarum ad umbram illius serenissimi ac beatissimi Marci evangeliste patroni et gubernationis alme dominationis Venetorum . . . reduxerit" (Vicenza, Biblioteca Civica Bertoliana, Arch. Torre 778, fol. 8v). I owe all these references to the kindness of James Grubb. Earlier examples of Mark's imposition on subject peoples are discussed by Ernst Kantorowicz in connection with Venice's control of Crete in the thirteenth century in *Laudes Regiae* (Berkeley: Univ. of California Press, 1958), 154. See also Edward Muir, *Civic Ritual in Renaissance Venice* (Princeton: Princeton Univ. Press, 1981), 88.

moted and reaffirmed? Why was the officiating bishop, by name Lorenzo Giustiniani, elevated in 1451 to a patriarchate, venerated himself as a holy presence, and soon after his death in 1456 promoted by his city as a candidate for sanctification? Answers to these questions may delineate some interconnected aspects of Venetian religious and political history.

Mark was, of course, *the* patron saint of Venice and had been since the ninth century. The story of his translation from Alexandria (827–828) was a favorite theme in Venetian legends and iconography.[4] Two Venetian merchants, driven by a storm into the port of Alexandria, heard that the Caliph was dismantling the church in which the remains of Mark were kept.[5] By an elaborate scheme and the connivance of two Alexandrine monks, they were able to smuggle the body out, covering it with pork meat so as to forestall investigation by the Moslems for whom that meat was repellent. Their justification lay in the legend that Mark had earlier preached in Aquileia and, in so doing, had founded the north Adriatic church.[6] There, it was also averred, he had written his Gospel. And there he had been visited by an angel in a dream who foretold his martyrdom, his *passio*, and the eventual return

---

[4] Geary, *Furta Sacra: Thefts of Relics in the Central Middle Ages*, (Princeton, N.J.: Princeton Univ. Press, 1978), for a general discussion of the translation of relics; and Muir, *Civic Ritual*, 78–92, for a good summary of the Marcian bibliographies.

[5] The Moslem danger, evidenced in their conquest of Sicily in 827, their occupation of Taranto and Bari in 839, and their sack of Rome in 846, made the Venetian rescue of St. Mark and his subsequent protection more urgent. Local ecclesiastical politics were a further impetus: Carolingian bishops were asserting ecclesiastical control over Venice by supporting Aquileia's primacy (as against Grado) at the Council of Mantua in 827. By having Mark's body, Venice-Grado would 'neutralize' Aquileia's importance. See Geary, *Furta sacra*, 108–10; and Silvio Tramontin, "San Marco," in *Culto dei Santi a Venezia*, ed. S. Tramontin et al. (Venice: Studium Cattolico Veneziano, 1965), 50–51. Shortly before, in 810, Pepin had made his unsuccessful bid to conquer the lagoons by attacking Malamocco (at that time the capital), and the government had been moved thereafter to the Rialto. St. Mark's presence would affirm the importance of the new site.

[6] Otto Demus, *The Church of San Marco in Venice* (Washington: Dumbarton Oaks Research Library and Collection, 1960), 37. Mark's visit to Aquileia is first described in Paul the Deacon's chronicle (783–86). See Tramontin, "San Marco," 48; and Muir, *Civic Ritual*, 80. See also Andrea Dandolo's *Chronica* (fourteenth century), ed. Esther Pastorello in *Rerum Italicarum Scriptores*[2], vol. 12, pt. 1:1 (Bologna: Nicola Zanichelli, n.d.), which begins with Mark's mission to Aquileia (p. 9).

of his body to these north Adriatic shores, populated by Christians re-markable for their piety.[7]

The translation of Mark's remains fulfilled this prophecy. The Vene-tians placed his body—now rescued from the infidels—in a chapel at-tached to the Doge's palace, rather than in the cathedral church of Ve-nice which was S. Pietro di Castello, located in the eastern section of the city. The great Basilica of St. Mark, the Doge's private chapel, arose around Mark's remains and came to represent the city's holy stat-us. To this church was brought the booty of subsequent campaigns: mosaics, jewels, precious icons, and statuary such as the giant bronze horses taken from Constantinople during the Fourth Crusade in 1204. Mark, as Peter's disciple, guaranteed the apostolicity of the Venetian Church and made it second only to Rome in antiquity.[8] Mark's pres-ence, as signified by his remains, served as an assertion of Venice's re-ligious independence from Rome as well as its political importance vis-à-vis Byzantium and its imperial pretensions vis-à-vis the other Italian city-states. But Mark had not always been the principal saint of the city. Theodore, a Greek warrior saint, had been (or by the fifteenth century was considered to have been) the original tutelary saint of the Dogate.[9] The *dux*, later doge, of Venice was, in his earliest phase, the

---

[7] Bernardo Giustiniani, *De divi Marci evangelista vita, translatione, et sepulturae loco*, vol. 5 of *Thesaurus antiquitatum et historiarum Italiae*, ed. J. G. Graevius (Leyden: Petrus Vander Aa, 1722), pt. 1, bk. 1, col. 175A: "Caeterum ut tibi gratio iste sit locus, quem tam humilem tenuemque nunc vides, nosse te velim, tempus adhuc fore, quum ossa tua e barbarorum manibus erepta, hic perpetua quiescant. Evadet in gentem magnam ope tua precibusque, tantum virtutem pietatemque colant."

[8] Because St. Peter had allegedly invested Mark with an episcopal office, the Venetian St. Mark was often portrayed in episcopal robes, an insistence upon St. Mark's sacerdotal office and an enhancement of the prestige of the Venetian bishops as heirs of St. Peter himself. See Staale Sinding-Larsen, *Christ in the Council Hall: Studies in the Religious Iconography of the Venetian Republic* (Rome: "L'erma" di Bret-schneider, 1974), 192.

[9] Theodore's early role remains uncertain. Marin Sanudo in his *Le Vite dei Dogi* writes of "Thòdaro, qual si dice fu primo protectòr di Venitiani, tamen di questo io non l'ho trovato scripto in alcun cronicha" (*Rerum Italicarum Scriptores*[2], vol. 22 [Città di Castello, 1900], 283–84). See Antonio Niero, "I santi patroni," in *Culto dei santi in Venezia*, ed. S. Tramontin et al. (Venice: Studium Cattolico Veneziano, 1965), 91–92, 232; and Silvio Tramontin, "Realtà e leggenda nei racconti marciani veneti," *Studi Veneziani* 12 (1970): 52–53, n. 44. See Muir, *Civic Ritual*, 93–94, on "the chronicle of confusions" between two saint Theodores. One was Theodore of Amasea in Pontus whose remains were buried with Nicholas and Nicholas's holy uncle (also St. Nicholas)

military commander of a Byzantine province, and therefore the Greek soldier Theodore was an appropriate symbol of militant Byzantine sovereignty. It seems that the first ducal chapel of Venice was dedicated to Theodore and built on the site later occupied by the Basilica of St. Mark.[10]

Even after Mark had displaced Theodore in the ninth century—his great church swallowing up the smaller chapel of St. Theodore—Theodore remained important, and his continuing presence was traced in mosaic and stone. In the mid-thirteenth century (1257), his reputed remains were secured by the Venetians (the most active among bodysnatchers in the Middle Ages), and some time later a statue of Theodore was raised upon a pillar in the piazzetta, the waterside ceremonial entrance to the great Piazza of St. Mark (1329). This first statue was replaced in the second half of the fifteenth century with a strange composite: an antique head, placed on a Roman armored torso, to which were added assorted arms and legs, the assembled figure standing triumphant over a fantastic crocodile-dragon with the muzzle of a dog.[11] It was an apt image of the fragmentary, composite, and collective quality of many of the saints dear to Venice, considered none the less efficacious in destroying the demonic, dragonic enemy and in defending the composite and collective Venetian empire. That is the statue we

---

in St. Nicholas on the Lido. This is the Theodore referred to in the twelfth-century invocation at the beginning of the essay. The other was Theodore of Heraclea, whose body was brought to Venice in 1267 and placed in the Church of St. Salvador. Muir indicates that the Venetian St. Theodore of the later fifteenth century may have become a fusion of these two, although in 1448 the two were still distinct.

[10] Demus, *Church of San Marco*, 21–22. See also Wladimiro Dorigo, *Venezia origini. Fondamenti, ipotesi, metodi* (Milan: Electa Editrice, 1983), 2:545–56. Dorigo dates the foundation of this early ducal chapel in 554. Muir, *Civic Ritual*, 94, dates the edifice about 819. Niero, "I santi patroni," 92–93, considers the existence of the church dubious.

[11] See Gaetano Cozzi and Michael Knapton, *La Repubblica di Venezia nell'età moderna* (Turin: UTET, 1986), illustration facing p. 16; Luisa Sartorio, "San Teodoro, statua composita," *Arte veneta* I (1947): 132–34. For an explanation of why this statue's spear was held in the left hand and the shield in his right hand, see Francesco Sansovino, *Venezia città nobilissima e singolare* (Venice: S. Curti, 1663; facsimile repr. Farnborough, Hants: Gregg Press Ltd., 1968), 317: "L'animo della Repubblica non fu di offendere alcuno ma si ben di difendersi dalle altrui l'offese, poi che ella tiene armata di difesa quella mano con la quale si fa per ordinario l'offesa." The militant aspect of saints such as Theodore is discussed by John R. Hale in *Renaissance War Studies* (London: Hambledon, 1983), 366–67.

see today, the famous "Tòdaro" (in Venetian dialect), set alongside another pillar which supports the lion of St. Mark. And it is interesting to note that between the two columns of the Piazzetta, between "Tòdaro e Marco," one with Theodore, the other supporting Mark's winged lion, justice was done. Here was the traditional place for the execution of criminals, of those who had harmed the Venetian state: in the judgmental presence of two of the city's holiest patrons.[12]

The third in this trio of saints, Nicholas, physically arrived in Venice at the beginning of the twelfth century, between the advent of Mark in the ninth century and Theodore in the thirteenth. Long associated with the sea, sailors, and commerce, Nicholas was venerated prior to the arrival of his remains; we know that the church on the Lido existed some decades before Nicholas' relics were taken from Myra in 1100 to be placed in his Venetian church.[13] The account of his translation from Myra to Venice provided the opening peroration of this essay: "Oh happy Venice! O blessed Venice!" Happy and blessed in her protectors, among which surely the saint of the sea had a predictably prominent role. The church of St. Nicholas on the Lido came to play a special part in the annual ceremony of the doge's marriage of the city

---

[12] Marin Sanudo, *De origine, situ et magistratibus urbis Venetae, ovvero la città di Venetia (1493–1530)*, ed. Angela Caracciolo Aricò (Milan: Cisaltino-La Goliardica, 1980), 25: "Ha un altra piazza—dil Palazzo—dove si tien, et dà rason a tutti et senta li officij, et va verso il Canal Grande dove, alla riva, sono due colonne altissime, et erette sopra alcuni gradi; sora di una è San Thodaro et sora di l'altra è San Marco. Qui in mezo si fa giustitia di tutti li ladri, traditori, o altri, sì brusar, impichar, come far altro malefi- cio." Sanudo discusses these two columns also in his *Le vite dei dogi* (in *Rerum Italicarum Scriptores²*, 430). Mark's lion may have arrived on his column a century sooner (mid-thirteenth) than Theodore's first statue was put on his (mid-fourteenth century). See J. B. Ward Perkins, "The Bronze Lion of St. Mark at Venice," *Antiquity*, vol. 21, no. 81 (March, 1947): 23–41.

[13] Wells of sweet water, used to provision ships, may have accounted for the church's location on this island at the mouth of the lagoon. Marin Sanudo describes these in his 1493 "List of Notable Things in Diverse Venetian Churches," ("Queste sono cosse notabile in diverse chiesie"), Museo Civico Correr, Venice, MS Cicogna 969, fols. 24v–26r, published by Wendy Stedman Sheard, "Sanudo's List of Notable Things in Venetian Churches and the Date of the Vendramin Tomb," *Yale Italian Studies*, vol. 1, 3 (Summer 1977): 255–57. The Church's date is given as 1043 by G. Musolino, "Feste religiose popolari," *Culto dei santi a Venezia* (Venice: Studium Cattolico Veneziano, 1965), 218. It was built by Domenico Contarini (1042–71) and it is with this doge that the formula *Dei gratia dux* replaces others suggestive of subservience to Byzantium. The acquisition of her own holy patrons went hand in hand with Venetian insistence on a sovereignty dependent on God alone.

to the sea. Each year, on the day of the Ascension, the doge cast a ring into the Adriatic in token of the *sposalizio*, the marriage in which Venice celebrated her dominion over the sea. The doge then returned from the open waters to the Church of St. Nicholas for a solemn act of worship in honor of the saint who was, in effect, patron of the Venetian fleet.[14]

Mark, Theodore, and Nicholas: these three, along with Mary, were among the most important saints of Venice. It was her saints who supplied what Venice had originally lacked: walls, gates, fortifications, and a heroic founder. It was their patronage and protection which rendered Venice invulnerable and unassailable, and by the middle of the fifteenth century, Venice's need for holy protection was especially pressing.[15]

The years 1447–1450 were years of intense diplomatic and military activity in the Italian peninsula. The death of the Milanese Duke Filippo Maria Visconti, on August 13, 1447, without male heirs, plunged Italy into a three-year war for the Milanese succession. The Milanese populace declared itself the "Ambrosian Republic," at times allied with the Venetian Republic, although not without suspicion and anxiety. For Venice had, over the past decades, acquired large parts of what was formerly Milanese territory. Francesco Sforza, a condottiere married to the last Milanese duke's illegitimate daughter, was determined to capture Milan for himself. Formerly employed by Venice, he spent these

---

[14] On the *sposalizio*, see Muir, *Civic Ritual*, 119–34 and 97–98, where he suggests that an earlier propitiation ceremony invoking Nicholas's protection of Venetian sailors evolved into the more elaborate *sposalizio*. See also the catalogue of an exhibit, *Monasteri Benedettini nella Laguna Veneta*, ed. Gabriele Mazzucco (Venice: Arsenale, 1983), 52; B. Tamassia Mazzarotto, *Le feste veneziane* (Florence: Sansoni, 1961), 181ff. Sometime in the centuries which followed, another festival developed in connection with the church of S. Nicolò dei Mendicoli, located in the poorer section of the city populated by fishermen and pauper nobility. This was the annual election of a popular doge, the doge dei Nicolotti, who was crowned and feted and even received by the proper doge of the city. So important was St. Nicholas to the maritime city of Venice that his worship has been seen as competitive with that of St. Mark (Roberto Cessi, *Storia di Venezia*, [Venice: C. Ferrari, 1958], 2:346–48). There was also a church, dedicated to St. Nicholas, in the ducal palace, important enough to be decorated with a fresco cycle. See Patricia Fortini Brown, *Narrative Painting in the Age of Carpaccio* (New Haven: Yale Univ. Press, 1988), 259–60.

[15] Bernardo Giustiniani, *De divi marci*, col. 171C: ". . . ut is ad urbem novam, vel muniendam, vel ornandam quasi conditor, sane protector nobilissimus accesserit, cuius munitione et patrocinio invicta tandem et inexpugnabilis redderetur."

three years warring sometimes with Venice against Milan, or with Milan against Venice, or against both, according to alliances so kaleidoscopic that even contemporary credulity was strained.[16] It was Sforza who inflicted on Venice a major setback to her *terraferma* ambitions, first destroying a large part of the Venetian inland fleet at Casalmaggiore on the Po on July 16–17, 1448, and then, two months later on September 15, inflicting an unanticipated and totally humiliating defeat on the Venetian military forces at the battle of Caravaggio (a battle at which Venice was said to have lost all but 1500 of her original 12,500 cavalry and saved not a single foot soldier of her 5000 infantry). This, in spite of her troops being led by ten condottieri (including Bartolomeo Colleoni) under the general captaincy of the experienced Michele Attendolo.[17]

A treaty between Sforza and Venice followed a month later, but relations with Sforza deteriorated so that eventually Sforza and his envoys began to issue forth a stream of anti-Venetian propaganda charging Venice with the ambition of dominating first the north and then all of Italy: "They remain obstinate and hardened and always with their

---

[16] See, for example, Bernardo Giustiniani's comment in his 1457 "Oratio funebris habita in obitu Francisci Fuscari Ducis," in *Orazioni, elogi e vite scritte da letterati veneti patrizi in lode di dogi, ed altri illustri soggetti* (Venice: A. Curti, 1798), 58: "Quis has fortunae vices credat? Tantas rerum temporumque tam brevi mutationes, ultra progredi fas non est."

[17] On June 13, 1448, the Venetian Senate wrote Pasquale Malipiero, their procurator with the army, that Venice's political honor and reputation rested upon its army's protection of Lodi (in the vicinity of Caravaggio) and the presence of its river fleet on the Po (ASV, Secreta, Reg. 18, fol. 6 n.m.). After these two stunning defeats of Casalmaggiore and Caravaggio, the Senate wrote Nicolò Canale, Venetian ambassador in Florence: "Denotamus vobis damnum et cladem dicti exercitus fuisse adhuc valde maiorem et graviorem quod crederemus. Nam omnes gentes nostrae confracte sunt et in maxima parte capte.... Res nostrae maxime et evidenti periculo constitutae sint" (ASV, Secreta, Reg. 18, fol. 38 n.m., Sept. 18, 1448). Giorgio Dolfin in his "Cronica di Venezia" (Biblioteca Nazionale Marciana, MS. Ital VII, 794 [8503], refers to the "gran melicanie e affanni" these defeats caused in Venice [fol. 412 n.m.]). On the battles of Casalmaggiore and Caravaggio, see Ercole Ricotti, *Storia delle Compagnie di Ventura in Italia* (Turin: G. Pomba, 1844–45), 3:126–35; and Bortolo Belotti, *La vita di Bartolomeo Colleoni* (Bergamo: Istituto d'Arti Grafiche, 1923), 176–81. Even two attending Venetian Procuratori were taken prisoner. Well might the Florentine government refer to the battle of Caravaggio in a letter (September 26, 1448) to its ambassador in Venice as a grim event for the Venetians, "il caso sinistro ... la qualcosa è stata molestissima a tucto questo popolo" (in Luigi Rossi, "Firenze e Venezia dopo la battaglia di Caravaggio," *Archivio Storico Italiano*, ser. 5, vol. 34 [1904], 158–79).

mouth open to acquire states and usurp the territories of their neighbors, to satisfy their appetite for dominating Italy."[18] In this war of words, Sforza came to be joined by the Florentine Republic, increasingly controlled by Cosimo de' Medici, under whose guidance Florence abandoned its traditional alliance with her sister republic of Venice. Together with Sforza, Florence inveighed against what was now labelled the threat of Venetian dominion, attempting to convince the remaining powers—Rome, Naples, and Genoa—that this label was indeed appropriate.

Pope Nicholas V, however, who succeeded the Venetian Eugenius IV in February of 1447, was chiefly concerned with establishing peace in the Italian peninsula and attempted to preserve a mediator's role. At the same time, he also sought to maintain the papacy against the claims of the Council of Basel, to encourage René of Anjou's claim to the kingdom of Naples as a counterpoise to Alfonso of Aragon's aggressive power there, and to establish the prestige and power of the Roman Catholic Church through a religious and cultural program. 1450 was to be celebrated as a Holy Year in Rome, and the remarkable collections of the Vatican Library were launched.

Further to the south, Alfonso of Aragon was proclaiming a testamentary right to the Milanese ducal throne and waging military campaigns in Tuscany against Florence. Eventually, however, he stated that his real enemy was Venice and declared war against her in July of 1449.[19] To the west there was the Republic of Genoa, to which the

---

[18] "E Veneziani ... come quelli che stanno obstinati e induriti e semper con la bocha aperta per acquistar Signoria e usurpare quello de tucti soi vicini per adimpire l'apetito de li animi soi de dominar Italia," Francesco Sforza writing from Milan to his ambassador Nicodemo in Rome on February 21, 1451, in Luigi Rossi, "Venezia e il re di Napoli, Firenze, e Francesco Sforza dal novembre del 1450 al giugno del 1451," *Nuovo Archivio Veneto*, fasc. 3 (anno 1905), 281. Even the Venetian chronicler, Giorgio Dolfin, confirmed Venetian cupidity—"cognosciuta la cupidita venetiana appetir al dominio di tutta Lombardia" ("Cronica di Venezia," fol. 408 n.m.).

[19] Alfonso's declaration of war against Venice was a threat to the important Venetian commerce in the southern region of Apulia where the city of Bari also claimed to have the body of St. Nicholas since 1087, a decade prior to the Venetian acquisition. There, as part of a fervent local cult, an elaborate church was built to accommodate the vast throngs of pilgrims. See Silvio Tramontin, "Influssi orientale nel culto de' santi a Venezia fino al secolo XV," in *Venezia e il Levante fino al secolo XV* (Florence: L. S. Olschki, 1973–74), 805–6; and Geary, *Furta sacra*, 124, on the rivalry between Bari and Venice in the grain trade from Apulia.

Venetians sent one of their most skilled ambassadors in order to gain Genoese adherence to a Venetian alliance. But Genoa opted to send aid to Francesco Sforza and echo the anti-Venetian propaganda which Sforza continued to sound.

In February of 1450, the Milanese, constrained by siege and famine, murdered the Venetian ambassador—an intolerable insult and shock to the Venetians—and shortly thereafter Francesco Sforza gained control of the Milan.[20] Given Venice's severe diplomatic and military failings, the swelling rancor and bitterness among the Italian city-states against Venice, the growing risk to the bulwarks of her eastern empire where the Ottoman power would, within a few years, overrun Constantinople, and the fact that within the city there had been, in 1447, a devastating recurrence of the plague, it is no wonder that at this mid-century point Venice should secure her spiritual alliances and supernatural connections.[21]

It was the relics of St. Nicholas, in their tomb on the Lido, which started the series of 'holy recognitions' in the mid-fifteenth century.[22] In 1449, St. Nicholas' tomb, his *arca*, began to ooze a sacred unguent

---

[20] Giorgio Dolfin, "Cronica di Venezia," fol. 417 n.m. Luigi Rossi assessed this as "un'umiliazione pe' Veneziani che essi per l'orgoglio e prestigio presso gli altri Signori e Signorie della Penisola in niun modo potevano tollerare" in "Niccolò V e le potenze d'Italia dal maggio del 1447 al dicembre del 1451," *Rivista di Scienze Storiche*, anno 3, vol. 1 (1906): 246.

[21] For a general review of the politics of this period, see Samuele Romanin, *Storia documentata di Venezia* (Venice: P. Naratovich, 1855), 4:207–30; and Nicolai Rubinstein, "Italian reaction to Terraferma expansion in the fifteenth century," in *Renaissance Venice*, ed. John R. Hale (London: Faber and Faber, 1973), 197–217. See also Gianni Zippel, "Ludovico Foscarini ambasciatore a Genova, nella crisi dell'espansione veneziana sulla terraferma (1449–50)," *Bolletino dell'Istituto Storico Italiano per il Medio Evo* 71 (1959): 181–255. Other complicating factors in this situation were Frederick III's claims to Milan as having devolved to the empire upon the death of the last male Visconti and Charles d'Orléans' claim through his mother Valentina Visconti, Filippo Maria's sister. For the plague of 1447, see Antonio Niero, "Pietà ufficiale e pietà popolare in tempo di peste," in *Venezia e la Peste* (catalogue of an exhibition in Venice, 1979), 287. Of some importance also for the religious activity of the next few years was the example of relics and hagiographical texts now arriving from the threatened Eastern Empire. Witness the transference to Venice from Constantinople in 1454 of the body of St. Athanasius of Alexandria.

[22] "Recognition" was most often formally practised as part of the beatification process. See "Reconnaissance des restes mortels d'un serviteur de Dieu" in *Dictionnaire de Droit Canonique*, vol. 7 (Paris: Librairie Letouzey et Ané, 1965), cols. 479–80. Here, it served rather to validate the presence and potency of the holy remains.

which apparently engendered marvelous cures and led to an investigation.[23] So on March 30, 1449, the doge went together with the bishop, Lorenzo Giustiniani, the higher clergy, and the chief governmental leaders, joining together in the kind of politico-ecclesiastical ceremony so familiar in Venice. The tomb was opened, and body of St. Nicholas was officially seen and verified in what an eyewitness described as a deeply religious event. Then the tomb was sealed with cramp-irons, so that it could not be opened again, and the city was filled with rejoicing and devotion.[24]

For St. Mark, shortly thereafter, similar ceremonies were planned—

---

[23] From an early period, Nicholas was a "myroblyte," a saint whose relics oozed a myrrh, or meliorative unguent. See Charles W. Jones, *Saint Nicholas of Myra, Bari, and Manhattan: Biography of a Legend* (Chicago: Univ. of Chicago Press, 1978), 66 and 206 for an extensive description of this miracle and the nineteenth-century procedures of priests in Bari for extracting "the manna" which was then given to pilgrims who bought vials for this purpose from the local merchants.

[24] The eyewitness account is in Giorgio Dolfin, "Cronica Di Venezia," fols. 413r–413v n.m. Dolfin's description may be found in Fernanda Sorelli, "Predicatori a Venezia (fine secolo XIV—metà secolo XV)," *Le venezie francescane*, n.s., anno 6, fasc. 1 (1989): 158. Marin Sanudo based his description on Dolfin's account (Cronica Veneta, pt. 5, carta 254). See Daniele Rosa, *Summorum Sanctissimorumque Pontificum . . . de Beati Laurentii Justiniani Venetiarum Patriarchae . . . vita sanctitate ac miraculis Testimoniorum centuria* (Venice: Pinelli, 1630), 144: "Il Dose andò con li piatti à San Nicolò de Lio con il Vescovo de Castello Domino Lorenzo Giustinan, e con il Clero, e zonto lì, doppo ditta una solenne Messa cantata per il prefatto Vescovo, e fatta processione, andò esso Dose con il predetto Vescovo, l'Abbate, la Signoria, e altri Prelati sotto Confessione dove è l'arca marmorea, nella quale si diceva che erano li Corpi de San Nicolo barba, de San Nicolo nipote, e de San Theodoro Martire, e apersero la detta arca, e cosi vedendo li detti corpi tre con gran devotione, e serrono la detta arca con arpesi, che più non si potesse aprir, li quali Corpi Santi se etiam furono visti in tempo de M. Antonio Venier Dose del 1399 li quali erano involtadi in panni de seda, si come appareva per una notade lettere scritte in marmoro, poste li sotto confession come se vide." The fact that there was an eyewitness account indicates the public and publicized aspect of the ceremony. See also Sanudo's shorter description in *Città di Venetia* (1980), 164. Further details are provided by Flaminio Corner, *Notizie storiche delle chiese e monasteri de Venezia e di Torcello* (Padua: Manfré, 1758), 58–59. G. Cracco, "Dai santi ai santuari: un'ipotesi di evoluzione in ambito veneto," in *Studi sul medioevo veneto* (Turin: Giappichelli, 1981), 42, characterizes this epoch as the "triumph of visuality." Was this Renaissance emphasis on visual piety, with its specific and local celebration of the saints and communion with Christ through the visible elevation of the host and the Corpus Christi processions, a consequence of the more than half-century of schism and conciliar conflict which weakened the claims and character of the abstract Church universal? On the presentation and visibility of imported relics in the later Middle Ages, see Hans Belting, *The Image and its Public in the Middle Ages* (New Rochelle: Aristide D. Caratzas, 1990), 203–21.

or so we are told by Lorenzo Giustiniani's biographer and nephew, Bernardo Giustiniani. This same nephew tells us that he had seen, in the episcopal apartments of his uncle, a secret document indicating where all the holy relics of the city were hidden and preserved.[25] This was especially important for St. Mark, whose body had already been lost once in the tenth century, during the reconstruction of the Basilica, after a fire in 972 made that rebuilding necessary. A century later, in 1094, after a three-day fast and much communal prayer, a pillar had miraculously opened and the saint revealed his hiding place.[26] He was then reburied in a location known only to the doge, the *primicerio*, and the procurator of the Basilica.[27] Now, once again in the mid-fifteenth century, it seemed appropriate to re-view, to see again, Mark's sacred relics. Accordingly, the bishop, together with the doge, planned such an event, but because of the pressure of politics and war—so we are told—and the demise of the two leaders, the ceremony never took place.[28]

---

[25] Giustiniani, *De divi Marci*, col. 191–92, 193A.

[26] On this inventio or *apparitio*, see Giustiniani, *De divi Marci*, col. 188B: "Lapides callopreciae cujusdam (ea est columna pluribus ex lapidibus compacta) loco sensim moveri caepti. Cadentibusque et admirantibus omnibus, arca ubi corpus latebat mira cum odoris fragrantia, omnium oculis sese videndam offert." Cf. Sanudo, *Città di Venetia*, 56. Tramontin, "Realtà e leggenda,'" 56–57, offers a plausible explanation for this miracle, suggesting that in the process of rebuilding the church, the body was exposed, venerated, seen to perform miracles and then hidden again; popular fantasy turned this event into a mysterious and miraculous "inventio." Geary, *Furta Sacra*, 126–27, points out the coincidence of this *inventio* with the building in Bari of the elaborate tomb for St. Nicholas and suggests that rivalry—commercial and hagiographical—may have played a significant role. See also Roberto Cessi, "L'apparitio Sancti Marci del 1094," *Archivio Veneto*, anno 110, ser. 5, vol. 85 (1964): 113–15, where Cessi argues that the arrival of St. Nicholas in Venice, and the competition Nicholas posed for Mark, may have prompted the rediscovery and reaffirmation of Mark's presence in his basilica. Muir, *Civic Ritual*, 87–88, suggests that the defeat of the Byzantine emperor by the Seljuk Turks in 1071 may have intensified the Venetian determination to distinguish themselves from the Byzantine heritage by this insistence on Mark's presence. Muir also points out that the same set of circumstances led to another Christian assertion, Pope Urban II's call for a crusade in 1095, the year after the "inventio."

[27] Giustiniani, *De divi Marci*, col. 186E: "Corpus Evangelistae sublatum ex ea columna, ubi per tot annos delituerat, novo alio delecto loco, est collocatum. Antiqua tamen lege ne quis locum cognoscat, nisi dux, primicerius, et Ecclesiae procurator." The *primicerio* was the dogal chaplain.

[28] Giustiniani, *De divi Marci*, col. 192F. The fact that the body was not verified at this time may have prompted Bernardo Giustiniani's long arguments as to the certainty of its presence in Venice, among which was the following: if the body were else-

As for Theodore, he was rediscovered—so to speak—in this same period. Prior to 1450, no written sources indicate that Theodore was the original protector of the city. But in 1450, the Venetian Senate itself declared that "in bygone times and ever thereafter St. Theodore was the protector of this our city, together with St. Mark the Evangelist." It appears from this decree that at some earlier time, Theodore's ensign had been removed from the armies of the Venetian Republic. Now, to compensate for this displacement and to make sure that from this time forth Theodore would receive due attention, his feast was made into a *festum solemne*, a holy day of obligation.[29]

Finally, as integral to the holy patronage and holy promotion of these years, there was Lorenzo Giustiniani, the officiating bishop at these viewings, recognitions, and saintly promotions, of which three were planned and two executed. Lorenzo Giustiniani was a member of one of the oldest and most distinguished families of the city, so old they were called apostolic and so distinguished they claimed descent from the imperial Justinians of Constantinople. The period of Giustiniani's episcopacy (1433–1456) is marked by renewal and reform which emanated from the piety associated with the small island of San Giorgio in Alga; here, as a young devotee, Lorenzo had gone to join other devout and later influential patricians.[30] His reputation for sanctity grew

---

where, why was there no great building elsewhere to house it? Giustiniani then fortifies his argument from architecture with a lengthy description of the extravagant dimensions and accoutrements of the Basilica (cols. 184–86).

[29] "Quia, ut notum est, per superiora et continua tempora Sanctus Theodorus fuit protector istius urbis nostrae una cum B. Marco Evangelista, ex quorum quidem Sanctorum intercessionibus res nostrae mediante divina clementia feliciter processerunt. Et sic res digna, et conveniens est, quod, postquam vexillum ipsius Sancti Theodori a nobis, sive ab ista Republica non defertur, saltem, et devotione, et veneratione hujus Beatissimi Sancti dies suae commemorationis, quae est die nono mensis Novembris, debeat celebrari" (September 21, 1450) in Corner, *Ecclesiae Venetae*, 13:399–400. The Senate's action was prompted by Bishop Lorenzo Giustiniani who, on October 12, 1450, in a supporting episcopal decree, mandated that on this holy day "a cunctis in nostra Dioecesi abstineatur mecanicis artibus exercendis. Quibus XL dies de Indulgentia observantibus misericorditer concedimus, ut pius et misericors Deus ejus intercessionis auxilio civitatem istam ejus gratia cum pace, et sospitato conservet" (Corner, *Ecclesiae Venetae*, 13:399–400). Niero suggests that the removal of Theodore's *vexillum*, his standard, from the Republic's armies occurred during the war of Chioggia with the Genoese (1378–81) to avoid confusion with Genoese standards bearing the emblem of St. George, Theodore's military brother saint ("I santi patroni," 94).

[30] Among the members of that early group were Ludovico Barbo, the great

even as his spiritual administrative influence was enlarged. In 1451, Lorenzo was promoted, against his deepest ascetic inclinations, to be the first Patriarch of Venice—an office now combined with the episcopacy. And upon his death, five years later, Lorenzo came to serve the same religious purpose of civic protection which he had, in his lifetime, pursued.

Called "beatus" even before he died, Lorenzo was, following his death, sculpted (perhaps by Jacopo Bellini) in a half-bust style after the manner of popes and saints, a bust the faithful could touch for its reputedly magical powers. A few months later, Lorenzo was represented in a Gentile Bellini painting on a processional panel, nimbed with rays and attended by celebratory angels.[31] In the following decades, there were active efforts by his family and city to have his sanctity proclaimed by the Church.[32] A hagiographical *Vita* was written by his

---

reformer of Santa Giustina in Padua, Angelo Correr, later Gregory XII (1406–14), and Gabriele Condulmer, later Eugenius IV (1431–47). Lorenzo Giustiniani shared with these men a belief in restoring religious discipline by implementing the ancient ecclesiastical canons through synods, apostolic visitations, and episcopal decrees. For a summary of Lorenzo's reforming activities, see A. Niero, *I Patriarchi di Venezia da Lorenzo Giustiniani ai nostri giorni* (Venice: Studium Cattolico Veneziano, 1961), 21–31. At the beginning of the fifteenth century, the Venetian authorities had firmly rejected the mystical popular movements represented by Domenico Dominici. Lorenzo Giustiniani's emphasis on the monastic ideal and austere canonical tradition, combined with carefully orchestrated public ceremonials such as these "recognitions," was entirely compatible with the oligarchic polity of the Venetian state and consonant with the spiritual intensification of the Alghense reform. Cf. G. Zarri, "Aspetti dello sviluppo degli Ordini religiosi in Italia tra Quattro e Cinquecento. Studi e problemi" in *Strutture ecclesiastiche in Italia e in Germania prima della Riforma* (Bologna: Il Mulino, 1984), 221.

[31] On the statue, see Jürg Meyer zur Capellen, "La 'Figura' del San Lorenzo Giustiniani di Jacopo Bellini," *Centro tedesco di studi veneziani, Quaderni* 19 (Venice, 1981): 5–33; and the documents cited in Colin Eisler, *The Genius of Jacopo Bellini* (New York: Harry N. Abrams, 1989), 59–60, 521. Cf. Antonio Niero, "Pietà popolare e interessi politici nel culto di S. Lorenzo Giustiniani," *Archivio Veneto*, ser. 5, vol. 117 (1981): 199. Marilyn Lavin has pointed out to me the presence of festive swags over the angels. The panel is now in the Gallerie dell' Accademia in Venice.

[32] See my essay "No Man But an Angel: Early Efforts to Canonize Lorenzo Giustiniani (1381–1456)" in *Continuità e discontinuità nella storia politica, economica e religiosa* (Vicenza: Neri Pozza Editore, 1993), 15–43. There was some previous association of the Giustiniani family with sanctity and the particular saints under discussion. An ancestor, Beato Nicolò Giustiniani, had prevented the extinction of his clan in the twelfth century by gaining permission to take a temporary leave from his monastery of St. Nicholas on the Lido, marry, and propagate a quantity of heirs before he

nephew and a *processo* for sanctification was initiated. Numerous miracles were recounted, among them that Lorenzo's body had lain uncorrupted for forty days, a felicitous symbol for his supposedly incorrupt and unassailable city. According to a holy hermit, it was Lorenzo's prayers and intercession which saved the city during her wars with Milan.[33] But it was not until 1524 that the papacy permitted his cult as "beatus" throughout the Venetian dominions.[34] Canonization proper had to wait until the next Venetian pope finally granted it in 1690.

What emerges from these accounts is the contemporary concept of sanctity as a living, active, and unifying force: Mark, Theodore, and Nicholas were understood to be still present among the living Venetians who venerated them and never more so than in a time of tribulation. Lorenzo, a chief participant in the events of 1449–1451, was, upon his death in 1456, immediately considered to have joined the company of Venetian patron saints. The Venetian liturgical calendar reminded Venetians throughout the year of these personalities: January 2, the dedication of the first Basilica of St. Mark; January 8, the death and later the feast of Lorenzo Giustiniani; January 31, the translation of Mark's body; April 25, Mark's feast day (his day of martyrdom); May 25, Nicholas's translation; June 25, Mark's reappearance in the pillar, his *inventio*; September 5, Lorenzo's birth date; October 8, the consecration of the rebuilt Basilica of St. Mark; November 9, Theodore's feast day; December 6, Nicholas's feast day.[35]

---

returned to that monastery, in which he was eventually buried. Lorenzo's own brother, Leonardo, had translated, in the early 1430s, the "Life of St. Nicholas" from Greek texts into Latin. He, too, was also buried in the Church of St. Nicholas. Lorenzo's other brother was called Mark; Bernardo's children included a Lorenzo and a Nicholas. The prevalence of saints' names such as Marco and Nicolò among the Venetian patricians is worth some attention.

[33] See Bernardo Giustiniani's *Vita Beati Laurentii Iustiniani Venetiarum Proto Patriarchae* (Rome: Officina Poligrafica Laziale, 1962), chap. 65, p. 131, and chap. 52, p. 104. This *Vita* is the primary source for San Lorenzo's life and was first published in Venice by Jacques Le Rouge in 1475.

[34] See Claudio Finzi's introduction to Domenico Morosini, *De bene istituta re publica* (Milan: Giuffré, 1969), 7–8. Finzi suggests that papal recognition of Lorenzo Giustiniani's cult may have been in exchange for Venetian support of the papal project of a crusade.

[35] For a more complete list of Venetian holy days, see S. Tramontin, "Il 'Kalendarium' veneziano," in *Culto dei Santi a Venezia* (Venice: Studium Cattolico Veneziano, 1965), 287–324. Other lists, however, indicate considerable variety in the dates

Only a century earlier, in 1341, it was believed—at least by the credulous—that St. Mark and St. Nicholas (this time together with St. George, the military brother saint of Theodore) had rescued the city from an *aqua alta* of threatening dimensions caused by hostile demons. The three saints on that occasion had given a ring to a poor fisherman in proof of their protection—another favorite subject for Venetian Renaissance painters.[36] Such continuing efficacy was reinforced when, in 1420, the very Gospel of St. Mark, purported to have been written by the saint's own hand, was brought to Venice from its newly-acquired territory of Friuli. With tremendous pomp and circumstance, it became another "relic" which the capital city insisted on removing from its dominions to its own safekeeping.[37]

So great was the faith vested in holy patronage, so interwoven were sacred and secular history, and so available were these protectors in moments of acute political stress and civic danger, that sanctity was viewed as a continuum, a part and parcel of daily life. Heavenly citi-

---

of some of the feast-days. See also idem, "Realtà e leggenda," 35–58; and idem, "San Marco," 41–73. Bernardo Giustiniani, at the end of his funeral oration for the defunct Francesco Foscari, called upon Christ, Mary, St. Mark, and the relics of seventy saints now collected from barbarous nations to preserve and protect the Venetian state: "Vosque septuaginta sanctorum felicissimae reliquiae, qui per varias orbis plagas dispersi, perque barbaras et infestas vestrae fidei nationes jactati, demum non minori veneratione quam labore collecti hic sedem, hic domicilium reperistis: vos item, sancti et sanctae omnes imploro atque obtestor" ("Oratio funebris," p. 58).

[36] Paintings depicting this legend by Palma il Vecchio and Paris Bordone are now both in Venice's Gallerie dell' Accademia. On St. George, see Muir, *Civic Ritual*, 95–97.

[37] This "Gospel" and a ring—possibly that purportedly given to the poor fisherman, or the one which was considered as received from the hand which St. Mark extended from the pillar at the time of his *inventio*—were paraded on Mark's ceremonial days, contained in an elaborate tabernacle and carried by the members of the Scuola Grande di San Marco (Muir, *Civic Ritual*, 88). The "Gospel," actually a sixth-century codex, is now partly in the library of Cividale and partly in Prague (Tramontin, "San Marco," 69–70). See also Marin Sanudo, *Le vite dei Dogi*, col. 933 (and Monticolo's notes 3 and 4 on p. 96 in the 1900 edition). A year earlier in 1419, the Senate had debated whether special measures should be taken to secure a relic from Egypt which was reported to be the head of St. Mark and which the Genoese were reputedly seeking to acquire. The proposal for such measures failed to pass by a wide margin, suggesting that the Venetian senators harbored some doubts as to the authenticity of this relic (Antonio Niero, "Questioni agiografiche su San Marco," *Studi Veneziani* 12 [1970]: 3–27). For Marin Sanudo's list of relics in Venice see *Le Vite dei Dogi*, 76–85.

zens of the *patria*,[38] the saints were there to be rediscovered, to be made tangible and visible, to have their potency promoted and confirmed, so that they, in turn, might validate the conquests, claims, and invulnerability of this most "miraculous city."

---

[38] ". . . ut coelestis patriae civibus ante Divinae majestatis thronum continue assistentibus." The expression is from Lorenzo Giustiniani's decree of October 12, 1450, as described in note 29.

Devotion to the Archangel Raphael in Renaissance Florence

KONRAD EISENBICHLER
for Māra Ezerkalns

he archangel Raphael plays a crucial role in the apocryphal book of Tobit, not only as the angel who guides and protects the young Tobias on his journey from Nineveh to Media, but also as the healing angel who cures Tobit (Tobias' father) of his blindness and Sara (Tobias' wife) of her demon.

Raphael's role as a "healing angel" is indicated by his name—Raphael is Hebrew for "God has healed"—and is reiterated in a variety of Patristic writings and in the *Glossa ordinaria*.[1] In the book of Enoch he is described as one of the "four presences," and specifically as "the second, who is set over all the diseases and all the wounds of the children of men" (Enoch 40:9). Because of his name and his role as the healing angel in the book of Tobit he has been identified in different legends as the angel who healed Abraham of the pain of circumcision (which the patriarch underwent as an adult), and Jacob of the injury to

---

[1] See, for example: St. Jerome, *Commentarii in Danielem* (bk. 2 chap. 8); Isidore, *Etymologiarum sive originum libri XX* (bk. 7, chap. 5, par. 13); Gregory the Great, *XL Homiliarum in Evangelia* (bk. 2, hom. 34, chap. 9).; and Nicolas de Lyra, *Biblia sacra cum glossa ordinaria* (Venetiis, 1603), vol. 2 col. 1514 where he writes "Raphael medicina Dei missus est" and then col. 1542 where he adds "et sic angelus iste vocatur Raphael, id est, medicus vel medicina Dei: quia missus fuit ad sanandum Tobiam."

his thigh (incurred when wrestling with the angel). He has also been seen as the angel who, after the flood, gave Noah a medical book, as well as the unnamed healing angel at the Probatic pool at Bethesda (John 5:2–4).[2] Given such wide-ranging medical references, it is surprising that the archangel Raphael is not venerated as the patron saint of doctors and other such healers, a role assumed, instead, by St. Luke, "the beloved physician" (Col. 4:14).[3]

This anomaly, if one may call it so, is evident in Medieval and Renaissance iconography—Raphael is generally depicted as Tobias' guide, rather than Tobit's or Sara's healer. In fact, paintings dealing with the healing of Tobit or Sara are very few and late for our period of interest. An early seventeenth-century example is the painting *Tobias Restores his Father's Sight* (Florence, Certosa del Galluzzo) attributed to the Florentine painter Ottavio Vannini (1585–1644).[4] Another is Orazio Fidani's 1654 *Tobias Healing his Father's Blindness* (Florence, Uffizi).[5]

Raphael's role as a guide was, and has remained, more important than his role as healer. The archangel becomes, in a way, an image of the Guardian Angel. The tenderness of his care for Tobias, for example, could easily suggest he is Tobias' guardian angel, with a continual, life-long commitment to protecting and guiding the young man. By the late sixteenth century, such a connection between the archangel

---

[2] Gustaf Davidson, *A Dictionary of Angels* (New York: The Free Press, 1967), 240.

[3] This and all subsequent citations from the Bible are taken from the Authorized King James translation (Oxford Univ. Press).

[4] Giovanni Leoncini attributes it to Vannini saying: "Non se ne conosce la provenienza. Il soggetto tratto dall'Antico Testamento, fu molto diffuso a Firenze nei primi decenni del Seicento. Per la chiarezza e la semplicità espositiva, sostenuta da un nitido disegno, per i gesti misurati, lo studiato panneggio dell'angiolo, una certa vivezza cromatica, il dipinto è riferibile al Vannini." Caterina Chiarelli and Giovanni Leoncini, eds., *La Certosa del Galluzzo a Firenze* (Milano: Electa Editrice, 1982), 239; see also fig. 38. I am indebted and grateful to dott. Ludovica Sebregondi for kindly pointing out to me both the wonderful painting and Leoncini's comments.

[5] Florence, Uffizi (Deposits). Inv. 1890 n. 7612. Shortly after its completion the painting was donated by Agnolo and Alessandro Galli to the youths' confraternity of the Arcangelo Raffaello detta della Scala (about which more will be said below), where it hung, until 1785, above the left altar in the entrance hall; Archivio di Stato di Firenze (henceforth ASF), Compagnie Religiose Soppresse (henceforth Crs) 164 fasc. 37 "Inventario, 1690" and also ASF, Patrimonio Ecclesiastico (1784) 43, fasc. 32 p. 1.

and the Guardian Angel had become fairly standard. We see it, for example, in the *Flos sanctorum*, a collection of saints' lives compiled in the 1570s–1580s by Alonso de Villegas Selvago (b. 1534), which replaced the medieval *Golden Legend* of Jacobus de Varagine. Under the entry for the feast of the Guardian Angel (at date 1 March in the collection), Alonso de Villegas Selvago narrates the story of Tobias, and then draws several connections between the actions of the archangel Raphael in that story and those of Guardian Angels in general saying:

> In this story we see, drawn from life, what happens to mankind with respect to the holy Guardian Angels. First, they take very great care of us in our adversities and travails, for they present to God the tears we shed at such times, and they pray continually for us and procure for us other advocates in Heaven so that our interests may have better results. They also keep us company in our journey in this world, and if by chance the fish, which is the sin that takes away the life of our soul, should rise against us to devour us, the Holy Angel comes immediately to our help and gives us courage to seize the fish and draw it from the river, cut it to pieces, and examine precisely what is to be found in sin, removing the gall and the liver. The liver, which is our culpability, must be burnt on the fire of our love of God, and thus the demon is put to flight. The gall, which is our pain, must be placed on our eyes to restore our sight, for it [leads us] to consider how God punishes mortal sin with eternal pain. [...] Another role of this Holy Angel is that he advises some [of us] to become priests, and others to get married. For those who get married, he advises them on the reason for marriage, which is to serve God in such a state, and not to give oneself over to sensual pleasures. This Holy Angel also ensures that, if we serve God truly, we will lack nothing of what is necessary for us, that is, both spiritual and material sustenance. Finally, he guides us, happy, to God when our journey in this world has ended. (my translation)[6]

---

[6] "Està aqui muy al vivo dibujado lo que passa à todos los hombres con los santos Angeles de la guarda. Lo priimero, tienen grande cuydado de nosotros en nuestros trabajos, y adversidades, adonde las lacrimas, que en tales tiempos derramamos, las pre-

Although tempting, the interpretation of Raphael as Tobias' guardian angel is, strictly speaking, incorrect, for the book of Tobit is very explicit in pointing out that Raphael undertook a scope- and time-limited mission, and, once this mission was completed, returned to whence he came (Tob. 12). As Raphael himself tells Tobias' family, he is "one of the seven holy angels, which present the prayers of the saints, and which go in and out before the glory of the Holy One" (Tob. 12:15). He is clearly a messenger, a courier, not Tobias' life-long guardian angel. And he himself sums up his recent intervention into that family's life not as the guardian for one or the other member of the family, but rather as the ferryman who carries their prayers and good deeds to God, and His rewards back to them:

> Now therefore, when thou didst pray, and Sara thy daughter in law, I did bring the remembrance of your prayers before the Holy One: and when thou didst bury the dead, I was with thee likewise. And when thou didst not delay to rise up, and leave thy dinner, to go and cover the dead, thy good deed was not hid from me: but I was with thee. And now God hath sent me to heal thee and Sara thy daughter in law.   (Tob. 12:12–14)

---

sentan delange de Dios, y de su parte interceden por nosotros, procurandonos siempre abogados en el Cielo, para que el negocio se haga mejor. Tambien en la jornada deste mundo vàn en nuestra compañia, donde si sale el peze a tragarnos, que es el vicio, y pecado, que nons quita la vida del alma, el santo Angel llega luego, y nos pone animo, para que saquemos el peze del rio, y le hagamos pedazos, considerando por menudo lo que se encierra en el pecado, y que tiene hiel, y higado. El higado se ha de quemar, que es la culpa, en el fuego del amor de Dios, y assi huye el demonio. La hiel, que es la pena, se ha de poner en los ojos con que cobran vista, viendo que por un pecado mortal dà Dios infierno para siempre. [. . .] Tambien es efecto deste santo Angel, que a unos aconseja que tomen estado de Sacerdotes, à otros, de casados. A los que se casan, amonesta el intiento con que se han de casar, que es, por servir à Dios en aquel estado, y no para darse à los deleytes sensuales. Tambien cobra nuestras deudas el santo Angel, siendo muy solicito, en que lo que se nos debe, si de veras servimos à Dios, que es el sustento en lo temporal, y espiritual, no nos falte. Finalmente, buelvemos alegres, y contentos à Dios, quando el viage, y carrera deste mundo se han concluìdo." Alonso de Villegas Selvago, *Flos sanctorum* (Barcelona: Por Pable Nadal y Pedro Escudèr, 1748), 612–13.

The work was translated into Italian at least as early as 1599 by Timoteo da Bagno under the title *Nuovo leggendario della vita, e fatti di N.S. Giesv Christo, e di tvtti i santi* (Venice: Appresso i Gverra, 1599); the above passage appears on p. 696 of that edition.

Nonetheless, the iconographic tradition prefers to present Raphael in the guise of Tobias' guardian angel. Paintings of Tobit and Tobias burying the dead, for example, do not show the archangel Raphael, in spite of the archangel's very clear statement that when they performed such deeds he was with them (Tob. 12:12–13). They show him, instead, as Tobias' companion on the journey.

Some details in the journey narrative are even altered in the iconographic tradition so as to emphasize the archangel's role as guide and guardian. The most obvious revision is that of Tobias' age. In the original, Tobias is a young man, yet old enough to undertake the long journey from Nineveh to Media and to get married to Sara (who is not necessarily young, for the text says she had already been married seven times—albeit briefly, each time). In Renaissance iconography Tobias is, in the vast majority of cases, a vulnerable and innocent young boy, hardly of marriageable age, and certainly not the type of man one would expect to be sent abroad to collect and bring back a sizeable sum of money.

A similar transformation occurs with the archangel Raphael. The narrative says that Tobit "gave [Tobias] the handwriting [i.e., the note of credit] and said unto him, Seek thee a man which may go with thee, ... and I will give him wages: and go and receive the money" (Tob. 5:3). In more modern terms, Tobit is sending Tobias to collect the money he had invested abroad, and tells him to find himself a paid body-guard for such a business trip. Rather than the reliable body-guard suggested by the book of Tobit, or the masculine angel of early Christian iconography, one finds instead in Renaissance iconography that the archangel is a sexless or effeminate adolescent, wearing beautifully flowing ankle-length robes, adorned with sparkling jewels, walking barefoot (or perhaps wearing a pair of rather ineffectual sandals); he is also encumbered with a pair of enormous wings more appropriate to flying than walking on the ground.[7] It is clear that the practical realities of overland travel have been ignored by Renaissance painters.

The fact that the archangel was Tobias' body-guard has also been

---

[7] See, for example, the Botticini panel (Florence, Accademia) or his altarpiece (Florence, Uffizi), or the Pollaiuoli panel (Turin, Galleria), all reproduced in Gertrude M. Achenbach, in "The Iconography of Tobias and the Angel in Florentine Painting of the Renaissance" *Marsyas* 3 (1943–45): 71–91.

ignored, unless one looks for it under the guise of "companion."
Raphael's enormous wings do, sometime, seem to enfold and hence
protect the young Tobias. This gesture, however, is more appropriate
to an image of the Guardian Angel than to that of the archangel who,
disguised as a man (hence without wings or long flowing robes), had
escorted Tobias to Media and back.

The concept of Raphael as a guide is thus removed from the physical reality of a journey to Media, or from the context of international
financial investments, in order to transfer it to the spiritual world of the
journey and enrichment of the soul. Tobias is no longer a real person,
but an image of our soul—vulnerable, lacking experience, childish—
and the archangel Raphael is no longer "one of the seven holy angels
... which go in and out before the glory of the Holy One" (Tob.
12:15), but an image of the Guardian Angel who walks beside us in
our life-journey. Once this change takes place, then the episode can be
extracted from its historical context and the two participants, Raphael
and Tobias, placed into a mystical context, as in Raphael's *Madonna of
the Fish* (1512–14; Madrid, Prado), where the two travellers are not depicted proceeding to Media, but rather taking part in an adoration of
the Madonna and Child—the archangel Raphael has just presented the
young Tobias to Mary and Jesus, and now gently helps the youth rise
from a kneeling position so as to offer the fish he has been carrying to
the Mother and Child.[8]

The concept of a "spiritual guide" is further suggested by the relationship between the two travellers. Often the archangel Raphael
seems hardly to touch Tobias, as if the physical contact between him
and the youth were unimportant. Such is the case in Andrea Verrocchio's *Tobias and the Angel* (c. 1470, London, National Gallery), or
Perugino's tryptich of *The Virgin, Child, and the archangels Michael and
Raphael* (c. 1507, London, National Gallery). What is more important,
instead, is the spiritual link between the two travellers, underlined by
the intent gaze that unites them. In Cima da Conegliano's rendition,
*The Archangel Raphael and Tobias between St. James the Greater and St.
Nicholas* (Venice, Gallerie dell'Accademia), the two figures are walking

---

[8] See Jeanne Villette, *L'Ange dans l'art d'occident du XIIe au XVIe siècle. France, Italie,
Flandre, Allemagne* (Paris: Henri Laurens, 1940), 293–96 for a more detailed discussion
of these aspects.

side by side, like friends.[9] Raphael speaks and Tobias listens. Raphael gestures vaguely as if to emphasize something he is saying; it seems the archangel is instructing the youth. His guidance is therefore spiritual, moral, not necessarily physical, or earthly.

The fact that the "business aspect" of the story is not emphasized, nor even suggested, in Renaissance iconography may be attributable (not without a sense of irony) to the people who were commissioning such paintings. Emile Mâle noted that after the fifteenth century the cult of the archangel Raphael was tied to the growing cult of the Guardian Angel, and then, drawing a charming image of such devotion, connected it to Florentine international banking and business interests.

> Since the 15th century, the archangel Raphael had often been represented accompanying the young Tobias to Rages. The Book of Tobit, this charming narrative in the Bible, where a sweet piety and a deep sense of family are joined to the fantasies of an oriental imagination, fascinated the Christian world. Fifteenth-century art multiplied these images [of the archangel Raphael accompanying Tobias] because the archangel Raphael was then considered to be something of a patron saint for travellers. The Florentine merchant who sent his son to his subsidiary in Bruges prayed the archangel to bring him back safe and sound, and commissioned in his honour a painting depicting the archangel leading Tobias's son by the hand. When the cult of the Guardian Angel began to expand, it came naturally to depict him as the archangel Raphael guiding the youth through unknown lands. (my translation)[10]

---

[9] See Luigi Menegazzi, ed., *Cima da Conegliano. Catalogo della mostra* (Venezia: Neri Pozza Editore, 1962), 66–67 and fig. 92; or Peter Humfrey, *Cima da Conegliano* (Cambridge: Cambridge Univ. Press, 1983), 64–65 and plate 159.

[10] "Depuis le XVe siècle, l'archange Raphaël était souvent représenté accompagnant le jeune Tobie à Ragès. Ce livre de Tobie, ce charmant récit de la Bible, où une douce piété et un sentiment profond de la famille s'associent aux fantaisies de l'imagination orientale, enchantait la chrétienté. L'art du XVe siècle multiplia ces images, parce que l'archange Raphaël était considéré alors comme le patron des voyageurs. Le marchand de Florence, qui envoyait son fils dans son comptoir de Bruges, priait l'archange de le lui ramener sain et sauf, et faisait peindre en son honneur un tableau qui le représentait conduisant le fils de Tobie par la main. Quand le culte de l'ange gardien commença à se répandre, on trouva naturel de le figurer sous les traits de l'archange Raphaël guidant le jeune homme à travers des pays inconnus."

A similar connection among the cult of the archangel Raphael, that of the Guardian Angel, Florentine business interests across Europe, and the ever-present reality of Italian exiles was echoed a few years later by another French scholar, Jeanne Villette, who pin-pointed the flowering of archangel Raphael iconography to late fifteenth-century Florence:

> The cult of angels had always been quite extensive in central Italy. That of the archangel who protects Tobias against the dangers of his journey and brings him back happy and full of life to his old father was especially suitable to those whose anxious hearts followed their absent loved ones on the road of exile. Are not political turmoil and the proscriptions that followed it, as well as the business voyages of Florentine and Lombard bankers whose subsidiaries were multiplying as far away as Flanders, at the roots of this passion for the traveller-archangel, and do they not explain the abundance of artworks that represent them? . . .
>
> It is in Tuscany, in the second half of the fifteenth century, in a time of fratricidal turmoil, that the first images of the archangel multiply. The subject then passes, at the end of the century, to Venetian lands, and from there it enters into lands North [of the Alps]. (my translation)[11]

Gertrude Achenbach, who examined closely the Raphael-Tobias iconography in Medieval and Renaissance Italy, suggested there was no possibility of seeing in these devotional paintings the Humanism and initiative for which Renaissance Florence is so famous:

Emile Mâle, *L'Art religieux après le Concile de Trente* (Paris: Armand Colin, 1932), 305.

[11] "Le culte des anges avait toujours été très répandu dans le centre de l'Italie. Celui de l'archange, qui protège Tobie exposé aux dangers du chemin et qui le ramène heureux et plein de vie à son vieux père, convenait spécialement à des coeurs anxieux dont la pensée cherche les absents sur la route de l'exil. Les luttes politiques et les proscriptions qu'elles entraînent, les voyages d'affaires aussi des banquiers florentins et lombards dont les comptoirs se multiplient jusqu'en la lointaine Flandre, ne seraient-ils pas à l'origine de cette ferveur à l'égard de l'archange-voyageur, et n'expliqueraient-ils pas l'abondance des oeuvres qui les représentent? . . .

C'est dans la Toscane de la deuxième moitié du XVe siècle, au temps des luttes fratricides, que se multiplient les premières images de l'archange. Puis le sujet passe, à la fin du siècle, sur les terres vénetiennes et, de là, gagne les pays du Nord." Villette, *L'Ange dans l'art d'occident*, 293. This connection is again mentioned by Achenbach, who also ties it in with sons going abroad to do business and gain experience in the family firm; Achenbach, "The Iconography of Tobias," 76.

The possibility of interpreting the subject as a humanistic theme is excluded by the class of patrons commissioning paintings of it, and by the type of artists who executed them. Instead, we must recognize in its popularity an expression of the beliefs and interests of an unprogressive and pious class of Florentine Renaissance society.[12]

Although there may be cause for argument with Achenbach's grounds for such conclusions, she did point correctly to the "popular" nature of such iconography.

An example of how the archangel Raphael entered into the popular imagination of the time is offered by a 1465 letter from Alessandra Macinghi negli Strozzi to her exiled sons. The mother, residing in Florence, brings the archangel Raphael to her distant children's attention:

Be sure to pray God for us; and do some good deeds in His honor and in honor of His blessed mother the Virgin Mary, and of the Angel Raphael who, as he protected little Tobias from danger and deceits, and then brought him back to his father and mother, so may he also bring you back to your mother, who awaits you eagerly. (my translation)[13]

A growing cult for the archangel Raphael in Renaissance Florence can be surmised, as well, from the establishment of two different confraternities named in his honor, one for adults and one for youths.[14]

---

[12] Achebach, "The Iconography of Tobias," 80.

[13] "Attendiano pure a raccomandarci a Dio; e disponetevi di fare qualche bene a onore suo e della sua benedetta madre Vergine Maria, e dell'Angiolo Raffaello, che come guardò Tubbiuzzo da pericolo e da inganni, e poi lo rimenò al padre e alla madre, che così rimeni voi a vostra madre, che con tanto disiderio v'aspetta." Alessandra Macinghi negli Strozzi, *Lettere di una gentildonna fiorentina del secolo XV ai figliuoli esuli*, ed. Cesare Guasti (Firenze: Sansoni, 1877), 517; also published in Alessandro D'Ancona "Una gentildonna fiorentina del secolo XV" in *Varietà storiche e letterarie* (Milano: Treves, 1883–85), 230.

[14] Confraternities were founded, in general, in order to offer their members a devotional outlet outside the standard liturgical/clerical context. Their activities consisted, primarily, of communal recitation of prayers (usually modelled on the monastic hours). Many confraternities fostered the singing of religious songs called *laude*, thus becoming known as *laudesi* confraternities (those who sing *laude*). Others preferred to practice penance, especially in the form of self-flagellation, and became known as *battuti* (those

Little is known of the adults' confraternity of the archangel Raphael, also known as "il Raffa" (a common Florentine abbreviation for "Raffaele"). Because the group seems not to have distinguished itself within the Florentine context, modern scholars have not examined closely the confraternity's extensive records at the Archivio di Stato.[15] They were a flagellant confraternity, meeting in the Oltrarno, in rooms facing via Maffia and backing against the convent of Santo Spirito (from whom the confraternity had received its site). The men of the Raffa did, like other Florentine confraternities, commission artworks for their oratory and meeting rooms, but little is known about this.[16]

The youths' confraternity of the archangel Raphael, also known as "la Scala" (from the name of the Ospice where it met in the fifteenth century), is much more important and consequently better known.[17] Musicologists, in particular, have cast their eyes upon it because, at the

---

who beat themselves). Beside prayers, singing, or flagellation, confraternities also performed works of mercy, such as burying the dead, comforting the afflicted, feeding the hungry, etc., according to their own specific inclination or calling.

For an excellent recent work on Italian confraternities see Christopher Black, *Italian Confraternities in the Sixteenth Century* (Cambridge: Cambridge Univ. Press, 1989); for a more specific and analytical study of the confraternal movement in Florence see Ronald F. E. Weissman, *Ritual Brotherhood in Renaissance Florence* (New York: Academic Press, 1982); for a good variety of recent articles on Italian confraternities see Konrad Eisenbichler, ed., *Crossing the Boundaries. Christian Piety and the Arts in Italian Medieval and Renaissance Confraternities*, Early Drama, Art, and Music Monograph Series, 15 (Kalamazoo: Medieval Institute Publications, 1991); for an excellent collection of essays on Italian confraternities associated with the Dominicans see Gilles Gerard Meersseman's fundamental *Ordo fraternitatis. Confraternite e pietà dei laici nel Medioevo* (Rome: Herder, 1977); Gennaro M. Monti's *Le confraternite medioevali dell'alta e media Italia* (Venezia: 1927) is old and, in many ways, has been superseded, however it remains an important source in the field. The bi-annual *Confraternitas* (Toronto: Centre for Reformation and Renaissance Studies, 1990–) is the official bulletin of the Society for Confraternity Studies and includes in each issue a good, though incomplete, bibliography of recent work.

[15] Documents for the Compagnia dell'Arcangelo Raffaello detta del Raffa are at the ASF, Crs 139–54. The earliest reference to it is in a 1454 processional list; see John S. Henderson, *Piety and Charity in Late Medieval Florence. Religious Confraternities from the Middle of the Thirteenth Century to the Late Fifteenth Century* (Ph.D. diss., Univ. of London, 1983), 396.

[16] Ernst Künnel, *Francesco Botticini* (Strasbourg: 1906), 203, makes a passing reference to the confraternity and cites briefly the 1542 inventory of the paintings at il Raffa; see also Monti, *Le confraternite medioevali* 1:183.

[17] The documents for the Compagnia dell'Arcangelo Raffaello detta della Scala are at the ASF, Crs 155–65.

turn of the seventeeth century a number of important musicians and composers belonged to it—Jacopo Peri and Marco da Gagliano, to mention just two.[18] Art historians have not yet examined it closely, though the youths of the archangel Raphael did possess a number of works by contemporary Florentine painters.[19]

Although in the Renaissance the archangel Raphael did not enjoy a universally-declared feastday of his own,[20] the youths of the archangel Raphael in Florence celebrated his feast on 31 December with special Masses, Vespers, music, food, and occasionally a small theatrical event. Theirs was such a fine feast that it attracted the attention of

---

[18] See John Walter Hill "Oratory Music in Florence, I: *Recitar Cantando*, 1583–1655," *Acta Musicologica* 51:1 (Januar–Juni 1979): 108–36; Edmond N. Strainchamps "Marco da Gagliano and the Compagnia dell'Arcangelo Raffaello in Florence: An Unknown Episode in the Composer's Life," in *Essays Presented to Myron P. Gilmore*, ed. S. Bertelli and G. Ramakus (Florence: La Nuova Italia, 1978), 2:473–87 (also published, without plates, in *Studies in Music from the University of Western Ontario* 3 (1978) 35–47); and his "Memorial Madrigals for Jacopo Corsi in the Company of the Archangel Raphael," in Eisenbichler, *Crossing the Boundaries* 161–78. See also the very recent work by Blake Wilson, *Music and Merchants. The Laudesi Companies of Republican Florence* (Oxford: Oxford Univ. Press, 1992).

[19] The different confraternity inventories indicate the youths had commissioned or received as gifts quite a number of paintings on a variety of subjects appropriate to the confraternity. To mention just a few: Lorenzo Lippi's panel of the *Crucifixion with the Virgin, St. Mary Magdalene, and St. John the Evangelist* (now in Florence, San Marco); a crucifix also by Lorenzo Lippi; Orazio Fidani's panel of *Tobias Healing his Father's Blindness* (recently restored and now in Florence, Uffizi); Jacopo Chimenti detto l'Empoli's *Our Lady Presenting a Member of our Confraternity*; ten large paintings on canvas, some by Lorenzo Lippi, others by Baccio del Bianco, illustrating stories touching on the Archangel Raphael; the panel *Virgin with Child and Saints Dominic and Jerome* (Cambridge, Mass., Yale University Art Gallery) attributed in the confraternity inventories to Domenico Ghirlandaio but in fact by Piero di Cosimo. They also possessed works by Giovanni di San Giovanni, Giovan Battista di Benedetto, Jacopo Ferretti, Bartolomeo Neri, Valerio Spada (calligraphy and illustrations on the *Capitoli* of 1636). ASF, Crs 164, fasc. 37 "Inventario . . . 1690." In my forthcoming book on the confraternity of the archangel Raphael there will be a detailed listing of artworks in this confraternity.

[20] Such a feast day was universally declared and set for 24 October only in 1921. Previous to that, there had been locally celebrated feasts in honor of the archangel Raphael on dates that varied according to country and diocese. In Spain, for example, the feast was celebrated on 7 May; in France on 9 or 15 July; in Venice on 22 April; Pietro de Natalibus gives the feast day of the archangel Raphael as 8 May; Molano, Canisius, and Ferraris, in their martyrologies, give 20 October; and so forth. For a summary of such variances see the *Enciclopedia cattolica* (Vatican City and Florence: Sansoni, 1948–53), 10:471, *ad vocem* "Raffaele."

non-members, as well. Christine of Lorraine, Grand-duchess of Tuscany, attended the event in 1589 and 1591. The second time she was
so impressed by the confraternity's devotion and celebrations she
immediately enrolled the young heir to the throne, Cosimo II de'
Medici, in the group.[21]

The festivities could be fairly ornate and extensive, so much so that
every year, in early December, the confraternity appointed a dozen
members to supervise the preparations for the feast and another dozen
to arrange for the little buns (*panellini*) that were to be distributed to all
present.

In 1563, for example, the feastday started with a solemnly sung
Mass celebrated at the confraternity's High Altar by one of the priests
from the near-by Dominican convent of Santa Maria Novella. Then
the Office of the Virgin Mary was recited (that is, the Canonical Hours
of Prime, Terce, Sext, None). The confraternity's own chaplain (*Padre
Correttore*) then celebrated a Low Mass, again at the High Altar, in
which he gave communion to past and present members of the confraternity ("padri et fratelli"). After this Mass the brothers charged with
providing the *panellini* came out dressed in their confraternal robes
bearing baskets full of bread to be blessed by the chaplain. Then, after
the youths had sung a religious song (*lauda*), another brother came out
dressed as the youth Tobias and recited some verses of admonition to
the confraternity's outgoing and incoming officers. He then declared
that he wished to distribute the buns himself, with the assistance of two
Virtues. At this point two more youths came out, dressed as the allegorical figures Humility and Obedience, and each recited some more
verses addressed this time to all members. Tobias then called upon the
youths bearing the baskets and, with the help of Humility and Obedience, distributed the bread to all present as all members sang the *Te
Deum* antiphonally. Tobias then gave licence to go, the Ave Maria was
sung, and everyone departed. The confraternity reconvened in the
afternoon for Vespers (sung with organ accompanyment), and then one
of the youths delivered a sermon. It reconvened a third time in the
evening to recite Matins and hear a sermon from the chaplain.[22]

---

[21] ASF, Crs 162, fasc. 21/22 fols. 143v–144v.
[22] ASF, Crs 160, fasc. 7/8, at date 31 Dec. 1563.

The feastday was such an important day in the confraternity's devotional calendar that it was attended by the adult supervisors of the other major Florentine youth confraternities (in particular the *Guardiani* of S. Marco, S. Giovanni Vangelista, and S. Niccolò). Occasionally, especially by the end of the sixteenth century, the event was also attended by members of the Grand-ducal family, such as the Grand-duchess Christina, who has been mentioned above.

Such a feast, however, did not lead to the creation of a special liturgy in honor of the archangel Raphael. As is evident from the description of the 1563 celebrations, the confraternity was satisfied, liturgically, with standard Masses, Vespers, and the recitation of the Office. These rites were accompanied by music and sermons, the recitation in costume of a few appropriate verses, and the distribution of buns. There is no indication in the surviving documents that the readings for the Masses, Vespers, or the Office had anything to do with the archangel Raphael, or the Tobias story. Christ and the Virgin Mary were at the center of the youths' liturgical devotions by virtue of the standard rites of Mass, Vespers, and Office; the archangel and his young charge were consigned, instead, to their devotees' non-liturgical imagination by having them literally walk into the hall, talk to those present, and distribute food. Tobias and the archangel entered into the youths' imagination, therefore, not so much as devotional objects, but rather as festive objects; they were part of a mythology created by costume, recitation, and acting.

Other times when the archangel Raphael and Tobias enter into the activities of this confraternity further support such conclusions. On Sunday, 3 June 1582, for example, the confraternity's records describe the representation of a dramatized dialogue between Tobias and a stranger. The dialogue ends with the appearance of the archangel Raphael who urges all present to remain faithful to the Lord:

We gathered in the morning at an appropriate time and in great numbers, the Matins of the Virgin were very solemnly sung with music, and when they were finished our Father Corrector celebrated Holy Mass, and after he had delivered a long and very beautiful sermon he gave Communion to 32 of our fathers and brothers, and then, after the usual offering to the altar, we made a small collection for our servant, and everyone was dismissed.

Returning in the afternoon after lunch, after the usual Vespers had been recited, Antonio di Lionardo Tempi read a lesson on Charity, the third theological virtue, then the usual offering to the altar was made, and our substitute Guardian Father, Zanobi Buonavolti, invited everyone to stay in the hall, and after the Ave Maria was sung, [everyone] stayed in the hall, and out come a youth and Sir Tobias dressed like a pilgrim, and after a long dialogue Tobias threw off his pilgrim's cloak and revealed who he was, and after he comforted the youth a little he began to say a prayer to the Archangel Raphael, and when this was done the said Archangel Raphael came out accompanied by two angels and a musical choir, and they began to sing a madrigal, and when this was finished the Archangel Raphael gave some advice to Tobias, and asked the two angels to give everyone a printed sheet of paper containing:

> the 12 articles of faith
> the Creed
> the 10 Comandments of the law
> the 7 sacraments of the church
> the 3 theological virtues
> the 4 cardinal virtues
> the 7 gifts of the Holy Spirit
> the 12 fruits of the Holy Spirit
> the 2 comandments of Charity
> the 7 spiritual works of mercy
> the 7 corporal works of mercy
> the 7 deadly sins
> the 4 things a Christian must always remember
> the 5 senses of the body
> the comandments of the Church
> the things a good Christian must observe
> the 6 sins against the Holy Spirit
> the 8 Beatitudes
> Praised be the Lord. (my translation)[23]

---

[23] "Ragunamoci la mattina per tempo e in gran numero, dissesi cantando di musica il mattutino della Vergine solennissimamente, il qual fornito dal nostro Padre

The youths also dressed up as angels with the archangel Raphael and Tobias on the morning of the 23rd of June for the great parade in honor of St. John the Baptist, the patron saint of Florence:

> We gathered in the morning at an appropriate time, and our Father Corrector recited Holy Mass, then we prepared ourselves to go to the procession, the Archangel Raphael and Tobias got dressed, with a choir of about 12 angels, who continually sang a madrigal ... composed by one of our beloved brothers. (my translation)[24]

Correttore fu celebrata la santa Messa, di poi doppo che hebbe fatto un lungo e bellissimo sermone communicò 32 de' nostri padri e fratelli, di poi si fece doppo la solita offerta all'altare un poco di limosina al nostro servo di poi ciascun fu licentiato.

Tornati al solito il giorno doppo mangiare detto che fu il solito vespro Antonio di Lionardo Tempi lesse una lettione sopra la Carità, terza virtù tèologale, di poi si fece l'offerta solita all'altare, e dal nostro sostituto [Guardiano] Zanobi Buonavolti fu commesso a ciascuno di fermarsi nello stanzone detto, e sonata che fussi l'Ave Maria, e fermoronsi a sedere nello stanzone, venne fuori un giovane e Ser Tobbia vestito in forma di pellegrino, e doppo un lungo lor discorso il detto Tobbia gettato via l'habito del pellegrino se li dimostrò quello che egli era, e riconfortato alquanto il giovane cominciò a far un'orazione all'Arcangelo Raffaello e finita che fu venne fuora il detto Arcangelo Raffaello accompagnato da 2 angeli e un coro di musica e cominciorno a cantare un madrigale il qual fornito dall'Arcangelo Raffaello fu consigliato Tobbia, e per mano de' 2 Angeli dette a ciascuno una carta stampata di questo tenore

Li 12 articoli della fede
Credo in deum Patrem omnipotentem creatorem celi et terre e quel che segue
i 10 comandamenti della legge
i 7 sacramenti della chiesa
le 3 virtù teologali
le 4 virtù cardinali
i 7 doni dello Spirito Santo
i 12 frutti dello Spirito Santo
i 2 comandamenti della Carità
le 7 opere spirituali della misericordia
le 7 opere di misericordia temporale
li 7 peccati mortali
le 4 cose si dee ricordare continuamente il christiano
li 5 sentimenti del corpo
li comandamenti della chiesa
le cose da osservarsi dal buon christiano
li 6 peccati contro lo Spirito Santo
le 8 beatitudini
Laus Deo"   ASF, Crs 162, fasc. 21/22, fols.12v–13r.

[24] "Ragunati la mattina per tempo, et il nostro Correttore disse la S. Messa, di poi ci mettemmo in ordine per ire alla processione, vestironsi l'Arcangelo Raffaello e

Although in theory a religious feast, St. John's was, in fact, an un-abashed celebration of Florentine civic pride. Parades and processions easily blended the secular with the spiritual, so much so that they al-lowed for the presence of costumed youths singing religious songs and, in certain years, staging religious pantomines or even plays.[25] As early as the mid-fifteenth century, the saintly archbishop Antoninus had sought to reform the celebrations by separating the secular elements from the relig-ious moments of the *festa*, but the nature of the three-day celebration retained an inextricably complex mixture of sacred and profane.[26]

As in the case of the St. John festivities, so too with the archangel Raphael—Florentine attitudes and practices contained a complex inter-twining of secular and religious interests.

There was, undoubtedly, a growing awareness among Florentines in general of the archangel and his role as guide, teacher, and protector. It is not suprising, therefore, that the archangel was seen as protector of Florentine youths, especially those travelling afar or those enrolled in the confraternity named in his honor. The archangel thus became a companion on the journey of life, a big brother, as it were, who looked over his young devotees.[27]

Florentines thus commissioned devotional paintings of the archangel and Tobias, and, as Gertrude Achenbach points out, some even had their sons portrayed on the canvas as the young Hebrew boy.[28] By promoting the image of Raphael as a guide to the young Tobias, rather than as healer of Tobit or Sara, Florentines drew attention to the theme of angelic protection on a business journey. In a way, they were connecting their business practices and extensive foreign financial inter-

---

Tobia, con un coro di 12 angeli in circa, che andavano continovamente cantando un madrigale ... composto per uno de' nostri amorevoli frategli." ASF, Crs 162, fasc. 21/22 fol. 15r–v.

[25] For a discussion of the theatrical aspects of the San Giovanni parade, see Nerida Newbigin's introduction to her *Nuovo corpus di Sacre Rappresentazioni fiorentine del Quat-trocento*, ed. Nerida Newbigin (Bologna: Commissione per i Testi di Lingua, 1983).

[26] For a dated, but still unsurpassed examination of the festivities for San Giovanni see Pietro Gori, *Le feste fiorentine attraverso i secoli*, vol. 1, *Le feste per San Giovanni* (Flor-ence: R. Bemporad & Figlio, 1926).

[27] The term "big brother" is perhaps more appropriate than may at first appear, for the well-known Florentine practice of late marriage for men did result in quite a number of children remaining orphaned in their youth.

[28] Achenbach, "The Iconography of Tobias," 76–77.

ests with their love for their sons who, on many occasions, gained business experience tending to Florentine interests abroad.

Many young Florentines enrolled themselves in the confraternity dedicated to the archangel. The group flourished in numbers, wealth, and prestige and became the preeminent lay religious youth organization in the city. It developed a cultic life around the archangel, but failed to turn it into an officially sanctioned devotional ritual. It celebrated a special feast in honor of the archangel, but did not develop a liturgy for it. Although the feast attracted illustrious spectators, it was limited to the confines of the confraternity. In line with the confraternity's "praise-singing" (i.e., *laudese*) background, the festivities were characterized by musical and theatrical elements more conducive to "staging" the archangel and Tobias than to developing a specific devotional ritual.

In conclusion, Florentine iconography and popular piety during the fifteenth and sixteenth centuries fostered but at the same time emasculated devotion to the archangel Raphael. The iconography, which focused on a particular episode and significantly revised the figures of its two major participants, eventually turned the event into an icon for a completely different concept—that of the Guardian Angel. The popular piety that brought into existence the youth confraternity of the archangel Raphael also belied its original intentions. Instead of fostering an independent devotional cult, it developed a festive imagination that lead the youths more to spectacle than to ritual. The young men of the archangel Raphael, like the figures of Raphael and Tobias in Renaissance paintings, thus became elegant actors on the stage of Florentine civic life. And the archangel under whose patronage they gathered became an excuse, rather than a reason for their meetings.

Praying to Saints in the Late Middle Ages*

VIRGINIA REINBURG

n their prayers, late medieval Christians addressed saints as relatives, friends, and lords. St. Barbara is "my honorable mistress" to the devotee in a prayer from fifteenth-century Lorraine. In another prayer St. Anne is told, "God is the son of your own daughter . . . , your daughter is queen and duchess of the heavenly saints." A text from Rouen has the devotee declare herself Mary Magdalene's "human goddaughter."[1] Not only were forms of address familiar from secular life, but the very modes of relating to saints suggested the support, responsibility, and protection expected within family and community. In this article I will outline some ways late medieval men and women understood their relationships to saints, as reflected in the prayers and devotional images in

* This article grows out of a book I am completing on the social history of prayer in fifteenth- and sixteenth-century France (forthcoming from Cornell Univ. Press). I am grateful to Thomas Head and Lucinda Smith for helpful comments made in the course of conversations about saints. Research for this article was supported by the American Council of Learned Societies and the Department of History, Princeton University.

[1] St. Barbara: Bibliothèque Municipale de Nancy MS. 35 (245), fols. 122v–123v (Hours, use of Toul, fifteenth century) (Pierre Rézeau, *Les prières en français à la fin du moyen age: Prières à un saint particulier et aux anges* [Geneva: Librairie Droz, 1983], no. 63). St. Anne: Bibliothèque Municipale de Dôle MS. 45, pp. 157–60 (Hours, undetermined use, fifteenth century; region of Langres) (Rézeau no. 45). Mary Magdalene: Fitzwilliam Museum, Cambridge (England), MS. 105, fol. 88v (Hours, use of Rouen, 1530) (Rézeau no. 166).

French and Flemish books of hours (ca. 1350–1550). In addition, I will comment on the role of the book of hours in nurturing relationships between human beings and the saints to whom they prayed.

The book of hours, a compilation of offices, litanies, and prayers originally adapted from the breviary, was the prayer book of the laity.[2] By the mid-fourteenth century it had distanced itself considerably from its clerical origins. The addition of vernacular texts, family diaries, and other personal material demonstrates the ability of the book of hours to accommodate the religious concerns of the literate laity. These additions are threads that link the book of hours to contemporary devotional practices such as pilgrimage, membership in confraternities, and pious bequests. For the historian of religious life the book of hours holds within its covers precious bits of information about the religious practices of a wide segment of late medieval society. For as a devotional object it is located at the intersection of literate and not necessarily literate religious experience—particularly the visual, aural, and tactile dimensions of medieval religious experience. Owners of books of hours sometimes pasted or sewed amulets and religious medallions inside their books. And both manuscript and printed prayer books often included devotional images. These visual and tactile features of the book, reinforced by the interiority of private reading by owners, created a physical and psychic space for meditative prayer.[3] In the devotional imagi-

---

[2] On the history of the book of hours see Roger S. Wieck, "Introduction," and V. Reinburg, "Prayer and the Book of Hours," in *Time Sanctified: The Book of Hours in Medieval Art and Life*, ed. Wieck (Baltimore and New York: The Walters Art Gallery and George Braziller, 1988), 27–32, 39–44; V. Leroquais, "Introduction," *Les Livres d'Heures manuscrits de la Bibliothèque Nationale*, 3 vols. and supplement (Paris and Mâcon: Bibliothèque Nationale, 1927–43); Joachim Plotzek, *Andachtsbücher des Mittelalters aus Privatbesitz* (Cologne: Schnütgen-Museum, 1987), especially 9–64; L. M. J. Delaissé, "The Importance of the Book of Hours for the History of the Medieval Book," in *Gatherings in Honor of Dorothy E. Miner*, ed. Ursula McCracken et al. (Baltimore: The Walters Art Gallery, 1974), 203–25; and James H. Marrow, "Introduction," *The Golden Age of Dutch Manuscript Painting* (New York: George Braziller, 1990), 9–16.

[3] My forthcoming book explores in detail the features of books of hours noted in this paragraph. On the use of devotional images and amulets in books of hours and related devotional books see especially Sixten Ringbom, "Devotional Images and Imaginative Devotions: Notes on the Place of Art in Late Medieval Private Piety," *Gazette des Beaux-Arts*, 6th series, 73 (1969): 159–70; Erwin Panofsky, "'Imago Pietatis,' Ein Beitrag zur Typengeschichte des 'Schmerzensmanns' und der 'Maria Mediatrix,'" in *Festschrift für Max J. Friedländer zum 60. Geburtstage* (Leipzig: E. A. Seemann, 1927), 261–308; Hans Belting, *Das Bild und sein Publikum im Mittelalter*

nation of the laity, this space became the world in which personal relationships with saints and God were forged.

Praying to a saint meant engaging in a dialogue with the saint, a dialogue in which both devotee and saint communicated through words and actions. Books of hours preserve examples of this dialogue in images and texts. A fifteenth-century miniature depicts an affectionate relationship between a woman and her patron, St. Catherine, and also explains how the saint helps her protégée. As the woman kneels in prayer before Jesus, Catherine stands behind her, resting a hand on her shoulder. The woman has the courage to approach Jesus himself because of the support and encouragement of her patron saint (fig. 1).[4] Texts of prayers also preserve the dialogue between supplicant and saint. One such text is entitled "Vow made by the city of Cervières in October 1628, to Saint Roch, confessor, taken as patron." Here the village appeals to St. Roch to preserve it from the plague, and pledges to honor him as patron in return for his protection. The villagers ask the saint "to be a very good friend to us, before Jesus, the heavenly king." In response, St. Roch replies that he has presented the petition to God, who, for his part, promised to curb the plague's spread.[5]

The hierarchy of appeal—from devotee to saint to God—conforms

---

(Berlin: Gebr. Mann Verlag, 1981); Kurt Köster, "Religiöse Medaillen und Wallfahrts-Devotionalien in der flämischen Buchmalerei des 15. und frühen 16. Jahrhunderts," in *Buch und Welt: Festschrift für Gustav Hofmann zum 65. Geburtstag dargebracht* (Wiesbaden: Otto Harrassowitz, 1965), 459–504; and Curt F. Bühler, "Prayers and Charms in Certain Middle English Scrolls," *Speculum* 39 (1964): 270–78. On the practices of reading see Paul Saenger, "Silent Reading: Its Impact on Late Medieval Script and Society," *Viator* 13 (1982): 367–414; Saenger, "Books of Hours and the Reading Habits of the Later Middle Ages," in *The Culture of Print*, ed. Roger Chartier and trans. Lydia Cochrane (Princeton: Princeton Univ. Press, 1989), 141–73; R. W. Scribner, *For the Sake of Simple Folk: Popular Propaganda for the German Reformation* (Cambridge: Cambridge Univ. Press, 1981), 1–13.

[4] Walters Art Gallery, Baltimore, MS. W. 220, fol. 150v (Hours, use of Rome, ca. 1450; produced in Bruges).

[5] "Voeu faict par la ville de Cervieres, en octobre 1628, a saint Roch, confesseur, prins pour patron." Bibliothèque Municipale de Lyon MS. 1402, fol. 128 (Hours, use of Rome, sixteenth century with seventeenth-century additions). I have used the text edited by Rézeau (*Les prières aux saints*, 442–44). Rézeau notes that Cervières (Lyonnais) suffered through the plague in 1628, and erected a chapel honoring St. Roch in that year. The vow was likely composed on the occasion of the chapel's dedication. This text resembles the vows to saints composed by the sixteenth-century Spanish villagers William Christian Jr. has written about in *Local Religion in Sixteenth-Century Spain* (Princeton: Princeton Univ. Press, 1981), especially chaps. 2–3, and app. A.

to late medieval notions of salvation, a business laboriously conducted through avenues of spiritual patronage, entailing intricate exchanges of favors and gifts. The village of Cervières hopes that St. Roch's friendship with God will enable the community to gain God's ear, while the villagers' gifts of prayers and a chapel should encourage the saint to listen to them. Reciprocity rules relationships between devotees and saints; in exchange for praise and donations, devotees receive spiritual and material assistance from the saints to whom they pray.

The concept of patron applied readily to saints. After all, saints were members of God's court and thus had his ear. Some saints were closer than courtiers, being either relatives (Anne, John the Baptist) or friends (John the apostle and Mary Magdalene). That saints were in principle able to intercede with God on a devotee's behalf was beyond question for most medieval Christians. But a devotee needed to establish a personal relationship with a saint, a relationship promising the saint's favor. This is the central goal of prayer to saints.

Spiritual patronage held out the promise of connection to God through someone close to him. Owners of books of hours were often identified as protégés of particular saints through special prayers or devotional portraits. Like the miniature of St. Catherine described above, many images depict the patron standing behind the devotee, resting a hand on the devotee's right shoulder (fig. 1). Isabelle de Coucy's prayer book portrays her praying before the Virgin Mary and child Jesus (fig. 2).[6] Far more than a standard devotional portrait, however, this painting states precisely that Isabelle and Jesus are engaged in a feudal relationship, as fifteenth- and sixteenth-century French society understood that kind of relationship. Mary inclines her head toward Isabelle, signalling attentiveness, while Jesus grasps Isabelle's folded hands in his hand. Each gesture performed here—Isabelle kneeling and folding her hands, Jesus holding her hands in his own—constitutes an element of the ritual of homage by which a lord and a vassal made a mutual vow of service and protection.[7]

---

[6] Walters Art Gallery MS. W. 89, fol. 3v (Hours, use of Paris, ca. 1380; Hours of Isabelle de Coucy, wife of Raoul II de Raineval).

[7] On this ritual see J. Russell Major, " 'Bastard Feudalism' and the Kiss: Changing Social Mores in Late Medieval and Early Modern France," *Journal of Interdisciplinary History* 17 (1987): 509–35; and Marc Bloch, *Feudal Society*, trans. L. A. Manyon, 2 vols. (Chicago: Univ. of Chicago Press, 1961), 1:145–62.

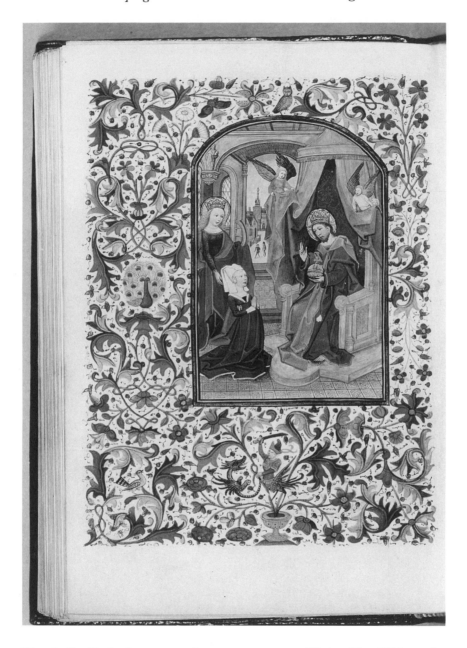

Fig. 1. St. Catherine presenting a patroness to Christ. The Walters Art Gallery, MS. Walters 220, fol. 150v (Hours, use of Rome, ca. 1450; produced in Bruges). Reproduced by permission of the Walters Art Gallery, Baltimore.

Fig. 2. Virgin Mary and child Jesus with patroness Isabelle de Coucy. The Walters Art Gallery, MS. Walters 89, fol. 3v (Hours, use of Paris, ca. 1380; Hours of Isabelle de Coucy). Reproduced by permission of the Walters Art Gallery, Baltimore.

A devotional portrait, however, might do more than record personal affiliation. Some paintings in books of hours were clearly intended to serve as aids to devotion. Iconic images of Veronica's veil or the *Ecce Homo* easily fall into this category: here the painting displays an object (Jesus' bleeding face, Jesus' crucified body) for veneration, in much the same way a priest would raise a consecrated host for adoration.[8] Other miniatures in books of hours function in a more complex way, primarily by depicting the relationship between the devotee and the person to whom she prays.[9] Devotionally rich paintings such as the portrait of the owner at prayer in the Hours of Mary of Burgundy represent the act of devotion itself. Gazing upon the image and reproducing it in the imagination would lead a viewer to create within herself the moment of rapt prayerful attention captured in the painting.[10]

The possible devotional function of owner portraits with patron saints is more obscure, however. Certainly many must have simply displayed the owner's wealth and name. But the portrait of Isabelle de Coucy, by recording visually an oath of loyalty between Isabelle and Jesus, offers a glimpse of spiritual relationship. Might the owner fashion in her interior world a dialogue with Jesus modelled on such an image? Images like this, that interweave the worldly and the celestial, the contemporary detail with the vaguely ancient, might encourage a devotee to incorporate the relationship into her spiritual life.

Relationships that devotees established with saints to whom they prayed mirrored relationships characteristic of late medieval and early modern patronage systems.[11] Both earthly and spiritual patronage

---

[8] On the *Ecce Homo* see Panofsky, " 'Imago Pietatis' "; and Belting, *Das Bild und sein Publikum.*

[9] On these kinds of paintings see James H. Marrow, "Symbol and Meaning in Northern European Art of the Late Middle Ages and Early Renaissance," *Simiolus* 16 (1986): 150–69; and Anne Hagopian van Buren, "The Canonical Office in Renaissance Painting, Part II: More About the Rolin *Madonna*," *Art Bulletin* 60 (1978): 617–33.

[10] Österreichischen Nationalbibliothek, Vienna, Cod. 1857, fol. 14v (Hours, use of Rome, ca. 1480; Hours of Mary of Burgundy). The miniature was painted by the Master of Mary of Burgundy. It is reproduced in F. Unterkircher and A. de Schryver, *Gebetbuch Karls des Kühnen vel potius Stundenbuch der Maria von Burgund, Codex Vindobonensis 1857*, 2 vols. (Graz: Akademische Druck- und Verlagsanstalt, 1969), 2: fol. 14v. On this manuscript see also Otto Pächt, *The Master of Mary of Burgundy* (London: Faber and Faber, 1948).

[11] On the language and workings of patronage see Kristen B. Neuschel's superb

required the exchange of gifts and favors, and in nearly identical manners. Devotees felt comfortable using forms of courtesy learned for negotiating noble or bourgeois society. Praising God or a saint was certainly a salutary activity. But here we can see the broad plausibility of "salvation through works" for late medieval Christians. If one offered flattery or gifts to social superiors hoping to receive favors in return, why not pray to saints for spiritual and material aid? And why not pray to saints in the same way one would humbly ask influential friends to intercede with earthly seigneurs? Devotees treated celestial patrons with the same combination of deference and familiarity they used with their aristocratic neighbors. Protection from persons of status and power—whether saints or nobles—promised the security fifteenth- and sixteenth-century men and women craved.

Of the many specific requests expressed in prayers, protection from the plague is perhaps the most common. Contemporary understandings about the causes and effects of an outbreak of the disease enrich prayer to the so-called plague saints, Sebastian and Roch. Distinctively late medieval concerns shape the cult of St. Roch. As one modern historian explains, Roch, having lived during the fourteenth century, had the advantage over other plague saints of understanding the "present miseries" devotees suffered.[12] Born of a noble family in Montpellier around the middle of the fourteenth century and orphaned in adolescence, Roch distributed his wealth to the poor, took the habit of a pilgrim, and travelled to Rome.[13] On his journey through Italy he nursed plague victims—several of whom recovered unexpectedly. On his jour-

---

study of the nobility: *Word of Honor: Interpreting Noble Culture in Sixteenth-Century France* (Ithaca: Cornell Univ. Press, 1989). See also J. Russell Major, "The Crown and the Aristocracy in Renaissance France," *American Historical Review* 69 (1964): 631–45, and "'Bastard Feudalism' and the Kiss"; P. S. Lewis, "Decayed and Non-Feudalism in Later Medieval France," *Bulletin of the Institute of Historical Research* 37 (1964): 157–84, and "Of Breton *Alliances* and Other Matters," in *War, Literature, and Politics in the Late Middle Ages*, ed. C. T. Allmand (New York: Barnes and Noble, 1976), 122–43.

Systems of patronage within the cult of the saints are explained beautifully by Christian, *Local Religion*; and Thomas Head, *Hagiography and the Cult of Saints: The Diocese of Orléans, 800–1200* (Cambridge: Cambridge Univ. Press, 1990).

[12] Augustin Fliche, *Saint Roch* (Paris: Henri Laurens, 1930), 6.

[13] The most reliable modern account of Roch's life is André Vauchez, "Rocco," *Bibliotheca Sanctorum*, 12 vols. (Rome: Istituto Giovanni XXIII del Pontificia Università Lateranense, 1961–69), 11:264–73.

ney back to Montpellier, Roch stopped in Piacenza, where he finally contracted the dread disease he had confronted fearlessly. Retreating from the city to the countryside, he languished until rescued by a dog belonging to a local noble. The dog brought food from his master's table to Roch's wretched shelter in the woods, and eventually brought his master to nurse Roch back to health. Roch met an ignominious end: after leaving Piacenza he was arrested in Angera, where he died in prison several years later.

Roch's cult flourished soon after his death. He appears in most French books of hours from the mid-fifteenth century, frequently coupled with St. Sebastian. Typical prayers emphasize the noble, heroic aspects of Roch's story: an outsider, Roch "cured by touching" those afflicted with a malady so fearful that they had been abandoned.[14] Roch not only healed the bodies of plague victims. He touched those no one else dared touch, demonstrating charity rare in a plague-ridden city. Boccaccio's graphic account of Florentine families and neighborhoods torn apart by the Black Death expressed contemporary fears about the plague's social consequences. During an outbreak, when people feared for their lives if they came near one another, St. Roch thought of his fellows. He not only nursed the sick; he also showed concern for the community by withdrawing from the city during his own illness. Prayers to St. Roch emphasize the plague's destruction of social bonds, which can only be remedied by selfless generosity such as Roch's. Individuals and communities alike appealed to him for protection from the social and spiritual effects of the plague.

Like St. Roch, Mary Magdalene appears in books of hours as a complex saintly figure. She was also an ambiguous one. Legends, prayers, and images describe her life as long and varied, full of contrasts and contradictions. Late medieval Christians knew her as the repentant

---

[14] Prayers to St. Roch may be found in Bibliothèque Sainte-Geneviève, Paris, MS. 2694, fol. 1v (prayer book, fifteenth to early seventeenth centuries; Rouen); Bibliothèque Nationale [hereafter: "B.N."], Paris, MS. nouvelles acquisitions latines [hereafter: "nouv. acq. lat."] 195, fol. 113 (Hours, use of Bourges, fifteenth century; belonged to the Verne-Corbeyeux family); Bibliothèque de l'Arsenal, Paris, MS. 415, fols. 160r–160v (Hours, undetermined use, 1540; belonged to Davaillolles-Fresneau family); Fitzwilliam Museum MS. 128, fol. 111 (Hours, use of Paris, ca. 1500). The last three texts are variations of the same Latin prayer whose incipit is "Ave Roche sanctissime nobili natu. . . ." The first is a French translation/paraphrase of the Latin prayer.

woman who bathed Jesus' feet with her tears, begged Jesus to resuscitate her brother Lazarus, sat at Jesus' knee while her sister Martha served their guest, watched with the Virgin Mary at the foot of the crucified Jesus' cross, and met the risen Christ on Easter morning.[15] But according to medieval hagiographers, Mary Magdalene's life did not end with Jesus' ascension into heaven. By the twelfth century a detailed *vita* had emerged, according to which Mary Magdalene was one of a small troupe of Christ's disciples who travelled to Marseille. After evangelizing the pagans there, she withdrew from human company to live as a hermit in the remote Provençal countryside.

Mary Magdalene provided ample material for discussion by scriptural commentators and devotional writers. Her attraction for French Christians grew from her role in Jesus' life and in the birth of the Christian community in France. But her identity as a former sinner also exerted a powerful attraction. Late medieval men and women were moved by Mary Magdalene's conversion from a life of sin to one of virtue. Prayers refer to her as "comfort of sinners," "mirror of repentant sinners," and "mother of sinners."[16] As Rabanus Maurus had put it, Mary Magdalene was "an example of conversion to sinners, a certain home of remission to penitents, a figure of compassion to the faithful and to all Christian people a proof of divine mercy."[17] She was a

---

[15] On the life and cult of Mary Magdalene see Victor Saxer, *Le culte de Marie-Madeleine en Occident des origines à la fin du moyen âge* (Paris/Auxerre: Clavreuil/Publications de la Société des Fouilles Archéologiques et des Monuments Historiques de l'Yonne, 1959); Helen M. Garth, *Saint Mary Magdalene in Mediaeval Literature*, The Johns Hopkins University Studies in Historical and Political Science, vol. 67, no. 3 (Baltimore, 1950); Marjorie M. Malvern, *Venus in Sackcloth: The Magdalene's Origins and Metamorphoses* (Carbondale: Univ. of Southern Illinois Press, 1975); M.-M. Sicard, *Sainte Marie-Madeleine* (Paris: Savaète, 1910); and *La Maddalena tra sacro e profano*, ed. Marilena Mosco (Florence: Arnaldo Mondadori, 1986; exhibition catalogue, Palazzo Pitti, 1986).

[16] "Comfort of sinners": New York Public Library MS. 56, fol. 376v (Hours, 1350–60; Hours of Blanche of France). On this manuscript see Léopold Delisle, "Les Heures de Blanche de France, duchesse d'Orléans," *Bibliothèque de l'École des Chartes* 66 (1905): 489–539. On the prayer itself see E. Hoepffner, "Une prière à sainte Marie-Madeleine," *Romania* 53 (1927): 567–68; and Rézeau, *Les prières aux saints*, 338. "Mirror of repentant sinners": Fitzwilliam Museum MS. 9–1951, fols. 117–22 (Hours, use of Toul, late fourteenth century) (Rézeau no. 162 *bis*). "Mother of sinners": *Louenges des benoistz sainctz et sainctes de paradis* (Paris, n.d. [early sixteenth century]), fol. xx5 (Rézeau no. 165).

[17] Quoted in Garth, *Saint Mary Magdalene*, 53.

mirror for sinners because she understood what it meant to reject sin.

A fourteenth-century Parisian woman's prayer book includes a particularly moving prayer addressed to Mary Magdalene, adapted and translated from a Latin text composed by Anselm.[18] The devotee tells the saint, "my very dear lady, you yourself have proven how a sinful soul is reconciled to its creator, what consolation a miserable sinner needs." Recalling the saint's "many sins" forgiven by Jesus, the devotee then pleads: "O most blessed lady, I, a disloyal sinner [*desleaus pecherresse*] recite your sins not to reproach you but ... I call to mind the great mercy by which your sins are blotted out." After asking the saint to request from God the same mercy and love she herself was shown, the devotee then turns her own voice to Jesus. She pleads: "Jesus, most compassionate redeemer of the world, please do not despise the prayer of an unworthy sinner, but aid the weak endeavors of the poor sick one who loves you, ... so that she might worthily and loyally serve you." Emphasizing the distance between God and herself, the devotee presents her petition in the most humble manner of late medieval supplication—spiritual or social. She is a "miserable," "disloyal" sinner who can only approach her lord through one of the lord's closest friends. The prayer's language suggests contemporary practices of charity, in which beggars customarily acknowledged absolute dependence on the generosity of their more fortunate benefactors.[19] And the re-

---

[18] B.N. MS. nouv. acq. lat. 592, fols. 78–85v (Hours, use of Paris, fourteenth century). Leroquais believes the book was composed for a princess or queen; Rézeau says a widow in *Les prières aux saints*, 635, 336. For a Latin text of Anselm's prayer see *S. Anselmi Cantuariensis Archiepiscopi Opera Omnia*, ed. F. S. Schmitt, 6 vols. (Edinburgh: Thomas Nelson and Sons, 1940–51), 3:64–67 (*oratio* 16). Benedicta Ward provides an English translation of Anselm's text in *The Prayers and Meditations of Saint Anselm with the Proslogion*, ed. B. Ward (Harmondsworth: Penguin Books, 1973), 201–6. The French prayer modifies Anselm's language by adding late medieval titles and forms of address.

[19] One prayer to Mary Magdalene calls her "doulce aulmonière," which may mean either almsgiver or alms-purse. *Louenges des benoistz sainctz et sainctes de paradis* (Paris, n.d. [early sixteenth century]), fol. xx5v (Rézeau no. 165). Explicit use of the contemporary language of charitable practices may also be found in an early sixteenth-century *palinod* to the Virgin Mary: B.N. MS. français 145 (*Chants royaux en l'honneur de la Vierge au Puy d'Amiens*). Here the Virgin is described as "des dons divins liberale Boucière," and a miniature depicts her holding a purse open to approaching human beings (fols. 34v–35). See also Jean Gerson's dialogue *La mendicité spirituelle* (1401), in which he describes devotional life as a quest for the spiritual alms of God and the saints (Jean Gerson, *Oeuvres complètes*, ed. P. Glorieux, 10 vols. [Paris: Desclée, 1960–73], 7:220–80).

peated requests for forgiveness show how penitential language resonates with the legal language of confession and pardon.

Prayers to Mary Magdalene linger lovingly on the saint's humble act of public penance: washing Jesus' feet with her tears. The fourteenth-century text discussed above opens with: "Saint Mary Magdalene, you came with a great fountain of tears to the fountain of mercy, dear sweet Jesus Christ." The devotee goes on to ask for "tears of humility," "the bread of pain and tears." Another prayer explicitly asks the saint for "tears of true contrition."[20] The attention lavished on the saint's tears would have had great spiritual significance for fifteenth- and sixteenth-century Christians. Tears expressed penance, and openness to the love of God. Presumably most devotional weeping was solitary, and thus signified a softened heart only to the weeper. But public weeping—by processants, pilgrims, and preachers—provided an important penitential model for witnesses.[21] For owners of books of hours, reading about another's tears might have served a similar function. Thus Mary Magdalene became a mirror for sinners not only by exemplifying conversion from sin. Reading about her tears might elicit the reader's tears, by creating a visual image for devout imitation.

By the late middle ages the concept of repentance had acquired a new social significance, in addition to its traditional religious one. Heightened interest in a specific set of urban problems—prostitution, open displays of wealth, the public life of women—gave new emphasis to elements of Mary Magdalene's life, and reshaped her cult. From the fourteenth through the early sixteenth centuries, a number of French and Italian cities attempted to legalize and supervise the practice of prostitution within their walls. As Leah Lydia Otis and Sherrill Cohen have shown, the transformation of prostitution from an unregulated occupation to a civic institution was accompanied by the establishment of religious communities of former prostitutes. Almost always dedicated to St. Mary Magdalene, these cloistered or semi-cloistered communities of "repentant" or "converted" women (*converties*) served as permanent

---

[20] Fitzwilliam Museum MS. 9–1951, fol. 120v (Hours, use of Toul, late fourteenth century) (Rézeau no. 162 *bis*).

[21] See William Christian, Jr., "Provoked Religious Weeping in Early Modern Spain," in *Religious Organization and Religious Experience*, ed. J. Davis (New York: Academic Press, 1982), 97–114.

homes for retired or "reformed" prostitutes, and sometimes as half-way houses for former prostitutes young enough to re-enter the respectable world.[22]

Mary Magdalene provided a focus for discussion about prostitution and related questions about women's lives. Preachers elaborated on the "wanton life" the saint had left behind, while religious dramatists depicted her as a "public woman" or courtesan. In their hands the story of Mary Magdalene's early years became a cautionary tale about the life of a young urban woman. Jacques Rossiaud has commented that these moralists "cleverly maintained the ambiguity of Mary Magdalene, and the figure they presented was so enigmatic that the spectators watching the *Passion* [of Jean Michel] in Angers or the crowds listening to Olivier Maillard or Michel Menot could imagine her either as a courtesan or as a spoiled young woman who led a free life for lack of family guidance."[23] This rich ambiguity seeped into devotional life; Mary Magdalene was imagined as a prostitute or "an honorable lady of the manor," as one sixteenth-century prayer described her.[24] She was all the more capable of being a mirror for repentant sinners if her social rank was open to interpretation.

Prayers to Saints Mary Magdalene and Roch exemplify the way saints held a mirror for devotees. Their lives provided examples of virtues treasured by late medieval men and women: conversion from sin

---

[22] Leah Lydia Otis, *Prostitution in Medieval Society: The History of an Urban Institution in Languedoc* (Chicago: Univ. of Chicago Press, 1985), and "Prostitution and Repentance in Late Medieval Perpignan," in *Women of the Medieval World: Essays in Honor of John H. Mundy*, ed. Julius Kirshner and Suzanne F. Wemple (Oxford: Basil Blackwell, 1985), 137–60; Sherrill Cohen, "Asylums for Women in Counter-Reformation Italy," in *Women in Reformation and Counter-Reformation Europe: Private and Public Worlds*, ed. Sherrin Marshall (Bloomington: Indiana Univ. Press, 1989), 166–88, and *The Evolution of Women's Asylums: From the Sixteenth Century to the Present* (New York: Oxford Univ. Press, 1992), chaps. 1–2. On prostitution see also Jacques Rossiaud, *Medieval Prostitution*, trans. Lydia Cochrane (Oxford: Basil Blackwell, 1988); and Bronislaw Geremek, *The Margins of Society in Late Medieval Paris*, trans. Jean Birrell (Cambridge: Cambridge Univ. Press, 1987), chap. 7.

[23] Rossiaud, *Medieval Prostitution*, 142.

[24] Fitzwilliam Museum MS. 105, fol. 87 (Hours, use of Rouen, 1530) (Rézeau no. 166). Another early sixteenth-century devotional text discusses the excessively luxurious style of dress and "worldly life" Mary Magdalene abandoned when she decided to follow Jesus. See Bibliothèque Municipale de Rouen MS. Y.226a, p. 117 (*Recueil de poésies palinodiques, exécutés pour Jacques Le Lieur*, Rouen, ca. 1520).

to grace, and selfless caring for others. Although conversion and charity were certainly spiritual themes of great antiquity, these prayers contain messages specific to late medieval urban culture—precisely the social world of owners of books of hours. For these people, conversion signalled moral and civic reform. Roch's charity and nursing repaired social bonds torn apart by the plague. And being a patron or "mirror" was more than symbolic. Prayers and images in books of hours not only depicted, but nurtured and even established ties of support and dependence between devotees and saints.

Martin of Tours:
A Patron Saint of Medieval Comedy

MARTIN W. WALSH

n the treasury of the church of Sint Maarten, Utrecht, there is a polished neolithic axe, hefted and encased in silver about 1300, bearing the inscription: *Ydola vana ruunt Martini cessa securi. Nemo deos esse credat qui sic fuerrant ruituri* (The false idols crash, having been cut down by Martin's axe. Let no one believe gods exist who thus had been ready to fall down).[1] It is a fitting tribute to the powerful fourth-century saint, this tool of the pagan past transformed into the very weapon he wielded in his heroic destruction of the shrines and idols of the recalcitrant Gauls. In a single concrete object, it embodies Pope Gregory's policy of appropriation of pagan practices and sites for the greater glory of the Christian God. But let us look at another thirteenth-century artifact, from not far away, the

---

[1] Photo in Mieke Breij, *Sint Maarten Schutspatroon van Utrecht* (Utrecht: Stichting Discodom, 1988), 27. For ritual use of neolithic axes by later ages, see Ralph Merrifield, *The Archaeology of Ritual and Magic* (New York: New Amsterdam Books, 1987). The most substantial work on the medieval Martin cult remains A. Lecoy de la Marche, *Saint Martin* (Tours: Alfred Meme et Fils, 1881). A recent hagiographical study in English is Christopher Donaldson, *Martin of Tours: Parish Priest, Mystic, and Exorcist* (London: Routledge and Kegan Paul, 1980). Much new work is emerging on the Martin of the Gallo-Roman and early Merovingian periods, most notably Clare Stancliffe, *St. Martin and his Hagiographer: History and Miracle in Sulpicius Severus* (Oxford: Clarendon Press, 1983). Neither the works of modern hagiography, nor specialized historical studies address the subject of this paper.

anonymous Old French fabliau *Les i.i.i.i. souhais Saint Martin.*

In this comic tale, a Norman peasant, much devoted to Martin, is met one morning by his patron saint who promises to reward him for his lifelong devotion:

> *"Lesse ton travail et ta herce,*
> *si t'en reva tout liement;*
> *je te di bien tout vraiement:*
> *ce qu'a .IIII. souhais diras,*
> *saches tu bien que tu l'avras; mes garde toi au souhaidie*
> *tu n'i avras ja recouvrier!"*

> "Leave off your labors and your plough
> and give free rein to dreams of bliss;
> in sober truth I tell you this:
> whatever you in wishes four
> may ask to have, you shall; before
> you make a wish, be careful, though:
> you cannot take them back, you know."[2]

The peasant foolishly allows his wife to have the first wish and she asks, for her frequent gratification, that his body erupt all over with penises. The peasant retaliates for his new monstrosity by wishing that the wife's body be pierced all over with vaginas. They are both in quite a fix, and proceed to wish away their multiple sex organs, resulting in their winding up with no sex at all. The fourth and final wish, of course, is spent in getting everything back to where it was before the miraculous gift. The saint is in a very peculiar context here, to say the least. Martin presides over a conspicuous example of that burgeoning, polymorphous, collective and communal Body at the center of Mikhail Bakhtin's theory of the carnivalesque.[3] At some level, it seems, the *Ydola* are taking revenge upon the austere missionary saint.

Nor is the fabliau an isolated example of this Martin motif. Jean Bodel (1165–1210) also employed it in *Des sohaiz que Sainz Martins*

---

² Robert Harrison, trans., *Gallic Salt: Eighteen Fabliaux Translated from the Old French* (Berkeley: Univ. of California Press 1974), 176–89.

³ As outlined in his influential work, *Rabelais and His World,* trans. Helene Iswolsky (Cambridge, Mass.: M.I.T. Press, 1968), esp. chaps. 5, 6.

dona Anvieus et Covietos.[4] Though decidedly more moralistic in tone, this fabliau again features the saint as ironic wish-giver. An envious man and a covetous man each get a wish from Martin. The covetous one is granted double whatever the other wishes for, and the envious, provoked into choosing first, wishes for the loss of an eye. This fabliau draws equally upon Martin's traditional association with cripples and beggars, as we shall see later. It is clear that these comic tales are proceeding from popular notions of St. Martin as a wish-bringer *cum* Trickster, this primitive form of "culture hero" being one of the most universal archetypes in world folklore.[5]

Trickster elements, and a consequently comic tone, are certainly not unknown in popular and even official saints' lives, especially where the protagonist encounters notable adversaries. Martin, like many other saints, repeatedly turns the tables upon the Devil.[6] When Emperor Valentinian refuses to honor Martin by rising from his throne, his unfortunate seat bursts into flames. Pine-worshipping pagans allow their cult object to be felled, provided that Martin stand in the way of its fall. Upon his making the sign of the cross, the crashing timber naturally reverses its direction and squashes the pagans—a scene rather amusingly portrayed on a twelfth-century capital at Vézelay.[7]

Martin's function in the above anonymous fabliau, however, is essentially different. His gift of the four wishes, with their promise of a life without toil, is common enough to the folktale, but certainly not to Christian hagiography; Martin is here a fairy benefactor, not an his-

---

[4] Harrison, *Gallic Salt*, 170–75. The basic situation goes back to the Roman fabulist Avianus.

[5] See esp. Paul Radin, Karl Kerenyi, and C. G. Jung, *The Trickster: A Study in American Indian Mythology* (New York: Bell Publishing, 1956).

[6] The classic example is Martin penetrating the disguise of Satan as Christ the King, *Vita Martini,* chap. 24. This and Martin's other encounters with the Devil were passed on to later *vitae* and esp. Jacobus de Varagine's *Legenda Aurea*. For the *Vita Martini*, I have used F. R. Hoare, trans., *The Western Fathers* (New York: Sheed and Ward, 1954) with reference to Jacques Fontaine, ed. and trans., *Sulpice Sévère: Vie de Saint Martin,* 3 vols. (Paris: Éditions du Cerf, 1967).

[7] Cf. Simone Martini's fresco in the Lower Church of Assisi, where the Emperor has fallen on his knees in terror before Martin. George Kaftal, *Iconography of the Saints in Tuscan Painting* (Florence: Sansoni, 1952), fig. 801. Detailed photos of the Vézelay capital can be found in Victor-Henry Debidour and E. M. Janet le Caisne's *Vézelay* (Paris: Plon, 1962), pl. 29.

torical saint. The seemingly blissful state of innumerable and complementary sex organs, for which he is responsible, is strongly suggestive
of something more than simple grotesque comedy. Like Panurge's plan
for fortifying Paris with an alternating work of penises and vaginas, the
fabliau seems to preserve a distant memory of those grotesque fertility
cult images not infrequently uncovered in areas of Roman occupation.[8] But even apart from this, Martin appears to be closely associated
with sexual humor throughout the fabliaux corpus. Though I cannot
pretend to any statistical rigor here, the significant oath, "by St. Martin" or "by the faith I owe St. Martin," which rhymed, not insignifi-
cantly with *vin*, appears quite frequently in comic narratives and monologues such as *Dit de Bigorne, Le Franc archer de Bagoulet, Auberee, Le
povre clerc, Des perdriz, Du segretain moine, Du bouchier d'Abeville, Des ii.
changeors, De la crote, Du chevalier a la robe vermeille, Le meunier et les deux
clercs*, to name but a few. In the latter fabliau, a source for Chaucer's
Reeve's Tale, the repeated expression *l'ostel saint Martin* stands for sexual
congress with the miller's women folk. Chaucer's lecherous monk in
The Shipman's Tale likewise swears "by God and seint Martyn." The
peasant marriage in Gautier Le Leu's *Del fol vilian* takes places at *le
Capele Saint Martin*, and in the *Segretain moine* St. Martin's altar becomes the trysting place of the lecherous sacristan. Swearing *par sainct
Martin*, as well as references to the *mal de saint Martin* (drunkeness) are
also quite common in the French farces of the fifteenth century,
together with the comic peasant name *Martin*. We have, for example,
the mythical *Martin Garant*, the man who stands for the drinks who is
evoked in *Pathelin*, or the title character of the *Farce de Martin de
Chambray*, who not only invokes his patron saint but has this connection mocked by his shrewish wife in the curtain lines: *Vous estes Martin
de Chambray/Vous en estes saint sus le cul* (with its play on "you're a
saint/ceint (= belt) down to your anus").[9]

---

[8] As described in chap.15 of Rabelais' *Pantagruel*. For images of multiple sex organs
resembling Panurge's plan, see esp. R. P. Knight's *Discourse on the Worship of Priapus*
(1894; repr. Secaucus, N.J.: University Books, 1974), pl. 25, fig. 4.

[9] See esp. Raymond Eichmann and John DuVal, eds. and trans.,*The French Fabliau
B.N. MS.837*, 2 vols. (New York: Garland Publishing, 1984); Guy Raynaud de Lage,
ed., *Choix de Fabliaux*. (Paris: Librairie Honore Champion, 1986); Robert Hellman
and Richard O'Gorman, trans., *Fabliaux: Ribald Tales from the Old French* (Westport,
Conn.: Greenwood Press, 1965); and Harrison, *Gallic Salt*. For the farces, see Gustave

To return to Rabelais, direct heir to the fabliau and farce tradition, St. Martin is directly associated with the phallic warrior Gargantua:

Then Gargantua mounted his great mare and ... went on his way, in the course of which he found a huge, tall tree—which was commonly called St. Martin's Tree, because it had grown from a pilgrim's staff once planted by Saint Martin. "This is just what I needed," he said. "This tree will serve me for a pilgrim's staff and a lance." And he easily rooted it up out of the ground, stripped off its branches, and trimmed it to his liking.

Gargantua, chap. 36.[10]

The mare's oceanic urination follows immediately, and Martin's Tree eventually becomes a major weapon in the war against the invading Picrochole. Rabelais, true to form, co-opts the military saint and wandering apostle into his lower-body humor and, curiously, preserves a cult-tree of the very saint dedicated to felling such abominations.[11]

In the French tradition, then, we have established some connection between St. Martin and grotesque sexual humor. Similar associations appear in Italian as well; witness a charivari on St. Martin's Eve in the Romagna known as *festa dei becchi* (feast of cuckolds), or the Venetian children's begging processional:

Cohen, ed., *Recueil de farces français inedités du XVe siècle* (Cambridge, Mass.: Mediaeval Academy of America, 1949), 110, 150, 225, 232–33, 305, 308, 325–26, 424–25.

[10] François Rabelais, *The Histories of Gargantua and Pantagruel,* trans. J. M. Cohen (Harmondsworth: Penguin Books, 1955), 117. See also Panurge's reference to the tempest-raising Devil as "St. Martin's running footman," p. 501 and his verb *martiner* = tipple, p. 258. Gustave Cohen discusses Rabelais' use of farcical elements from Martin drama in "Rabelais et la legende de saint Martin," *Revue des Études Rabelaisiennes* 8 (1910): 331–49. Martin was in competition with Gargantua in shaping the French landscape. See H. Fromage, "Rapports de saint Martin avec Gargantua," *Bulletin de la Société de Mythologie Française* 74 (1969): 75–84. There is a Rabelaisian phallic joke in the Poitou folksong where the monk Martin cuts off his frozen nose only to have it appropriated by three nuns. "Le Nez de Martin" in Jerome Bujeaud, ed. *Chants et chansons populaires des provinces de l'Ouest* (Niort: L. Clouzot, 1895), 1:293–94.

[11] Jean Fournée cites several *arbres Martin* for Normandy in *Enquête sur le cult populaire de saint Martin en Normandie* (Nogent-sur-Marne: Cahiers Leopold Delisle, 1963), 41–43. Fournée also catalogs Martin springs and stones (some being menhirs), as well as votive offerings of horse-shoes for veterinary help and journeys safely completed. Similar Martinian sites are found in other regions of France.

San Martin xe anda in soffitta
A trovar la so novizza
La novizza no ghe gera
L xe casca col cul per tera
El s'a roto una culata
El s'a messoin boletin,
Viva viva San Martin!

St. Martin went to the garret
To find his novice nun
The novice wasn't there
His ass hit the ground
He broke one butt
He came up empty-handed
Viva, viva Saint Martin![12]

More important, however, is Martin's role as wish-granter, anterior to his role of trickster. This places him, folklorically speaking, among the denizens of that nebulous Third Realm between Christian Heaven and Hell, the world of Faerie. Already in the dream life of early suppliants at his tomb, Martin was an extraordinary otherworldly personage, clothed in purple and wreathed as if in swan feathers. Gregory of Tours likewise records the hysteric experience of an official who knew he was violating a St. Martin hostel:

> As I walked into the courtyard . . . , I saw an old man holding in his hand a tree, the branches of which spread out until they soon covered the whole yard. One of the branches . . . touched me, and I was so affected by the contact that I collapsed.[13]

---

[12] See Piero Camporesi, *Bread of Dreams: Food and Fantasy in Early Modern Europe,* trans. David Gentilcore (Chicago: Chicago Univ. Press, 1989), 98. Angela Nardo Cibele, "Canzone di San Martino nel Veneto," *Archivio per le tradizioni popolari* 5 (1886): 363, and cf. the song on page 239 from Belluno. The Venetian rhyme employs further sexual puns on "sausage," "little knife" and giving "charity." Thanks to Prof. Raymond Grew, University of Michigan, for the translation and Prof. Samuel Kinser, Northern Illinois University for the original reference.

[13] Gregory of Tours, *De Virtutibus sancti Martini* (bk. 2:56) quoted by Jacques LeGoff in *The Medieval Imagination,* trans. Arthur Goldhammer (Chicago: Univ. of Chicago Press, 1988), 220; Gregory of Tours, *The History of the Franks,* trans. Lewis Thorpe (London: Penguin, 1974), 426.

Martin is clearly imagined here as an arboreal deity, a virtual burgeoning "Green Man." There is a report from the reign of King Stephen, recorded by William of Newburgh, (collected, it seems, from Ralph of Coggeshall and repeated by later chroniclers) which evidently reflects the discovery of a pair of "wild children." Near Bury St. Edmunds was a village called *Wolfpittes* named for "certain trenches of immemorial antiquity":

> One harvest-time when the harvesters were gathering in the corn, there crept out from these two pits a boy and a girl, green at every point of their body, and clad in garments of strange hue and unknown texture. These wandered distraught about the field, until the harvesters took them and brought them to the village.

The children refuse all human food until they are given newly shelled beans, upon which provender they subsist until they learn to eat bread. They also learn to speak English:

> The children as soon as they learned our speech, were asked who and whence they were, and are said to have answered: "We are folk of St. Martin's Land; for that is the chief saint among us."[14]

Upon further interrogation it is learned that they inhabit a twilight region separated from the realms of the sun by a river of great breadth—a traditional description of Fairyland, apart from the fact that Christian churches also seem to exist there. What is particularly germane to our inquiry is the season of the year (Martin's festival time), the magic bean-food, and the green-hued wanderers in the field. Whether this represents a garbled account of an atavistic folk ritual or of the actual discovery of feral children is impossible to say. In any case, Martin's patronage over the *viridi pueri* is extremely significant. The saint's position in the liturgical calendar apparently coincided with

---

[14] Translated in G. G. Coulton, ed. *Social Life in Britain from the Conquest to the Reformation* (Cambridge: Cambridge Univ. Press, 1938), 537–38. Other chroniclers, Walsingham, Gervase of Tilbury, and Giraldus Cambrensis, record the incident. See also Norman Scarfe, *Suffolk in the Middle Ages* (Woodbridge, Suffolk: Boydell Press, 1986), 165–67.

other, older and deeper calendars, allowing him to sink, as it were, into the realm of Faerie and rule over its outer provinces: the *Pays de cocagne, Schlaraffenland,* and the Land of Plenty.

Martinmas and Carnival

Martin's feast of November 11th coincides with the beginning of the Anglo-Germanic winter, and is little more than a week after the Celtic New Year of *Samhain.* While it is tempting to link the Christian saint with a pagan deity at this turning of the year, Martin might well have supplanted or been grafted onto any number or combination of local tribal deities over the centuries of Christian proselytization. The historical Martin worked against rural Gallo-Roman paganism, but became the wonder-working patron of the Germanic Franks as well as the *Urvater* of Western monasticism. His cult eventually stretched from Portugal to Finland, and from Ireland to Sicily. Never simply a destroyer of idols, Martin would seem to have served some other, more mediating function in the great transformation of mythologies in Europe. We have, for example, the *Minnetrunk* in honor of Martin, instituted by the Norwegian King Olaf in 996 after dreaming of the saint, presumably on his feast day:

> The night before the Assembly [summoned at Moster, South Hordaland] was appointed to meet, there appeared to King Olaf in a dream, a vision of St. Martin the Bishop, who said to him: "It is a custom in this land, as in many other lands where the people are heathen, to consecrate ale to Thor and Odin at feasts and banquets, and to dedicate full cups to the Anses. It is my desire that you make a change in this custom at banquets and feasts where toasts are drunk, so that the evil habit exist no longer as heretofore; and that you cause my name to be proposed as a memorial toast with God and his Saints. I will then, when morning comes, support and strengthen your mission [to Christianize Norway], so that it may have success."[15]

---

[15] J. Sephton, trans., *The Saga of King Olaf Tryggwason* (London: David Nutt, 1895), 191. The saga is a twelfth-century compilation from earlier Latin and Norse sources.

While it is risky to reduce all popular manifestations of Martin to hypothetical pagan sources on this Scandinavian model, on the other hand it is clear that the various activities of a pastoral/agricultural economy that lined up with his festival season would come under his protection in a Christian or predominantly Christian context.[16] Martinmas thus coincided with the time for slaughtering a certain percentage of cattle newly brought in from summer pasturage, since not enough winter fodder could be stored for the entire herd. Such a scene is wonderfully evoked by Brueghel in "The Return of the Herd" (1565), where the cloaked rider on a white horse perhaps encodes the saint himself.[17] November was indeed the pagan Anglo-Saxons' *blotmonað*, as Bede records, and *Slachtmaand* (slaughter month) survives as a synonym for November in early modern Dutch. It was also the season for *pannage*—driving the swine into the forest for a good feed on beech mast or acorns, the beating down of which became one of the "Labors" of the month. The choice meat, sausages and blood-puddings not destined for the brine-tub or smoke-house afforded the materials for a carnivorous feast. Thus we have such comic personifications as "Martin Martlemas-beefe," one of the godfathers of Gluttony in Marlowe's *Faustus*, or "the martlemas your master," Sir John Falstaff himself in *2 Henry IV* (2.2); together with such expressions as the Franconian "Gut-pudding Feast;" the proverb found in French, Portuguese and Spanish and which appears in the *Quixote*—"Every pig has his Martinmas;" or the French idiom for living on Easy Street (or to flirt), *faire la Saint Martin*. Johannes Boemus recorded Martinmas wild boar fights in sixteenth-century Würzburg. Meat from the defeated animals would afterwards be distributed to the people.[18] Stamford, Lincolnshire pre-

---

[16] For Martinmas see articles in R. T. Hampson, *Medii Ævi Kalendarium or, Dates, Charters and Customs of the Middle Ages* (London: Henry Kent Causton, 1841), 1:378–83; John Brand, *Observations on the Popular Antiquities of Great Britain* (London: Henry G. Bohn, 1853), 1:399–404; William S. Walsh, *Curiosities of Popular Customs* (Philadelphia: J. B. Lippincott, 1897), 662–69; Clement A. Miles, *Christmas Customs and Traditions* (1912 repr. New York: Dover Publications, 1976), 202–8; and Hanns Bächtold-Stäubli, *Handwörterbuch des deutschen Aberglaubens*, ed. E. Hoffmann-Krayer (Berlin: Walter DeGruyter, 1932–1933), 5:1707–26.

[17] The figure parallels the Carnival revelers in the early spring canvas of the cycle, "Gloomy Day." On the realistic level, of course, this white horse rider is the owner of the herd or overseer of the drovers.

[18] For Martinmas proverbs see Ida von Düringsfeld and Otto Freiherrn von Reins-

served until fairly recent times a bull-running within the Octave of St. Martin (13 November), which in the fourteenth century was under the auspices of a Guild of St. Martin and likewise involved charitable distribution of fresh meat.[19]

In the weeks before Martinmas the migration of wild geese signalled a final round-up of the domestic gaggles who were allowed to glean the newly harvested fields to fatten them up. Thus in some medieval cuisines the goose became the principal festive dish, particularly in the Germanic north. It was well established in seventeenth-century Denmark and even in countries adjacent to the Germanic language area such as Poland and Hungary. In Germany the Martinmas goose goes back a long way. Othelricus de Swalenberg presented a silver image of the bird to the monks of Corvey for the Martinmas feast of 1171.[20] The goose is found nuzzling episcopal images of the saint in later medieval German paintings and scupture. Its bones were used for weather prognostication by the Teutonic Knights in their conquest of Prussia, and a Swabian knightly order founded during a Martinmas feast in 1367 took the jocular name of *die Martinsvögel*. Martinmas was often represented in early peasant calendars by the picture of a plucked goose rather than by a mitred head.[21] The tradition of goose dinners persists

---

berg-Düringsfeld, *Sprichwörter der germanischen und romanischen Sprachen* (Leipzig: Hermann Fries, 1872), 1:433. The Scots dialect word for a cow or ox slaughtered for winter provision is *mart*. Johannes Boemus Aubanus, *Mores, leges, et ritvs omnivm gentivm* (Paris: Hieronymus de Marnef, 1561), 130v.

[19] George Burton, ed., *Chronology of Stamford* (Stamford: Robert Bagley, 1846), 449–55; and Toulmin Smith, ed., *English Gilds: The Original Ordinances of More Than One Hundred Early English Gilds* (Oxford: Early English Text Society, 1870), 192.

[20] Anton von Snakenburg (d. 1476), *Annals of the Monastery of Corvey*. Cited by Gottlieb Samuel Treuer, *Untersuchung des Ursprungs und der Bedeutung des Märten-Mannes* (Helmstadt: Christian Friedrich Weygand, 1733), 74.

[21] For Denmark see Robert Molesworth, *An Account of Denmark as It Was in the Year 1692* (London, 1694), 11. A sanctified goose from Eckenhagen is re-produced in Carl Vossen, *Sankt Martin: Sein Leben und Fortwirken in Gesinnung, Brauchtum und Kunst* (Düsseldorf: Rheinisch-Bergische Druckerei, 1974), 43. For goose-bone: Jacob Grimm, *Teutonic Mythology*, trans. J. S. Stallybrass (London: George Bell & Sons, 1888), 4:1776–77. For *Martinsvögel* : Christian F. Sattler, *Geschichte des Herzogthums Würtenberg* (Tübingen: Georg Heinrich Reiss, 1773), 4:10–13. For typical *Bauernkalender* (Augsburg: Hans Hofer's heirs, 1584) see British Library, Tab. 597.d.I.(10) and *St. Lambrecht Wooden Calendar* (c. 1475) in Hellmut Rosenfeld, "Kalender, Einblattkalender, Bauernkalender und Bauernpraktik," *Bayerisches Jahrbuch für Volkskunde* (1962), 8.

to this day, especially in the Rhineland, where it is bound up with the number magic of 11/11, inaugurating the official Carnival season.

The feast in later medieval centuries also marked the expiration date of agricultural laborers' and herdsmen's contracts, particularly in northern Europe and Britain. It was thus a significant turning point for the lowest members of rural society, providing an opportunity for earnest pay in the form of meat and drink. In East Yorkshire, for example, the Sunday of Martinmas was called *Rive-kite* (i.e., split-stomach) *Sunday*, and from the same area comes the protest rhyme:

> Good Morning, Mr. Martinmas
> You've come to set me free,
> For I don't care for master
> And he don't care for me.[22]

As with other "liminal" periods in the medieval calendar, Martinmas was a time for re-examining, and ultimately reaffirming, the high and low of social structure. The lowly farm laborers, moreover, could see in the Beggar of the well-known icon of the "Charity of St. Martin" a precise image of their own condition.

Martinmas was also traditionally the date upon which the new wine, pressed out the month before, could first be broached. In this respect it paralleled, for northern Europe, the Roman new-wine feast of *Vinalia* (late August) under Venus's patronage, although aspects of it adumbrated features of the *Saturnalia* as well, as we shall examine shortly. With regard to Martin's patronage of the new-wine, comparison with a pagan deity was consciously drawn in the later Middle Ages and early Renaissance. The sixteenth-century antiquarian, Ambrosio Novidio Fracco, for example, makes this gloss on Martinmas:

Martinalia, *geniale Festum. Vini delibantur et defecantur.*
Vinalia, veterum festum huc translatum. Bacchus in Martini figura.

(*Martinalia,* joyous feast. Wines are tasted and drawn from the lees. The Vinalia, a feast of the ancients, removed to this day. Bacchus in the figure of Martin.)[23]

---

[22] Charles Knightly, *The Customs and Ceremonies of Britain: An Encyclopedia of Living Traditions* (London: Thames and Hudson, 1986), 158.

[23] Ambrosio Novidio Fracco, *Ferentinatis sacrorum fastorum* (Antwerp: J. Bellerus, 1559),

The great neo-Latin poet Pontano would likewise draw upon classical analogies in his *De festis martinalibus* (1492).

The West of Ireland, one of the most conservative areas for folklore in Europe, preserves an animal sacrifice ritual on Martinmas that has some claim to being a genuine pagan survival. Specific documentation for it, at any rate, can be pushed back well into the fifteenth century, with evidence for an even earlier continuity with pre-Christian practice.[24] An addendum to the *Tripartite Life of Patrick* (c. 900) proports to account for the Martinmas pig:

> Martin, it is he that conferred a monk's tonsure on Patrick: wherefore Patrick gave a pig for every monk and every nun to Martin on the eve of Martin's feast, and killing it in honour of Martin and giving it to his community if they should come for it. And from that to this, on the eve of Martin's feast, every one kills a pig though he be not a monk of Patrick's.[25]

The sacrifice, as recorded by recent folklorists, involves the segregation of a choice animal, originally a pig, later a sheep, cow, goose or other fowl, and the dedication of same to the saint on his vigil. Blood from the animal is used to sign the hearth, the corners, the thresholds, the outer buildings, and even the members of the family, as a particularly potent prophylaxis. The family partakes of the flesh on the following feast day. Sharing of this meat with one's poorer neighbors is also a conspicuous feature, as Humphrey O'Sullivan indicates for Tipperary when it was still an Irish-speaking county. Similar Martinmas rites were found in Scotland, with cock sacrifices reported from as far away as Latvia. The old French practice of hanging up a goat by the legs and

---

155; Johannes Oeschger, ed., *Pontano: Carmina* (Bari: G. Laterza, 1948), *Eridanus* 35.

[24] For the Irish Martinmas blood-ritual, see esp. Henry Morris, "St. Martin's Eve," *Béaloideas* 9 (1939): 230–35; Seán Ó Súilleabháin, "The Feast of St. Martin in Ireland," in *Studies in Folklore in Honor of Stith Thompson*, ed. W. Edson Richmond (Bloomington: Univ. of Indiana Press, 1957), 252–61; and Patrick C. Power, *The Book of Irish Curses* (Cork: Mercier Press, 1974), 21. For Tipperary see *The Diary of Humphrey O'Sullivan*, trans. Tomás de Bhaldraithe (Cork: Mercier Press, 1979), 65, 98.

[25] Whitley Stokes, ed. *Tripartite Life of Patrick with Other Documents Relating to that Saint* (London: HM Stationary Office, 1887), 2:560–61. O'Davoren's *Glossary* of 1569 lists the rare word *lupait* (Cf. Welsh *llwpai*, "sow"?) which specifically designated this Martinmas pig.

slowly bleeding it to death is further evidence that the Irish blood-sacrifice was not an isolated phenomenon in earlier centuries. Even today in Canton Lucerne there is a Martinmas contest involving one severing the neck of a suspended goose with a saber, while blindfolded.[26]

Attendant folktales make much of Martin's jealousy regarding his prerogative in Ireland. Farmers who sacrifice less than their best are punished with poor times, those who sacrifice beyond their means in the saint's honor are rewarded with prosperity. In the latter category, there are even tales of the sacrifice of infants, no other victims being available, with the saint resurrecting the slaughtered child. Strict time limits prevail as well, the blood offering being totally unacceptible *after* Martinmas. Malignant curses against the one who first partakes of the Martinmas victim, which then double back upon their authors, are also recorded.

The saint himself, moreover, is seen not only as patron, but literally as provider of the feast: cut up and eaten in the form of an ox, or lumps of his flesh being placed under a tub and thus producing the first pig or other animals. Like John Barleycorn, he too is supposed to have been ground up in a mill, and a prohibition against turning wheels of any sort belongs to his day as well. This may have something to do with Martin's position on the Year Wheel—that milling of the harvest must be over before the Celtic New Year can proceed. There is a nineteenth-century record from Devon of the application of cock's blood to mill machinery, thus uniting these two principal folkloric motifs of insular Martinmas. Such multiple features allowed one Irish antiquarian to seriously compare Martin to Dionysus, and indeed it seems likely that some lord-of-the-animals with agricultural associations stands behind this very complete and very archaic blood-sacrifice.[27]

---

[26] For Latvia see Lena Neuland, *Motif-Index of Latvian Folktales and Legends. FF Communications* 229 (1981): 431. For the French custom, Walsh, *Curiosities,* 665. For custom in Sursee, Canton Lucerne see Otto Swoboda, *Alpenländisches Brauchtum im Jahreslauf.* (Munich: Süddeutscher Verlag, 1979), 151–53. Contestants wear a red mantle and gold sun-mask. One suspects an antiquarian overlay upon genuine folk custom. Cf. painting *L'Automne* by Sebastien Vranx (1573–1647) where a goose-decapitation contest is under way.

[27] David Fitzgerald, "Early Celtic History and Mythology," *Revue celtique* 6 (1883–85): 254, also 235. Finding a Celtic "Dionysus" would of course not explain Martin's appropriation by Germanic peoples on the Continent. Devon record, *Folk-Lore* 54 (1943): 408.

Certainly Martin's connection with Faerie can be reinforced from Irish material, for a cow who fell sick from the well known malevolence of the fairies was then dedicated to the saint by the letting of a few drops of its blood.[28] If it recovered, it was from then on, literally, a "sacred cow."

Another feature that links Martin's calendar position with Faerie, that realm of opposites, is *St. Martin's Summer:* periods of mild weather on or about his feast. The expression is common to French and Italian, and Shakespeare speaks of "St. Martin's summer, halcyon days." (*1 Henry VI*, 1.2). In the early Middle Ages, unusually mild weather in early winter which caused trees and fields to sprout was directly attributed to Martin's influence.[29] In the ambivalent manner characteristic of ancient dieties, Martin is the harbinger of spring at the onset of winter. The strange *St. Martin's Land* recorded by William of Newburgh, then, has its mundane equivalent in the common phenomenon of Indian summer. Nor is it surprising to find "Martin fires" surviving particularly in the Low Countries, Rhineland, and Mosel, linking Martin to the renewal of the solar cycle and fecundity in general.[30]

Martinmas indeed was one of the oldest sacred *cum* profane festivals of the Western Christian calendar. As Advent was largely an innovation of sixth-century Gaul, the penitential season was reckoned from the Feast of St. Martin. It became known as *Quadragesima S. Martini,* and conspicuous feasting prior to "St. Martin's Lent" thus considerably predates the evolution of the medieval carnival season at the other end of winter. Sexual abstinence enjoined upon the laity during this autumnal lent might also help account for the saint's association with sexual humor, previously noticed in the French and Italian traditions.[31]

---

[28] E. Estyn Evans, *Irish Folk Ways* (London: Routledge & Kegan Paul, 1957), 304. Martin's exorcism of a mad cow was recorded by Sulpicius Severus without, however, much understanding of the "miracle's" importance for an agricultural community.

[29] C. Grant Loomis, *White Magic: An Introduction to the Folklore of Christian Legend* (Cambridge, Mass.: Medieval Academy of America, 1948), 45. The feast had its share of weather pronostication and Martin plays a major role as weather-guardian. He shields vineyards from hailstones in France, where the rainbow is also called *l'arc de Saint Martin.*

[30] For bonfires see Freidrich Mossinger, "Martinsfeuer," *Volk und Scholle* 15 (1937): 285–88; Bächtold-Stäubli, *Handwörterbuch,* 5:1716–17; and René Meurant and Renaat van der Linden, *Folklore en Belgique* (Brussels: Paul Legrain, 1974), 36–39, 158.

[31] John Dowden, *The Church Year and Kalendar* (Cambridge: Cambridge Univ.

The split of a "secular" from a "sacred" Martin may have begun as early as the Gallican liturgies of the sixth to seventh centuries where, if E. Catherine Dunn's speculations are correct, recitation of the saint's *vita* was a species of late antique pantomimic art, possibly even performed by professional entertainers. The Council of Auxerre, in 573, clearly prohibited all-night vigils on Martin's feast in its Canon 5, with Canons 3 and 9 helping us piece out the evident abuses: private oblations, "secular" choral song and dance, and feasts within the church building.[32] Notker the Stammerer records an unfortunate St. Martin's Eve debauch by one of Charlemagne's new ecclesiastical appointees in the *Gesta Karoli Magni* (c. 885.), and about 1130 there is a record of a drink-inflamed argument over Martinmas hospitality between the bishop of Chichester's men and their hosts, the monks of Battle Abbey. The German crusaders garrisoned at Jaffa were so incapacitated by their *Martinsnacht* of 1198 that they were surprized by the Muslims under al-'Adil and massacred.[33] The double association of the saint with wine and meat-feasting clearly assured him a place in popular imagination on the opposite end of the spectrum from the historical saint in his habitual frugality and abstinence.

Martinian lore even appropriated the Jesus-miracle of turning water into wine. The seventeenth-century traveler Sir John Reresby, for example, in describing Martin's monastery of Marmoutier, records a "St. Martin's tub, as big as a little room, which the saint ... caused to be filled with water, and converted it into wine."[34] Such folklore gave

---

Press, 1910), 76–77. See also *O.E.D.* (Compact Edition, 1971) "St. Martin's Lent," quoting Chamber's *Cyclopedia*. For sexual abstinence during the period see Jonas, Bishop of Orléans, *De institutione laicali* quoted by Pierre Riche in *Daily Life in the World of Charlemagne*, trans. JoAnn McNamara (Princeton: Princeton Univ. Press, 1978), 51.

[32] E. Catherine Dunn, *The Gallican Saint's Life and the Late Roman Dramatic Tradition* (Washington, D.C.: Catholic Univ. of America Press, 1989), esp. 80–86, 97, 108–9. Dunn's hypothesis has not gone unchallenged however.

[33] Hans F. Haefele, ed. *Notkeri Balbuli, Gesta Karoli Magni Imperatoris* (Berlin: Weidmannsche Verlagsbuchhandlung, 1959), 7–8; Eleanor Searle, ed. *The Chronicle of Battle Abbey* (Oxford: Clarendon Press, 1980), 138–39; S. Tolkowsky, *The Gateway to Palestine: A History of Jaffa* (London: George Routledge & Sons, 1924), 115.

[34] Albert Ivatt, ed. *The Memoirs and Travels of Sir John Reresby, Bart.* (London: Kegan Paul, Trench & Trübner, 1904), 23. Cf. *The Diary of John Evelyn*, ed. E. S. de Beer (Oxford: Oxford Univ. Press, 1955), 2:147.

rise to a German folk custom (Halle) where children fill vessels with
water on the saint's vigil to find them filled with wine and topped with
a special pastry, the *Martinshorn,* on the morrow. In a quite literal sense,
the miracle of the rapid transformation of mere pressed juice into
musty new-wine is what is celebrated. To quote the Elizabethan translation of Naogeorgus (1511–1563):

> To belly cheare yet once againe doth Martin more encline,
> Whom all the people worshippeth, with rosted Geese and wine:
> Both all the day long and the night, now ech man open makes
> His vessels all, and of the Must oft times the last he takes,
> Which holy Martyn afterwards, alloweth to be wine,
> Therefore they him unto the skies extoll, with prayse deuine:
> And drinking deepe in tankardes large, and bowles of compasse
>   wide.   *The Popish Kingdome,* bk.4.[35]

As Naogeorgus also indicates, this Rhenish practice was accompanied
by songs and processions "Not praysing Martyn much, but at the goose
rejoyceing tho'." Indeed the *Martinslied* had become a sub-genre of the
German medieval lyric. As early as 1216, Thomas of Cantimpre complained of a *cantus de Martino turpissimus* which he claimed was composed by the devil himself and spread widely throughout France and
Germany, clear evidence of an international popular tune.[36] Oswald
von Wolkenstein in 1420 attests to the antiquity of vernacular *Martins-
lieder* by quoting one: « *Des besten vogel, den ich weiss, das was ain ganns* »
vor zeiten ward gesungen ("The best bird I know of, that's the goose"
was sung of old). Several early examples are associated with the fourteenth-century Monk of Salzburg.[37] These are purely secular in tone

---

[35] For the folk custom see Walsh, *Curiosities,* 666. Cf. Paolo Veneziano's Chioggia
panel, in George Kaftal, *Iconography of the Saints in the Painting of North East Italy* (Florence: Sansoni, 1978), fig. 888, where Martin makes the sign of the cross over a large
wine tun. Robert Charles Hope, ed., *The Popish Kingdome or Reigne of Antichrist* (London: Chiswick Press, 1880), 55, a reprint of 1570 Barnaby Googe translation of the
Regnum papisticum (1553).

[36] Thomas de Cantimpre, *Bonum vniversale de apibus* (Douai: Baltazar Belleri, 1627)
456–57. (*Obscoenas cantilenas componi a daemonibus*).

[37] See esp. entry in *Die deutsche Literatur des Mittelalters Verfasserlexikon* 6. (Ber-
lin/New York: Walter de Gruyter, 1985); Karl Kurt Klein, ed., *Die Lieder Oswald von
Wolkenstein* (Tübingen: Max Niemeyer, 1975), no. 28, no. 67; F. Arnold Mayer and
Heinrich Rietsch, eds., *Die Mondsee-Wiener Liederhandschrift und der Mönch von Salzburg*

with titles like *Von sand Marteins frewden,* their refrains enjoining one to *geus aus, schekch ein* (pour out, hand around) much *kuelen wein,* to dig into roast goose, wear gay apparel, and generally make merry. The saint himself is that *milde man* (compassionate man), or ones *lieber, czarter, trawer herre mein* (my beloved, tender, and true lord). They reflect a decidedly tavern environment where group participation in singing elaborate part-songs and rounds is called for, witness *Ain radel von drein stymmen* (a "wheel" or round for three voices) or *Ein radel von wirtten* (a round for barmen). The songs moreover are infused with the democratic spirit of Saturnalia: *Dy grossen/dye klainen/gemainen* (the great/ the lowly/together). Later songs would even reproduce the sounds of the festival goose—*das best gesang das sie kan da da da da dz ist gick gack gick gack gick gack . . . singen wir zu sant Mertens tag* (the best song they know tha tha tha tha that is gick gack gick gack gick gack . . . we sing on St. Martin's day).[38] Through the anthologizing of Georg Forster in the *Frische Teutsche Liedlein* (1540) and Melchior Francken in the *Newes Teutsches Musicalisches Fröhliches Convivium* (1621), the *Martinslied* continued as a subgenre of German lyric resulting in a substantial body of folk song collected from the Romantic period onward, for instance by Brentano and von Armin in *Des Knaben Wunderhorn* (1806).

The strength of this secular tradition can best be seen in a work by Thomas Stoltzer (c.1480–1526), Kapellmeister to the king of Hungary. It is also an excellent example of the symbiotic relationship between the sacred and profane aspects of the saint's festival. In a sacred anthem for the feast of St. Martin, an unusual fifth vocal line employs a bilingual pun. The bastard Latin—*Nimis denegans, his denegans, nimis denegans* is simultaneously a repeated reference to the festival bird in German—*Nun ist deine Gans, hier ist deine Gans,* and so on.[39] Stoltzer's choristers in the chapel royal were evidently, in the midst of the service, also ruminating upon their festival meal.

A seasonal piece, *Die Martinsnacht,* by the early thirteenth-century poet known as Der Stricker, is worth examining in some detail. Not a

---

(Berlin: Mayer & Müller, 1894), 511–23.

[38] M. Elizabeth Marriage, ed., *Georg Forsters Frische Teutsche Liedlein* (1540; repr., Halle a.d.S.: Max Niemeyer, 1903), 2:6.

[39] Thomas Stoltzer, *Sämtliche lateinischen Hymnen und Psalmen,* ed. Hans Albrecht and Otto Gombosi (Weisbaden: Breitkopf and Hartel, 1959), no. 31.

Martinslied but rather a *Märe* or fabliau, it combines many of the popular cultural motifs we are examining. A rich peasant celebrating St. Martin's Eve hears some commotion in his cow-barn and closes in on the thief. The cattle rustler, as a ruse, strips himself naked and proceeds to bless all the animals in their stalls. He informs the half-drunk peasant that he is St. Martin himself, newly arrived from Heaven, and instructs him to rejoin his household and joyfully carouse with the new-wine that is Martin's gift to mankind. The peasant ecstatically returns to the house to inspire a orgy of celebration, during which time the thief makes off with the entire herd.[40] The evidently plausible appearance of a naked saint blessing the cows, links us back to the strange world of the "four wishes" in the French tradition with its trickster amalgam of boon-giving and practical jokes.

The Martin-disguise motif, moreover, can be found surviving in nineteenth-century Irish folklore, and Martinmas as a season for comic action is also the frame for the well-known Child ballad, "Get Up and Bar the Door:"

> It fell about the Martinmas time
>   And a gay time it was then,
> When our goodwife got puddings to make
>   And she's boiled them in the pan.

Such carnivalesque elements as night wanderers who gorge themselves on puddings "white" and "black," the threat of shaving and befouling the husband as well as of kissing and abducting the goodwife, together with the ultimate triumph of Woman over Man, indicate that the festival reference is far from arbitrary in this ballad already considered "ancient" in the eighteenth century.[41] Some three hundred years after Der Stricker, the rich peasant's *Martinsnacht* was still available for coarse jocular situations, as in several tales from Georg Wickram's *Das Roll-*

---

[40] Wolfgang Wilfried Moelleken, Gayle Agler-Beck, and Robert E. Lewis, eds., *Die Kleindichtung des Strickers* (Göppingen: Alfred Kümmerle, 1975), 3:128–41.

[41] A servant boy takes revenge on a miserly mistress by appearing under her window on St. Martin's Eve chanting: "Nancy Farrell, are you within? I am Saint Martin outside your house; Unless you kill the black wether, I'll be at your wake a week from tonight!" (Ó Súilleabháin, "The Feast of St. Martin," 257); Francis James Child, ed., *English and Scottish Popular Ballads* (New York: Dover Publications, 1965), 5:98.

wagenbüchlin (1555) where the *sussen Martinsmilch,* or new-wine, is rendered scatalogical, or a Martinmas sausage becomes a kind of tail on a priest during the Elevation of the Mass, and Martin is linked with such carnivalesque mock saints as St. *Schweinhardus.*[42]

Early sixteenth-century churchwardens' accounts from St. Martin Outwich in London show payments for singers and rose garlands, as well as copious drink on Martinmas, a major festival date as well for London's Vintners' Company. Burgh records for the same period in Aberdeen suggest that Martinmastide was a time for reappointing the "Abbot" and "Prior" of "Bonaccord," two carnival officers that reappear in the spring as "Robin Hood" and "Little John." The Chester cordwainers' and shoemakers' records also note regular payments for "menstrels on martenes dey," together with collections for drink, throughout the latter half of the same century.[43] Roger Vaultier in *Le folklore pendant la guerre de Cent Ans* collected several, unfortunately not very specific, records of Martinmas revelry in France. One, however, does involve a dancing priest in red shoes and a crown of flowers. In Venice one could find *canzoni in barzeletta per i putti da cantar per San Martino* (jesting songs to be sung by putti on St. Martin's) in 1571.[44] All this is evidence that the German revelling tradition was certainly not an isolated phenomenon.

A Swiss folk drama, *Ein Streit zwischen Herbst und Mai*—a variation on the common winter vs. summer combats—clearly belongs to Martinmastide.[45] *Herbst* (autumn) is obviously the month of November, six months away from May. His attributes are long bratwursts and bumpers of wine, and he vaunts himself as a true King Carnival: *Hie win und wurst und wecke!/Da von bin ich ein recke* (valiant hero or giant).

---

[42] Georg Wickram, *Das Rollwagenbüchlin*, ed. Johannes Bolte (1555; repr., Stuttgart: Phillip Reclam, 1968), no. 62, no. 103, no. 104.

[43] Brand, *Observations,* 401. For Aberdeen records see Anna Jean Mill, *Medieval Plays in Scotland* (St. Andrews: St. Andrews Univ. Press, 1924), 133–42; Lawrence M. Clopper, ed., *Chester: Records of Early English Drama* (Toronto: Univ. of Toronto Press, 1979), 48–49. See also Alan H. Nelson, ed., *Cambridge: Records of Early English Drama* (Toronto, Univ. of Toronto Press, 1989), 1:189.

[44] Roger Vaultier, *Le folklore pendant la guerre de Cent Ans d'après les lettres de rémission du Trésor des Chartes* (Paris: Guénéguad, 1965), 152–54; Anon., *Dve Canzoni* from a rare pamphlet with woodcut (Venice, 1571) in Houghton Library, Harvard.

[45] S. Singer, ed., *Schweizerisches Archiv für Volkskunde* 23 (1921): 112–16.

His twelve "knights" sport such carnivalesque names as Neverfull, Drink-up, Full-bag, and Goose-gobbler. The piece may date from as early as the fourteenth century, and if so, closely anticipates the processional *Fastnachtspiele* of the fifteenth century. This piece has an analogue in the early Tudor *Debate and stryfe betwene Somer and Wynter* (c. 1530) where Lord Winter boasts that "Men make greate Joy what tyme I com in/For copanyes gadareth togyther on eue of/seynt martyn/Ther is nother great not small but than they/wyll drinke wyne."[46] The great carnivalist Hans Sachs did not neglect the feast: his *Der faisten gens sorgfeltig clag/Auf den kunfting sant Mertens-tag* (1569) is a dream vision of the suffering geese on Martinmas, a later version of the blackened swan's lament in the *Carmina Burana*. The French dramatic monologue *Sermon fort joyeux de saint Raisin* (c. 1450) also refers to the Martinian festival on which it was likely performed.[47] In seventeenth-century Amsterdam, Martin received the ultimate accolade of popular culture: he became the sponsor of a jest-book, *De Gaven van de milde St. Marten* (1654) whose frontispiece is conceived in completely burlesque terms. There Martin splits his cloak on an actual theatrical stage to the applause of a mixed crowd of men and women. The "naked" beggar of the Charity becomes a literally naked young Bacchus who flogs the humorous publication. The Martinmas roast goose and new-wine are also prominently and quite literally "on stage"[48] (fig. 1).

Martinmas then was a fairly well established period of feasting and conviviality in the medieval period, over many language areas, with its own literary products, and an enduring influence upon folk culture. It is not surprising that it took on many of the customs associated with the winter revels proper, usually commencing on the neighboring and collateral feast of St. Nicholas. We have records from the recent folklife

---

[46] *Debate* reproduced in E.W. Ashbee, ed. *Occasional Fac-simile Reprints of Rare English Tracts* 12 (London, 1868–1870). Cf. the ballad version of *Gawain*, "The Grene Knight:"—"he cheered the Knight & gave him wine/& said, 'welcome, by St. Martine'!" John W. Hales and Frederick J. Furnivall, eds., *Bishop Percy's Folio Manuscript: Ballads and Romances* (London: N. Trübner, 1868), 2:70.

[47] Hans Sachs, *Werke,* eds. A. von Keller and E. Goetze (Hildesheim: G. Olms, 1964), 23:456–57. For *sermon joyeaux,* Anatole de Montaiglon, ed. *Recueil de poésies françoises des XVe et XVIe siècles* (Paris: P.Jannet, 1855), 2:112–17.

[48] *De Gaven van de milde St. Marten: bestaende in kluchten koddereyen en andre vermakelykheden.* Amsterdam: Kornelis Last, 1654. (Columbia Univ. Library).

Fig. 1. A burlesque St. Martin. Frontispiece of a Dutch jest-book, 1654. (Columbia University Library).

of Europe which mention: Martinmas begging processions with lanterns together with "ridings" of the saint on a white horse; bonfires
and candle-lit windows; ritual noise-making; gifts to children, especially
apples and nuts, with accompanying discipline threats; anthropomor-
phic baked goods or pastries skewered on Martin's "sword" (Tournai).
There were Martinmas guisers in straw suits (Orkney and Shetland),
and other anticipations of shaggy, winter demon masquerades in the
Swabian *Pelzmärte* (Furry Martin), the Salzburger *Kasmandel*, and the
"Wolf" in the *Wolfauslassen* of the Bavarian Woods, with cognate creatures from Latvia and Estonia.[49] Dunkirk had an odd "Hunting of the
Ass," supposedly derived from an incident in the saint's life when,
praying at a wilderness shrine on the site of the future city, his donkey
wandered off to munch thistles in the dunes. On St. Martin's Eve and
the following night, Dunkirkers search for the beast with lanterns,
blowing horns in imitation of its bray, and generally having a wild old
time.[50] This may preserve a memory of the medieval *festa asinorum*,
and tempts one again to draw parallels with Bacchus and his retinue.

It is clear then that Martinmas represents for the later medieval centuries a kind of shadow Carnival—on the opposite side of the season,
but at the point where specifically indoor, winter revels may properly
commence. "Between Martinmas and Yule, water's wine in every
pool," as a Scottish proverb runs.[51] In a sixteenth-century German
almanack we find this prognostication for the month of November: *Es
werden ouch vil Düppel, Narren vnd Trunckenböltz allenthalben in der
gantzen welt gefunden werden* (Many idiots, fools and drunkards will be
found everywhere throughout the world), which indeed sounds like
Mardi Gras. Jacob Frey felt that Martinmas was a particularly appropriate time to dedicate his 1556 jest-book, *Gartengesellschaft* , as it ushered
in the great winter festivals including the "kingdoms" of the Epiphany
and Carnival itself—*bey den newen wein, Martins nächten, königreichen,*

---

[49] See esp. Miles, *Christmas Customs;* Swoboda, *Alpenländisches Brauchtum*; the British Calendar Customs series of the Folk-Lore Society; and Jennifer M. Russ, *German
Festivals and Customs*. (London: Oswald Wolff, 1982), 74–77.

[50] Walsh, *Curiosities,* 666–67. For the current Martin festival see Maurice Millon,
Les legendes de l'histoire de Dunkerque et de la Flandre maritime (Saint-Omer: L'Independ-
ant, 1972), 21–23.

[51] Dwight Edwards Marvin, *Curiosities in Proverbs* (New York: G. Putnam's Sons,
1916), 147.

kottfleischen und fassnachten allerhand (with new-wine, Martin's nights, kingdoms, tripe feasts and Shrovetides of all sorts).[52] As lord of a goose-eating, wine-bibbing Cockaigne, Martin takes on some of the mystique of King Carnival, and can thus be more easily appreciated as an ally of Gargantua and source of priapic humor. This popular mytho-logical dimension is secure, whether or not we are able to read a palimpsest of Bacchus, the cattle protector Silvanus, or some cognate Teutonic or Celtic diety behind him. Indeed, it could well be that Martin's mythic persona is principally a creation of the Christian centu-ries at the level of popular culture, taking only minimal cues from aboriginal paganism.

Martin-Beggar/Martin-Poet

St. Martin the popular icon, however, would be little more than an abstraction, like King Carnival, were it not for the contribution of spe-cific aspects of his official hagiography which gave him his own unique features. The single most important image of Martin, of course, is the "Charity": the saint astride a warhorse before the gates of Amiens, sev-ering his military cloak to share it with a naked beggar. In a dream that night, Christ appeared bearing the remnant and praising Martin for his exemplary action. The half-cloak became the most precious relic and battle flag of the Merovingians, but it is the beggar that concerns us. He became more and more grotesque, and as the Middle Ages pro-gressed, was pushed further in the direction of *genre* interest. To the simple "naked man" of the original *vitae* were added withered limbs, goiter, slings and bandages, little carts, crutches and walkers of all sorts. By the Elizabethan age it had become almost proverbial "to stand, like Saint *Martin's* beggar, upon two stilts." His number multiplied about the saint's horse. He might even have an old peasant mother behind him or a dying child in swaddling in his arms. The multiplication of these images closely corresponds to the "explosion" of mendicancy and vagabondage in the generations after the Black Death, so amply chron-

---

[52] Jacob Bächtold, "Quellen zu 'Aller Praktik Grossmutter,'" *Vierteljahrsschrift für Litteraturgeschichte* 3 (1890), 234; Johannes Bolte, ed., *Jacob Freys Gartengesellschaft* (1556; repr., Tübingen: Literarischen Verein in Stuttgart, 1896), 4. Martin Montanus dedicat-ed two of his jest-books on Martinmas 1557, indicating a sense of "holiday book trade" in sixteenth-century Strasbourg.

icled by Michel Mollat in *Les pauvres du Moyen Age*.[53] It is the grotesque element in the iconic composition that serves as the valve
between the fluid popular materials, examined above, and the more
compact official hagiography, with its heavy investment in the ecclesi-
astically controlled mechanisms of charity.

Charity toward the poor is of course a commonplace in saints' lives,
but the historical Martin appears to have had unusually strong associations with the socially marginal. He is credited with adventures with
brigands in the Alps, resuscitating a hanged servant, releasing debtors
and other convicts from prison, passing on a wine cup proffered him
by the emperor to a lowly clerk, kissing lepers, and other divestments
for the sake of the poor. His favoring of the underdog extends even to
his quite numerous later associations with animals. There is, for example, the bizarre account of freezing in their tracks a brace of hounds
that had "hunted a hare vnder his hors wombe."[54]

This insistence upon marginality in the official *vitae* and later legends indeed creates an interesting tension within Martin's dominant
icon. The Charity, as composition, poses a considerable formal problem: how to turn the classical equestrian pose of the Roman cavalry-
man trampling the naked barbarian, the very epitome of military
might, into its opposite? The solution, for the vast majority of medieval
painters and sculptors, was to have Martin face backwards—over his
horse's rump, towards the beggar—in the act of parting his cloak. The
saint is, in effect, halfway toward that universal *topos* of Folly: the backwards rider.

The earliest images of the Charity, in tenth-century sacramentaries,
follow Sulpicius Severus' account closely, and portray Martin on foot
in front of the city gate.[55] It is only after the First Crusade, apparently, that the familiar equestrian image appears, possibly due to the influence of the newly imported figure of St. George. In its development

---

[53] Elizabethan quote, see Francis O. Mann, ed., *The Works of Thomas Deloney* (Oxford: Clarendon Press, 1912), 207. Michel Mollat, *The Poor in the Middle Ages,* trans.
Arthur Goldhammer (New Haven: Yale Univ. Press, 1986).

[54] From an early fifteenth-century Martinmas sermon. Theodor Erbe, ed., *Mirk's
Festial: A Collection of Homilies* (London: Kegan Paul, Trench, Trübner, 1905), 272–74.

[55] The two sacramentaries from the monastery of Fulda, c. 975 are housed in the
Universitäts Bibliothek, Göttingen and the Staatliche Bibliothek, Bamberg.

from the twelfth through fourteenth centuries we can discern the creation of a truly archetypal construct of young, resplendent Chevalier and
wild, distorted Beggar, fully the equal in power, ambivalence, and lon-
gevity to that perennial team of king and fool.[56] For example, in a
painting composed c. 1440, now in the Rottenburg Diocesan Museum, Martin's mantle passes, upper left to lower right, from the hands of
God himself, through the splendid equestrian figure, into the hands of
a slavering cripple, forming in the process a cursive letter M. Significantly, this Martin faces toward his beggar, his golden, knightly pano-
ply rendered superbly ambivalent by the "alternating current" of red
drapery. The slippery, reversible quality of the Charity is nowhere
more apparent than in the production of a counter-image to Christ in
the person of the least of one's brethren. Later legendary accretions,
following Martin's reported willingness to preach to the Devil himself,
replay the Charity with Satan now in the beggar disguise. This curious
subject even attracted the pencil of Raphael.[57]

Reversal/inversion indeed pervades the Martin *vita* with its multiple
disguisings—the beggar is really Christ, the Roman officer, really a
pacifist; Satan masquerades as Christ the King; Martin proves a dead
"martyr" to be really a thief; and he returns as an "old fayre man" to
translate his own relics—and the proto-Trickster elements noted above
in relation to antagonistic figures. My suggestion here is that the
Martin legend had, inherently, somewhat more comic ambivalence
than the typical saint's life. Even in Martin's contemporary biographer,
Sulpicius Severus, the cornerstone of all Martin hagiography, there are
moments of almost farcical grotesquery. For instance, when the saint
encountered a white-shrouded funeral bier and *mistook* it for a pagan
cult object, he made the sign of the cross to prevent the procession's
forward progress: "Then, they tried with all their might to advance
but, being quite unable to move forward, they kept turning round in
the most ridiculous whirligigs," (an incident for which Edward Gibbon

---

[56] See esp. William Willeford, *The Fool and His Sceptre* (London: Edward Arnold,
1969) for detailed discussion of the King-Fool archetype. The George and Martin
icons together present an almost text-book illustration of Levy-Strauss' structuralist in-
versions: dragon to beggar/killing lance to sheltering sword/wilderness to city gate.

[57] Drawing reproduced in Lecoy de la Marche, pl. 16.

likens Martin to Don Quixote).[58] During a trying exorcism Martin
thrust his fingers between the demoniac's teeth, making it impossible
for the demon to leave by the man's mouth and resulting in a massive
diabolical fart. Nor should one forget that, in Severus, the climactic
moment of the Charity is punctuated by laughter. Martin's companions
(seldom represented in the visual arts) laugh at him for the now ridiculous figure he cuts in a mutilated cloak.

These mild absurdities of the *vita* (certain anti-establishment tendencies and near approximation to the type of Holy Fool in the historical
figure), coupled with the strong festive connotations afforded by calendar position, made Martin readily available for the comic/ironic purposes of secular artists.[59] It is not surprizing then to find Martin prominent, in later centuries, in the *exempla* of popular sermons: that fertile
middle ground between sacred and secular literary culture. Even before
the heyday of the Preaching Friars, Martin was used repeatedly by
Jacques de Vitry in his *Sermones Vulgares* (c. 1230). Only one of his
three examples is indisputably "sacred." The others (including the
ironic cure of the blind and lame man to be discussed later) show
Martin rubbing shoulders with Aesop animals, Eastern tricksters, and
fabliaux prototypes.[60] From there it was a short step for him to the
world of misericords and manuscript marginalia.

At the beginning of secular lyric in Europe the Martin's-beggar
image was embraced, even to the point of identification, by those itinerant minor clerics known as the "Goliards," who were said to "con-

---

[58] Hoare, *The Western Fathers*, 26. Gibbon's comment is found in a footnote to
chap. 28 of *Decline and Fall of the Roman Empire*.

[59] As a frequent self-humiliator enduring blows and insults gladly, as a contemplative subject to absent-mindedness, and as a very reluctant bishop who dressed in hair
cloth tunic and ragged black cloak (an appearance capable of spooking pack animals),
the historical Martin certainly approximates the type of Holy Fool as delineated by
John Saward in *Perfect Fools: Folly for Christ's Sake in Catholic and Orthodox Christianity*
(New York: Oxford Univ. Press, 1980). Strangely, Saward does not discuss Martin
whose medieval images, whether as young cavalier or dignified bishop, gloss over the
distinctly odd character in Sulpicius Severus. It is the suggestion of this paper that the
"alternative" tradition, in a sense, recovered him.

[60] Thomas Frederick Crane, ed. *The Exempla or Illustrated Stories from the Sermones
Vulgares of Jacques de Vitry* (London: Folk-Lore Society, 1890), 42 & 173; 52 & 182;
79 & 209–10. See also the Dominican Herolt's *Promptuarium Exemplorum* (c. 1440) for
a variant on the reluctent recipient of a Martin cure.

sume as much in one evening as St. Martin in his entire lifetime."[61] Frequently in their verses an unfavorable comparison is made between present ecclesiastical patron and legendary magnaminous saint. In an all-purpose begging poem, complete with a blank space for inserting the patron's name, we find the Martin cloak in a conspicuous position:

> *Ille meus tenuis*
> *nimis est amictus,*
> *sepe frigus patior*
> *calore relictus.*

> *Ergo mentem capite*
> *similem Martini,*
> *vestibus induite*
> *corpus peregrini.*

> My poor cloak, so very thin,
> fails to keep the cold out:
> drained of warmth, against the wind
> I can hardly hold out.

> May St. Martin's deed inspire:
> bear in mind what he did:
> draped upon a pilgrim's back,
> something warmly needed.[62]

The great goliardic poet, Hugo of Orleans, known as Primas (fl. 1140), even conducted a dramatic dialogue (*Pontificum spuma*) with the miserable piece of mantle given him by an ecclesiastic who all-too-inadequately embodied the saint:

> —Pauper mantelle, macer absque pilo, sine pelle,
> si potes, expelle boream rabiemque procelle!

---

[61] From Simon of Tournai, *Summa* (c. 1202) quoted in Helen Waddell, *The Wandering Scholars* (New York: Henry Holt, 1926), 200n. Cf. Johannes de Bromyarde: *sicut Martinus, non dicit Mimum, uel ioculatorem: sed nudum pauperem* in *Summa Praedicantium* [c. 1365] (Venice: Domenico Nicolino, 1586), under "Eleemosyna."

[62] David Parlett, trans. *Selections from the Carmina Burana* (Harmondsworth: Penguin Books, 1986), 129.

(Poor mantle, what abuse could thin you?/No fur, no
padding in you!/Think you, thus sadly aging,/To fend
me from the blast, the storm's mad raging?)

Primas with his "mean appearance and twisted face" was particularly
well equipped to impersonate the Martin-beggar. His poem no. 18
indeed opens with praise of the city of Amiens for charities done him;
Amiens being the site of St. Martin's famous Charity.[63] The Archpoet
of Cologne (fl. 1165) was also known for his cloak-begging verses. In
a serio-comic vision of Heaven he actually meets St. Martin, persuad-
ing him to turn his wrath from the archbishop of Cologne. That pre-
late was guilty of tyrannizing over St. Martin's monastery, where the
threadbare poet had often received generous measures of wine.[64]

The funeral of the itinerant Minnesinger, Heinrich von Meissen,
known as "Frauenlob," also appears to have been influenced by the
more carnivalesque aspects of the Martinmas season. When the poet
was interred in the cloister of St. Martin's in Mainz (where saint and
beggar prominently enact their scene on the roof ridge), in late November 1318, the women of the city turned out *en masse* to carry and
accompany his bier. The cloister was said to be "swimming" in wine
dispensed in his honor.[65]

There was, then, some amelioration of the marginality experienced by
these early secular poets in the archetype of the Martin-beggar, but the
figure was always fraught with comic irony. In a scurrilous complaining
verse, for example, a Provençal poet could wittily subvert the Charity:

Et enojam, per saint Marti,
Trop d'aiga en petit de vi;
E quan trob escassier mati
M'enoja, e d'orp atressi,
Car nom azaut delor cami.

---

[63] George F. Whicher, trans., *The Goliard Poets: Medieval Latin Songs and Satires* (Norfolk, Conn.: New Directions, 1949), 80–83, 74. See also Therese Latzke, "Die Mantelgedichte des Primas Hugo von Orleans und Martial," *Mittellateinisches Jahrbuch* 5 (1968): 54–58, and "Der Topos Mantel-gedicht," *Mittellateinisches Jahrbuch* 6 (1970): 109–31.

[64] Edwin H. Zeydel, ed. and trans., *Vagabond Verse: Secular Latin Poems of the Middle Ages* (Detroit: Wayne State Univ. Press, 1966), 247–65.

[65] See entry "Frauenlob" in *Die deutsche Literatur des Mittelalters Verfasserlexikon.*

I hate, by good St. Martin's sign
a pint of water drowning my wine!
To meet the lame in morning-shine
annoys, and blind men I decline
because their way does not suit mine.

Monk of Montaudon (fl. 1195)[66]

Under the sign of the shared mantle, Martinmas feasting naturally became an occasion for mass charity in the democractic spirit of carnival—*dy grossen, /dye klainen, /gemainen* (the great, the lowly, together) as the *Martinslied* enjoins. In anticipation of the midwinter revels, it appropriated some of the "liminality" of the Roman Saturnalia with its anarchic mingling of masters and slaves. A painting in the Brueghel school from the brush of Pieter Balten, "The Wine of St. Martin," depicts a fantasy scene of mass wine distribution to the Flemish poor. A great barrel high on a scaffold is stormed by a seathing anthill of empoverished humanity, wrangling, guzzling, spewing, reaching aloft their recepticles for the alchoholic dole. The saint is present on horseback, but off to one side and deliberately turned away from the scene. In a related Vienna fragment, evidently closer in format to the Elder Brueghel's lost original, the saint wears a face of resigned world-weariness. A few cripples anticipate his act of cloak-sharing, but the vast majority of the "welfare recipients" are clearly in it only for the booze. The effect here is not one of unreserved, jovial celebration, but like Bosch's "Haywain," whose compositional structure it approximates, of a pathos-laden comment upon human folly and perversity; creating, moreover, an ambivalent attitude toward the saint himself, dissociating him from the melee but compromising him at the same time. A thematically related canvass, Martin van Cleve's "St. Martin's Bonfire," shows a group of boys fighting over possession of the saint's banner while a solitary drunk, or "Martinsman," wanders past with his little

---

[66] Emil Philippson, ed., *Der Mönch von Montaudon, ein provenzalische Troubadour* (Halle a.d.S.: Max Niemeyer, 1873), no. 19, ll. 23–27. Hubert Creekmore, ed. and trans., *Lyrics of the Middle Ages* (New York: Grove Press, 1959), 54–57. The great ironist of our century, Bertolt Brecht, has both Martin and the beggar perish from the cold since the mantle is, practically speaking, only large enough to cover one ("Solomon Song" in *Mother Courage*).

flag, singing away, a crown of vineleaves in his hair.[67] Some decades earlier an engraving attributed to Bosch grafted the Charity upon the *Narrenschiff* tradition, as Martin and horse stand placidly in a rowboat surrounded by fighting beggar-grotesques with musical instruments and wine jugs.[68] These internal contradictions of the Martin/Beggar construct which are simultaneously its comic possibilities, only intensify when we follow them into the drama.

Martin Drama

One Provençal and three French medieval Martin plays survive, together with a *sacre rappresentatione* from Orvieto, and a Martin *auto* from the pen of Gil Vincente. Records of other plays or pageants exist from Barcelona (1424), Lanark (1490), Colchester (1527), and Leicester and Aberdeen from the first half of the sixteenth century.[69] The earliest of the extant plays is the most elaborate and most humorous and was written by Andrieu de la Vigne for the Burgundian town of Seurre in 1496. It had 152 roles for about 120 actors, and took three days to perform.[70] The eve of this major event was devoted to a farce on the

---

[67] George Marlier, *Pierre Brueghel le Jeune* (Brussels: Robert Finck, 1969), 324–27 and 353–54. The "Wine of St. Martin" engraving by N. Guerard appears to preserve the original Brueghel design, and is even more violent and crowded.

[68] Reproduced in Louis Maeterlinck, *Le genre satirique dans la peinture flamande* (Brussels: G. Van Oest, 1907), pl. 23.

[69] For French Martin plays, see Lynette R. Muir's checklist in "The Saint Play in Medieval France," in *The Saint Play in Medieval Europe,* ed. Clifford Davidson (Kalamazoo: Medieval Institute Publications, 1986), 171. For Barcelona see Peter Meredith and John E. Tailby, eds., *The Staging of Religious Drama in the Later Middle Ages: Texts and Documents* (Kalamazoo: Medieval Institute Publications, 1983), 127–28. For English plays see Ian Lancashire, ed., *Dramatic Texts and Records of Britain: A Chronological Topography to 1558* (Toronto: Univ. of Toronto Press, 1984) and Davidson, *The Saint Play in Medieval Europe,* 69. For Scotland: Mill, *Medieval Plays in Scotland,* 74, 261. A highpoint of Elkanah Settle's *Lord Mayor's Show* of 1702 was a Martin-and-beggar scene in honor of the Vintners' Company. There is also record of a lost Martin play by Lope de Vega.

[70] A. de la Vigne, *Le Mystère de Saint Martin, 1496,* ed. André Duplat (Geneva: Librairie Droz, 1979). Translation of *L'Aveugle et le Boiteux,* in R. S. Loomis and Henry W. Wells, eds., *Representative Medieval and Tudor Plays* (New York: Sheed & Ward, 1942), 13–14, 49–60. For the play in performance, see Ernest Serrigny, *La representation d'un Mystère de Saint-Martin à Seurre, en 1496* (Dijon: Librairie Lamarche, 1888). See also Graham A. Runnalls, "The Staging of André de la Vigne's *Mystère de Saint Martin,*" *Treteaux* 3 (1981): 68–79, for corrections to Duplat's theoretical staging.

fabliau theme of the Devil mistaking a miller's turd for his soul. The *mystère* proper had its share of *diableries* and comic passages, particularly the adventures of *Hannequin le Hasardeur* who became the hanged man of the Martin miracle. But the episode from the legend which de la Vigne chose to decant and serve up as a separate farce or *moralité joyeuse* at the end of the entire festival, exemplifies the comic ambivalence of the popular tradition of St. Martin. This is the miracle of *L'Aveugle et le Boiteux* (The Blind Man and the Cripple), which had found its way into Jacques de Vitry's *exempla*, the *Golden Legend,* John Mirk's Martinmas sermon, the eponymous work of the Master of the Brucker Martin-Panel, a rondel of the *St. Martin Embroideries,* and many other "official" treatments of the saint's life and works.[71] A widespread folkloric motif, the symbiosis of frail cripple and sturdy blindman can be found from Celtic Ireland to Hopi Arizona, and apparently entered the Martin *vita* through one of the miracle accounts in a twelfth-century chronicle on the return of Martin's relics to Tours after the Viking era.[72]

As de la Vigne skillfully dramatizes the tale, the two unfortunatès are presented in split focus: the blind man lamenting that he has been abandoned by his boy, the cripple that he is now stuck without any means of locomotion, his helper having absconded as well. Gradually they distinguish each other's voices and gropingly come together. They can now, after much grumbling and tumbling, form a perfect union of one *complete* human being, with the frail, though sighted cripple riding atop the sturdy blind man. With the reality of live actors, this odd couple becomes one of the funniest, and most touching, emblems of human need and cooperation ever produced by medieval art. And yet there is a twist. The cripple is immediately wary of the procession

---

[71] Margaret B. Freeman, *The St. Martin Embroideries* (New York: Metropolitan Museum of Art), 18 & pl. 31. The work is c. 1440. The Brucker Martin Panel (1518) is reproduced in *Gotik in der Steiermark* (St. Lambrecht: Kulturreferat der Steiermarkischen Landesregierung, 1978), color pl. 5. Rabelais may refer to the begging pair in the *Tiers Livre,* chap. 47.

[72] Pseudo-Odo, *Reversione beati Martini a Burgundia Tractatus.* This "forgery" by the monks of Martin's monastery of Marmoutier is discussed in Sharon Farmer, *Communities of St. Martin: Legend and Ritual in Medieval Tours.* (Ithaca: Cornell Univ. Press, 1991), chap. 3. It is a brief account of how two (unspecified) cripples are cured against their will.

bearing St. Martin's relics. The pair would be sure to be cured, thus ending their now carefree existence as one accomplished and mobile beggarman. The climax of the action is that, in their efforts to flee the crowds, they tumble down directly in front of the reliquary and are instantly cured. (In the embroidery rondel mentioned above, they cannot see the saintly apparition who is about to collide with them at the street corner.) Back to being two separate voices again, the blind man gives copious thanks to the saint for his vision, but the cripple curses his new strength of limb. He has the last word, and even plans to anoint himself with a poison that will raise hideous boils. The play ends with him rehearsing a new pitch for the compassionate suckers to come. The playwright is certainly not trying to underscore the obvious moral here, that of Christ's parable of the lepers made clean. At some level he wishes us to admire the comic resiliency of the unregenerate cripple for whom the saint is not the great thaumaturge but a wry, fabliau trickster.

There is, moreover, impressive metatheatricality in the piece, with its internal procession figuring the three days of the celebration as a whole and its very human—and contradictory—relationship to the heroic and miraculous representing the self-reflections of the itinerant playwright himself. Blind man and cripple, indeed, embody the two fundamental aspects of the Martinus cult: the one, "officially" aligning itself with the active life of the Church Militant, the other facing wistfully toward that impossible life of perpetual Carnival. They are not self-annihilating, however, but mutually coexisting. The saint provides a curious hinge between the two.

The shaggy, not to say repellant appearance of the historical bishop of Tours simply underscores the fact that, *vis-à-vis* the eternal, all earthy splendor and power is relative and on a very sliding scale. The effect that de la Vigne achieves is the polar opposite, if not the deliberate subversion, of the "official" culture's reading of Martin iconography. The powerful archbishops of Mainz in their Cathedral of St. Martin, for example, invariably included an image of the Charity on their elaborate tombs—Martin dressed as a bishop with a miniature beggar tucked into the composition at his feet. A sixteenth-century altar panel, now in the Mainzer Landesmuseum, epitomizes this trend. There Martin is a well-fed, resplendent prince of the Church who drops a coin into a begging box conspicuously bearing a seal, proof that this beggar (back to the viewer) is an officially registered member of the "worthy poor." The farce cripple will have none of this. He is an irreducible vagabond giving the lie to such patronizing images and maintaining himself tenaciously in the foreground of his composition. The power of the paradoxical relationship created by de la Vigne's can be gauged by the fact that his blind man and cripple team was directly taken up by several twentieth-century dramatists, by J. M. Synge in *The Well of the Saints,* by W. B. Yeats in *The Cat and the Moon,* and by such diverse theatre artists as Samuel Beckett (*Theatre I*) and Dario Fo (*Mistero Buffo*) after them.[73] The legacy of the Martin-beggar is indeed a rich one, and still with us.

To conclude this rough mapping of one hinterland of hagiography, it is clear that we are not dealing with a subversive counter culture in these popular manifestations, but with phenomena that coexist with, indeed feed off of "official" or "elite" culture. The relationship is perhaps best imagined as symbiotic rather than parasitic; something which the medieval mind apparently felt quite at home with, exploiting the contradictions, ritualistically and artistically, rather than denying or surpressing them. Because of the peculiar features—multiple disguisings and *peripeteitia,* anti-establishment and Holy Fool traits—in the "official" legend, coupled with a particularly strong calendar position, rich in practices possibly overlaying an aboriginal paganism, St. Martin became a curious kind of spiritual benefactor: a provider of feasts of meat and wine at the portal of winter; a patron to the most marginalized members of society from whom he did not even expect gratitude; a granter of wishes, infantile or pubescent, priapic or gastronomic; and a historical figure of major importance for European Christendom but with one foot still in the land of Faerie.[74] If the comic spirit of the Middle Ages then lacks a patron saint, let it be Martin, bishop of Tours and Lord of Misrule.

---

[73] See esp. Toni O'Brien Johnson, *Synge: The Medieval and the Grotesque* (Gerrards Cross: Colin Smythe, 1982), 29–53.

[74] Comic exploitation of beggars and cripples seems to occur naturally around Martin, but not around other saints with similar retinues: Elizabeth of Hungry, for example, or even the conspicuously "theatrical" St. Nicholas. An interesting work on the position of Martin in the development of attitudes toward the poor is Sara Hansell MacGonagle, *The Poor in Gregory of Tours: A Study of the Attitude of Merovingian Society towards the Poor, as Reflected in the Literature of the Time.* (Ph.D. diss., Columbia University, 1936).

Bibliography

Index

Bibliography

Abate, Giuseppe. "Le fonti biografiche di S. Antonio. VII. I frammenti della 'Benignitas' e la 'Vita S. Antonii' edita dal Surio." *Il Santo* 10, fasc. 3 (Sept–Dec. 1970): 223–72; ibid., 12, fasc. 1–2 (Jan–Aug. 1977): 3–106.

———. "Le fonti biografiche di S. Antonio. V. La 'Vita Sancti Antonii' di Fra Pietro Raymondina da San Romano, c. 1293." *Il Santo* 10, fasc. 1–2 (Jan–Aug. 1970): 3–34.

———. "Le fonti della biografia di S. Antonio. VI. Legenda Rigaldina." *Il Santo* 10 (1970): 35–77.

———. "Le fonti biografiche di S. Antonio (cont.). II. L'Ufficio ritmico di S. Antonio di Fra Giuliano da Spira, O.M.I. c. 1235." *Il Santo* 9, fasc. 2 (May–Aug. 1969): 149–89.

———. "Le fonti biografiche di S. Antonio. I. La 'Vita Prima' di S. Antonio." *Il Santo* 8, fasc. 2–3 (May–Dec. 1968): 185–201.

Achenbach, Gertrude M. "The Iconography of Tobias and the Angel in Florentine Painting of the Renaissance." *Marsyas* 3 (1943–1945): 71–91.

Ahl, Diane Cole. "Benozzo Gozzoli's Santa Rosa da Viterbo Cycle: The Decorum of Saintly Narrative," in *Decorum in Renaissance Narrative Art*, eds. Francis Ames-Lewis and Anka Bednarek (London: Caldra House Ltd., 1992): 61–69.

———. "Benozzo Gozzoli's Frescoes of the Life of Saint Augustine in San Gimigniano: Their Meaning in Context." *Artibus et historiae* 13 (1986): 35–53.

Aigraim, René. *L'hagiographie.* Paris: Bloud et Gay, 1953.

Airaldi, Gabriella. *Jacopo da Voragine: tra santi e mercanti.* Milan: Camunia, 1988.

Alvarez Bresciani, G. "L'Architettura e l'arredo della cappella di S. Giacomo ora detta di S. Felice al Santo." *Il Santo* 5 (1965): 131–41.

———. et al. *La Cappella del Beato Luca e Giusto dè Menabuoi nella Basilica di Sant'Antonio.* Padua: Messagero, 1988.

Ambrose. *Epistola 20, Patrologia Latina* 16.

Amos, Thomas L. "Monks and Pastoral Care in the Early Middle Ages," in *Religion,*

Culture, and Society in the Early Middle Ages: Studies in Honor of Richard E. Sullivan, eds. Thomas F. X. Noble and John J. Contreni (Kalamazoo: Medieval Institute Publications, 1987): 165–80.

Analecta Hymnica, vols. 5, 13, 14b, 17, 24 (ed. Guido M. Dreves), 25 (ed. Clemens Blume), 26, 28, 45a (Blume and Dreves), 52 (Blume), Leipzig: R. Reisland, 1886–1922.

Andreozzi, Gabriele. "S. Rocco in Montefalco." *Analecta T. O. R.* 5–6 (1949–1952): 81–89, 169–75, 345–47.

Arndt, W., ed. *Historia Francorum,* vol. 1 in *Monumenta Germaniae Historica Scriptores Rerum Meronvigiarum* 1.

Arnold, T. *Symeonis Monachi Opera,* Rolls Series vol. 75. London, 1882.

Arnold-Foster, Francis. *Studies in Church Dedications.* London: Skeffington and Son, 1899.

Ashbee, E. E., ed. *Occasional Facsimile Reprints of Rare Tracts 12.* London, 1868–1870.

Aspetti dell'agiografia nell'Alto Medioevo, Testi del II Colloquio medievale, Palermo, 2–21 marzo 1983, published in *Schede Medievali* 5 (luglio–dicembre, 1983): 303–82.

Athanasius. *History of the Arians,* in J. Stephenson. *A New Eusebius.* London: SPCK, 1957.

Aubanus, Johannes Boemus. *Mores, leges, et ritus omnium gentium.* Paris: Hieronymus de Marnef, 1561.

Auda, Antoine. *L'école musicale liégeoise au Xe siècle: Etienne de Liège.* Brussels: Maurice Lamertin, 1923.

Bachtold-Staubli, Hanns. *Handworterbuch des deutschen Aberglaubens,* ed. E. Hoffmann-Krayer. Berlin: Walter De Gruyter, 1932–1933.

Baker, A. T., ed. *An Anglo-Norman Life of Saint Paul the Hermit,* Modern Language Review 4 (1909): 491–504.

———, ed. *Vie de Saint Panuce,* Romania 38 (1909): 418–24.

Baker, Derek, ed. *Medieval Women.* Oxford: Basil Blackwell, 1978.

Baker, Donald C., John Murphy, and Louis B. Hall Jr. *The Late Medieval Religious Plays of Bodleian MSS Digby 133 and e museo 160.* EETS, vol. 283. Oxford, 1982.

Bakhtin, Mikhail. "Problema teksta." *Voprosy literatury* 10 (1976): 122–50.

Balaguer, Jordi Rubió. *Ramón Llull i el lullisme.* Montserrat: Publicacions de l'Abadia, 1985.

Balsdon, J. P. V. D. *Roman Women.* New York: John Day Co., 1963.

Barbero, Alessandro. *Un santo in famiglia. Vocazione e resistenze sociali nell'agiografia latina medievale.* Turin: Rosenberg and Sellier, 1991.

Barlow, Frank. *The English Church, 1000–1066.* London: Longmans, 1979.

Barnes, Timothy D. *Constantine and Eusebius.* Cambridge: Harvard Univ. Press, 1981.

Barstow, Anne Lllewellyn. *Married Priests and the Reforming Papacy: The Eleventh-Century Debates,* vol. 12 of *Texts and Studies in Religion.* New York: Edwin Mellen Press, 1982.

Batllori, M., T. and J. Carreras Artau, and J. Rubió Balaguer, eds. *Llull's Obres essencials,* 2 vols. Barcelona: Selecta, 1977–1960.

Becker-Nielsen, Hand, Peter Foote, Jørgen Højgaard Jørgensen, and Tore Nyberg, eds. *Hagiography and Medieval Literature*. Odense: Odense Univ. Press, 1981.

Bede. *A History of the English Church and People*. Trans. Leo Sherley-Price. Baltimore: Penguins Books, 1968.

Belting, Hans. *The Image and its Public in the Middle Ages*. New Rochelle: Aristide D. Caratzas, 1990.

———. *Das Bild und sein Publikum im Mittelalter*. Berlin: Gebr. Mann Verlag, 1981.

Benvenuti Papi, Anna. *"In castro poenitentiae." Santità e società femminile nell'Italia medievale*. Roma: Herder, 1990.

———, and Elena Gennarelli, eds. *Bambini santi*. Turin: Rosenberg and Sellier, 1991.

Berlière, Ursmer. "L'exercise du ministère paroissial par les moines dans le haut moyen âge." *Revue Bénédictine* 39 (1927): 227–50.

Betto, Bianca. *Il collegio dei notari, dei giudici, dei medici e dei nobili in Treviso (secc. XIII–XIV)*. Venice: Deputazione Veneta di Storia Patria, Miscellanea di Studi e Memorie, 1981.

Bevington, David, ed. *Medieval Drama*. Boston: Houghton Mifflin, 1975.

Bihl, Michele. "La leggenda antoniana di Fra Giuliano da Spira OFM e il suo epilogo inedito." *Studi francescani*, 3rd ser., 4 (1932): 429–53.

Bischoff, Bernard. "Literarische und künstlerisches Leben in St. Emmeran." *Studien und Mitteilungen zur Geschichte des Benediktiner-ordens* 51 (1933): 102–42, reprinted in *Mittelalterliche Studien, Ausgewählte Aufsätze zur Schriftkunde und Literaturgeschichte* (Stuttgart, 1966–1981): 2: 77–115.

———. "Otloh," in *Die Deutsche Literatur des Mittelalters. Verfasserlexikon*, ed. Karl Langosch, vol. 3 (1943): cols. 658–70.

Blach, Christopher. *Italian Confraternities in the Sixteenth Century*. Cambridge: Cambridge Univ. Press, 1989.

Blair, Peter Hunter. *Anglo-Saxon England*. Cambridge: Cambridge Univ. Press, 2nd ed., 1977.

Bloch, Marc. *Feudal Society*, trans. L. A. Manyon, 2 vols. Chicago: Univ. of Chicago Press, 1961.

Blume, Dieter. *Wandmalerei als Ordenspropaganda. Bildprogramme im Chorbereich franziskanische Konvente italiens bis zur Mittes des 14. Jahrhunderts*. Worms: Werner'sche Verlagsgeselleschaft, 1983.

Boesch Gajano, Sofia. *Chelidonia. Storia di un culto*. Turin: Rosenberg and Sellier, 1992.

———, and Lucetta Scaraffia, eds. *Luoghi sacri e spazi di santità*. Turin: Rosenberg and Sellier, 1990.

———, ed. *Le raccolte di vite di santi dal XIII al XVIII secolo. Strutture, messaggi, fruizione*. Collana del Dipartimento di Studi Storici dal Medioevo all'Età contemporanea dell'Università degli Studi di Roma "La Sapienza". Fasano: Schena, 1988.

———, and Lucia Sebastiani, eds. *Culto dei Santi, istituzioni e classi sociali in età preindustriale*. Rome/L'Aquila: Japadre, 1984.

———. *Agiografia altomedioevale*. Bologna: Il Molino, 1976.

Bolte, Johannes, ed. *Jacob Freys Gartengesellschaft*. 1556; repr. Tubingen: Literarischen Verein in Stuttgart, 1896.

Bonner, Anthony and Lola Badia. *Ramón Llull: Vida, pensament i obra literària*. Barcelona: Empuries, 1988.

Bonser, Wilfrid. *The Medical Background of Anglo-Saxon England: A Study in History, Psychology, and Folklore*. London: Wellcome Historical Medical Library, 1963.

Boorsook, Eve and Johannes Offerhaus. *Francesco Sassetti and Ghirlandaio at Santa Trinità, Florence. History and Legend in a Renaissance Chapel*. Doornspijk: Davaco, 1981.

Borgehammer, S. *How the Holy Cross was Found. From Event to Medieval Legend* (Ph.D. diss., Univ. of Stockholm, 1991).

Boschetto, Antonio. *Benozzo Gozzoli nella chiesa di San Francesco di Montefalco*. Milan: Istituto Editoriale Italiano, 1961.

Boureau, Alain. *La légende dorée. Le système narratif de Jacques de Voragine*. Paris: Editions du Cerf, 1984.

Bozon, Nicholas. *Three Saints' Lives by Nicholas Bozon*, ed. Sister Amelia Klenke. St. Bonaventure: The Franciscan Institute, 1874.

Brand, John. *Observations on the Popular Antiquities of Great Britain*. London: Henry G. Bohn, 1853.

Breij, Mieke. *Sint Maarten Schutspatroon van Utrecht*. Utrecht: Stichting Discodom, 1988.

Bremond, Claude, Jacques Le Goff, and Jean-Claude Schmitt. *L'Exemplum*, Typologie des Sources du Moyen Age Occidental, 40. Turnhout, Belgium: Brepols, 1982.

Brooke, C. N. L. "Gregorian Reform in Action: Clerical Marriage in England, 1050–1200." *Cambridge Historical Journal* 12 (1956): 1–21.

Brooke, Rosalind B. "Recent Work on St. Francis of Assisi." *Analecta Bollandiana* 100 (1982): 653–76.

———. "The Lives of St. Francis of Assisi," in *Latin Biography*, ed. T. A. Dorey (New York: Basic Books Publishers, 1967): 177–98.

Brooks, N. P. "England in the Ninth Century: The Crucible in the Ninth Century: The Crucible of Defeat." *Transactions of the Royal Historical Society* 5th ser., 29 (1978): 1–20.

Brown, Patricia Fortini. *Narrative Painting in the Age of Carpaccio*. New Haven: Yale Univ. Press, 1988.

Brown, Peter. *Furta Sacra: Thefts of Relics in the Central Middle Ages*. Princeton: Princeton Univ. Press, 2nd ed., 1990.

———. *The Body and Society: Men, Women and Sexual Renunciation in Early Christianity*. New York: Columbia Univ. Press, 1988.

———. *The Cult of the Saints: its Rise and Function in Latin Christianity*. Chicago: Univ. of Chicago Press, 1981.

———. *Relics and Social Status in the Age of Gregory of Tours*. Reading: Univ. of Reading, 1977.

———. "The Rise and Function of the Holy Man in Late Antiquity." *Journal of Roman Studies* 61 (1971): 80–101.

Brummer, Rudolph. "Sobre les fonts literàries del *Blanquerna* de Ramón Llull." *Iberoromania* 9 (1979): 1–11.

Bühler, Curt F. "Prayers and Charms in Certain Middle English Scrolls." *Speculum* 39 (1964): 270–78.

Bujeaud, Jerome, ed. *Chants et chansons populaires des provinces de l'Ouest*. Niort: L. Clouzot, 1895.

Burton, George, ed. *Chronology of Stamford*. Stamford: Robert Bagley, 1846.

Bynum, Caroline. *Holy Feast and Holy Fast: The Religious Significance of Food to Medieval Women*. Berkeley: Univ. of California Press, 1987.

———. *Jesus as Mother: Studies in the Spirituality of the High Middle Ages*. Berkeley: Univ. of California Press, 1987.

———. *Docere verbo et exemplo*. Missoula: Scholars Press, 1979.

Cambell, Jacques. "Le Culte liturgique de Saint Antoine de Padoue." *Il Santo* 11, fasc. 2–3 (May–Dec. 1971): 3–70; 155–97 and ibid., 12 (1972): 19–63.

Camporesi, Piero. *Bread of Dreams: Food and Fantasy in Early Modern Europe*, trans. David Gentilcare. Chicago: Chicago Univ. Press, 1989.

Capezzali, Walter, ed. *"Magisterium et Exemplum": Celestino V e le sue fonti più antiche*, Atti del 5 Convegno storico internazionale, L'Aquila, 31 agosto–1 settembre 1990. L'Aquila: Centro Celestiniano, 1991.

———, ed. *Celestino e le sue immagini del Medio Evo*, Atti del 6 Convegno storico internazionale, L'Aquila, 24–25 maggio 1991. L'Aquila: Centro Celestiniano, 1993.

———, ed. *Celestino V e i suoi tempi: realtà spirituale e realtà politica*, Atti del 4 Convegno storico internazionale, L'Aquila, 26–27 agosto 1989. L'Aquila: Centro Celestiniano, 1990.

———, ed. *S. Pietro del Morrone. Celestino V nel medioevo monastico*, Atti del 3 Convegno storico internazionale, L'Aquila, 26–27 agosto 1988. L'Aquila: Centro Celestiniano, 1989.

———, ed. *Celestino V Papa Angelico*, Atti del 2 Convegno storico internazionale, L'Aquila, 26–27 agosto 1987. L'Aquila: Centro Celestiniano, 1988.

Carli, E. *Gli affreschi di Belverde*. Firenze: Edam, 1977.

Castro, Américo. *España en su historia*. Barcelona: Crtitica, 1984.

Cazelles, Brigitte, trans. *The Lady as Saint: A Collection of French Hagiographic Romances of the Thirteenth Century*. Philadelphia: Univ. of Pennsylvania Press, 1991.

Celestino a Vieste, Atti del Convegno storico, Vieste, 24 maggio 1992. Vieste: Centro di Cultura "N. Cimaglia," 1993.

Cenci, Cesare. *Documentazione di vita assisiana, 1300–1530*, vol. 1. Grottaferrata: Editiones Collegii S. Bonaventurae ad Claras Aquas, 1974.

Cerulli, Enrico and Raffaello Morghen, eds. *Agiografia nell'Occidente cristiano, secoli XIII–XIV*. Rome: Accademia Nazionale dei Lincei, 1980.

Cessi, Roberto. "L'Apparitio Sancti Marci del 1094." *Archivio Veneto*, anno 110, ser. 5, vol. 85 (1964): 113–15.

———. *Storia di Venezia*. Venice: C. Ferrari, 1958.

Chaney, W. A. *The Cult of Kingship in Anglo-Saxon England*. Manchester: Manchester Univ. Press, 1970.

Charlier, Celestin. "Les manuscrits personnels de Florus de Lyon et son activité littéraire." *Mélanges E. Podechard* (Lyon: Facultés catholiques, 1945): 71–84.

Chartier, Roger. "Intellectual History and the History of Mentalites: a Dual Re-evaluation," in *Cultural History* (Ithaca: Cornell Univ. Press, 1988): 39–40.

Chazan, Robert. *Daggers of Faith*. Berkeley: Univ. of California Press, 1989.

Chiarelli, Caterina and Giovanni Leoncini, eds. *La Certosa del Galluzzo a Firenze*. Milano: Electa Editrice, 1982.

Chibnall, Majorie. "Monks and Pastoral Work: A Problem in Anglo-Norman History." *Journal of Ecclesiastical History* 18 (1967): 165–72.

Child, Francis James, ed. *English and Scottish Popular Ballads.* New York: Dover Publications, 1965.

Chiuini, Giovanna. "Montefalco," in Federico Zeri, ed. *Storia dell'arte italiana: inchieste su centri minori,* vol. 8 (Turin: Einaudi, 1980): 206–18.

Christian, William, Jr. "Provoked Religious Weeping in Early Modern Spain," in *Religious Organization and Religious Experience,* ed. J. Davis (New York: Academic Press, 1982): 97–114.

———. *Local Religion in Sixteenth-Century Spain.* Princeton: Princeton Univ. Press, 1981.

Cibele, Angela Nardo. "Canzone di San Martino nel Veneto." *Archivio per le tradizioni popolari* 5 (1886): 363–64.

Clark, Elizabeth A. *Jerome, Chrysostom and Friends.* New York: Edwin Mellen Press, 1979.

Clementi, Alessandro, ed. *Indulgenza e perdonanza di papa Celestino,* Atti del Convegno storico internazionale, L'Aquila, 5–6 ottobre 1984. L'Aquila: Centro Celestiniano, 1987.

Clemoes, Peter. "Liturgical Influence on Punctuation in Late Old English and Early Middle English Manuscripts." *Old English Newsletter: subsidia* 4 (1980): 1–44.

Clopper, Lawrence M., ed. *Chester.* Records of Early English Drama. Toronto: Univ. of Toronto Press, 1979.

Coakley, Hohn Wayland. *The Representation of Sanctity in Late Medieval Hagiography* (Ph.D. diss., Harvard Divinity School, 1980).

Cohen, Gustave, ed. *Recueil de farces françaises inédites du XVe siècle.* Cambridge: Mediaeval Academy of America, 1949.

———. "Rabelais et la légende de Saint Martin." *Revue des Etudes Rabelaisiennes* 8 (1910): 331–49.

Cohen, Jeremy. *The Friars and the Jews.* Ithaca: Cornell Univ. Press, 1982.

Cohen, Sherrill. *The Evolution of Women's Asylums: From the Sixteenth Century to the Present.* New York: Oxford Univ. Press, 1992.

———. "Asylum for Women in Counter-Reformation Italy," in *Women in Reformation and Counter-Reformation Europe: Private and Public Worlds,* ed. Sherrill Marshall (Bloomington: Indiana Univ. Press, 1989): 166–88.

Coldewey, John C. "Plays and 'Play' in Early English Drama." *Research Opportunities in Renaissance Drama* 28 (1985): 181–88.

Colgrave, B. "The post-Bedam Miracles and Translations of At. Cuthbert," eds. C. Fox and B. Dickens. *The Early Cultures of North-West Europe* (Cambridge: Cambridge Univ. Press, 1950): 305 32.

———, and R. A. B. Mynors, eds. and trans. *Bede's Ecclesiastical History of the English People.* Oxford: Oxford Univ. Press, 1969.

———, ed. and trans. *Two Lives of St. Cuthbert.* Cambridge: Cambridge Univ. Press, 1940.

Constable, Giles. *Monastic Tithes.* Cambridge: Cambridge Univ. Press, 1964.

Corbet, P. *Les saints ottoniens.* Sigmarinsen: J. Thorbecke, 1986.

Corner, Flaminio. *Notizie storiche delle chiese e dei monasteri di Venezia e di Torcello.* Padua: Manfre, 1758.

————. *Ecclesiae Venetae Antiquis Monumentis . . . Illustratae.* Venice: Typis Jo. Baptistae Pasquali, 1749.

Cortese, Dino. "Sisto Quarto Papa Antoniano." *Il Santo* 12 (1972): 211–72.

Coulton, G. C., ed. *Social Life in Britain from the Conquest to the Reformation.* Cambridge: Cambridge Univ. Press, 1938.

Cousins, Ewert, trans. *Bonaventure. The Soul's Journey into God. The Tree of Life. The Life of Saint Francis.* New York: Paulist Press, 1978.

Cozzi, Gaetano and Michael Knapton. *La Repubblica di Venezia nell'età moderna.* Turin: UTET, 1986.

Cracco, G. "Dai santi ai santuari: un'ipotesi di evoluzione in ambito veneto." *Studi sul medioevo veneto* (Turin: Giappichelli, 1981): 25–42.

Craddock, Lawrence G. "Franciscan Influences on Early English Drama." *Franciscan Studies* 10 (1950): 399–415.

Crane, Thomas Frederick, ed. *The Exempla or Illustrated Stories from the Sermones Vulgares of Jacques de Vitry.* London: Folk-Lore Society, 1890.

Craster, E. "The Patrimony of St. Cuthbert." *English Historical Review* 271 (1954): 177–99.

Creekmore, Hubert, ed. and trans. *Lyrics of the Middle Ages.* New York: Grove Press, 1959.

Cremascoli, Giuseppe, ed. Uguccione da Pisa. *De dubio accentu.* Biblioteca degli Studi Medievali, vol. 10. Spoleto: Centro Italiano di Studi sull'Alto Medioevo, 1978.

Curtius, Ernst Robert. *European Literature and the Latin Middle Ages,* trans. W. R. Trask. Princeton: Univ. Press, 1973.

D'Alatri, Mariano. "La figura di San Francesco nella predicazione di San Bernardino," in Cardaropoli and Conti, *Lettura delle fonti francescane,* 283–98.

D'Avray, L. D. *The Preaching of the Friars.* Oxford: Clarendon Press, 1985.

Da Campagnola, Stanislao. *Francesco d'Assisi nei suoi scritti e nelle sue biografie dei secoli XIII–XIV.* Assisi: Porziuncola, 1981.

————. *L'Angelo del sesto sigillo e "l'alter Christus."* Rome: Ed. Antonianum, 1971.

Da Ponte, Ippolito, trans. *Compendio volgare della vita et delle opere.* Venice: Guglielmo da Fontaneto, 1532.

Da Bagno, Timoteo. *Nuovo leggendario della vita e fatti di N. S. Giesu Christo, e di tutti i santi.* Venice: Appresso i Guerra, 1599.

Dahl, Ellert. "Heavenly Images: The Statue of St. Foy of Conques and the Significance of the Medieval 'Cult-Image' in the West." *Acta ad archael. et artium hist. pertinentia* 8 (1978): 175–91.

Daniel, Emmett R. *The Franciscan Concept of Mission in the High Middle Ages.* Lexington: Univ. Press of Kentucky, 1975.

Darlington, R. R. *The Cartulary of Worcester Cathedral Priory (Register I),* Publications of the Pipe Roll Society, n.s., 38. London, 1968.

————. "Ecclesiastical Reform in the Late Old English Period." *English Historical Review* 51 (1936): 385–428.

————. *The Vita Wulfstani of William of Malmesbury.* London: Royal Historical Society, 1928.

Davidson, Clifford, ed. *A Tretise of Miraclis Pleyinge.* Early Drama, Art, and Music,

Monograph Series, n. 19. Kalamazoo: Medieval Institute Publications, 1993.

———, ed. *Iconoclasm vs. Art and Drama*. Early Drama, Art, and Music, Monograph Series, n. 11. Kalamazoo: Medieval Institute Publications, 1989.

———. "The Middle English Saint Play and Its Iconography," in *The Saint Play in Medieval Europe*, ed. Clifford Davidson. Early Drama, Art, and Music, Monograph Series, n. 8 (Kalamazoo: Medieval Institute Publications, 1986): 45–52.

———, ed. *The Saint Play in Medieval Europe*. Kalamazoo: Medieval Institute Publications, 1986.

Davidson, Gustaf. *A Dictionary of Angels*. New York: The Free Press, 1967.

Davis, Norman, ed. *Non-cycle Plays and Fragments*. EETS, supplementary series, vol. 1. Oxford, 1970.

Dawson, Giles E. *Records of Plays and Players in Kent, 1450–1642*. Malone Society Collections, vol. 7. Oxford, 1965.

De Beer, E. S., ed. *The Diary of John Evelyn*. Oxford: Oxford Univ. Press, 1955.

De Cantimpre, Thomas. *Bonum universale de apibus*. Douai: Balthazar Belleri, 1627.

De Gaiffier, Baudoin. *Recueil d'hagiographie*, Subsidia Hagiographica 61. Brussels: Société des Bollandistes, 1977.

De Kerval, Léon. *L'Évolution et le développement du merveilleux dans les légendes de S. Antoine de Padoue*. Paris: Opuscules de Critique Historique, fasc. 12–14, Avril, 1906.

———. *Sancti Antonii de Padua Vitae duae quarum altera huisque inedita*. Paris: Librairie Fishbachr, 1904.

De la Marche, A. Lecoy. *Saint Martin*. Tours: Alfred Meme et Fils, 1881.

De la Vigne, A. *Le Mystère de Saint Martin, 1496*, ed. André Duplat. Geneva: Librairie Droz, 1979.

De Lage, Guy Raymond, ed. *Choix de Fabliaux*. Paris: Librairie Honoré Champion, 1986.

De Lyra, Nicolas. *Biblia sacra cum glossa ordinaria*. Venetiis, 1603.

De Montaiglon, Anatole, ed. *Recueil de poésies francoises des XVe et XVIe siècles*. Vol. II. Paris: P. Jannet, 1855.

De Riquer, Martí. *Historia de la literatura catalana*, 6 vols. (Barcelona: Ariel, 1964): 1: 197–352.

Delaisse, L. M. J. "The Importance of the Book of Hours for the History of the Medieval Book," in *Gatherings in Honor of Dorothy E. Miner*, ed. Ursula McCracken et al. (Baltimore: The Walters Art Gallery, 1974): 203–25.

Delaruelle, Etienne. *La piété populaire au Moyen Age*. Turin: Bottega d'Erasmo, 1975.

Delcorno, Carlo. "Il racconto agiografico nella predicazione dei secoli XIII–XV," *Agiografia nell'occidente cristiano secoli XIII–XV*, Atti dei Convegni lincei, 1–2 marzo 1979, Rome (Rome: Accademia Nazionale dei Lincei, 1980): 79–112.

Delehaye, Hippolite. *The Legends of the Saints*. trans. V. M. Crawford. South Bend: Univ. of Notre Dame Press, 1961.

———. *Cinq leçons sur la méthode hagiographique*, Subsidia Hagiographica 21. Brussels: Société des Bollandistes, 1934.

———. *Les légendes hagiographiques*. Brussels: Société des Bollandistes, 1905.

Delisle, Léopold. "Les Heures de Blanche de France, duchesse d'Orléans." *Bibliothèque de l'Ecole de Chartres* 66 (1905): 489–539.

Delooz, Pierre. *Sociologie et canonisations*. Liège-The Hague: Faculté de droit, 1969.

———. "Notes sur les canonisations occitanes à l'époque de la croisade des Albigeois." *Annales de l'Institut d'études occitanes* 4 em. série 1 (1965): 106–12.

———. "Pour une étude sociologique de la saintété canonisée dans l'Eglise catholique." *Archives de sociologie des religions* 13 (1962): 17–43.

Demus, Otto. *The Mosaics of San Marco in Venice*, 2 vols. Chicago and London: Univ. of Chicago Press, 1984.

———. *The Church of San Marco in Venice*. Washington: Dumbarton Oaks Research Library and Collection, 1960.

Desbonnets, Th. "*Legenda trium sociorum*," critical edition in *Archivum Franciscanum Historicum* LXVII (1974): 38–144.

Deyermond, Alan. "The Sermon and its Uses in Medieval Castilian Literature." *La Corónica* 8, 2 (1980): 127–45.

Di Febo, Giuliana. *Teresa d'Avila: un culto barocco nella Spagna franchista*. Naples: Liguori, 1988.

Didi-Huberman. "Un sang d'images." *Nouvelle Revue de Psychanalyse* XXXII (1985): 137–38.

Donaldson, Christopher. *Martin of Tours: Parish Priest, Mystic, and Exorcist*. London: Routledge and Kegan Paul, 1980.

Doob, Penelope B. R. *Nebuchadnezzar's Children: Conventions of Madness in Middle English Literature*. New Haven: Yale Univ. Press, 1974.

Dorigo, Wladimiro. *Venezia origini. Fondamenti, ipotesi, metodi*. Milan: Electa Editrice, 1983.

Dowden, John. *The Church Year and Kalendar*. Cambridge: Cambridge Univ. Press, 1910.

Draper, Peter. "King John and St. Wulfstan." *Journal of Medieval History* 10 (1984): 41–50.

Drijvers, Jan Willem. *Helena Augusta: The Mother of Constantine the Great and the Legend of Her Finding the True Cross*. Leiden: Brill, 1991.

Duby, Georges. *The Knight, the Lady and the Priest: The Making of Modern Marriage in Medieval France*, trans. Barbara Bray. New York: Pantheon, 1985.

———. *The Early Growth of the European Economy: Warriors and Peasants, 7th to 12th Centuries*. Ithaca: Cornell Univ. Press, 1974.

Dunn, E. Catherine. *The Gallican Saint's Life and the Late Roman Dramatic Tradition*. Washington: Catholic Univ. of America Press, 1989.

Dunn-Lardeau, Brenda, ed. *Legenda Aurea: sept siècles de diffusion*, Actes du Colloque International sur la "Legenda Aurea: texte latin et branches vernaculaires," Université de Québec à Montréal, 11–12 mai, 1983. Montréal-Paris: Bellarmin et Vrin, 1986.

Dutka, JoAnna. *Music in the English Mystery Plays*. Early Drama, Art, and Music, Reference Series, n. 2. Kalamazoo: Medieval Institute Publications, 1980.

Eadmer. *History of Recent Events in England*, trans. G. Bosanquet. London: Cresset Press, 1964.

Eckenstein, Lina. *Women Under Monasticism*. New York: Russell & Russell, 1963.

Eder, C. E. "Die Schule des Klosters Tegernsee in frühen Mittelalter im Spiegel der

Tegernseer Handschriften." *Studien und Mitteilungen zur Geschichte des Benediktiner-ordens und seine Zweige* 83 (1972): 8–155.

Eisenbichler, Konrad, ed. *Crossing the Boundaries. Christian Piety and the Arts in Italian Medieval and Renaissance Confraternities.* Early Drama, Art, and Music, Monograph Series, 15. Kalamazoo: Medieval Institute Publications, 1991.

Eisler, Colin. *The Genius of Jacopo Bellini.* New York: Harry N. Abrams, 1989.

Elliott, Dyan. *Spiritual Marriage.* Princeton: Princeton Univ. Press, 1993.

Erbe, Theodor, ed. *Mirk's Festial: A Collection of Homilies.* London: Kehan Paul, Trench, Trubner, 1905.

Eusebius. *Life of Constantine.* Trans, John H. Bernard, in The Churches of Constantine at Jerusalem. London: Palestine Pilgrims Text Society, 1986.

Evans, E. Estyn. *Irish Folk Ways.* London: Routledge & Kegan Paul, 1957.

Fabris, Giovanni. "Il Cardinal legato Guido d'Alvernia e l'ultima traslazione di S. Antonio (15 febbraio 1350)," in his *Scritti di arte e storia padovana* (Quarto d'Altino: Rebellato, 1977): 303–11.

Facinger, Marion F. "A Study of Medieval Queenship: Capetian France 987–1237." *Nebraska Studies in Medieval and Renaissance History* 5 (1968): 1–48.

Farmer, Sharon. *Communities of St. Martin: Legend and Ritual in Medieval Tours.* Ithaca: Cornell Univ. Press, 1991.

Farmer, D. H. "Two Biographies by William of Malmesbury," in *Latin Biography*, ed. T. A. Dorey (London: Routledge and Kegan Paul, 1967): 165–74.

Fassler, Margot. "Accent, Meter, and Rhythm in Medieval Treatises *De rithmis.*" *Journal of Musicology* 5 (1987): 164–90.

Felder, Hilarin. *Geschichte der wissenschaftlichen Studien im Franziskanordern bis um die Mitte des 13. Jahrhunderts.* Freiburg im Breisgau: Herdersche Verlagshandlung, 1904.

Finucane, Ronald C. *Miracles and Pilgrims: Popular Beliefs in Medieval England.* London: Rowman and Littlefield, 1977.

Fiocco, Giuseppe. " 'Storia e storie' della Cappella di S. Giacomo." *Il Santo* 6 (1966): 261–66.

———, and Antonio Sartori. "La Rivincita di Altichiero." *Il Santo* 3 (1963): 284–326.

Fitzgerald, David. "Early Celtic History and Mythology." *Revue celtique* 6 (1883–1885): 194–206.

Fleming, John. *An Introduction to the Franciscan Literature of the Middle Ages.* Chicago: Franciscan Herald Press, 1977.

Fletcher, Alan J. "Layers of Revision in the N-Town Marian Cycle." *Neophilologus* 66 (1982): 469–78.

Fliche, Augustin. *Saint Roch.* Paris: Henri Laurens, 1930.

Fontaine, Jacques, ed. and trans. *Sulpice Sévère: Vie de Saint Martin.* 3 vols. Paris: Editions du Cerf, 1967.

Foot, Sarah. "Parochial Ministry in Early Anglo-Saxon England: The Role of Monastic Communities," in W. J. Sheils and D. Wood, *The Ministry: Clerical and Lay*, vol. 26 of *Studies in Church History* (Oxford, 1989): 43–54.

Fortunatus, Venantius. *Vitae sanctae Radeguntis, Liber I, c. 2*, ed. B. Krusch, *Monumenta Germaniae Historica, Scriptores Rerum Merovingiarum*, 2. Hannover, 1988.

Fournée, Jean. *Enquête sur le culte populaire de saint Martin en Normandie.* Nogent-sur-Marne: Cahiers Léopold Delisle, 1963.

Fracco, Ambrosio Novidio. *Ferentinatis sacrorum fastorum.* Antwerp: J. Bellerus, 1559.

Francesco d'Assisi, Storia e Arte, Catalogue of the Franciscan Exhibitions of 1982 in Assisi. Milano: Electa, 1982.

Frend, W. H. C. *The Rise of Christianity.* Philadelphia: Fortress Press, 1984.

Frere, Walter H., ed. *Antiphonale Sarisburiense.* London: Plainsong and Mediaeval Music Society, 1901–1924, reprinted 1966.

Fridenperger, Paul. *Vita e miracoli di Sant'Antonio da Padova.* Verona: Paul Fridenperger, 1532.

Friese, Eckhard. "Kalendarische und annalistische Grundformen der Memoria," in *Memoria: Der geschichtliche Zeugniswert des liturgischen Gedenken im Mittelalter,* ed. Karl Schmid and Joachim Wollasch (Munich: W. Fink, 1984): 469–70.

———, Dieter Genenich, and Joachim Wollasch, eds. *Das Martyrolog-Necrolog von St. Emmeran zu Regensburg.* Hannover: Hahnsche Buchhandlung, 1986.

Fromage, H. "Rapports de Saint Martin avec Gargantua." *Bulletin de la Société de Mythologie Française* 74 (1969): 75–84.

Frugoni, Chiara. *Francesco: un'altra storia.* Genoa: Marietti, 1988.

———. "La giovinezza di Francesco nelle fonti (testi e immagini)." *Studi Medievali* XXV, 1 (1984): 115–43.

Gaiffier, Baudoin. "Les revendications de biens dans quelques documents hagiographiques du XIe siècle." *Analecta Bollandiana* 50 (1932): 123–28.

Galbraith, V. H. "Notes on the Career of Samson Bishop of Worcester (1096–1112)," *English Historical Review* 82 (1967): 86–101.

Gamboso, Vergilio. "Ricerche sulla leggenda Antoniana, 'Benignità'." *Il Santo* 15 (1975): 13–879; 17 (1977): 3–106.

———. "La 'Sancti Antonii Confessoris de Padua vita'." *Il Santo* 11 (1971): 199–283.

Gardner, J. "The Louvre Stigmatization and the Problem of the Narrative Altarpiece." *Zeitschrift für Kuntgeschichte* XLV (1982): 217–47.

Garth, Helen M. *Saint Mary Magdalene in Medieval Literature,* The Johns Hopkins University Studies in Historical and Political Science, vol. 67, n. 3. Baltimore, 1950.

Gasparotto, Cesira. "Guide e illustrazioni della Basilica di sant'Antonio in Padova." *Il Santo* 2 (1962): 369–87.

Gatch, Milton McCormick. *Preaching and Theology in Anglo-Saxon England: Aelfric and Wulfstan.* Toronto: Univ. of Toronto Press, 1977.

Gélis, J. and O. Redon, eds. *Les miracles des corps.* Paris: Presses et Publications de l'Université de Paris VIII, 1983.

Genolini, Antonio Palmucci. "S. Bernardino da Siena a Montefalco." *Miscellanea Francescana* 1 (1886): 185–86.

Geremek, Bronoslaw. *The Margins of Society in Late Medieval Paris,* trans. Jean Birrell. Cambridge: Cambridge Univ. Press, 1987.

Ghinato, Alberto. "La predicazione francescana nella vita religiosa e sociale del Quattrocento." *Picenum seraphicum* 10 (1973): 24–98.

Giannarelli, Elena. *La tipologia femminile nella biografia e nell'autobiografia cristiana del IV secolo*, Studi Storici, fasc. 127. Rome: Istituto Storico Italiano per il Medio Evo, 1980.

Gibson, Margaret. *Lanfranc of Bec.* Oxford: Clarendon Press, 1978.

Gibson, Gail McMurray. *The Theater of Devotion: East Anglian Drama and Society in the Late Middle Ages.* Chicago: Univ. of Chicago Press, 1989.

Giese, Elizabeth. *Benozzo Gozzolis Franziskuszyklus in Montefalco: Bildkomposition als Erzahlung.* Frankfurt am Main: Lang, 1986.

Gilson, E. "L'Interprétation traditionnelle des stigmates." *Revue d'Histoire Franciscaine* II (1925): 467–79.

Giustiniani, Lorenzo. *Vita Beati Laurentii Iustiniani Proto Patriarchae.* Rome: Officina Poligrafica Laziale, 1962.

Giustiniani, Bernardo. *De divi Marci evangelistae vita, translatione, et sepulturae loco*, vol. 5 of *Thesaurus antiquitatum et historiarum Italiae*, ed. J. G. Graevius. Lyden: Petrus Vander Aa, 1722.

Gloria, Andrea, ed. *Statuti del comune di Padova dal secolo XII all'anno 1285.* Padua: F. Sacchetto, 1873.

Goffen, Rona. *Spirituality in Conflict: Saint Francis and Giotto's Bardi Chapel.* University Park: Pennsylvania State Univ. Press, 1987.

Golinelli, Paolo. *Città e culto dei santi nel Medioevo italiano.* Bologna: Clueb, 1991.

———. "Indiscreta sanctitas." *Studi sui rapporti tra culti, poteri e società nel pieno Medioevo.* Roma: Istituto Storico Italiano per il Medioevo, 1988.

———. *Culto dei santi e vita cittadina a Reggio Emilia, secoli IX–XII.* Modena: Aedes Muratoriana, 1980.

González-Casanovas, R. J. *Predicacion y narrativa en Ramón Llull: De imagen a semejanza en Blanquerna* (Ph.D. diss., Harvard Univ., 1990).

Gonzati, Bernardo. *La Basilica di S. Antonio di Padova. I.* Padua: A. Bianchi, 1852–1853.

Goodich, Michael. *Vita Perfecta: The Ideal of Sainthood in the Thirteenth Century.* Stuttgart: A. Hiersemann, 1982.

———. *The Dimensions of Thirteenth-Century Sainthood* (Ph.D. diss., Columbia Univ., 1972).

Gori, Pietro. *Le feste fiorentine attraverso i secoli*, vol. 1, *Le feste per San Giovanni.* Florence: R. Bemporad & Figlio, 1926.

Grandsen, Antonia. "Traditionalism and Continuity during the Last Century of Anglo-Saxon Monasticism." *Journal of Ecclesiastical History* 40 (1989): 159–207.

———. "Cultural Transition at Worcester in the Anglo-Norman Period." *British Archaelogigal Association Conference Transactions*, vol. l, *Medieval Art and Architecture at Worcester Cathedral* (1978): 1–14.

———. *Historical Writing in England c. 550 to 1307.* Ithaca: Cornell Univ. Press, 1974.

Graus, František. *Volk, Herrscher und Heiliger im Reich der Merowinger: Studien zur Hagiographie der Merowingerzeit.* Prague: Nakladatelstvi Ceskoslovenske akademie ved, 1965.

Gravdal, Kathryn. *Ravishing Maidens: Writing Rape in Medieval French Literature and Law.* Philadelphia: Univ. of Pennsylvania Press, 1971.

Green, Victor. *The Franciscans in Medieval English Life (1224–1348).* Paterson: St. Anthony Guild Press, 1939.

Grégoire, Réginald. *Manuale di agiologia. Introduzione alla letteratura agiografica.* Fabriano: Monastero San Silvestro, 1987.

Gregory of Tours. *The History of the Franks,* trans. Lewis Thorpe. London: Penguin, 1974.

Gregory. *Oratio funebris in Flacillam Imperatricem,* ed. Spira (Jaeger-Langerbeck, vol. 9).

Grim, Jacob. *Teutonic Mythology,* trans. J. S. Stallybrass. London: George Bell & Sons, 1888.

Gurevich, Aaron. *Medieval popular Culture: Problems of Belief and Perception.* Cambridge: Cambridge Univ. Press, 1988.

Hackel, Sergei, ed. *The Byzantine Saint.* London: Fellowship of St. Alban and St. Sergius, 1981.

Haefele, Hans F., ed. *Notkeri Balbuli Gesta Karoli Magni Imperatoris.* Berlin: Weidmannsche Verlagsbuchhandlung, 1959.

Hale, John R. *Renaissance War Studies.* London: Hambledon, 1983.

Hales, John W. and Frederick J. Furnivall, eds. *Bishop Percy's Folio Manuscript: Ballads and Romances.* London: N. Trubner, 1868.

Halkin, F. "L'Hagiographie byzantine au service de l'histoire." *XIII International Congress of Byzantine Studies* (Oxford, 1966): 345–54.

Hampson, R. T. *Medii Aevi Kalendarium or, Dates, Charters and Customs of the Middle Ages.* London: Henry Kent Canston, 1841.

Hanning, Robert W. *The Vision of History in Early Britain From Gildas to Geoffrey of Monmouth.* New York: Columbia Univ. Press, 1974.

Harrison, Robert, trans. *Gallic Salt: Eighteen Fabliaux Translated from the Old French.* Berkeley: Univ. of California Press, 1974.

Head, Thomas. *Hagiography and the Cult of the Saints in the Diocese of Orleans, 800–1200.* Cambridge: Cambridge Univ. Press, 1990.

Hearne, Thomas, ed. *Hemingi Chartularium ecclesiae Wigornensis.* 2 vols. Oxford: Sheldonian Theatre, 1723.

Heffernan, Thomas J. *Sacred Biography: Saints and their Biographers in the Middle Ages.* Berkeley: Univ. of California Press, 1982.

Heinzelmann, Martin. *Translationsberichet und andere Quellen des Reliquienkultes,* Typologie des Sources du Moyen Age occidental, no. 33. Turnhout: Brepols, 1979.

———, François Dolberau, and Joseph-Claude Poulin. "Les sources hagiographiques narratives composées en Gaule avant l'an mil (SHG): Inventaire, examen critique, datation." *Francia* 15 (1987): 701–31.

———, and Joseph-Claude Poulin. *Les vies anciennes de sainte Geneviève de Paris: Etudes critiques.* Paris: H. Champion, 1986.

Heist, William H. " 'Irish Saints' Lives, Romance, and Cultural History." *Mediaevalia et Humanistica* 6 (1975): 25–40.

Helgaud of Fleury. *Vita Aedwardi Regis qui apud Westmonasterium requiescit: S. Bertini ascripta,* ed. and trans. Frank Barlow. London: Nelson's Texts, 1962.

———. *Epitome Vitae Regis Rotberti Pii,* ed. and trans. R.-H. Bautier and Gillette Labory. Paris: Sources d'Histoire Médiévale, 1955.

Helias. "Epistola encyclica de transitu s. Francisci." *Analecta Franciscana* X (1926–1941): 525–28.

Hellman, Robert and Richard O'Gorman, trans. *Fabliaux: Ribald Tales from the Old French*. Westport: Greenwood Press, 1965.

Henderson, John S. *Piety and Charity in Late Medieval Florence. Religious Confraternities from the Middle of the Thirteenth Century to the Late Fifteenth Century* (Ph.D. diss., Univ. of London, 1983).

Hernández, Miguel Cruz. *El pensamiento de Ramón Llull*. Valencia: Castalia, 1977.

Hesbert, René-Jean. *Corpus antiphonalium officii I: Manuscripti 'Cursus romanus' II: Manuscripti 'Cursus monasticus' III: Invitatoria et antiphonae IV: Responsoria, versus, hymni et varia V: Fontes earumque prima ordinatio. Rerum ecclesiasticarum documenta, ser, major, Fontes* 7–11. Rome: Herder, 1963–1975.

——, ed. *Antiphonale Missarum Sextuplex*. Brussels: Vromant, 1935.

Hewlett, Maurice. "A Medieval Popular Preacher." *Nineteenth Century* 28 (1890): 471–77.

Hieatt, Constance. "A Case for *Duk Moraud* as a Play of the Miracles of the Virgin." *Mediaeval Studies* 32 (1970): 345–51.

Hill, John Walter. "Oratory Music in Florence, I: *Recitar Cantando*, 1583–1655." *Acta Musicologica* 51 (1979): 108–36.

Hillgarth, Jocelyn N. *The Spanish Kingdoms, 1250–1516*. Vol. I. Oxford: Clarendon, 1976.

——. *Ramón Llull and Lullism in Fourteenth-Century France*. Oxford: Clarendon, 1971.

Hoare, F. R., trans. *The Western Fathers*. New York: Sheed and Ward, 1954.

Hoepffner, E. "Une prière à sainte Marie-Madeleine." *Romania* 53 (1927): 567–68.

Holum, Kenneth. *Theodosian Empresses: Women and Imperial Dominion in Late Antiquity*. Berkeley: Univ. of California Press, 1982.

Hoogewerff, G.-J. *Benozzo Gozzoli*. Paris: Collection Art et Esthétique, 1930.

Hope, Robert Charles, ed. *The Popists Kingdome or Reigne of Antichrist*. London: Chiswich Press, 1880.

Horstmann, C., ed. *Editha sive Chronicon Vilodunense im Wiltshire, dialekt aus ms. Cotton-Faustina B. III*. Heilbronn: Hinninger Verlag, 1883.

Hrotswitha. *De Gestis Ottonis I*, in *Hrotswithae Opera*, ed. Paulus de Winterfeld. Berlin: Weidmann, 1902.

Huber, Raphael M. *A Documented History of the Franciscan Order (1182–1517)*. Milwaukee: Nowing Publishing Apostolate, 1944.

Hughes, Andrew. *Late Medieval Liturgical Offices: Resources for Electronic Research: Texts LMLO Subsidia mediaevalia*, vol. 23. Toronto: Pontifical Institute for Mediaeval Studies, 1994.

——. "Word Painting in a 12–Century Office," in *Beyond the Moon: Festschrift Luther Dittmer*, eds. Bryan Gillingham and Paul Merkley, Musicological Studies, vol. 53 (Ottawa: The Institute of Medieval Music, 1990): 16–27.

——. "Research Report: Late Medieval Rhymed Offices." *Journal of the Plainsong and Mediaeval Music Society* 8 (1985): 33–49.

Humfrey, Peter. *Cima da Conegliano*. Cambridge: Cambridge Univ. Press, 1983.

Hunt, E. D. *Holy Land Pilgrimage in the Later Roman Empire, AD 312–460*. Oxford: Clarendon Press, 1982.

Ingram, R. E., ed. *Coventry. Records of Early English Drama*. Toronto: Univ. of Toronto Press, 1981.

Iogna-Prat, Dominique. *Agni immaculat. Recherches sur les sources hagiographiques relatives à Saint Maieul de Cluny 954–94*. Paris: Editions du Cerf, 1988.

Jacopo da Voragine. Atti del I Convegno di Studi. Varazze: presso la Sede del Centro, 1987.

James, M. R., trans. *The Apocryphal New Testament*. Oxford: Clarendon Press, 1924.

————. *The Sculpture in the Lady Chapel at Ely*. London: D. Nutt, 1895.

Jameson, Anna. *Legends of the Madonna as Represented in the Arts*. rev. ed. London: Longmans, Green, 1890.

Jeffrey, David L. *The Early Franciscan Lyric and Franciscan Spirituality*. Lincoln: Univ. of Nebraska Press, 1975.

John, E. "The King and the Monks in the Tenth-Century Reformation," in *Orbis Brittaniae* (Leicester: Leicester Univ. Press, 1966): 177–80.

Johnson, Phyllis and Brigitte Cazelles. *Le Vain Siècle Guérpir: A Literary Approach to Sainthood through Old French Hagiography of the Twelfth Century*, North Carolina Studies in Romance Language and Literature. Chapel Hill, 1979.

Johnson, Toni O'Brien. *Synge: The Medieval and the Grotesque*. Gerrards Cross: Colin Smythe, 1982.

Johnson-South, T. "The Norman Conquest of Durham: Norman Historians and the Anglo-Saxon Community of St. Cuthbert." *Haskins Society Journal* 4 (1991): 87–97.

————. *The "Historia de Sancto Cuthberto": A New Edition and Translation, with Discussions of Surviving Manuscripts, the Text, and Northumbrian Estate Structure* (Ph.D. diss., Cornell Univ., 1990).

Johnston, Alexandra F. "What If No Texts Survived? External Evidence for Early English Drama," in *Contexts for Early English Drama*, eds. Marianne G. Briscoe and John C. Coldewey. Bloomington: Indiana Univ. Press, 1989.

————, and Margaret Rogerson, eds. *York*. Records of Early English Drama. Toronto: Univ. of Toronto Press, 1979.

Johnston, Mark D. *The Spiritual Logic of Ramón Llull*. Oxford: Clarendon, 1987.

Jones, Charles W. *Saint Nicholas of Myra, Bari, and Manhattan: Biography of a Legend*. Chicago: Univ. of Chicago Press, 1978.

————. *Saints' Lives and Chronicles in Early England*. Ithaca: Cornell Univ. Press, 1947.

Josa, Antonio Maria. *Legenda seu vita miracula S. Antonii de Padua*. Bologna: Pontificia Mareggiani, 1883.

Kaftal, George. *Iconography of the Saints in the Painting of North West Italy*. Florence: Sansoni, 1985.

————. *Iconography of the Saints in the Painting of North East Italy*. Florence: Sansoni, 1978.

————. *Iconography of the Saints in Central and Southern Italian Schools of Painting*. Florence: Sansoni, 1965.

————. *Saint Francis in Italian Painting*. London: Allen and Unwin, 1950.

Kahrl, Stanley, ed. *Records of Plays and Players in Lincolnshire, 1300–1585*. Malone Society Collections, vol. 8. Oxford, 1974 for 1969.

Kantorowicz, Ernst. *Laudes Regiae*. Berkeley: Univ. of California Press, 1981.

Kapelle, W. E. *The Norman Conquest of the North*. Chapel Hill: Univ. of North Carolina Press, 1979).

Kedar, Benjamin Z. *Crusade and Mission*. Princeton: Univ. Press, 1982.

Kemp, B. R. "Monastic Possession of Parish Churches in England in the Twelfth Century." *Journal of Ecclesiastical History* 31 (1980): 144–45.

Ker, Neil. "Old English Notes Signed 'Coleman'." *Medium Aevum* 18 (1949): 29–31.

Kieckhefer, R. *Unquiet Souls: Fourteenth Century Saints and their Religious Milieu*. Chicago: Univ. of Chicago Press, 1984.

———, and George D. Bond, eds. *Sainthood: its Manifestation in World Religions*. Berkeley: Univ. of California Press, 1988.

Klein, Karl Kurt, ed. *Die Lieder Oswald von Wolkenstein*. Tübingen: Max Niemeyer, 1975.

Kleinschmidt, P. Beda. *Antonius von Padua in Leben und Kunst, Kult und Volkstum*, vols. 6–8 of Forschungen zur Volkskunde, ed. Georg Schreiber. Dusseldorf: L. Schwann, 1931.

Klenke, Sister Amelia, ed. *Seven More Poems by Nicholas Bozon*. St. Bonaventure: The Franciscan Institute, 1951.

Knightly, Charles. *The Customs and Ceremonies of Britain: An Encyclopedia of Living Traditions*. London: Thames and Hudson, 1986.

Koch, Hugo. *Die Ehe Kaiser Heinrichs II mit Kunigunde*. Köln: Cologue, 1908.

Köster, Kurt. "Religiöse Medaillon und Wallfahrts-Devotionalien in der flämischen Buchmalerei des 15. und frühen 16. Jahrhunderts," in *Buch und Welt: Festschrift für Gustav Hofmann zum 65. Geburtstag dargebracht* (Wiesbaden: Otto Harrassowitz, 1965): 459–504.

Kurth, Godefroid. *Sainte Clotilde*. Paris, 2nd ed., 1897.

La pittura in Italia. Le origini. Milano: Electa, 1985.

Labalme, Patricia H. "No Man But an Angel: Early Efforts to Canonize Lorenzo Giustiniani (1381–1456)," in *Continuità e discontinuità nella storia politica, economica e religiosa* (Vicenza: Neri Pozza Editore, 1993): 15–33.

Lacarra, María Jesús. *Cuentística medieval en España*. Zaragoza: Univ. de Zaragoza, 1979.

Ladis, Andrew. *Taddeo Gaddi. Critical Reappraisal and Catalogue Raisonné*. Columbia: Univ. of Missouri Press, 1982.

Lagaisse, Marcel. *Benozzo Gozzoli*. Paris: Henri Laurens, 1934.

Lambert, Malcom D. *Franciscan Poverty, The Doctrine of the Absolute Poverty of Christ and the Apostles in the Franciscan Order, 1210–1323*. London: SPCK, 1961.

Lancashire, Ian. *Dramatic Texts and Records of Britain: A Chronological Topography to 1558*. Toronto: Univ. of Toronto Press, 1984.

Lapanski, D. "The Autographs on the 'Chartula' of St. Francis of Assisi." *Archivum Franciscanum Historicum* LXVII (1974): 18–37.

Laquer, Erika J. "Ritual, Literacy and Documentary Evidence: Archbishop Eudes Rigaud of St. Eloi." *Francia* 13 (1986): 625–37.

Latzke, Therese. "Der Topos Mantel-gedicht." *Mittelateinisches Jahrbuch* 6 (1970): 109–31.

———. "Die Mantelgedichte des Primas Hugo von Orleans und Martial." *Mittelateinisches Jahrbuch* 5 (1968): 54–58.

Lavin, Marilyn Aronberg. *The Place of Narrative-Mural Decoration in Italian Churches, 431–1600*. Chicago: Univ. of Chicago Press, 1989.

Le Blant, E. *Les inscriptions chrétiennes de la Gaule*. Paris, 1856.

Leclercq, Dom Jean. "Prédicateurs bénédictins aux XIe et XIIe siècles." *Revue Mabillon* 33 (1943): 48–73.

Legge, Dominica M. "Clerc Lisant." *Modern Language Review* 47 (1952): 554–55.

———. *Anglo-Norman Literature and Its Background*. Edinburgh: Univ. Press, 1950.

LeGoff, Jacques. *The Medieval Imagination*, trans. Arthur Goldhammer. Chicago: Univ. of Chicago Press, 1988.

Leroquais, V. *Les Livres d'Heures manuscrits de la Bibliothèque Nationale*, 3 vols. and supplement. Paris and Mâcon: Bibliothèque Nationale, 1927–1943.

Les fonctions des saints dans le monde occidental (IIIe–XIIIe siècles), Actes du Colloque organisé par l'Ecole Française de Rome avec le concours de l'Université de "La Sapienza," Rome, 27–29 octobre 1988. Rome: Ecole Française de Rome, 1991.

Levison, Wilhelm. "Conspectus codicum hagiographicorum." *MGHSSRM* (Hannover and Lepzig: Hahnsche Buchhandlung, 1920): 7: 529–706.

Levy, Brian J., ed. *Nine Verse Sermons by Nicholas Bozon*, Medium Aevum Monographs New Series, vol. 11. Oxford, 1981.

Lewis, P. S. "Of Breton *Alliances* and Other Matters," in *War, Literature, and Politics in the Late Middle Ages*, ed. C.T. Allmand (New York: Barnes and Noble, 1976): 122–43.

———. "Decayed and Non-Feudalism and Other Matters," in *War, Literature, and Politics in the Late Middle Ages*, ed. C. T. Allmand (New York: Barnes and Noble, 1976): 122–43.

Llull, Ramón. *Libre de Evast e Blanquerna*, 4 vols., eds. S. Galmés, A. Caimari, and R. Guilleumas. Barcelona: Els Nostres Clàssics, 1935–1954.

Lobrichon, G. *Les fresques de la Basilique inférieure*. Paris: Cerf, 1985.

Lomax, Derek W. "The Lateran Reform and Spanish Literature." *Iberoromania* 1, 4 (1969): 299–309.

Longhi, R. *La pittura umbra della prima metà del Trecento*. Firenze: Sansoni, 1973.

Loomis, C. Grant. *White Magic: An Introduction to the Folklore of Christian Legend*. Cambridge: Medieval Academy of America, 1948.

Loomis, R. S. and Henry W. Wells, eds. *Representative Medieval and Tudor Plays*. New York: Sheed & Ward, 1942.

Lorenzoni, Giovanni, ed. *L'Edificio del Santo di Padova*. Vicenza: Neri Pozza, 1981.

Lotter, Friedrich. *Severinus von Noricum: Legende und historische Wirklichkeit*, Monographien zur Geschichte des Mittelalters 12. Stuttgart: A. Hiersemann, 1976.

Lutolf, Max, ed. *Analecta Hymnica: Register*, 2 vols. in 3. Bern: Francke, 1978.

MacGonagle, Sara Hansell. *The Poor in Gregory of Tours: A Study of the Attitude of Merovingian Society towards the Poor, as Reflected in the Literature of the Time* (Ph.D. diss., Columbia Univ., 1936).

Mackay, Angus. *Spain the Middle Ages*. London: Macmillan, 1977.

Maeterlinck, Louis. *Le genre satirique dans la peinture flamande*. Brussels: G. Van Oest, 1907.

Major, J. Russell. "'Bastard Feudalism' and the Kiss: Changing Social Mores in Late Medieval and Early Modern France." *Journal of Interdisciplinary History* 17 (1987): 509–35.

————. "The Crown and the Aristocracy in Renaissance France." *American Historical Review* 69 (1964): 631–45.

Mâle, Emile. *L'Art religieux après le Concile de Trent.* Paris: Armand Colin, 1932.

Malvern, Majorie. *Venus in Sackcloth: The Magdalene Origins and Metamorphosis.* Carbondale and Edwardsville: Southern Illinois Univ. Press, 1975.

Manitius, Max. *Geschichte der lateinische Literatur des Mittelalters,* 2 vols. Munich: Beck, 1928.

Mann, Francis O., ed. *The Works of Thomas Deloney.* Oxford: Clarendon Press, 1912.

Mannix, Mary Dolorosa. *Sancti Ambrosii Oratio de Obitu Theodosii.* Washington: Catholic Univ. of America Press, 1925.

Manselli, Raoul. *Nos qui cum eo fuimus,* Bibliotheca Seraphico-Capuccina, vol. 28. Rome: Istituto Storico dei Cappuccini, 1980.

————. *San Francesco.* Roma: Bulzoni, 1980.

Marangon, Paolo. "Traslazioni e ricognizioni del corpo di S. Antonio nelle fonti storico-letterario." *Il Santo* 21, fasc. 2 (May–Aug. 1981).

Marchini, G. *Corpus vitrearum medii aevi, Italia,* vol. I. *L'Umbria. Le Vetrate dell'Umbria.* Roma: De Luca, 1973.

Marinangeli, Bonaventura. "Descrizione e memorie della Chiesa e del Convento di San Francesco a Montefalco." *Miscellanea Francescana* 14 (1913): 129–53.

Marlier, George. *Pierre Brueghel le Jeune.* Brussels: Robert Finck, 1964.

Marriage, Elizabeth, ed. *Georg Forsters Frische Teutsche Liedlein.* 1540. repr. Halle a. d. s.: Max Niemeyer, 1903.

Marrow, James H. *The Golden Age of Dutch Manuscript Painting.* New York: George Braziller, 1990.

————. "Symbol and Meaning in Northern European Art of the Late Middle Ages and Early Renaissance." *Simiolus* 16 (1986): 150–69.

Marsan, Rameline E. *Itinéraire espagnol du conte médiéval.* Paris: Lincksieck, 1974.

Marvin, Dwight Edwards. *Curiosities in Proverb.* New York: G. Putnam's Sons, 1916.

Mason, Emma. *St. Wulfstan of Worcester, c. 1008–1095.* Oxford: Basil Blackwell, 1990.

————. "Change and Continuity in Eleventh-Century Mercia: The Experience of St. Wulfstan of Worcester," in *Anglo-Norman Studies VIII: Proceedings of the Battle Conference 1985,* ed. R. Allen Brown (Woodbridge, Suffolk: Boydell Press, 1986): 154–76.

————. "St. Wulfstan's staff: a legend and its uses." *Medium Aevum* 53 (1984): 157–79.

Matanic, Atanasio G. "Le fonti francescane conosciute dagli storici del 1400," in Gerardo Cardaropoli and Martino Conti, eds. *Lettura delle fonti francescane attraverso i secoli: il 1400* (Rome: Ed. Antonianum, 1981): 107–18.

Matthew, D. J. A. *The Norman Monasteries and Their English Possessions.* Oxford: Oxford Univ. Press, 1962.

Mayer, F. Arnold and Heinrich Pietsch, eds. *Die Mondsee-Wiener Liederhandschrift und der Monch von Salzburg.* Berlin: Mayer & Muller, 1894.

Mazzarotto, B. Tamassia. *Le feste veneziane.* Florence: Sansoni, 1961.

Mazzucco, Gabriele, ed. *Monasteri Benedettini nella Laguna Veneta.* Venice: Arsenale, 1983.

McHam, Sarah Blake. *The Chapel of St. Anthony at the Santo and the Development of*

Venetian Renaissance Sculpture. Cambridge: Cambridge Univ. Press, 1994.

———. "Donatello's High Altar in the Santo, Padua," in *Andrea del Verrocchio and late Quattrocento Sculpture: The Acts of Two International Symposia commemorating the 500th Anniversary of his Death*, ed. Steven Bule (Florence: Licosa-Sansoni, 1990).

———. "Donatello and the High Altar in the Santo, Padua," in *IL60. Essays Honoring Irving Lavin on his Sixtieth Birthday*, ed. Marilyn Aronberg Lavin (New York: Italica Press, 1990): 73–96.

———. "La Decorazione della Cappella dell'Arca di Sant'Antonio nella Basilica del Santo, Padova, e sue relazioni coll'arte antica," in *Rivista di Archeologia. Supplementi 7. Convegno Internazionale Venezia e l'Archeologia*, ed. Gustavo Traversari (Venice: Giorgio Bretschneider, 1988): 195–98.

———. "La decorazione cinquecentesca della Cappella dell'Arca di S. Antonio," in *Le Sculture del Santo di Padova* (Vicenza: Fonti e studi per la storia del Santo a Padova, Neri Pozza, 1984): 110–11.

McIntyre, Elizabeth E. A. *Early-Twelfth-Century Worcester Cathedral Priory, with special reference to the manuscripts written there* (Ph.D. thesis, Oxford Univ. 1978).

McLaughlin, T. P. *Le très ancien droit monastique de l'occident*, vol. 38, *Archives de la France monastique*. Paris: Liguge, 1935.

McNamara, Jo Ann. "Living Sermons: Consecrated Women and the Conversion of Gaul," in *Peaceweavers: Medieval Religious Women*, vol. 2, eds. Lillian Thomas Shank and John A. Nichols (Kalamazoo: Cistercian Publications, 1987): 19–38.

———, John E. Halborg, and Gordon Whatley. *Sainted Women in the Dark Ages*. Durham: Duke Univ. Press, 1992.

Meersseman, Gilles Gerard. *Ordo fraternitatis. Confraternite e pietà dei laici nel Medioevo*. Rome: Herder, 1977.

Menegazzi, Luigi, ed. *Cima da Conegliano. Catalogo della mostra*. Venezia: Neri Pozza Editore, 1962.

Meredith, Peter., ed. *The Mary Play from the N. Town Manuscript*. London: Longman, 1987.

———, and John Tailby, eds. *The Staging of Religious Drama in Europe in the Later Middle Ages: Texts and Documents in English Translation*. Early Drama, Art, and Music, Monograph Series, n. 4. Kalamazoo: Medieval Institute Publications, 1983.

———, and Stanely J. Kahrl, eds. *The N-Town Plays: A Facsimile of British MS Cotton Vespasian D. VIII*. Leeds: Univ. of Leeds School of English, 1977.

Merrifield, Ralph. *The Archaeology of Ritual and Magic*. New York: New Amsterdam Books, 1987.

Meurant, Rene and Renaat van der Linden. *Folklore en Belgique*. Brussels: Paul Legrain, 1974.

Miles, Clement A. *Christmas Customs and Traditions*. 1912 repr. New York: Dover Publications, 1976.

Miles, Margaret. "Vision: The Eye of the Body and the Eye of the Mind in St. Augustine's *De trinitate* and *Confessions*." *Journal of Religion* 63 (1983): 125–42.

Mill, Anna Jean. *Medieval Plays in Scotland*. 1924; reprint, New York: Benjamin Bloom, 1969.

———. *Medieval Plays in Scotland*. St. Andrews: St. Andrews Univ. Press, 1924.

Millon, Maurice. *Les légendes de l'histoire de Dunkerque et de la Flandre maritime*. Saint-Omer: L'Indépendant, 1972.

Mirk, John. *Festial*. ed. Theodor Erbe. EETS, extra series, vol. 96. 1905.

Mitchell, Charles. "The Imagery of the Upper Church at Assisi," in *Giotto e il suo tempo*, Atti del Congresso internazionale per la celebrazione del VII centenario della nascita di Giotto, 24 settembre–1 ottobre 1967 (Rome: De Luca, 1971): 113–34.

Mockridge, Diane. *From Christ's Soldier to His Bride: Changes in the Portrayal of Women Saints in Medieval Hagiography* (Ph.D. diss., Duke Univ., 1984).

Modica, Marilena, ed. *Esperienze religiose e scritture femminili tra Medioevo ed età moderna*. Acireale, Bonanno, 1991.

Moelleken, Wolfgang Wilfred, Gayle Agler-Beck, and Robert E. Lewis, eds. *Die Kleindichtung des Strickers*. Goppingen: Alfred Kummele, 1975.

Mollat, Michel. *The Poor in the Middle Ages*, trans. Arthur Goldhammer. New Haven: Yale Univ. Press, 1986.

Monks of Solesmes, eds. *Les vers latins iambiques et trochaïques au moyen âge et leurs répliques rhythmiques*, Filologiskt Arkiv, vol. 32. Stockholm: Almquist & Wiksell International, 1988.

——, eds. *Antiphonaire monastique, XIIe siècle, Codex F. 160 de la bibliothèque de la cathédrale de Worcester*, Paléographie musicale, ser. l, vol. 12. Tournai: Société de Saint Jean l'Evangéliste, 1922.

——, eds. *Codex 121 de la Bibliothèque d'Einseideln*, Paléographie musicale, ser. l, vol. 4. Solesmes: Imprimerie Saint-Pierre, 1894.

Monti, Gennaro M. *Le confraternite medioevali dell'alta e media Italia*. Venezia, 1927.

Moorman, John. *A History of the Franciscan Order from its Origins to the Year 1517*. Oxford: Clarendon Press, 1968.

Morghen, Raffaello. "Tradizione religiosa e Rinascimento nel ciclo degli affreschi francescani a Montefalco," *Atti del V Convegno internazionale di studi sul Rinascimento*, Palazzo Strozzi, Florence, 2–6 settembre 1956 (Florence: Sansoni, 1956): 149–56.

Morosini, Domenico. *De bene istituta re publica*. Milan: Giuffre, 1969.

Morris, Henry. "St. Martin's Eve." *Bealoideas* 9 (1939): 230–35.

Mosco, Marilena, ed. *La Maddalena tra sacro e profano*. Florence: Arnaldo Mondadori, 1986.

Mossinger, Freidrich. "Martinsfeuer." *Volk und Scholle* 15 (1937): 285–88.

Muir, Lynette R. "The Saint Play in Medieval France," in *The Saint Play in Medieval Europe*, ed. Clifford Davidson (Kalmazoo: Medieval Institute Publications, 1986): 123–80.

Müller, Gerard Ludwig. *Gemeinschaft und Verehrung der Heiligen*. Freiburg: Herder, 1991.

Murphy, James J. *Rhetoric in the Middle Ages*. Berkely: Univ. of California Press, 1974.

Murray, Alexander. *Reason and Society in the Middle Ages*. Oxford: Clarendon Press, 1978.

Neaman, Judith S. *The Distracted Knight: A Study of Insanity in the Arthurian Romance* (Ph.D. diss., Columbia Univ., 1968).

Nelson, J. L. "'A King Across the Sea': Alfred in Continental Perspective," *Transactions of the Royal Historical Society* 5th ser., 36 (1986): 45–68.

———. "Queens as Jezebels: The Careers of Brunhild and Balthild in Merovingian History," ed. Derek Baker, *Medieval Women* (Oxford: Basil Blackwell, 1978): 31–78.

Nelson, Alan H., ed. *Cambridge: Records of Early English Drama*. Toronto: Univ. of Toronto Press, 1989.

Nessi, Silvestro. *Montefalco e il suo Territorio*. Spoleto: Arti Grafiche Panetto e Petrelli, 1980.

———, and Pietro Scarpellini. *La Chiesa-museo di S. Francesco a Montefalco*. Spoleto: Arti Grafiche Panetto e Petrelli, 1972.

———. "La Confraternita di San Girolamo in Perugia." *Miscellanea Francescana* 67 (1967): 78–115.

———. "Storia e arte delle chiese francescane di Montefalco." *Miscellanea Francescana* 62 (1962): 232–332.

———. "La vita di San Francesco dipinta da Benozzo Gozzoli a Montefalco." *Miscellanea Francescana* 61 (1961): 467–92.

Neuschel, Kristen B. *Word of Honor: Interpreting Noble Culture in Sixteenth-Century France*. Ithaca: Cornell Univ. Press, 1989.

Newbigin, Nerida, ed. *Nuovo corpus di Sacre Rappresentazioni fiorentine nel Quattrocento*. Bologna: Commissione per i Testi di Lingua, 1983.

Nicolini, Ugolino, ed. *Memoriale di Montefalco*. Assisi: Casa Editrice Francescana, 1983.

Niero, Antonio. "Pietà popolare e interessi politici nel culto di S. Lorenzo Giustiniani." *Archivio Veneto*, ser. 5, vol. 117 (1981): 197–224.

———. *I Patriarchi di Venezia da Lorenzo Giustiniani ai nostri giorni*. Venice: Studium Cattolico Veneziano, 1961.

Norberg, Dag. "Les vers latins iambiques et trochaïques au moyen âge et leurs répliques rythmiques." *Filologiskt Arkiv* 35 (Stockholm, 1988): 5, 15.

———. "L'accentuation des mots dans le vers latin du Moyen Age." *Filologiskt Arkiv* 32 (Stockholm, 1985): 39–50.

Notker the Stammerer. *Charlemagne*, trans. Lewis Thorpe. New York: Penguin Books, 1971.

O'Callagham, Joseph F. *A History of Medieval Spain*. Ithaca: Cornell Univ. Press, 1975.

O'Suilleabhain, Sean. "The Feast of St. Martin in Ireland," in *Studies in Folklore in Honor of Stith Thompson*, ed. W. Edson Richmond (Bloomington: Univ. of Indiana Press, 1957): 252–61.

Odilo of Cluny. *Epitaphium Adalheidae Imperatricis* 18, *Patrologia Latina* 142, cols. 974–75.

Oeschger, Johannes, ed. *Pontano: Carmina*. Bari: G. Laterza, 1948.

Oost, Stewart I. *Galla Placidia Augusta*. Chicago: Univ. of Chicago Press, 1968.

Osbern. *Miraculi Sancti Dunstani*, in *Memorials of Saint Dunstan*, ed. William Stubbs, Rolls Series 63. London: Public Record Office, 1874.

Otis, Leah Lydia. "Prostitution and Repentance in Late Medieval Perpignan," in *Women of the Medieval World: Essays in Honor of John H. Mundy*, ed. Julius Kirshner and Suzanne F. Wemple (Oxford: Basil Blackwell, 1985): 137–60.

———. *Prostitution in Medieval Society: The History of an Urban Institution in Languedoc.* Chicago: Univ. of Chicago Press, 1985.

Ozment, Steven. *The Age of Reform, 1250–1550.* New Haven: Yale Univ. Press, 1980.

Pacetti, Dionisio. "La predicazione di S. Bernardino da Siena a Perugia e ad Assisi nel 1425." *Collectanea Franciscana* 10 (1940): 5–28.

Pächt, Otto. *The Master of Mary of Burgundy.* London: Faber and Faber, 1948.

Palou, Sebastián Garcías. *Ramón Llull en la historia del ecumenismo.* Barcelona: Herder, 1986.

———. *Ramón Llull y el Islam.* Madrid: Graficas Planisi, 1981.

———. "El Papa Blanquerna de Ramón Llull e Celestino V." *Estudios Lulianos* 20 (1976): 71–86.

Panofsky, Erwin. *Early Netherlandish Painting.* Cambridge: Harvard Univ. Press, 1953.

———. " 'Imago Pietatis', Ein Beitrag zur Typengeschichte des 'Schmerzensmanns' und der 'Maria Mediatrix'," in *Festschrift für Max J. Friedlander zum 60. Geburstage* (Leipzig: E. A. Seemann, 1927): 261–308.

Parlett, David, trans. *Selections from the Carmina Burana.* Harmondsworth: Penguin Books, 1986.

Passarelli, G., ed. *Il santo patrono nella città medievale: il culto di S. Valentino nella città di Terni,* Atti del Convegno di Studi, 9–12 febbraio, 1974. Rome: La Goliardica, 1984.

Pasti, Stefania. "Lo scomparso ciclo di affreschi di S. Rosa da Viterbo di Benozzo Gozzoli e la sua influenza nel Viterbese: Gli affreschi dell'Isola Bisentina." *Il Quattrocento e Viterbo,* 11 giugno–10 settembre 1983 (Rome: De Luca, 1983): 159–78.

Patlagean, E. "A Byzance: Ancienne hagiographie et histoire sociale." *Annales ESC* 23 (1968): 106–26.

———, and Pierre Riché, eds. *Hagiographie, cultures et sociétés. IVᵉ–XIIᵉ siècles,* Actes du Colloque organisé à Nanterre et à Paris, 2–5 mai, 1979. Paris: Etudes Augustiniennes, 1981.

Pavone, Mario. *Iconologia Francescana. Il Quattrocento.* Todi: Ediart, 1988.

Peers, Edgar Allison. *Ramón Llull: A Biography.* London: Society for Promoting Christian Knowledge, 1929.

———. *Studies of the Spanish Mystics.* London: Sheldon, 1927.

Peile, H. F. *William of Malmesbury's Life of St. Wulfstan.* Oxford: Basil Blackwell, 1934.

Perkins, J. B. Ward. "The Bronze Lion of St. Mark at Venice." *Antiquity* 21, no. 81 (March, 1947): 23–41.

Pernoud, Regine. *Les saints au Moyen Age.* Paris: Presses-Pocket, 1988.

Philippson, Emil, ed. *Der Monch von Montaudon, ein provenzalische Trouhadour.* Halle a.d.s.: Max Niemeyer, 1873.

Phythian-Adams, Charles. *Desolation of a City: Coventry and Urban Crisis of the Late Middle Ages.* Cambridge: Cambridge Univ. Press, 1979.

Piana, Celestino. "Scritti polemici fra Conventuali ed Osservanti a meta' del 1400 con la partecipazione dei giuristi secolari." *Archivum Franciscanum Historicum* 72 (1979): 41–51.

Pierce, Frank. "*Blanquerna* and *The Pilgrim's Progress* Compared." *Estudis Romanics* 3 (1951–1952): 88–98.

Pioppi, Antonio, ed. *Liturgia, pietà e ministeri al santo di Padova fra il XIII e il XX secolo.* Verona: Neri Pozza Editore, 1978.

Pisanus, Bartholomeus. *Liber de conformitate vitae beati Francisci ad vitam domini Jesu, Analecta Francescana*, vols. 4 and 5 (1906, 1912).

Piza, M. Arbona. "Los exemplis en el *Libre de Evast e Blanquerna.*" *Estudios Lulianos* 20 (1976): 53–70.

Platelle, Henri. *Terre et ciel aux anciens Pays Bas: Recueil d'articles de . . . Platelle publié à l'occasion de son élection à l'Académie royale de Belgique.* Lille: Faculté des Lettres, 1991.

Plotzek, Joachim. *Andachtbücher des Mittelalters aus Privatbesitz.* Cologne: Schnutgen-Museum, 1987.

Polentone, Sicco. "La 'Sancti Antonii Confessoris de Padua Vita' of c. 1435," ed. Vergilio Gamboso, *Il Santo* 11 (1971): 198–283.

Pope-Hennessy, John. "Italian Gothic Sculpture," *Introduction to Italian Sculpture*, vol. 1. New York: Vintage Books, 3rd ed. rev. 1985.

Portenari, Angelo. *Felicità di Padova.* Padua: P. P. Tozzi, 1623.

Poulin, Joseph-Claude. *L'idéal de sainteté dan l'Aquitaine carolingienne d'après les sources hagiographiques (750–950).* Laval: Presses de l'Univ. de Laval, 1975.

Power, Patrick C. *The Book of Irish Curses.* Cork: Mercier Press, 1974.

Powicke, F. Maurice and E. B. Fryde. *A Handbook of British Chronology.* London: Royal Historical Society, 2nd ed., 1961.

Pring-Mill, R. D. F. "The Trinitarian World-Picture of Ramón Llull." *Romanistiches Jahrbuch* 7 (1955–1956): 229–56.

Prinz, Friedrich. "Heiligenkult und Adelsherrschaft im Spiegel merowingischen Hagiographie." *Historische Zeitschrift* 204 (1967): 529–44.

Pulgram, Ernst. *Latin-Romance Phonology: Prosodics and Metrics*, Ars grammatica, vol. 4. Munich: W. Fink, 1975.

Pulignani, Michele Faloci. S. Francesco e S. Domenico." *Miscellanea Francescana* 9 (1902): 13–15.

Radin, Paul, Karl Kerenyi, and C. G. Jung. *The Trickster: A Study in American Indian Mythology.* New York: Bell Publishing, 1956.

Raine, James, ed. *Testamenta Eboracensia*, Part 2. Durham: Surtees Society, vol. 30, 1855.

Rampolla, Mary Lynn. " 'A Pious Legend': St. Oswald and the Foundation of Worcester Cathedral Priory." *Oral Tradition in the Middle Ages*, ed. W. F. H. Nicolaisen (Binghamton: Medieval & Renaissance Text & Studies, 1995): 187–210.

Reames, Sherry. *The Legenda Aurea: A Re-examination of its Paradoxical History.* Madison: Univ. of Wisconsin Press, 1985.

Reinburg, Virginia. "Prayer and the Book of Hours," in *Time Sanctified: The Book of Hours in Medieval Art and Life*, ed. Roger S. Wieck (Baltimore and New York: The Walters Gallery and George Braziller, 1988): 39–44.

Rézeau, Pierre. *Les prières en français à la fin du moyen âge: Prières à un saint particulier et aux anges.* Geneva: Librairie Droz, 1983.

Riché, Pierre. *Daily Life in the World of Charlemagne*, trans. Jo Ann McNamara. Princeton: Princeton Univ. Press, 1978.

Rico, Francisco. *Prédicacion y literatura en la España medieval.* Cadiz: UNED, 1977.

Ricotti, Ercole. *Storia delle Compagnie di Ventura in Italia.* Turin: G. Pomba, 1844–1845.

Ridyard, Susan. *Royal Saints of Anglo-Saxon England.* Cambridge: Cambridge Univ. Press, 1988.

Ringbom, Sixten. "Devotional Images and Imaginative Devotions." *Gazette-des-Beaux-Arts* 73 (1969): 159–70.

Rizzo, Anna Padoa. *Benozzo Gozzoli pittore fiorentino.* Florence: Editrice Edam, 1972.

Rollason, D. W. *The Mildrith Legend: A Study in Early Medieval Hagiography in England.* Leichester: Univ. of Leichester Press, 1982.

Romanin, Samuele. *Storia documentata di Venezia.* Venice: P. Naratovich, 1855.

Rosenfeld, Hellmut. "Kalendar, Ein blattkalendar, Bauern-kalendar und Bauernpratik." *Bayerisches Jahrbuch für Volkskunde* (1962): 7–23.

Rosenthal, Joel T. "Edward the Confessor and Robert the Pious: 11th Century Kingship and Biography." *Mediaeval Studies* 33 (1971): 7–20.

Rossi, Luigi. "Firenze e Venezia dopo la battaglia di Caravaggio." *Archivio Storico Italiano,* ser. 5, vol. 34 (1904): 158–79.

Rossiaud, Jacques. *Medieval Prostitution,* trans. Lydia Cochrane. Oxford: Basil Blackwell, 1988.

Rouche, Michel. "Miracles, maladies, et psychologie de la foi à l'époque carolingienne en France." *Hagiographie, cultures et sociétés. IVe–XIIe siècles* (Paris: Etudes Augustiniennes, 1981): 319–37.

Rubinstein, Nicolai. "Italian Reaction to Terraferma Expansion in the Fifteenth Century," in *Renaissance Venice,* ed. John R. Hale (London: Faber and Faber, 1973): 197–217.

Ruf, Gerhard. *Franziskus und Bonaventura: die heilsgeschichtliche Deutung der Fresken im langhaus der Oberkirche von San Francesco von Assisi aus der Theologie des Heiligen Bonaventura.* Assisi: Casa Editrice Francescana, 1974.

Runnalls, Graham A. "The Staging of André de la Vigne's *Mystère de Saint Martin.*" *Tréteaux* 3 (1981): 68–79.

Rusconi, Roberto. "San Francesco nelle prediche volgari e nei sermoni latini di Bernardino da Siena," eds. Domenico Maffei and Paolo Nardi. *Atti del simposio internazionale cateriniano-bernardiniano,* 17–20 aprile 1980, Siena (Siena: Accademia Senese degli Intronati, 1982): 793–809.

Russ, Jennifer M. *German Festivals and Customs.* London: Oswald Wolff, 1982.

Ryan, Granger and Helmut Ripperger, trans. *The Golden Legend of Jacopus da Voragine.* New York: Longmans, Green and Co., 1941.

Sachs, Hans. *Werke,* eds. A. Von Keller and E. Goetze. Hildsheim: G. Olms, 1964.

Saenger, Paul. "Books of Hours and the Reading Habits of the Later Middle Ages," in *The Culture of Print,* ed. Roger Chartier and trans. Lydia Cochrane (Princeton: Princeton Univ. Press, 1989): 141–73.

———. "Silent Reading: Its Impact on Late Medieval Script and Society." *Viator* 13 (1982): 367–414.

Sanford, W. A. C. "Medieval Clerical Celibacy in England." *The Genealogists' Magazine* 12 (1957): 371–73.

Sankt Elisabeth: Fürstin Dienerin Heilige Aufätze Dokumentation Katalog. Sigmariensen: Thorbecke, 1981.

Sansovino, Francesco. *Venezia città nobilissima e singolare.* Venice: Curti, 1663; facsimile repr. Farnborough, Hants: Gregg Press Ltd., 1968.

Santi e demoni nell'Alto Medioevo occidentale, Settimane di Studio del Centro Italiano di Studi sull'Alto Medioevo, Spoleto, 7–13 aprile 1988, vols. 1–2. Spoleto: Presso la Sede del Centro, 1989.

Sartori, Antonio. "La 'Ratio Studiorum' al Santo," in *La Storia e la cultura al Santo fra il XII e il XX secolo,* ed. Antonio Pioppi, Fonti e studi per la storia del Santo a Padova, Studi 3 (Vicenza: Neri Pozza, 1976): 120–21.

———. "La Cappella di S. Giacomo al Santo di Padova." *Il Santo* 6 (1966): 267–361.

———. "La festa della traslazione di S. Antonio e il culto alla sua sacra lingua nel corso dei secoli." *Il Santo* 3, no. 1 (Jan–Apr. 1963): 67–98.

Sartorio, Luisa. "San Teodoro, statua composita," *Arte veneta* I (1947): 132–34.

Sattler, Christian F. *Geschichte des Herzogthums Wurtenberg.* Tubingen: Georg Heinrich Reiss, 1773.

Saward, John. *Perfect Fools: Folly for Christ's Sake in Catholic and Orthodox Christianity.* New York: Oxford Univ. Press, 1980.

Sawyer, P. *The Age of the Vikings.* London: St. Martin's Press, 1962.

Saxer, Victor. *Le culte de Marie-Madeleine en Occident des origines à la fin du moyen âge.* Paris/Auxerre: Clavreuil/Publications de la Société des Fouilles Archéologiques et des Monuments Historiques de l'Yonne, 1959.

Sbaraleae, Johannis Hyacinthi. *Bullarium Franciscanum Romanorum pontificum, constitutiones, epistolas, ac diplomata continens Tribus Ordinibus Minorum, Clarissarum, et Poenitentium a S. Patre Francisci institutis concessa,* vol. 4. Rome: Typis Sacrae Congregationis de Propaganda Fide, 1768.

Scaraffia, Lucetta. *La santa degli impossibili. Vicende e significati della devozione a Santa Rita.* Turin: Rosenberg and Sellier, 1990.

Scarfe, Norman. *Suffolk in the Middle Ages.* Woodbridge, Suffolk: Boydell Press, 1986.

Scarpellini, Pietro. "Iconografia francescana nei secoli XIII e XIV," in *Francesco d'Assisi. Storia e Arte* (Milan: Electa, 1982): 91–126.

Schauwecker, Helga. *Otloh von St. Emmeran. Ein Beitrag zur Bildungs-und Frömmigkeitsgeschichte des 11. Jahrhunderts.* Munich: Verlag der Bayer. Benediktiner-Akademie, 1965.

Schiller, Gertrude. *Ikonographie der christlichen Kunst,* 2 vols. Gutersloh: Gutersloher Verlagshaus G. Mohn, 1966.

Schleicher, Wolfgang. *Ramón Lulls Libre de Evast e Blanquerna: Eine Untersuchung über den Einflusss der Franziskanisch-Dominikanischen Predigt auf die Prosawerke des Katalanischen Dichters.* Genève: Librairie Droz, 1958.

Schmid, Karl. "Welfisches Selbstverständnis." *Gebetesgedenken und adliges Selbstverständnis im Mittelalter. Ausgewählte Beiträge* (Sigmarinsen: Thorbecke, 1983): 424–53.

Schmitt, Jean-Claude, ed. *Les saints et les stars: le texte hagiographique dans la culture populaire.* Paris: Beauchesne, 1983.

———. *Le saint lévrier. Guinéfort guérisseur d'enfants depuis le XIIIe siècle.* Paris: Flammarion, 1979.

Schneyer, Johannes B. "Lateinische Sermones-Initien des Hochmittelalters fur die heiligenfeste des Franziskanerordens." *Archivum Franciscanum Historicum* 61 (1968): 3–78.

Schulte Van Kessel, Elisja, ed. *Women and Men in Spiritual Culture, XIV–XVII Centuries. A Meeting of South and North*. The Hague: Netherlands Govt. Pub. Office, 1986.

Scribner. R. W. *For the Sake of Simple Folk: Popular Propaganda for the German Reformation*. Cambridge: Cambridge Univ. Press, 1981.

Searle, Eleanor, ed. *The Chronicle of Battle Abbey*. Oxford: Clarendon Press, 1980.

Selvago, Alonso de Villegas. *Flos sanctorum*. Barcelona: Por Pable Nadal y Pedro Escuder, 1748.

Sephton, J., trans. *The Saga of King Olaf Tryggwason*. London: David Nutt, 1895.

Serrigny, Ernst. *La représentation d'un Mystère de Saint-Martin à Seurre, en 1496*. Dijon: Librairie Lamarche, 1888.

Sharpe, Richard. *Medieval Irish Saints' Lives*. New York: Oxford Univ. Press, 1991.

Sheingorn, Pamela. *The Easter Sepulchre in England*. Early Drama, Art, and Music, Reference Series, n. 5. Kalamazoo: Medieval Institute Publications, 1987.

Sicard, M.-M. *Sainte Marie-Madeleine*. Paris: Savaete, 1910.

Sidney, Allen W. "Accent and Rhythm: Prosodic Features of Latin and Greek." *Cambridge Studies in Linguistics*, vol. 12. Cambridge: Cambridge Univ. Press, 1973.

Sigal, Pierre André. *L'homme et le miracle dans la France médiévale (XIe–XIIe siècles)*. Paris: Editons du Cerf, 1985.

———. "Un aspect du culte des saints; le châtiment divin aux XIe et XIIe siècles d'après la littérature hagiographique du Midi de la France." *Cahiers de Fanjeaux* 11 (1976): 39–59.

Silk, Mark. *Scientia Rerum: The Place of Example in Later Medieval Thought* (Ph.D. diss., Harvard Univ., 1982).

Simioni, Attilio. *Storia di Padova dalle origini alla fine del secolo XVIII*. Padua: Giuseppe e Pietro Randi Librai, 1968.

Simpson, L. "The King Alfred/St. Cuthbert Episode in the *Historia de Sancto Cuthberto*; Its Significance for Mid-Tenth Century English History," eds. G. Bonner, D. Rollason and C. Stanclife. *St. Cuthbert, His Cult and his Community to AD 1200* (Woodbridge: Boydell and Brewer, 1989): 397–411.

Sinding-Larsen, Staale. *Christ in the Council Hall: Studies in the Religious Iconography of the Venetian Republic*. Rome: "L'erma" di Bretschneider, 1974.

Smart, Alastair. *The Assisi Problem and the Art of Giotto*. Oxford: Clarendon Press, 1971.

Smith, Toulmin Lucy, ed. *English Gilds: The Original Ordinances of More Than One Hundred Early English Gilds*. Oxford: EETS., 1870.

———, and Paul Meyer, eds. *Les Contes Moralisés de Nicole Bozon*, 1889; Paris: Johnson Reprint Corp., 1968.

Socrates. *Ecclesiastical History*. Library of Nicene and Post-Nicene Fathers, ser. 2, vol. 2. Grand Rapids: Wm. B. Eerdmans, 1979.

Sorelli, Fernanda. "Predicatori a Venezia (fine secolo XIV–metà secolo XV)." *Le venezie francescane*, n. s., anno 6, fasc. 1 (1989): 131–58.

Southern, R. W. *The Making of the Middle Ages*. London: Century Hutchinson Ltd., 1988.

———. "Aspects of the European Tradition of Historical Writing: 4. The Sense of the Past." *Transactions of the Royal Historical Society*, 5th ser., 23 (1973): 243–63.

———. *St. Anselm and his Biographer: A Study of Monastic Life and Thought 1059–c. 1130*. Cambridge: Cambridge Univ. Press, 1963.

Sozomen. *Ecclesiastical History*. Trans. C. D. Harranft, vol. 2 of Nicene and Post-Nicene Fathers.

Spector, Stephen. "The Composition and Development of an Eclectic Manuscript: Cotton Vespasian D. VIII." *Leeds Studies in English*, n.s. 9 (1977): 62–83.

Spiegel, Gabrielle. "History, Historicism and the Social Logic of the Text in the Middle Ages." *Speculum* 65 (1990): 59–86.

———. "The Cult of St. Denis and Capetian Kingship," in *Saints and Their Cults*, ed. Stephen Wilson (Cambridge: Cambridge Univ. Press, 1983): 141–68.

Stafford, Pauline. *Queens, Concubines and Dowagers*. Athens: Georgia Univ. Press, 1983.

Stancliffe, Clare. *St. Martin and his Hagiographer: History and Miracle in Sulpicius Severus*. Oxford: Clarendon Press, 1983.

Stephany, Christie F. "The Meeting of Saints Francis and Dominic." *Franciscan Studies* 47 (1987): 218–33.

Stevens, John. *Words and Music in the Middle Ages: Song, Narrative, Dance and Drama*, 1050–1350, Cambridge Studies in Music. Cambridge: Cambridge Univ. Press, 1986.

Stokes, Whitley, ed. *Tripartite Life of Patrick with Other Documents Relating to That Saint Martin*. Vol. II. London: HM Stationary Office, 1887.

Stoltzer, Thomas. *Samtliche lateinischen Hymnen und Psalmen*, eds. Hans Albrecht and Otto Gombosi. Wiesbaden: Breitkopf and Hartel, 1959.

Stoneman, William P. "Another Old English Note Signed 'Coleman'." *Medium Aevum* 56 (1987): 78–82.

Strainchamps, Edmond N. "Marco da Gagliano and the Compagnia dell'Arcangelo Raffaello in Florence: An Unknown Episode in the Composer's Life," in *Essays Presented to Myron P. Gilmore*, eds. S. Bertelli and G. Ramakus (Florence: La Nuova Italia, 1978): II, 473–87.

———. "Memorial Madrigals for Jacopo Corsi in the Company of the Archangel Raphael," in Eisenbichler, *Crossing the Boundaries*, 161–78.

Stroncone, Antonio da. "L'Umbria serafica." *Miscellanea Francescana* 4 (1889): 158–87; ibid., 5 (1890): 86–90.

Sumption, Jonathan. *Pilgrimage: An Image of Mediaeval Religion*. Totowa: Rowman & Littlefield, 1976.

Swanton, Michael. *Three Lives of the Last Englishmen*. New York: Garland Publishing, 1984.

Swoboda, Otto. *Alpenlandisches Brauchtum im Jahreslauf*. Munich: Suddeutscher Verlag, 1979.

Szarmach, Paul, ed. *An Introduction to the Medieval Mystics of Europe*. Albany: State Univ. of New York Press, 1984.

Talbot, Charles Hugh. *Medicine in Medieval England*. London: Oldbourne History of Science Library, 1967.

Terry, Arthur. *Catalan Literature*, vol. 7 of *A Literary History of Spain* (London: Ernst Benn, 1972): 12–22.

Theodoret. *Ecclesiastical History*, trans. B. Jackson, vol. 3 of Nicene and Post-Nicene Fathers. Grand Rapids: Wm. B. Eerdmans, 1979.

Thiébaux, Marcelle. *The Writings of Medieval Women*. New York: Garland Publishing, 1987.

Thomas, C. B. C. "The Miracle Play at Dunstable." *Modern Language Notes* 32 (1917): 337–44.

Thomas, Antoine. "Nicole Bozon, Frère Mineur." *Histoire Littéraire de la France* 36 (1924): 400–424.

Thompson, A. Hamilton, introductory essay and notes, *Liber vitae ecclesiae Dunelmensis: A Collotype facsimile of the original manuscript*. Surtees Society, vol. 163. Durham, 1923.

Thomson, Rodney. *William of Malmesbury*. Woodbridge, Suffolk: Boydell Press, 1987.

Thorn, A. Chr., ed. *Les Proverbes de Bon Enseignement de Nicole Bozon*, Lunds Universitets Arsskrift. Lund: C. W. K. Gleerup, 1921.

Tolkowsky, S. *The Gateways to Palestine: A History of Jaffa*. London: George Routledge & Sons, 1924.

Torriti, F. *La pinacoteca nazionale di Siena*. Genova: Sagep, 1977.

Toscano, Bruno, ed. *Museo Comunale di San Francesco a Montefalco*. Perugia: Electa, 1990.

Townsend, David. "Anglo-Latin Hagiography and the Norman Transition." *Exemplaria* 3 (1991): 385–433.

Tramontin, Silvio. "Realtà e leggenda nei racconti marciani veneti." *Studi Veneziani* 12 (1970): 25–58.

———. et al., eds. *Culto dei Santi a Venezia*. Venice: Studium Cattolico Veneziano, 1965.

———. "Il 'Kalendarium' veneziano," in *Culto dei Santi a Venezia*, 287–324.

Treuer, Gottlieb Samuel. *Untersuchung des Urpsrung und der Bedeutung des Marten-Mannes*. Helmstadt: Christian Friedrich Weygand, 1733.

Trexler, Richard. *Public Life in Renaissance Florence*. New York: Academic Press, 1980.

———. "Ritual in Florence: Adolescence and Salvation in the Renaissance," in C. Trinkaus and H. A. Oberman, *The Pursuit of Holiness in Late Medieval and Renaissance Religion* (Leiden: Brill, 1974): 200–264.

———. "Florentine Religious Experience: The Sacred Image." *Studies in the Renaissance* 19 (1972): 7–41.

Tyrannus, Rufinus. *Historia monachorum in Aegypto, Patrologia Latina* 21, cols. 387–462.

Uitti, Karl D. "Women Saints, the Vernacular, and History in Early Medieval France," in *Images of Sainthood in Medieval Europe*, eds. Renate Blumenfeld-Kosinski and Timea Szell (Ithaca: Cornell Univ. Press, 1991): 247–67.

Unterkircher, F. and A. de Schryver. *Gebetbuch Karls des Kühnen vel potius Stundenbuch der Maria von Burgund, Codex Vindobonensis 1857*, 2 vols. Graz: Akademische Druck-und Verlagsanstalt, 1969.

Van Dijk, Stephen J. P., ed. *Sources of the Modern Roman Liturgy: The Ordinals of Haymo of Faversham, and Related Documents (1243–1307), Studia et documenta Francescana*, vols. 1, 2. Leiden: E. J. Brill, 1963.

————. *Handlist of the Latin Liturgical Manuscripts in the Bodleian Library, Oxford* (typescript in the Bodleian Library, no date): 2: 234.

Van Os, Henk. "St. Francis of Assisi as a Second Christ in Early Italian Painting." *Simiolus* 7 (1974): 115–32.

Van Buren, Anne Hagopian. "The Canonical Office in Renaissance Painting, Part II: More About the Rolin *Madonna.*" *Art Bulletin* 60 (1978): 617–33.

Vauchez, André. *La sainteté en Occident aux derniers siècles du moyen âge.* Rome: Ecole Française de Rome, revised edition, 1988.

————. *La sainteté en Occident aux derniers siècles au moyen âge.* Rome: Ecole Française de Rome, edition of 1980.

————. *Les laïcs au Moyen Age.* Paris: Les Editions du Cerf, 1978.

————. *La spiritualité du moyen âge occidental VIIIe–XIIe siècles.* France: Presses Universitaires Françaises, 1975.

————. "Les stigmates de saint François et leurs détracteurs dans les derniers siècles du Moyen Age." *Mélanges d'archéologie et d'histoire* LXXX (1968): 595–625.

————. "Rocco." *Bibliotheca Sanctorum,* 12 vols. (Rome: Istituto Giovanni XXIII della Pontificia Università Lateranense, 1961–1969): 11: 264–73.

————. "Lay People's Sanctity in Western Europe: Evolution of a Pattern (Twelfth and Thirteenth Centuries)," in Blumenfeld-Kosinski and Szell, *Images of Sainthood,* 21–32.

Vaultier, Roger. *Le folklore pendant la guerre de Cent Ans d'après les lettres de remission du Trésor des Chartes.* Paris: Gueneguad, 1965.

Verci, Giovanni Battista. *Storia della Marca Trevigiana.* Venice: G. Storti, 1786–1789.

Viera, David J. *Medieval Catalan Literature: Prose and Drama.* New York: Twaine, 1988.

Villette, Jeanne. *L'Ange dans l'art d'occident du XIIe au XVIe siècle. France, Italie, Flandre, Allemagne.* Paris: Henri Laurens, 1940.

Vita sanctae Genovefae virginis Parisiis, Acta Sanctorum, 3 January, 137–53.

Vitz, Birge E. "1215 The Fourth Lateran Council: The Impact of Christian Doctrine on Medieval Literature," in *A New History of French Literature,* ed. Denis Hollier (Cambridge: Harvard Univ. Press, 1989): 82–88.

Von Duringsfeld, Ida and Otto Freiherrn von Reinsberg-Duringsfeld. *Sprichwörter der germanischen und romanischen Sprachen.* Leipzig: Hermann Fries, 1872.

W. G. B. " 'Seynt Martyns Pley' at Colchester." *Essex Review* 48 (1939): 83.

Wace. *The Conception Nostre Dame of Wace,* ed. William Ray Ashford. Chicago: Univ. of Chiacago Press, 1993.

————. *La Vie de Sainte Marguerite,* ed. Elizabeth A. Francis. Paris: Edouard Champion, 1932.

Waddell, Helen. *The Wandering Scholars.* New York: Henry Holt, 1926.

Walsh, William S. *Curiosities of Popular Customs.* Philadelphia: J. B. Lippincott, 1897.

Ward, Benedicta. *Harlots of the Desert: A Study of Repentance in Early Monastic Sources.* Kalamazoo: Cistercian Publications, 1987.

————. "Miracles and History: A Reconsideration of the Miracle Stories Used by Bede," ed. G. Bonner. *Famulus Christi* (London: SPCK., 1976): 70–76.

————, ed. *The Prayers and Meditations of Saint Anselm with the Proslogion.* Harmondsworth: Penguin Press, 1973.

Wasson, John, ed. *Devon*. Records of Early English Drama. Toronto: Univ. of Toronto Press, 1986.

——. "The Morality Play: Ancestor of Elizabethan Drama?" *Comparative Drama* 13 (1979): 210–21.

Watt, W. Montgomery and Pierre Cachia. *A History of Islamic Spain*. Edinburgh Univ. Press, 1965.

Wattenbach, Wilhelm and Robert Holtzmann. *Deutschlands Geschichtsquellen in Mittelalter: Die Zeit der Sachsen und Salien*. Part I revised by Franz-Josef Schmale. Darmstadt: Cologne-Graz: Bohlau, 1967.

Weinstein, Donald and Rudolph M. Bell. *Saints and Society: The Two Worlds of Western Christendom, 100–1700*. Chicago: Univ. of Chicago Press, 1982.

Weissman, Ronald F. E. *Ritual Brotherhood in Renaissance Florence*. New York: Academic Press, 1982.

Whatley, Gordon, ed. and trans. *The Saint of London: The Life and Miracles of St. Erkenwald*. Binghamton: Medieval & Renaissance Texts & Studies, vol. 58, 1989.

——. "North American Research in Hagiography." *Analecta Bollandiana* 105 (1987): 425–44.

Whicher, George F., trans. *The Goliard Poets: Medieval Latin Songs and Satires*. Norfolk: New Directions, 1949.

Whitelock, D., ed. *English Historical Documents c. 500–1042*. London: Oxford Univ. Press, 1955.

Wickersheimer, E. "Une vie des saints Côme et Damien dans un manuscrit médical du IXe siècle suivie d'une recette collyre attribuée à la mère des deux saints." *Centaurus* 1 (1950): 38–42.

Willeford, William. *The Fool and His Sceptre*. London: Edward Arnold, 1969.

William of Malmesbury. *De gestis pontificum Anglorum*, ed. N. E. S. A. Hamilton, Rolls Series 90. London: Public Record Office, 1870.

——. *Gesta Regum Anglorum*. London: Camden Society, 1846.

Williams, Ulla and Werner Williams-Knapp. *Die Elsässische "Legenda Aurea"*. Tübingen: Niemeyer, 1980–1983.

Wilson, Blake. *Music and Merchants. The Laudesi Companies of Republican Florence*. Oxford: Oxford Univ. Press, 1992.

Wilson, S., ed. *Saints and their Cults. Studies in Religious Sociology, Folklore and History*. Cambridge: Cambridge Univ. Press, 1983.

Wossen, Carl. *Sankt Martin: Sein Leben und Fortwirken in Gesinnung, Brauchtum und Kunst*. Dusseldorf: Rheinisch-Bergische Druckerei, 1974.

Wright, Stephen. "The Durham Play of Mary and the Poor Knight: Sources and Analogues of a Lost English Miracle Play." *Comparative Drama* 17 (1983): 254–65.

Young, Karl. *The Drama of the Medieval Church*. 2 vols. Oxford: Clarendon Press, 1933.

Zarri, Gabriella. *Le sante vive. Cultura e religiosità femminile nella prima età moderna*. Turin: Rosenber and Sellier, 1990.

——. "Aspetti dello sviluppo degli Ordini religiosi in Italia tra Quattro e Cinquecento. Studi e problemi," in *Strutture ecclesiastiche in Italia e in Germania prima della Riforma*. Bologna: Il Mulino, 1984.

————, ed. *Falsi santi. Santità e simulazione in età moderna.* Turin: Rosenberg and Sellier.

Zawart, Anscar. "The History of Franciscan Preaching and of Franciscan Preachers (1209–1927)." *Franciscan Studies* 7 (1928): 241–589.

Zeydel, Edwin H., ed. and trans. *Vagabond Verse: Secular Latin Poems of the Middle Ages.* Detroit: Wayne State Univ. Press, 1966.

Zink, Michel. *La Prédication en langue romane avant 1300.* Paris: Honoré Champion, 1976.

Zippel, Gianni. "Ludovico Foscarini ambasciatore a Genova, nella crisi dell'espansione veneziana sulla terraferma (1449–1450)." *Bolletino dell'Istituto Storico Italiano per il Medio Evo* 71 (1959): 181–255.

Zoepf, Ludwig. *Das Heiligen-Leben im 10. Jahrhundert.* Leipzig and Berlin: B. G. Teubner, 1908.

Zur Capellen, Jurg Meyer. "La 'Figura' del San Lorenzo Giustiniani di Jacopo Bellini." *Centro tedesco di studi veneziani, Quaderni* 19 (Venice, 1981): 5–33.

Index

ꝏRTS

ꝏedieval & renaissance texts & studies
is the publishing program of the
Center for Medieval and Early Renaissance Studies
at the State University of New York at Binghamton.

ꝏrts emphasizes books that are needed —
texts, translations, and major research tools.

ꝏrts aims to publish the highest quality scholarship
in attractive and durable format at modest cost.